DATE DUE

Changing Aesthetic Views of
Instrumental Music in
18th-Century Germany

Studies in Musicology

George Buelow, Series Editor

Professor of Musicology
Indiana University

Other Titles in This Series

Changing Aesthetic Views of
Instrumental Music in
18th-Century Germany

by
Bellamy Hosler

RESEARCH PRESS

Produced and distributed by
UMI Research Press
an imprint of
University Microfilms International
Ann Arbor, Michigan 48106

Library of Congress Cataloging in Publication Data

Hosler, Bellamy.
Changing aesthetic views of instrumental music
in 18th century Germany.

(Studies in musicology ; no. 42)
Revision of thesis (Ph.D.)–University of Wisconsin,
Madison, 1978.
Bibliography: p.
Includes index.
1. Instrumental music–Germany–History and criticism.
2. Music–History and criticism–18th century. 3. Music–
Philosophy and aesthetics. I. Title. II. Series.

ML499.H67 1981   780'.943   81-4754
ISBN 0-8357-1172-2   AACR2

Contents

Acknowledgments

An endeavor such as this cannot be brought to completion without the help and support of many people. And, for me, the task cannot truly be declared accomplished until I acknowledge and thank those who contributed so much to its progress.

First, I wish to acknowledge the steady support and encouragement of my major professor, Lawrence Gushee. Throughout the long process he promptly read and thoughtfully commented on the labors of the fledgling scholar. An exacting taskmaster, he has the rare gift of combining incisive criticism and genuine respect.

Without Helen Hay, my friend and typist, there might never have been a completed project. She patiently and efficiently made her way through the forest of umlauts into which I enticed her.

Libraries and librarians were not only essential but most helpful. Lenore Coral, at the University of Wisconsin-Madison, most generously arranged for the quick acquisition of microfilms for distant and obscure sources. The staff of the library at the University of Wisconsin Center-Marathon County, where I teach, did all they could to minimize my geographical separation from the research libraries upon which I was so dependent. Inter-library loan request after inter-library loan request was sent off, article after article was copied, and countless overdue reminders were graciously tendered by Nyla Weitzman, Judy Strebig, and John Schmitt.

The ultimate debt I owe to my family, not only for support, but for very real sacrifice. My parents always provided me the unconditional support and trust that seems peculiar to parenthood. They never doubted or pressured. They allowed me to have the joy of intellectual endeavor for its own sake. This precious gift I must acknowledge.

Lastly, there is the family to whom I am mother and wife: Amy, Jacob, and Doug. Even in the face of the burden of research and writing, the children made life seem beautiful. Doug enthusiastically encouraged my "liberation." And though there were times when he must have wondered if he could live with the consequences, he persevered with the rest of us, at times stepping into the role of wife and mother. This capacity for metamorphosis, along with his unfailing understanding, provided the basis for my ability to work and to lead a full life at the same time. Without Doug there would have been neither joy nor completed work.

Introduction

Music historians often think of the eighteenth century as the time when instrumental music developed into an autonomous and flourishing art, reaching by the end of the century a new level of artistic significance and prominence in the "classical style" of Haydn, Mozart, and the young Beethoven. Historians of aesthetics and criticism see during this same time a great flowering of art criticism and the beginnings of "aesthetics" as such—a time when reflection on art became an independent and respected department of philosophical inquiry. The relation between these two phenomena has not, however, been fully explored.

I have undertaken to investigate one central aspect of this relation: the changing critical views of instrumental music's aesthetic function and status in Germany. For not only did musical style and patterns of musical consumption change radically (there is a world of difference between a Bach concerto movement and a movement of a Haydn symphony, and between the concert in private princely chambers and the concert in the public concert hall), but aesthetic attitudes towards instrumental music were also undergoing a profound change. During the eighteenth century instrumental music rose from being considered the poor, insignificant sister of vocal music, the "handmaid of poetry," and the ready source of appropriate dance, dinner, and festive fanfare sounds—from functioning to provide the "allowable recreation" of the bourgeoisie and the "ear-tickling" divertissement of bored aristocrats—to be viewed by the early Romantics as the symbol of the multifarious, mysterious stream of man's inner life: the highest and "most romantic of all the arts," as E. T. A. Hoffmann was to write in the early nineteenth century.

Two questions are fundamental to the cross-disciplinary nature of this study: What, if any, was the effect of the aesthetic views on the music itself, and what, if any, the effect of the music on the aesthetic ideas?

It is only natural that students of music history, should ask what all these aesthetic views and critical opinions have to do with the music that was actually created. What, for example, does Forkel's theory of music's formal analogy with the emotions have to do with any of the contemporary masterpieces in the classical style?

I do not attempt to show or suggest any causal connection between the attitudes we shall be surveying and the creative forces of men like Haydn, Mozart, or Beethoven. At the same time I do not believe that attitudes as to instrumental music's aesthetic function and worth remain solely within the admittedly absorbing arena of aesthetic speculation. For truly to study eighteenth century music is to study not only the engaging artworks themselves, but also the larger cultural phenomenon of which these compositions were the central part.

Ideas did play a role in this spectacle of the concert hall filled with listeners attending to "mere sounds" and finding in them something of significance or worth. Ideas could even have contributed to the fact that certain works were composed at all. Certainly composers of instrumental music were responsive to the existence of audiences who believed that such music was significant, or in some way worthwhile.

As Leonard Meyer pointed out, the "attention given to a work of art" and even the "perception itself" are affected by "beliefs as to the nature and significance of aesthetic experience in general and the expected musical experience in particular"—by what he calls the "preparatory set" of the listener.[1] "The power of most journalistic criticism," wrote Meyer, "derives not so much from its ability to influence judgment as from its power to enhance or weaken belief."[2] The eighteenth-century music lover formed his beliefs in substantial part from his reading on the critical issues surrounding instrumental music, and from the climate of opinion formed by current music-critical ideologies—sources of opinion which form the object of this study. Thus, the ideas about music which we shall uncover played a significant role in the "preparatory set," and hence the perceptions and beliefs of eighteenth-century listeners. And it was these listeners who filled the concert hall, for whom the composer in part wrote, who were central figures in the larger cultural phenomenon of eighteenth-century music—and who, we may choose to believe, through attentive and appreciative listening, had some positive effect on the creation of those musical masterpieces which are part of the rich musical endowment of Western culture.[3]

Let us now turn the tables and ask, what effect might the music have had on those aesthetic views which form the object of this investigation? In the course of my research it became clear to me that the most telling issues in the critical debate over instrumental music's aesthetic status revolved around problematic aspects of contemporary instrumental music itself—those aspects of accepted, even popular, musical practice which were not explained or justified by theories of the fundamental nature and purpose of music. That is, the very issues of the debate grew out of a confrontation of aesthetic theory with actual musical practice. I found, moreover, that it was only by focusing on the aesthetic issues implied by rejections or characterizations of actual practice that I was able to devise an approach which promised to illuminate the course and causes of instrumental music's dramatic rise in aesthetic significance and importance. Therefore I chose to proceed with my research on the assumption that the train of critical thought leading to the Romantics' uniquely high apprisal of instrumental music in effect concerned itself with the challenge of explaining, or rendering meaningful, a successful contemporary musical phenomenon: the "new" Italian instrumental style and its offspring, the "classical style" itself.

This fundamental assumption was confirmed by the thrust of the critical literature to which I turned as a source of aesthetic views. For critics and others who wrote about music were rarely considering a priori the value of music without words. Abstract, rigorous speculation on the aesthetics of music was not the rule in the eighteenth century. Critics were most often trying to construe the artworks at hand, especially the artworks in the controversial new style, as sense or nonsense; they wanted to sanction or condemn—to render significant or meaningless. It was typically on the basis of these occasional observations and arguments, lacking in speculative rigor and in awareness of the larger issues involved, that positions on the fundamental nature, function, and worth of instrumental music were actually taken.

Fortunately, for the general reader, as well as for the musicological specialist, the main issues of the debate over instrumental music's status relate only to the most fundamental changes in musical style. In order to understand the relevance of the aesthetic issues of this debate to the music itself, one need know little more than the basic facts (which can be illustrated with only a few recordings or scores): the style of a baroque concerto movement, for example, characterized by thematic unity and rhythmic continuity, richness of harmonic detail, contrapuntal complexity, and an evident seriousness of compositional purpose—a style widely noted (then as now) for its clear, intense and sustained characterization of a single "affect"—was to be supplanted (as Quantz, the contemporary composer and critic, recognized had already occurred by 1752) by a "new" Italian instrumental style derived from the opera buffa. This new style eschewed the heavy pathos and the elaborate long-winded vocal lines of the contemporary opera seria in favor of a series of short, catchy, and tuneful ideas of a light-hearted, comic, even frivolous, character. In addition, the new music was typified by strong thematic and affective contrasts (a trait viewed, alternatively, as highly entertaining, or highly confusing); its simplicity and the ready accessibility of its harmonic language was in marked reaction to baroque complexity; its "pleasing," tuneful melodiousness and its transparent homophonic textures, a reaction to the weight and seriousness of baroque style. Contemporaries often spoke of its simple "sensual" appeal and its "ear-tickling" charm, but it was also frequently faulted for its "meaninglessness." Subsequently, this contrast-dominated "new" Italian style came to constitute the fundamental language of the more serious, complex, and more masterly-crafted compositions in the "classical style" of Haydn, Mozart, and Beethoven—works exploiting and displaying the many compositional techniques of thematic development (or "thematische Arbeit") and using a richer harmonic palette than that of the Italians, and yet retaining the instrumental elan and quick pace of the Italian style, as well as much of its tuneful symmetry and simplicity. It was this "classical style" which was to form the basis for the Romantic reappraisal of instrumental music.

If then one could have at hand a movement of a Bach Brandenburg concerto, one of Tartini's or one of Sammartini's middle symphonies, and a mature Haydn symphony, one would have the musical reference points needed in order to understand the aesthetic issues central to the eighteenth-century German debate over instrumental music's function and status.

The central issue of this debate was that of the meaningfulness and function of a sensual, non-representative musical medium, with the discussion focusing especially on the issue of the intelligibility of the contrasts so essential to the character of the new Italian instrumental style, as well as to the later classical style. The primary thesis of this study specifies the way in which eighteenth-century German music criticism dealt with this issue so that there emerged by the end of the century a new vision of instrumental music's significance. Over the course of the later eighteenth century, new theories of the emotions as themselves full of change and contrasts, new theories of man's spiritual well-being, and a new view of man's whole inner self as inscrutable, complex, and mysterious, came to justify—to render meaningful and useful—certain problematic aspects of contemporary instrumental music: its lack of a clear cognitive content, hence its reliance on the sheer sensual stimulation afforded by its non-referential and idiomatic materials; its growing compositional complexity, far surpassing the formal simplicity and unencumbered expressivity of mere vocal utterance; and especially its characteristic but confusing affective contrasts. The specific nature of instrumental music was seen by the end of the century to be most like the soul's; the Romantics saw music and the soul as sharing an analogously elusive and ever-changing essence. Indeed, the very idea that instrumental music was the highest art was based on the new appreciation of the affinity between the characteristic features, the "specific nature," of the classical instrumental style and the dynamic, complex, and ineffable reality of the inner emotional life itself. This change of attitude can also be seen in geographical terms. The contrast-dominated, "meaningless," brilliant, and idiomatic new Italian instrumental style clashed on German soil (where it had become well entrenched) with the French intellectual culture of the Enlightenment (by mid-century, the new ideology of the German intelligentsia as well), which demanded of music an intelligible meaning, reference to the extra-musical world, and most often the imitation of the natural utterances of passion. German musicians, music critics, and music lovers, who were raised in the traditional beliefs that music possessed an innate significance, that the "art" or craft of music was of unquestionable worth, that there was a "secret association" or "secret affinity" between the soul and music, and who were willing neither to violate Enlightened principles nor to abandon their fondness for Italian (and other non-representative) music, effected a kind of reconciliation of French critical theory and Italian musical style which finally took the form of a uniquely German critical synthesis. Borrowing new theories from the English, and relying on their own intellectual energy and thoroughness, as well as on traditional beliefs, the Germans evolved a new view of instrumental music. By virtue of its very nature and by virtue of the materials and procedures characteristic of the classical style, instrumental music was seen to possess an isomorphism with the inner life of man which could stimulate and symbolize the reality of the listener's own inner experience. Just as the "grand symphonies with their manifold elements" were a result of a distinctively German mixture of styles, so was the early Romantics' recognition of the significance of instrumental music based on a distinctively German blend of musical experiences and attitudes.

It should come as no surprise that two of the central roles in this study are played by contrast and what, for lack of a better term, I shall call "counterpoint." (In the eighteenth century, the various sorts of contrapuntal activity—ranging from strict fugue to the free contrapuntal textures created by thematic development—would have been called "harmony," a misleading term to use today.) Thematic and affective contrast has long been recognized by musicologists as a distinctive trait of the classical style, one which clearly separates it from the earlier Baroque style. Most recently, Charles Rosen, in his study *The Classical Style*, has reaffirmed the importance of thematic, dynamic, and rhythmic contrast for this essentially "dramatic" idiom.[4] Certain relatively complex compositional techniques are also considered characteristic of the masterpieces in the classical style. Einstein characterized Mozart's style as a fusion of the galant and the "learned," that is, of the merely pleasing and the compositionally challenging (which includes, in Mozart's case, both the older techniques of strict counterpoint and the newer contrapuntal art of "thematic work").[5] That Haydn's innovative and imaginative use of the techniques of thematic development not only distinguishes his mature style but also formed one of the cornerstones of the classical style itself is also well known. The homophonic idiom and harmonic simplicity of the pre-classic period, which constituted a reaction to the thick textures of baroque music, and upon which this new type of contrapuntal and thematic development was often imposed, are also considered basic distinguishing traits of classical, as opposed to baroque, style. Strangely, however, studies in the history of music aesthetics seem to have ignored the extent to which eighteenth-century music criticism was grappling with some of the very musical style features which we now recognize as essential and distinctive ones. We have been told many times about the emotional theory upon which the baroque unity of style was based, namely the so-called *Affektenlehre* of Mattheson and Descartes; we are frequently told of the mid-eighteenth-century rejection of counterpoint in the interests of more natural emotional expression; and we are told repeatedly that the classical style incorporates contrasting themes, changing affects, and thematic development. But the aesthetic and emotional theories vindicating some of the most essential traits of the classical style receive little attention, whereas in fact much critical attention in eighteenth-century Germany was devoted to the development and implementation of a new "doctrine of the soul," or "Seelenlehre" (as Wackenroder called it), with which one could account for the expressive function of such things as contrast and counterpoint.

The organization of this study grew out of a dissatisfaction with existing frameworks for investigation within the area of eighteenth-century aesthetic criticism. In the secondary literature in this field there is much talk of imitation and expression, and of rationalism, the Enlightenment, and Romanticism. Initially I expected to follow instrumental music's changing fortunes along a path moving away from rationalism and towards Romanticism, away from the espousal of imitation theories and towards the nineteenth-century view of art as emotional expression. I expected to find the explanation for the Romantics' elevation of instrumental music to the highest of the arts in the growing recognition of instrumental music's peculiar aptness as a vehicle of emotional self-expression. But I was to find in ways I shall try to describe that such historical categories as Romanticism and rationalism, expression and imitation, proved confusing and unilluminating when used to explain changing attitudes towards instrumental music, in spite of the fact that they play central interpretive roles in much recent literature dealing with eighteenth-century music criticism.

The concepts of imitation and expression are frequently found in the secondary literature, where they often have been used as a dichotomy which serves as the basis for the determination of what is old and what is new in eighteenth-century music criticism. The currency of this interpretative framework in recent literature is due in large part, I feel, to the impact of M. H. Abrams's *Mirror and the Lamp*, a history of the evolution of the Romantic theory of poetry, first published in 1953. Abrams identifies Romantic poetic theory as founded on the self-expression of the artist ("expressive" theory), and earlier theories as based on either the moving of the audience ("pragmatic" theory) or the representation of objects in the world outside of the artist ("mimetic," or "imitative," theory). Each theory, according to Abrams, is marked by a distinctive "critical orientation": expressive theories are oriented to the artist himself; mimetic theories to the object of imitation, or the content; and pragmatic theories to the audience. The ascendance of Romantic ideas and the demise of neoclassic criticism he dates around 1800 with Wordsworth's description of poetry as "the overflow of spontaneous feelings."[6]

In her study of the eighteenth-century music critic Karl Ludwig Junker, Roye Wates used the imitation vs. expression dichotomy to label Junker as progressive. Since Junker saw music not as tone-painting, but as "the communication of powerful feeling," she argues, he was clearly participating in one of the "major developments of critical thought of the second half of the eighteenth century": namely, the "gradual evolving of music's function from imitation to expression."[7] Unfortunately, by equating musical tone-painting with musical imitation, Wates ignored the primary musical doctrine of the eighteenth-century neoclassic critics: that music should represent the emotions by imitating the inarticulate utterances of human passion. When the Romantics objected to the notion of art as imitation, it was to the idea that music should represent definite feelings. The vanquishing of *Tonmalerei* (tone-painting) as an important musical function was one of the more insignificant skirmishes of eighteenth-century music criticism.

Another recent study borrows more heavily from Abrams. Howard Serwer, in his dissertation on Marpurg, makes explicit use of Abrams's framework in order to interpret Marpurg's historical position as a critic.[8] Serwer does not rely on the imitation-expression dichotomy but uses his own amended version of Abrams's categories of critical orientation. He merges the mimetic and objective theories, since they are both seen to focus on the work itself; the mimetic theory is then identified as a "catalyst for change" in that it redirected the critic's view away from the audience and towards the work itself. For Serwer it is the pragmatic, or what he calls "affective" theories—those focusing on the effects of the music on the audience—that represent the more conservative viewpoint. (It seems that he would use the term "affective" to suggest a correspondence between Abrams's audience-oriented, or pragmatic, theory and the *Affektenlehre* of Mattheson's generation, with its close dependence on rhetorical theory.) In keeping with his revision of Abrams, Serwer proceeds to interpret Marpurg's historical role as a progressive one. He asserts that Marpurg's late periodicals show "a change in critical approach when compared with his early ones," explaining that "the critical attention shifts from the effect the work has on the audience to the qualities of the work itself." Significant as this change may be, Marpurg is generally considered to be conservative in his aesthetic outlook, as his championing of Batteux's ideas in Germany attests.

The real question is that of the very applicability of Abrams's theory to the history of the eighteenth-century critical treatment of instrumental music. That the imitation-expression dichotomy is of fundamental importance in understanding and isolating trends in eighteenth-century poetic theory is undeniable. Abrams has fully documented this change in critical orientation—the change from art as the imitation of an action, as in the epic and tragedy, to art as the "spontaneous overflow of powerful feelings," as in the lyric poem, the Romantic literary genre par excellence. It is not clear, however, that the dichotomy is equally useful in understanding the specific nature of eighteenth-century music criticism. It is plausible enough to say that a self-expression theory of art can account for the lyric poem, but one wonders how it would account for, or lead to an appreciation of, the highly-developed, specifically musical form of the classical symphony—the favorite musical genre of the German Romantic writers, Tieck, Wackenroder, and E. T. A. Hoffmann. And indeed, it is not clear that the early Romantics, whose ideas were basic to a whole new vision of music, especially instrumental music, viewed music

as essentially a mode of self-expression. Thus both Serwer and Wates are hampered in any application of Abrams's framework, which worked so well for him in
explaining the field of the history of poetic theory, by the fact that they have naive-
ly taken Abrams's account of the trends toward literary Romanticism around 1800
for a workable and essentially correct account of the development of fundamental
Romantic musical attitudes. We have no reason to assume that Abrams's imitation
vs. expression framework is appropriate to the study of eighteenth-century music
criticism until we take an unprejudiced look at its applicability, and until we see
what that framework is able to elucidate.

All of this is not to say that the terms "imitation" and "expression" are not
prevalent ones in eighteenth-century music criticism, as they are in the other arts.
But any usefulness they provide today as an indication of eighteenth-century
musical thought must be carefully qualified by a recognition and understanding of
the immense confusion surrounding their changing and ambiguous usage in the
specific area of music criticism. (We have already seen how Wates so easily fell
into this terminological confusion.) For what we now refer to, in light of Abrams's
and others' formulations, as imitation and expression theories, do not correspond
to the sometimes radically different eighteenth-century meanings of these terms.

According to the mid-eighteenth-century usage of Batteux and his numerous
German followers, "imitation" as applied to music meant primarily the imitation,
or representation, of the tones of passionate utterance; the words "painting" and
"depiction" were often used as alternates in this prescription for music's proper
function.[9] Later (as in Sulzer's encyclopedia of the seventies), when the term "imitation" acquired negative connotations and went out of fashion, the same type of
musical representation came to be called "expression"; the term "depiction" remained, significantly, as an alternate.[10] In other words both the terms "imitation"
and "expression" were widely used to denote the depiction, or representation, of
passionate utterances—or, to add to the confusion, the representation of emotional
self-expressions. The meanings of the terms were so inextricably bound together
that one can even say that a musical "expression" most often meant "imitation"
in its mid-eighteenth-century musical sense. One encounters the additional confusion that the term "expression," taken as meaning the imitation of passionate
utterance, was sometimes used in deliberate opposition to the more trivial pursuit
of tone-painting (that is, the representation of inanimate nature), which some
theorists later in the century began to label musical "imitation."[11]

But even when "expression" was opposed to "imitation," eighteenth-
century theories of musical "expression" certainly did not correspond to the
Romantic poetic theory of self-expression. Moreover, any meaning the term "imitation" might have had distinct from a real theory of self-expression, would have
been somewhat weakened by the fact that mimetic theorists held that music imitated first and foremost emotional self-expressions. In literary theories of imitation the most important genres, the epic and the tragedy, were seen to imitate an

action, not an expression of emotion. Thus "imitation" and "expression" could be much more distinctly defined categories in the case of eighteenth-century literary criticism. And even if we would make the tidy distinction (one which Abrams might approve) that imitative music has other people's feelings as its content, whereas expressive music is a representation of the composer's own feelings, we would run into yet another specifically musical problem: for, as Wagner asked, who can say whose emotions are represented in a given piece of music, since by virtue of music's specific nature if cannot specify the possessor of the emotions in question? In sum, it seems there are many problems with the viability of the imitation-expression distinction which are specific to the field of music criticism itself—problems which Abrams did not encounter in his researches into the field of literary criticism, and for which his theory understandably makes no allowance.

But even if we document and clarify the eighteenth-century musical meanings of the terms "imitation" and "expression," and acknowledge their fundamental role in eighteenth-century aesthetic discourse, and even if we could agree on what the eighteenth-century musical equivalents were for Abrams's distinct critical orientations, the possibility would remain that if we continue to address the data of eighteenth-century music criticism with these categories foremost in our minds, we might fail to recognize the existence of more significant themes and issues. The study of instrumental music's changing aesthetic fortunes reveals most clearly the fact that there were indeed other issues of immense importance in eighteenth-century German music criticism. For the imitation-expression dichotomy does not exhaust the possibilities open to the composer of instrumental music; he need do neither, and in the eyes of many eighteenth-century critics this was precisely the problem with instrumental music: it did neither, or it could do neither, in a sufficiently intelligible manner. The issue of whether instrumental music had meaning or not eclipsed any discussion of the relative merits of imitation theories vs. expression theories, however the terms might be interpreted. Moreover, those critics who believed that music could or must represent the emotions, that the emotions were the fitting and proper content of music—and these critics were in the majority—were not very concerned to distinguish whether the content was infused into the music by an act of imitation or by an act of expression. Rather, they were concerned with such issues as what in fact the emotions were, what aspects of the emotions and which emotions could be musically represented and with what musical means, how the listener was made cognizant of this emotional content, how precise and intelligible this representation could be or needed to be, whether words were necessary to make music's content clear, and whether music had moral or spiritual value, and if so, of what kind. These questions were the crucial ones for an aesthetic appreciation of instrumental music; they cut across the imitation-expression issue and far over-shadowed it in eighteenth-century music criticism generally.

By becoming aware of these other issues we might make different judgments from those made solely on the basis of an Abramsian framework. Certainly, in the case of the Romantic elevation of instrumental music to the highest art, the change in aesthetic attitude neither hinged on nor was directly related to the issue of imitation vs. expression, no matter how critical this issue was for English poetic theory of the same time. Thus, this dichotomy cannot serve as a useful investigative framework for understanding the changing aesthetic attitudes towards instrumental music.

Another framework frequently borrowed for the purpose of providing some overall historical orientation to the facts of music criticism comes from the field of intellectual history. We have inherited a whole family of roughly congruent dichotomous pairs which are useful in characterizing the changing positions in eighteenth-century musical thought, as well as in eighteenth-century intellectual culture generally: Enlightenment vs. Romanticism, Rationalism vs. Romanticism, rationalism vs. emotionalism, head vs. heart, intellect vs. sentiment, objective truth vs. subjective intuition, and so on. (The imitation vs. expression dichotomy itself can be seen as a specific manifestation of these broader conflicts.) Many musicological accounts of eighteenth-century musical thought label positions conservative insofar as they can be subsumed under the rationality of the Enlightenment and progressive insofar as they anticipate the emotionalism of Romanticism. The problem with using the rationalism vs. Romanticism dichotomy, or any of its roughly equivalent alternates, as an investigative framework is that there was simply no agreement as to the real content of musical rationalism in the eighteenth century, or Enlightened views of instrumental music. The same situation existed with respect to Romanticism. Confusion in the use of these categories abounded.

Especially problematic is the labeling of theories of emotional representation, or "expression." The eighteenth-century view that music should imitate nature (in music's case this usually meant the imitation of the passions) is a view of art which is generally labeled "rationalistic" by virtue of its association with the rule-conscious, rationalistic attitude of mind typical of neoclassic aesthetics; it is a view of art which Abrams and others would easily label as opposite to the Romantic theory of art as emotional self-expression. And yet Batteux, who himself claimed to have demonstrated that all the arts could be reduced to the "single principle" of imitation, held as well that musical sounds represented, or even constituted, natural utterances of the passions; such sonal utterances, Batteux argued, were "natural signs" of the passions and hence communicated them more universally and powerfully than the "arbitrary signs" of verbal language.[12] Now this theory of musical sounds as declamatory expressions of real passions not only reminds us of Abrams's expressive theory, it is essentially the same one Schmid calls Romantic when he speaks of C. P. E. Bach's "speaking expression," his "free declamatory outpouring of feeling";[13] and it is the same one Sulzer used, though he was full of anti-imitation rhetoric, when he said that music must be the expression of feeling.[14]

And yet, such a declamatory theory of the emotional expression, or communication, of real-life emotions was explicitly rejected by the early Romantics as a prostitution of the purity of the art of instrumental music. What shall we call Romantic and what not? If we proceed on the basis of historical association, then this passionate utterance theory of musical expression, as I call it, must be viewed as part of the Enlightened set of attitudes towards instrumental music; furthermore, it appears that the early Romantic attitudes towards emotional expression in music need to be carefully re-examined.

Another confusion surrounds the issue of music's affective power, its power to move the listener. Abrams would hold that orientation toward affect is the opposite of orientation toward origin (namely, the artist's feelings) characteristic of Romantic criticism. But in early Romantic writings which find instrumental music to be a highly significant art the peculiar effects of music are seen to constitute a large portion of its significance; the idea that music is the expression of the artist's feelings does not figure at all prominently in their new appreciation of the power of instrumental music.[15] Is affective response to music after all then a mark of Romantic musical orientation, as Wates held in the case of Junker? But if so, then what do we make, for example, of Mattheson's confessions of his own emotional transport when listening to certain instrumental compositions?[16]

We must remember that the emotions have almost always played a central role in theories of music. Both the reasonable men of the Enlightenment and the intuitive Romantics felt that the content of music had to do with the emotions in some sense, and both expected to be moved by music. But then, if we consider Romantic views as resting essentially on emotionalist modes of thought and Enlightened ones on rational modes of thought, how do we distinguish the role of the emotions in Enlightened theories of music from the role of the emotions in Romantic theories? Certainly theories implying emotional content and emotionalism of response do not have to be viewed as exclusively Romantic. Moreover, the deliberate communication of definite emotions was anathema to the early Romantics who viewed instrumental music as the highest musical art. What exactly would musical emotionalism include—subjectivity of response, emotional content, emotional self-expression, communication of an emotional content from composer to listener, intuitive grounds for the assessment of musical worth? Indeed, is it really useful or informative to think of the early Romantic view of music as emotionalist? And to what extent were Germans ever completely rationalistic in their attitudes toward music?

If all these questions are faced, and if the confusions attendant on the use of these common dichotomies are sorted out, I believe we can clear the way for a workable and fitting definition of what the labels "Enlightened" and "Romantic" should be taken to mean in the specific case of the changing aesthetic views of instrumental music.

Eventually I came to my own understanding as to the relation of the Enlightenment and of Romanticism to the changing eighteenth-century attitudes towards instrumental music, and to a classification and definition of what "Enlightened" and "Romantic" could properly be taken to mean insofar as they applied to these changing attitudes. The final organization of my study relies heavily on these two concepts.

In general, I interpreted the terms historically: as standing for certain sets of ideas which at some time were associated together within commonly recognized schools of opinion; and I relied more on the term "Enlightened" than "rationalistic," with its often narrow meanings, as a contrasting partner to "Romantic." I then proceeded to label "Enlightened" the individual elements of that set of negative attitudes towards instrumental music which were largely associated with neoclassic aesthetics, and which dominated critical discussions of instrumental music around the middle of the century; and I called "Romantic" the elements of the later view of the *Frühromantiker*, who accorded to instrumental music such remarkably high aesthetic significance. Most of the individual views surveyed I then saw historically as possessing elements of one or both of these two opposing sets of attitudes or as contributing to the demise of the older view or the ascendance of the later one.

After wading through the confusions caused by trying to see the debate over instrumental music as an instance of the imitation vs. expression conflict or of the Enlightened vs. Romantic conflict, it became clear to me that the problems encountered by music lovers and critics in appreciating the new instrumental music centered on certain issues which were for the most part peculiar to discussions of music and thus were independent of the widely used interpretive frameworks borrowed from other fields. I therefore saw as my first task the isolation and definition of the issues which were in fact the determining ones in the critical debate over instrumental music's function and worth.

In order to construct this new framework for research and interpretation I looked to the body of eighteenth-century German music criticism itself. There I searched for the themes characteristically played upon in discussions of instrumental music.

In probing for possible elements for my own framework of issues, I hit upon two promising sources: the complaints against the "new" Italian instrumental style, and the commonly recognized characteristics of instrumental music which played no obvious role in the aesthetic ideologies to which all music was supposed to conform. Assuming that theory follows practice, and recognizing that the classical style (specifically, the idiom of the symphonies which so attracted the admiration of the early Romantics) incorporated certain essential features of the new Italian instrumental style of the latter eighteenth century, we can see that one of the tasks of eighteenth-century music aesthetics, if it was to prepare for a new appreciation of instrumental music as a significant art, was to come to terms with those features of this immensely successful new instrumental style which had elicited so many complaints: its lack of clearly intelligible extra-musical content, its seemingly unbridled contrasts, and the sheer sensuality of its appeal. Thus, in order to explain the new practice aesthetic theory had to wrestle with such issues as representation, intelligibility, contrast and coherence, and the role of sheer sensual enjoyment. For example, if the new Italian instrumental music was full of sudden and "senseless" contrasts, as many complaints attested, what sense could theory, especially a theory committed to some kind of musical embodiment or communication of the emotions, make of these puzzling elements—elements we know form a cornerstone of the classical style?

Other features of instrumental music, which did not appear so much in complaints, but which were widely recognized as somehow inhering in its specific nature (at least the specific nature of the current instrumental styles), also constituted problems for aesthetic theory because they made no obvious contribution to music's agreed-upon function in the mid-eighteenth century: to depict the vocal utterances of passion and thereby move the listener. For example, if a typical quality of an eighteenth-century symphony was seen to be fire and brilliance, or compositional complexity, then how could theory make a place for such non-vocal and non-expressive gestures in an art presumably addressed to man's emotional and spiritual nature?

Thus, the complaints against instrumental music and the aesthetically unjustified characteristics of the instrumental idiom served to define the aspects of instrumental practice which aesthetic theory had to explain before instrumental music could be accorded a high aesthetic status. These problematic aspects of practice also generated the set of issues which were to constitute my investigative and interpretive framework. The first and last chapters are devoted to this framework of issues: the first to their isolation and to a statement of the typical "Enlightened" position on each issue; the last, among other things, to a summary statement of the typical Romantic positions on the same issues—positions which served to vindicate the features of classical style previously considered problematic by Enlightened critics. Without a definition of these issues and without a spelling out of the typical Enlightened and Romantic positions on these same issues, I could not have begun to use the concepts of the Enlightenment and of Romanticism. I had found, as research progressed, that these broader cultural movements were clearly related to the changing aesthetic views of instrumental music; therefore I had to make their role in the study a meaningful one. The second and penultimate chapters provide an inner frame to the study in that they characterize, with specific reference to the issues surrounding instrumental music, the two actual schools of thought standing at either chronological end of my study: French neoclassicism and the Romanticism of the *Frühromantiker*.

The main body of the study examines and analyzes in succession the individual views of a selected number of writers. With the help of many concrete examples from these individuals' writings I attempt to substantiate and illustrate the historical progression between the ideological poles of Enlightened ideas about instrumental music and Romantic ideas—the progression from the rejection of instrumental music as a significant art to its virtual glorification. By focusing on the development of the themes isolated in the first chapter one can see the manner in which new theories arose to explain the new practice. On some issues there was a real evolution of thought, and on others the older ideas persisted so strongly that Romantic ideas can be seen as constituting a revolution in thought (though in these latter cases there was often a reactionary element at work). Thus there was not a single simple historical progression, but a complex progression, made up of various changing positions on various issues.[17] By studying in some depth the views of relatively few individuals we can better understand the complex reality of this change; for it was the norm that within one individual's thought progressive ideas should be qualified by conservative ones and vice versa. Though devoting some time to the views of each individual selected, I have not pretended to give a full and self-sufficient treatment of each person's ideas. My emphasis throughout has been on the currency and interaction of ideas bearing on the aesthetic issues which surrounded instrumental music; I wanted to find those ideas which German audiences, performers, and even composers, were exposed to, and which functioned in the evolution of a new aesthetic understanding of instrumental music. Nevertheless, as a consequence of focusing on a relatively small number of individuals, and of trying to provide a context for their views about instrumental music, the study does contribute to a new understanding of certain figures. For example, Krause's ideas are given a fuller treatment than is available elsewhere. Also, the historical roles of some individuals are reinterpreted. Baumgarten and Forkel, for example, certainly not heretofore considered progressive spirits, appear in my analysis to be important figures in the growth and evolution of new attitudes favorable to the acceptance of instrumental music as a serious art.

The writers to whom I have given a separate individual treatment were selected because they all spoke to the same crucial issues and because their specific views illustrate and illuminate the currency, interaction, and progression of ideas fundamental to the eighteenth-century debate over the aesthetic function and status of instrumental music.

Certain writers were selected who have not before figured prominently in secondary studies, such as Krause and Ruetz; other prominent critics were almost ignored, for example Marpurg and Schubart. One writer, Baumgarten, who scarcely mentioned music, was selected because he treated certain themes in such a way as to create a new climate of understanding for instrumental music. Moreover, my interest in the currency and interaction of views (rather than in the time and place of their origin) has led to the inclusion of some views which originated before the eighteenth century but which were still functioning in the eighteenth-century debate, as in the case with Luther's ideas, as well as to the inclusion of some views which originated outside of Germany, but which actually played an important role in German music criticism, as in the case with Marpurg's translation of Pluche and the many translations of Batteux. Whether implicitly or explicitly, most of the individuals selected adopt, revise, or react to positions taken by others among them.

A coherent discourse addressed to the philosophical problems of an aesthetic of instrumental music seems to have in effect taken place despite the disparate sources of the individual views examined, and despite their sometimes occasional and largely unsystematic character.

The desire to bring reason to bear on the aesthetic problems of music was widespread in eighteenth-century Germany. From around the middle of the century on, many of the more literate German musicians and music lovers were conversant with contemporary philosophical and critical issues and were anxious to enlighten the musical scene with the spirit of reason and reflection. Nicolai took issue with Gottsched, Krause put Baumgarten to good use, Hiller spoke for the application of Batteux's ideas to music, Junker relied heavily on Webb's psychology, and Forkel often cited Lessing as an authority on various matters. To be sure, the writers surveyed were not engaged in an explicit and closed debate with each other on the sole subject of instrumental music. But we can see even within this selection a mutual awareness that a debate of sorts was under way. The commonality of issues addressed bespeaks a common concern to deal with the aesthetic problems surrounding the new instrumental style.

The challenge to instrumental music posed by Batteux's mimetic theory can be sensed in all the German writings which followed him. Krause, Nicolai, and Sulzer all use Baumgarten's ideas to defend music, though Baumgarten's name barely appears in their writings. The problem of the intelligibility of contrasts is addressed by virtually all the writers; Baumgarten, Sulzer, and Forkel, in assigning a positive role to variety and contrasts, are answering Gottsched, Batteux, Lessing, and Junker. Nicolai responded explicitly to Gottsched's condemnation of instrumental music; Ruetz to Hiller's advocacy of Batteux. Junker was inspired by Lessing's identification of each art's peculiar potentialities; Forkel was infuriated by the neoclassicists' condemnation of counterpoint. Krause, Nicolai, Ruetz, Junker, Forkel, and Wackenroder all fall back on traditional pre-Enlightenment German musical ideas to defend music against rationalistic strictures. Even the Romantics, for all their iconoclastic and anti-speculative sentiments, speak to positions taken by earlier figures in this ongoing debate. Tieck is especially anxious to vanquish the utterance theory of musical expression, which Sulzer had advocated so effectively.

Although my task relied on a general survey, I have tried to illustrate my points as concretely as possible. This entailed the inclusion of many direct quotations, some of which are rather long. By giving the English-speaking reader access to much previously unavailable primary source material, I hope to open up more debate on the actual character of eighteenth-century music criticism and to enable the interested reader to test some of my interpretations with some of his own. The value of this study would be much enhanced if it could indeed contribute to a re-examination of eighteenth-century German musical thought.

I have seen no need to bring the German or French quotations into line with modern orthography; many spellings may therefore seem errant to the eye accustomed only to the modern spellings. Unless otherwise noted, the translations are my own. In most cases I have chosen to err on the side of literalness, so the reader not fluent in German or French might nevertheless, at certain key points, gain some hold on the original mode of expression.

1

Isolation of Themes: Problematic Aspects of Instrumental Music in the Eighteenth Century

In order to understand the changing aesthetic views of instrumental music in eighteenth-century Germany we need to determine what issues provided the framework for these judgments. Let us begin our investigation then by looking for these issues in eighteenth-century writings themselves, focusing only on those which bear specifically on the question of instrumental music's function and worth. For just as many of the difficulties experienced by eighteenth-century thinkers in appreciating instrumental music resulted from their desire to subsume all the arts under one common mission (one ill-befitting instrumental music), so our understanding of the history of music aesthetics and criticism has been hampered by the use of investigative frameworks belonging not to music, but to disciplines such as the history of ideas or the history of poetic theory. There has been undue emphasis placed on the shift from rationalism to Romanticism and on the shift from imitation theories of art to expression theories; the discovery and exploration of other, perhaps more appropriate and revealing, frameworks has thus been preempted.[1]

In eighteenth-century Germany the most widespread and outspoken commentary on music without words took the form of complaints against the "new" Italian style of instrumental music—against what was derisively called "blosses Geräusch" ("mere noise"), "unförmliches Geklängel" ("formless clanging"), "unverständliches Mischmasch" ("incomprehensible mishmash"), or "ohrkitzelndes Klingklang" ("ear-tickling jingle jangle"). The complaints are significant, for they attest to the enormous popularity of this newer style, and, most importantly, reveal the specific nature of the problematic stance contemporary writers adopted toward it. Here we have the classic theoretical scenario of an immensely successful artistic phenomenon, which is at odds with, indeed is an affront to, the prevailing aesthetic ideologies: hence the need to construct a new theory to justify or explain the new practice.

Of course, more than one theory of instrumental music's significance actually emerged, just as there were various ways of viewing the ear-tickling enigma; and the musical style implicated in the complaints was itself also changing. Nevertheless, the concept of a "new" Italian style runs throughout the century; and the traits identified with this music continued to constitute a challenge to the prevailing music-aesthetic ideology: that music must express the passions and move the listener.

The "new" Italian instrumental style was many things. For Georg Muffat in 1701, Italian "ear-tickling" music meant the contrast-dependent style of Corelli.[2] Marpurg, in 1749, complained about the unnatural excesses and the imaginative freedom of the "new" Italians; he expressly mentions Veracini, Paganelli, and Scarlatti.[3] For Quantz, writing in 1752, it was late Vivaldi and Tartini, who, by injecting the comic and the simple-minded into their instrumental music, had undermined the true singing style.[4] Hiller, in 1768, even singled out Germans who wrote in the new *tändelnd* (playful) style for complaint; he could not enjoy that "strange mixture of the serious and the comic, the sublime and the pretty," found in the music of composers such as Dittersdorf, Filtz and Haydn. (The symphonies of Galuppi, Jomelli and Sarti he hardly deigned to dismiss.)[5] And Rochlitz, in 1798, mentioned Cimarosa, Paisiello and Grétry as composers in the pretty, new, light, and playful style which delighted in teasing the listeners' expectations; he warned German composers not to follow the fad of mixing this style with the serious German style. (Only Haydn could get away with that, without becoming absurd.)[6]

But if in each generation the specific target changed, the nature of many of the complaints and the problematic style features remained. No matter to what degree, or on what compositional level manifested, Italian instrumental music's penchant for bold unvocal gestures, rich unbridled variety, strong startling contrasts, original and novel ideas, comic playfulness—in short, for what was seen as sheer aural delight—remained an aesthetic enigma. The persistent complaints attest to this, and so do the increasing attempts to integrate these features into acceptable theoretical frameworks. The theories will occupy us in later chapters. Let us address ourselves now to the complaints.

The most radical complaint against the new music was that it had no content at all. It did not even attempt to imitate or represent objects or passions. It bore no reference to the real world, whether physical or psychological. It did not possess what in French neoclassic aesthetics was called verisimilitude: it possessed no "truth."[7] To the quite rationalistically oriented Noël Antoine Pluche, whose views were promulgated at some length in Marpurg's *Beyträge*, the separation of words from music, of the instruction of the mind from the pleasure of the ear, was responsible for the ruin of music and the abandonment of music's central mission: to impress upon its listeners intellectually comprehensible moral principles.[8] Instrumental music, by its very nature, was intellectually and morally bankrupt. He had nothing but scorn for

l' usage qui est extrémement étendu depuis quelques siècles, de se passer de la musique vocale et de s'appliquer uniquement à amuser l'oreille sans présenter à l'esprit aucune pensée; en un mot de prétendre contenter l'homme par une longue suite de sons destitués de sens; ce qui est directement contraire à la nature même de la musique, qui est d'imiter, comme sont tous les beaux arts, l'image et le sentiment qui occupent l'esprit.[9]

the practice, which has been extremely widespread for several centuries, of doing without vocal music, and of attempting solely to amuse the ear without presenting any thought to the mind; in a word, of pretending to please the listener by means of a long series of sounds devoid of sense: which is directly contrary to the very nature of music, which is to imitate, as do all the fine arts, images and feelings which occupy the mind.

Johann Christoph Gottsched, the importer of French rationalistic ideas into Germany's literary life, expressly singled out the newer Italian instrumental pieces as meaningless; they were ''labyrinths of tones expressing nothing,'' which sounded neither happy nor sad. Pieces with titles such as ''Largo,'' Moderato,'' ''Allegro,'' and the like

bedeuten gar nichts: ein blosses Geklingel vorstellen, das einem weder kalt noch warm machet.[10]

mean absolutely nothing: they represent a mere jangle, which makes one neither cold nor warm.

Such instrumental pieces resemble a ''body without a mind,'' or a ''dead thing,'' because they require words to ''explain distinctly'' their meaning, if indeed they have any.[11] Johann Georg Sulzer, who wrote the most widely read encyclopedia of arts of the last part of the eighteenth century, compared the invention of French characteristic pieces and of overtures and symphonies intended for use before a theatrical production, where the composer had some guidelines as to the appropriate content, to the invention of concertos, trios, solos, sonatas and such, where the compositional process was left almost completely to chance. Since in these Italian instrumental genres the composer had no intent to represent anything,

die meisten Stücke dieser Art sind nichts anders, als ein wohlklingendes Geräusch, dass stürmend oder sanft in das Gehör fällt.[12]

most pieces of this type are nothing other than a pleasant sounding noise which enters the ear calmly or tempestuously.

Let the composer remember, he warns, that these pieces, in which no passion or feeling is uttered in ''understandable language,'' are ''nothing but mere noise.''
    Most Germans, however, were predisposed to sense some representative or affective essence in instrumental music. (We got a glint of this in Sulzer's ''stürmend oder sanft.'') Still, the Enlightened intellect balked at the absence of an ''understandable language.'' Thus there are many comments which assert instrumental music's inferiority because its content could be only confusedly

sensed—that is, its content could not be comprehended clearly and distinctly. Again it is the "new" style that is singled out for complaint, this time by one of the central characters of our story, Christian Gottfried Krause:

> Die allermeisten Stücke nach dem neuen Geschmack, ganz nicht rühren, kein *deutliches* Bild ausdrücken, and nicht nur bloss die Ohren kützeln, sondern auch wo nicht gar Uberdruss erwecken, doch wenigstens bloss languissant machen.[13] [My italics]

> Most of the pieces according to the new taste, are not at all moving, do not express a *distinct* picture, and not only merely tickle the ears, but, if they do not arouse outright disgust, at best they bring about boredom. [My italics]

The prominence of the word *deutlich* (distinct) in both Gottsched's and Krause's complaints, as well as the qualifier "understandable" in Sulzer's warning, must be noted.[14] It was part of the Cartesian epistemology, which was adopted into most neoclassic criticism, that only what was clear and distinct could be known with certainty. The "preparatory set" of many eighteenth-century listeners was such that they could not be moved by something they could not clearly and distinctly understand. Thus, if music's content was not distinct or determinate, not only was its epistemological status in question; the music itself was reduced to ear-tickling impotence, for it could not move the listener.

Johann Adam Hiller, who, in the midst of a defense of the applicability of Batteux's imitation of nature theory to music, took time out to make a special exception for non-imitative aspects of instrumental music, still ranked instrumental music below vocal because of its lack of determinate content:

> Worte . . . and Töne, zu einem Zwecke genau vereinigt, sind der Charakter der Vocalmusik, und hierinnen übertrift sie alle Instrumente.
> . . . Die Instrumentalmusik erhält von der Vocalmusik eine bestimmtere und gewisser Bedeutung. . . . Wie schön ist dieser Vereinigung, und wie vermag sie nicht über unser Herzen![15]

> Words . . . and tones utterly united towards one goal constitute the character of vocal music, and herein does it surpass all instrumental music.
> . . . Instrumental music receives from vocal music a more determinate and certain meaning. . . . How beautiful this unification is, and how powerful over our hearts!

Another similar complaint comes from a music critic of that antirationalistic movement, the Sturm und Drang. Karl Ludwig Junker's words of 1770 sound surprisingly like Hiller's above, of 1755:

> Weil die musikalische Nachahmung der Leidenschaften ohne Poesie schwankend ist, d.h., weil erst Poesie, jede Leidenschaft deutlich bestimmen kann, so muss sich der Setzer, dem Dichter unterwerfen, wie Lulli dem Quinault,—Vinci dem Metastasio, Gluck demselben,—und Schweitzer Wielanden.[16]

> Because without poetry the musical imitation of the passions is ambiguous, i.e., because only

poetry can distinctly define each passion, the composer must subordinate himself to the poet, as Lully did to Quinault, Vinci and Gluck to Metastasio, and Schweitzer to Wieland.

Even Herder, who is often seen as the originator of the Romantic movement in Germany, and who treasured music's arousal of "obscure" inner forces ("obscure" [*dunkle*] was the term opposite to "clear," in the Cartesian formula, "clear and distinct"), said that instrumental music needed an "explainer" to make its content more "definite" (*bestimmt*).[17] Instrumental music was thus inferior to vocal music.

The two complaints we have so far isolated can be viewed as based on the French neoclassic aesthetic theory that all art is an imitation of nature, and on the Cartesian epistemological demand for clearness and distinctness. Music which failed to meet these standards was, in short, a "dunkles Nichts."[18]

A third shortcoming of instrumental music can be related to another feature of neoclassic aesthetics: the glorification of drama, specifically the tragedy, as the highest form of art. Affects expressed in instrumental music not only lack the distinctness conferred by words, they lack a subject and an object, thus making it difficult for the listener to enter sympathetically into the affect being expressed. They also lack a cause and an effect, thus rendering communication of moral wisdom difficult. Lessing, who argued persistently against the tyranny of the dramatic unities of the French classic theater, and who championed the rights of genius over "the rules," still wanted the affects expressed in pure tones to have a specificity based on the dramatic determinants of subject, object, cause, and effect. He denied explicitly that music's obscure meanings—the nonverbalizability of its content—constituted an aesthetic defect; these dark feelings were even pleasant, he admitted. However, he could not respond to a succession of feelings, with no motivation, subject, or object:

> Itzt zerschmelzen wir in Wehmut, und auf einmal sollen wir rasen, Wie? warum? wider wen? wider eben den, für den unsere Seele ganz mitleidiges Gefühl war? oder wider einen andern? Alles das kann die Musik nicht bestimmen; sie lässt uns in Ungewissheit und Verwirrung; wir empfinden, ohne eine richtige Folge unserer Empfindungen wahrzunehmen; wir empfinden wie im Traume; und alle diese unordentliche Empfindungen sind mehr abmattend als ergötzend.[19]

> Now we are melting with woefulness, and all of a sudden we are supposed to rage. How so? Why? Against whom? Against the very one for whom our soul was just full of sympathy? Or against another? All these things music cannot specify; it leaves us in uncertainty and confusion; we have feelings, but without perceiving in them a correct sequence; we feel as in a dream; and all these disorderly feelings are more exhausting than delightful.

Similarly, Heinrich Christoph Koch, in his *Musikalisches Lexikon* of 1802, denied to instrumental music the power to evoke the listener's "interest" in the feelings which the tones themselves admittedly expressed; for tones alone could not express the objects or causes of the passions. To be sure, music can evoke the specific feelings of pleasantness, or unpleasantness;

wenn sie es aber unternehmen soll, in uns Gefühle anzufachen, wozu in der Lage, in welcher wir uns befinden, keine Ursache vorhanden, wofür unser Herz nicht aufgeschlossen ist, so fehlt es ihr, wenn es bloss durch die unartikulirten Töne der Instrumentalmusik geschehen soll, an Mitteln, unsern Herzen diese Gefühle interessant zu machen. Sie kann uns unter diesen Umständen nicht begreiflich machen, warum sie uns in sanfte oder traurige, in erhabene oder fröhlicher Empfindungen versetzen will; sie kann in uns weder die Bilder desjenigen Gutes, dessen Genuss uns ergötzen, noch die Bilder desjenigen Übels darstellen, welches Furcht oder Betrübnis veranlassen soll. Kurz, kein merkliches Interesse an den Empfindungen, die sie ausdrückt, einflössen.[20]

if it however should undertake to arouse in us feelings for which there are no causes in the situation where we find ourselves, and towards which our heart is not inclined, then music, using only the inarticulate tones of instrumental music, lacks the means to make these feelings interesting to our hearts. Under these circumstances music cannot make it comprehensible to us why it wants to impart to us serene or sorrowful, elevated or gay, feelings; neither can it awaken in us the images of that good which delights us, nor can it present the images of that evil which causes fear or distress. In short, music can confer no perceptible interest in the feelings which it expresses.

Sulzer's rationale for the lower status of instrumental music is similar to Koch's. When passions possessed subjects and objects, he held, they had far greater potency in a work of art.[21]

There were many among eighteenth-century music critics and connoisseurs who could accept the above defects. Although the ascription of inferiority to instrumental music because of its lack of distinct or determinate content was surprisingly persistent, many, like Lessing, found this defect to be nevertheless pleasant and justifiable. But the succession of contrasting—even contradictory—affective contents, or connotations, especially the apparent arbitrariness with which the ideas in the newer Italian instrumental pieces were arranged, presented still another, often more insurmountable, obstacle to appreciative listening. In Lessing's quotation above, it is as much the unexplained affective variety, the "unordentliche Empfindungen," as the lack of specificity of the affects, which bothers him. As far back as Muffat's *Auserlesene mit Ernst und Lust gemengte Instrumentalmusik* (1702), contrast was a recognized feature of the "new," "eartickling," Italian instrumental music. For Muffat, these contrasts (he lists those between loud and soft, tutti and solo, fast and slow) were a worthwhile aural diversion, no questions asked.[22] But the German *aufgeklärte Mensch* took Kant's injunction, "Aude sapere" seriously: he dared to know the why and the wherefore. How could a piece of instrumental music have any sense at all when it expressed contradictory contents, when it included both the serious and the joking, the agitated and the tranquil? Certainly one would not want to pay the price of an understandable content in order merely to get one's ears tickled. Sulzer damningly asserted that most Italian sonatas were characterized by

ein Geräusch von willkührlich aufeinander folgenden Tönen . . . phantastische plötzliche

Übergänge vom Fröhlichen zum Klagenden, vom Pathetischen zum Tändelnden, ohne dass man begreift was der Tonsetzer damit haben will.[23]

a bustling of tones in an arbitrary sequence . . . fantastic sudden transitions from the happy to the complaining, from the pathetic to the trifling, beyond anyone's comprehension of what the composer means by them.

In 1739 Johann Mattheson was already describing most Italian sonatas in uncomplimentary terms. They were ''unnatural''—a mere ''patchwork'' of stuck-together ideas.[24] Lessing called a symphony in which different movements expressed contradictory passions a ''musical monster.''[25] The stylish new multi-colored tidbits were a threat to the integrity of earlier, more carefully wrought and orderly—more German—artworks. Similarly, Johann Friedrich Reichardt defended the moving and unified character of Berlin music against the ''thousandfold multiplicity'' of this fashionable new style.[26] Quantz warned students against most of the new pieces, which consisted only of a ''Mischmasch'' of borrowed and stuck-together ideas.[27] They did not have the unified ''Charakter'' of the much recommended French characteristic pieces.[28] And a piece without unity was without order. Thus, Marpurg, who is urging German composers to be more French than Italian, speaks of the ''allerneuesten italienischen Geschmack'' as one wherein nothing but ''Unordnung'' reigns. It was a question of the Italians' having allowed their famed inventiveness to run to excess.[29] And Mattheson warned composers of instrumental music against abusing their freedom from words and producing only ''unförmliches Geklängel.''[30] Hiller respected the right of the instrumental composer to a certain amount of freedom to give his ideas free play, but with one qualification:

Nur hüte er sich vor jenem seltsamen Gemische des Comischen und Ernsthafften, des Lustigen und Traurigen, des Hohen und Niedrigen, das so lange abgeschmakt bleiben wird, als es unnatürlich ist, zugleich zu lachen und weinen.[31]

Let him beware of that strange mixture of the comic and the serious, the happy and the sad, the elevated and the lowly, that will remain tasteless as long as it is unnatural to laugh and cry at the same time.

As we shall later see, this unwillingness to accept contrasts, or certain kinds of contrast, was not only a matter of intelligibility in the cognitive sense. To be sure, affective variety was treated as clouding the act of cognition—both of form and of content. But a whole view of man's emotional behavior was also involved. Hiller believed that it was unnatural to experience opposing emotions in quick succession. Lessing, we saw, felt that the contradictory emotional states expressed in the movements of a symphony did not correspond to what he could recognize as a ''correct'' sequence of feelings.[32] (On the other hand, Beethoven's teacher, Neefe, virtually bragged that he often experienced contradictory feelings in quick

succession.)[33] In this regard, Pluche again points the finger directly at instrumental music:

> Le plus beau chant, quand il n'est qu'instrumental, devient presque nécessairement froid, puis ennuyeux, parce qu'il n'exprime rien . . . . On n'eut jamais bonne opinion d'un esprit qui passe de la tristesse aux grands éclats de rire, et du badinage à l'air grave, à l'air tendre, à la colère, et à la rage sans avoir aucun sujèt de rire ni de se fâcher. Or les sonates et bien d'autres musiques font-elles autre chose que ce que nous venons de dire? Elles sont une musique comme le papier marbré est une peinture. Il semble même que plus elles seront passionées moins elles doivent paroître raisonnables.[34]

> The most beautiful melody, when it is only instrumental, becomes necessarily cold, and then boring, because it expresses nothing. . . . One would never have a good opinion of a person who passed from sadness to great outbursts of laughter, from jesting to a serious manner, then to a tender manner, to anger, and then to rage, without having any subject [object] for laughter or grief. Now, are sonatas and many other kinds of music anything other than what I have just said? They are music just as marbled paper is a painting. It even seems that the more they become passionate, the less they seem reasonable.

An interesting case is Junker, who proclaimed loudly that all emotions contained contrasts, that emotional life is in a constant state of ebb and flow, but who denied that instrumental music had the ability to communicate more than four basic emotional states. Words were required to make clear sense out of emotional variety. For example, when in a piece where the main theme is love, another theme representing anger is brought in,

> so entstehet die letze Leidenschaft ohne Vorbereitung, sie ist also unbestimmte, unerklärliche Leidenschaft, sie verdunkelt die, ihr entegegen gesetzte, statt dass sie in ein stärkerers Licht setzen sollte, und das ganze Stück verliert seine bestimmte Bedeutung.[35]

> then the latter passion arises without preparation, it is thus an undefined, unexplained passion; it obscures the opposing passion instead of putting it in a stronger light, and the whole piece loses its definite meaning.

Many people, towards the end of the century, expected, and understood as natural, a certain amount of affective variety in instrumental music; but the complaint, such as Sulzer's above, against fantastic sudden transitions persisted. In 1798, Rochlitz (not by most standards a conservative) was still warning German composers against attempting to combine the "cute" Italian style with the serious style; again only Haydn could get away with that.[36] For a time, as with Forkel and Junker in the seventies and eighties, there is much talk of the art of transitions; the linking of contrasting characters is discussed as a special aesthetic and compositional problem. We owe perhaps our most well-defined awareness of the new Italian instrumental style to the acute practical musician, Johann Joachim Quantz. Quantz lamented the popularity of this new style, which he pinpointed as having arisen in the later works of Vivaldi and in the works of Tartini. The chief distin-

guishing feature of this style, Quantz regretted, was that it had altogether abandoned "das sangbar" (the cantabile) as a compositional model. Whereas earlier instrumental composers had tried to imitate "die guten Singart" (the good manner of singing), the newer composers relied on virtuosity, arbitrary ornamentation, extreme height, wild runs, a vulgar and comic tone, vacuous harmonies, and a string of brazen and disorderly ideas. The new pieces, according to Quantz, had

> mehr Frechheit und verworrene Gedanken, als Bescheidenheit, Vernunft und Ordnung. Sie suchen zwar viel Neues zu erfinden; sie verfallen aber dadurch in viele niederträchtige und gemeine Gänge, die mit dem, was sie noch Gutes untermischen, wenig Gemeinschaft haben. . . . Sie suchen nicht die Leidenschaften so auszudrücken und zu vermischen, wie es in der Singmusik üblich ist.[37]

> more boldness and confusion of thoughts, than discretion, reason, and order. They attempt, I must confess, to invent much that is new; but they are thereby led into many vulgar and common ideas, which have little in common with the good things they also mix in. . . . They do not seek to express and mix together the passions according to the usual practice of vocal music.

To be sure, such music had aroused wonderment (*Verwunderung*), but in departing from the lyrical character of vocal music it had lost its power to move—which is, of course, the very goal of music. Mattheson, too, identified music's power to move with vocal melody, as his expression "herzrührenden Gesang" itself implies. He called upon both Saint Paul and the patron saint of neoclassicism, Horace, in condemning merely pleasant sounds. When a composer writes with no intention to move, to reach the seat of human virtue, which is the passions, his music is

> nichts anders, ob es gleich, dem äusserlichen Ansehen nach, schöner als die Venus wäre, denn ein feiner, niedlicher Leib, ohne eine verständliche Seele; es sind angenehme Noten, liebliche Klange, ohne herzrührenden Gesang. Ist es demnach ein Wunder, dass bey so gestalten Sachen . . . den Zuhörern nur die blossen Ohren gekitzelt, nicht aber gehöriger Maasen das Hertz und Nachdencken rege gemacht werden. Es sind, nach dem Ausspruch des Horaz, *nugae canorae*, und nach Pauli Worten, klingende Schellen; auf gut Frantzösisch, des *niaiseries harmonieuses*, welches ich mich nicht zu verteutschen unterfange, aber wol verstehe.[38]

> nothing other than a pretty and graceful body without an intelligent soul, even though its exterior appearance be more beautiful than Venus; one hears pleasant notes and charming sounds, but no heart-moving melody. Is it therefore a wonder that in such pieces . . . the listeners only get their ears tickled, rather than their hearts and minds justly stimulated? One hears, after the dictum of Horace, *nugae canorae* [melodious nonsense], and in Paul's words, tinkling cymbals; in good French, *niaiseries harmonieuses [harmonious inanities]*, which I will not venture to translate, but which I understand quite well.

Mattheson's remarks were largely directed against that older, "barbaric," German style described by Quantz as made more for the eye than for the ear—that dry pedantic style of counterpoint devoid of the pleasing and touching qualities of vocal lyricism.[39] The natural, vocal style of writing was also recommended by Marpurg to German composers who wanted to free themselves from the "Gothic"

style of the past, which for Marpurg meant that style characterized by excessive ornamentation. But the German composer must also avoid the excesses of the new Italian instrumental style as described by Quantz. All these stylistic preferences are integrated into Marpurg's mid-century prescription for tasteful music, with its decided emphasis on vocal lyricism, and with its shunning of compositional or instrumental artifice on the one hand, and of the comic and the vulgar on the other:

> Man schreibe nur natürlich und singbar, ohne gemein und trocken zu werden; angenehm, ohne lappisch; männlich, ohne frech zu seyn; ausdrückend, ohne Zwang, und künstlich ohne auszuschweifen. Man höre einmahl auf, zu lärmen, und bestrebe sich etwa mehr der Zärtlichkeit, und suche nicht das Ohr zu übertauben, sondern zu kützeln, und nicht sowohl das Ohr zu kützeln, als die Neigungen zu lenken; . . . man betrachte die überflüssigen Zierathen, als ein Ueberbleibsel des Göthischen Geschmacks; man lasse nicht die Stimme arpeggiren und schaffe die ungeheuren Sprünge ab, bey deren Anhörung sich mancher einbilder mögte, als ob er sich in einer cabriolirenden Seiltantzerbude befände.[40]

> Let us just write music that is natural and melodious but not common and insipid; pleasant but not puerile; masculine but not obtrusive; expressive but without undue force: artfully, but in moderation. Let us stop, once and for all, making so much noise, and rather strive more for delicacy; let us not seek to drown the ear, but rather to tickle it, and indeed not so much even to tickle the ear as to govern the disposition;. . . let us regard superfluous ornamentation as a relic of the Gothic taste; let us not make the voice sing arpeggios, and let us get rid of those monstrous leaps, which make many feel as though they were in the presence of a somersaulting tightrope-walker.

The enlightened composer would avoid the "unnatural" gestures so natural, as we view things today, to instrumental utterance. C. P. E. Bach, who is said to have played such an important role in the development of Haydn's style, also clung to the *sangbar* as the key to creating a moving music. The unvocal features of his style (i.e., "filling the ear [with enough notes]") he characterized apologetically as a practical necessity; he tried to avoid mere "drumming," arpeggios, and the Alberti bass; such things could never "touch the heart."[41]

Thus, forthright lyrical utterance, even before Rousseau's famous condemnation of harmony, was seen as the model for the only moving and "natural"—in short, tasteful—form of music. Thus, we often hear, from Mattheson (1739) through Koch (1802), not so much that instrumental music must imitate nature, but that instrumental music is an imitation of vocal music.[42] Christian Daniel Schubart, who was a proud rebel of the *Geniezeit*, asserted that all instrumental music was an imitation of vocal music and defined the sonata as the "imitation of human conversation with dead instruments."[43] And Koch even went so far as to define a symphony as a chorus without words.[44]

Whether because of its neglect of "herzrührenden" song, its lack of a clear didactic content, or its failure to evoke sympathy with characters in situations of moral import, the new instrumental music was generally held to be incapable of moving, hence affecting morally, the heart of the listener.[45] Most of it displayed a

complete lack of moral qualities; it was "mere noise," "useless junk."[46] It simply could not live up to the standards of the other arts. It was as pointless and insignificant as marbled paper, or a painting of mere colors, with no recognizable shapes. It was mere ear-tickling *Klingklang*. If it was not downright boring, as Lessing, Pluche, and Krause contended, then it bore the equally damning designation of "idle pastime."[47] Krause, in a poem quoted by Reichardt, identifies the appeal of merely ear-tickling or sensually appealing music with the degenerate life at court. Thus, he would banish the composers of such music:

> I implore you with your inanity
> And ear-tickling jingle-jangle to go.
> You Buffoons! . . .
> . . . You defilers of noble harmony!
> Away to the degenerate court, where absurdity,
> Where boredom, satiety, and petty conceit reside;
> There will you capture your fill of bravos,
> Of princely gold and princely laughter—away with you![48]

These sounds divest of sense were at best a cure for boredom. Sulzer spoke of the custom of amateurs' getting together and playing for their own pleasant pastime, or for the sake of the free flitting around of their fantasies; neither "use" of instrumental music appeared worthwhile to the moralistic Sulzer. Art must confer some permanent uplift. Music must not be a mere transitory play of the emotions.[49]

Indeed, one did not have to specify all the defects listed above. Even disregarding all these deficiencies, the sheer sensuality of a music without words was in itself ground for condemnation. Aural delight or pleasure simply had no self-sufficient role to play in most aesthetic theories of eighteenth-century Germany. Some feared music's direct sensual appeal more than others. Some wanted to replace it with an act of cognitive communication or transmute it into an emphatic embodiment of useful and intelligible concepts (the more rationalistic approach); some wanted to exploit it or impress it into service of moral ends (as did Mattheson and Sulzer). For others it was an unavoidable stigma. It is significant that even Schiller, who condemned a work of art as invalid insofar as it succeeded merely in its intention to communicate a definite, specific representation, a cognitively comprehensible content, or a moral lesson, and who enjoined the other arts to make use of the nonconceptual immediacy of music's sensual appeal medium, nevertheless found that the sheer sensuality of music was unbefitting to the true work of art and that

> die geistreichste Musik durch ihre Materie noch immer in einer grossern Affinität zu den Sinnen steht, als die wahre aesthetische Freiheit duldet.[50]

> even the most clever music possesses by virtue of its medium a closer affinity to the senses than true aesthetic freedom can allow.

He therefore spoke out strongly against the "animalian" sensation of pleasure afforded by the "sweet melodiousness" and "agreeable tickling" of music in the predominant taste. The "principle of freedom" was eclipsed by the sheer force of the sensual and quasi-emotional involvement elicited by music.[51]

Given instrumental music's divorce from the world of intellectual and moral realities, given its failure to occupy the head or the heart, and given its appeal only to the ear and its resulting reliance on sheer sensual diversion, it almost naturally (some would have said inevitably) fell into certain abuses. The undesirable features—such as an excessive display of virtuosity and of compositional intricacy and inventiveness; reliance on sheer variety and novelty in order to elicit the listener's attention; the use of the unexpected and illogical in order to engage the listener in an entertaining game of expectation-play; its sheer ear-tickling triviality and playfulness; and its dance-like, base, comic, even "cute," character—all these undersirable natural proclivities of instrumental music formed the subjects for another group of complaints. This group of complaints will bring us into closer contact with the actual features of the Italian instrumental music which German critics found offensive. The first group listed, as it were, instrumental music's sins of omission; the second will list its sins of commission.

One fascination with the art of pure sounds manifested itself in the form of counterpoint and well worked-out harmony; and although there were no excessive displays of counterpoint in the new Italian style (indeed, we shall see, it was faulted for its insipid harmony), the age of a contrapuntally dominated musical style was close enough so that we find complaints against music, and especially instrumental music, because it was such a ready and natural vehicle for the display of the composer's skill, and thus so easily fell into neglect of its true goal of moving the listener. Rousseau's diatribes against counterpoint, indeed, against any contrapuntal independence at all in a song's accompaniment, are legion; since the only fit subjects for musical expression were the natural accents of passion, such compositional elaborations could only serve, on Rousseau's account, to obscure the true meaning of music.[52] John Brown, whose aesthetic tract on poetry and music was translated into German in 1769, accounted for the downfall of music, and its current neglect of "expression and true pathos," by explaining that counterpoint gave instrumental music such a new and appealing form that it led people to consider instrumental music as a complete form of music in itself, independent of poetry and song. This preoccupation with an art of pure sounds naturally led then to the downfall of music; for instrumental music's independence

> gab ihr eine künstliche und ausgearbeitete Wendung. Der Componist dachte nur auf neue Harmonie, Dissonanzen, Auflösungen, Fugen und Canons, und brüstete sich, wie der Dichter, mit einer prahlerischen Ausübung der Kunst, mit Hintansetzung des Ausdrücke und des wahren Pathos.[53]

gave it an artificial and elaborate character. The composer thought only of new harmonies, dis-

sonances, resolutions, fugues and canons; and he prided himself, as did the poet, on an ostentatious exercise of art, disregarding all expression and true pathos.

The contrapuntal arts were besmudged with the mannered, heartless, and "barbaric" pedanticism of Germany's past. They were by definition not in good taste; they were neither pleasing nor moving. They were mere *Künstelei* (petty artifice).

A whole host of complaints arose against another display of skill, which was quite common to Quantz's "new Italian instrumental" style. Virtuosity was viewed as a poison to the one and only "true, good taste"; and this poison came from Italy, Quantz tells us in no uncertain terms[54] Another German writer, Christoph Nichelmann, who espoused the popular imitation of nature doctrine and then attempted to construe contrapuntal music as the only natural music (to most mid-century critics "contrapuntal" and "natural" were by definition terms of opposition), also pointed his finger at Italy. The performers in Italy had too much power, he explained, and they insisted on a style providing opportunity for "excessive" ornamentation with which they could show off their virtuosity; an artificial style with offensively barren harmonies (the harmonies had to be simple to allow for the ornamentation) resulted. The desire merely to flatter the ear and to awaken only wonderment had found a ready partner in this new, brazenly homophonic style; the "noble simplicity of nature" and the only truly moving music had thus been undermined.[55] Hiller isolated the new virtuoso-dominated style as that type of music which could not be subsumed under the "imitation of nature" doctrine. Solos and concertos do not imitate, he said; they only seek to amaze, to arouse *Verwunderung*. He then warned against this tendency to indulge in the *wunderbar* (as opposed to the *wahrscheinlich*, or verisimilitudinous, which alone was sanctioned by the mimetic doctrine of neoclassic aesthetics). Sheer acrobatics he opposed to "the true"—music which expressed the passions. As with the other arts, music had sunk into a "night of bombast and barbarity." Although in one context he seems to equate musical bombast (*Schwulst*) with the contrapuntal *Künstelei* we discussed above, it is clear from the quotation below that it is the "unnaturalness" of certain instrumental gestures that constituted the greater threat to his values:

Je mehr man glaubte, dass man für das ausserordentliche und übernatürliche zu sorgen hatte, desto mehr verfiel man in eine Art von Unregelmässigkeit und Schwulst, wenn man sich anders dieses Ausdruckes in der Musik bedienen kann. Es wurden nicht allein die natürlichen Grenzen der Instrumenten überstritten, so dass man auf Bassinstrumenten Discant-und Violinnoten spielen musste, um sich durch übernatürliche Höhe hören zu lassen: sondern die Zusammensetzung der Noten ward durch allerhand ungewöhnliche Sprünge so holpricht, und durch eine übertriebene Geschwindigkeit so finster und schwer, dass man gar oft, statt des Vergnügens oder der Bewunderung, mit Angst und Schrecken erfüllt wurde.[56]

The more one believed that one had to be concerned only with the unusual and the unnatural, all the more did one fall into a kind of irregularity and bombast, if one can apply this word to music.

> Not only were the natural limitations of the instruments violated, so that one had to play discant and violin notes on bass instruments in order, by virtue of their unnatural height, to make oneself heard; but the connection of the notes was made so clumsy by all kinds of unusual leaps, and so obscure and burdensome by an exaggerated speed, that one quite often upon hearing such music was filled with fear and trembling instead of pleasure or wonderment.

Many complaints had to do with the "freedom" of instrumental music. As we already saw, many found the variety and contrasts typical of the newer music incomprehensible or confusing. And the instrumental medium, where music was free of the compulsion of a text, seemed only to heighten the tendencies of composers to indulge in sudden surprising contrasts and novel, unusual, and striking ideas—to indulge in the sheer exhilarating exercise of their powers of creativity. Thus, complaints against lack of unity and lack of coherent succession were complemented by those decrying the "brazen and bizarre" ideas of the new music, its "sudden transitions," its "weird mixtures," and its "thousandfold multiplicity." Italian music had long been noted for its wealth of invention and its bold and *frappant* ideas (many would have preferred to call it arbitrariness and incoherence). But these fecund and disorderly instincts of the Italians had been allowed too much room to develop, given the dangerous freedom of instrumental music. Thus, Marpurg wrote:

> Ich billige alles, was wahrhaftig schön ist. . . . Dass ich aber nicht bekennen sollte, dass die meisten Italiäner das wahre verlassen, dass sie ihrer Einbildung zuviele Freyheit erlauben, dass sie sich gar zu oft vergessen, und ein dunkles Nichts schreiben, dass sie nach einem prächtigen und erhabenen Ausdruck durch einen jähen Fall ins matte und kriechende gerathen, dieses wird man vor mir nicht fordern.[57]

> I value everything which is truly beautiful. . . . No one can demand of me, however, that I must not proclaim that most Italians forsake the true, that they allow their imagination too much freedom, that they too often forget themselves and write an obscure nothingness, that they often, after a splendid and sublime expression, fall precipitously into insipid and servile ideas.

And when summing up the character of Italian music in order to compare it to the French, Quantz refers to it as too varied:

> Denn so wie die Italiäner in der Musik fast zu veränderlich sind; so sind die Franzosen zu beständig, und zu sklavisch.[58]

> For just as the Italians are almost too variable in their music; so are the French too constant and too servile.

Too many contrasts and too much variety often mean incoherence. Reichardt gives a vivid picture of the implausibility which resulted from the "thousandfold multiplicity" of the clever new ear-tickling style: the pieces are nothing but

neumodischen, buntschäckigten Sächelchen . . . wo in einem Stücke bald ein cosackischer
Tanz, bald ein englischer, bald ein polnischer, bald wieder ein Husarenmarsch, und dann wieder
einer Tyrade aus einem Kirchencomponisten ausgeschrieben, um auch Bart und Mantel zu
haben.[59]

new-fangled, gaudy-checked knick-knacks . . . where in one piece are pilfered first a Cossack
dance, then an English, then a Polish one, then again a Hussar's march, and then again a tirade
from a church composition, in order to have a beard and cloak as well.

French character pieces, on the other hand, were recommended by Sulzer as excellent interpretative etudes; each piece possessed a definite "Charakter," that is, each piece expressed only one affect. C. P. E. Bach recommended them as studies in "coherent performance."[60] Indeed, the Italian penchant for disunity was pointed out early in the century by François Raguenet; he called the Italian style "incoherent" and the French "coherent."[61] Similarly, Quantz, in his autobiography, likened his travelling from Italy to France to a trip "out of variety into unity."[62] Part of the essential appeal of this "incoherent" style was of course the pleasant surprises it afforded, as Muffat in 1702 had pointed out. In 1713 Mattheson had summed up the essence of Italian music by saying "The Italians surprise; the French charm; the Germans study; and the English pay."[63] And Quantz, in his *Versuch*, remarked that one could always predict what would happen next in a piece of French music.[64] Quantz as we know had mixed feelings about this abundant and often surprising variety of Italian music. Many others reacted more strongly. Surprises could be entertaining, to be sure, but they only occasioned *Verwunderung*, which was not considered among "the passions" which all true music was supposed to "rouse and still." The frank expectation-play generated by this "arbitrary" style offended many serious German connoisseurs. Karl Ludwig Junker, for example, who saw contrast as essential to any work of expressive music, nevertheless could not countenance expectation-play for its own sake. To intensify a calm, depressed passion merely for the sake of eliciting expectations or creating a "pleasant deception" was wrong. Even the stock-in-trade deceptive cadence was aesthetically suspect:

Bizarrerie ist's: wenn der Bass, an statt in die Oktav wieder einzufallen, und die Empfindung zu
endigen, in die Sexte eintritt. Dieser Fall ist unvermuthet, und selbst durch eine Art von Neuheit
interessant.[65]

It is an oddity: when the bass progresses to the sixth [scale degree] instead of ending the feeling
and progressing to the tonic. This progression is unexpected and is only interesting by virtue of a
kind of novelty.

Finally, we come to a group of complaints which condemns the character itself of the new instrumental style. Of course, in eighteenth-century terms it had no "Charakter" at all. Nevertheless contemporary writers did find adjectives to de-

scribe it. By far the most common are the already familiar "ohrkitzelnd," or "ear-tickling," and the work "tändelnd," or "playful," which can also be translated in a derogatory sense as "trifling" or "frivolous." Even if the new musical inventions had been presented in an orderly and coherent way, and had not been designed to display the performer's skill or the composer's inventiveness, they would still apparently have been rejected due to their simple-minded, insignificant character. The new Italian music was not serious; it was common and trivial, rather than noble and elevating. Thus Germans such as Schubart idolized C. P. E. Bach's high-mindedness; for he stood above the "reigning spirit of triviality."

> Alles tändeln . . . alles süssliche geistentnervende Wesen, alles Berlockengeklingel der heutigen Tonmeister ist seinem Riesengeiste ein Greuel.[66]

> All trifling, all saccharine brainlessness, all the trinket-tingling of today's composers is an abomination to his mighty intellect.

As early as 1753 Quantz had isolated this "common," "comic" quality as typical of the new Italian instrumental taste. Not only was it a bold and bizarre taste; not only was its harmony insipid; not only was there too much emphasis on arbitrary ornamentation and virtuosity; not only did it depart from the truly good taste in trying to please by means other than singing: it was not serious—it was even comic. Tartini's music, he writes, contains

> nichts, als trockene, einfältige, und ganz gemeine Gedanken . . . welche sich allenfalls besser zur komischen, als zur ernsthaften Musik, schicken möchten.[67]

> nothing but dull, simple and altogether common ideas, which would be more appropriate to comic music than to serious music.

In 1795, in his article "Ueber den modegeschmacke in der Tonkunst," Koch was still not reconciled to this fashionable triviality:

> So viele der Modetonstücke erhalten ihren ganzen Reiz nur durch niedere Tändeleyen.[68]

> So many of the fashionable pieces owe all their charm to common frivolities.

He objected, as had Reichardt in his critique of Berlin music, to the absence of intense emotions, and to the absence of "higher beauties which elevate the spirit."[69] Even the style of such prominent German composers as Haydn, Dittersdorf and Filtz was criticized in Hiller's *Wochentliche Nachrichten* as too *komisch* and *tändelnd*.[70] And when C. P. E. Bach, late in his life, began to write rondos, a genre long identified with this *Tändelei* (playfulness or frivolity), he was widely criticized for stooping to such a low level, and he self-consciously had to explain to his friend, C. F. Cramer,

Wenn man alt wird, so legt man sich aufs spassen![71]

When one becomes an old man, then one devotes oneself to having fun!

How could mere trifling or sheer playfulness serve the ennobling ends of art? This was the question posed by the many complaints against "blos Tändelei."[72]

In order to isolate the themes of our investigation, I have concentrated so far on complaints against the phenomenon of instrumental music as it existed in the eighteenth century; for they show in the most colorful language the enigmatic nature of an art form at once successful and uncomprehended. The complaints show us what it was about the new music which critics found ideologically unacceptable, and what specific attributes of this successful music would have to find some aesthetic sanction, for instrumental music to be accounted for as a significant art.

But complaints aside, there were other qualities of instrumental music which had not found sanction within contemporary critical theories. These qualities emerge from more neutral and practical discussions of the instrumental idiom. For there were of course many who accepted the new style and who spoke approvingly, if not enthusiastically, of its peculiar attributes. But insofar as these typical attributes were slow to become justified in terms of more abstract aesthetic principles, they too constituted problems for the critic or philosopher who sought to reconcile aesthetic theory and musical practice. Thus, in the remainder of this chapter I would like to examine various eighteenth-century remarks which reveal the contemporary conception of the specific nature of instrumental music. It must be remembered that this nature, even when accepted, remained for most of the eighteenth-century an aesthetic anomaly: many characteristic features of the instrumental style, whether accepted or rejected, could only with difficulty be accommodated within the prevailing aesthetic ideology of Enlightenment Germany. It is these difficulties which we shall be studying in later chapters.

The most persistent style characteristic mentioned in the more neutral and practical contemporary accounts is *Abwechselung*, a term we did not come across in our survey of complaints. Translated in most dictionaries as "alternation," "succession," "change," or "variety," the word suggests, it seems, only a vague quality of changingness over time, which we might see as typical of all music. However, as we examine its usage in eighteenth-century musical criticism, it becomes apparent that often the most apt translation is "contrast," a quality we know is widely recognized today as a hallmark of the new Italian instrumental style.[73] That *Abwechselung* was a necessary ingredient in music was clearly grasped by practical musicians of the eighteenth-century. Leopold Mozart refers to it as "liebliche Abwechselung," and "angenehme Abwechselung." He even countenances a type of music whose goal would not be the usual expression of an affect, but merely the making of a "beliebte Abwechselung."[74] Quantz expressly

recognized *Abwechselung* as an absolutely essential feature of any pleasant and tasteful music:

> Man erwägt nicht, dass die Annehmlichkeit der Musik, nicht in der Gleichheit oder Aehnlichkeit, sondern in der Verschiedenheit bestehe. Wenn es möglich wäre, dass alle Tonkünstler, in gleicher Stärke, und in gleichem Geschmacke singen oder spielen könnten; so würde, wegen Mangels einer angenehmen Abwechselung, der grösste Theil des Vergnügens und der Musik nicht empfunden werden.[75]

> One does not reflect on the fact that the pleasantness of music consists not in uniformity or consistency, but in diversity. If it were possible for all players to play in uniform loudness, or for all singers to sing according to a uniform taste, then the greatest part of pleasure and of music would not be felt, because of the lack of pleasant contrast.

Quantz uses the term *Abwechselung* to indicate contrasts on several levels. In the quotation immediately above the contrasts recommended are those between musical compositions themselves. Elsewhere he speaks of the *Abwechselung* of dissonance and consonance, of forte and piano, and most importantly of the singing and the brilliant. These contrasts enable the composer, respectively, to keep the listener's attention, to "distinctly" portray the passions, and to move the listener. It is the last type of contrast, that between the characters or moods of various musical ideas within a piece, which Quantz repeatedly emphasizes and recommends. In explaining how an "adagio spiritoso" has more liveliness than other adagios, he reminds his reader that good taste requires some contrast:

> Sollten aber, ausser dieser [lebhaften] Art, einige cantable Gedanken, so wie es der ins Feine gebrachte Geschmack in der Setzkunst erfordert, mit untergemischet seyn; so muss man sich alsdenn im Spielen auch darnach richten, und das Ernsthafte mit dem Schmeichelnden abwechseln.[76]

> If, in addition to this [lively] mood, several singing ideas were intermingled, as the present refined taste requires, then the performer must observe these changes and alternate the serious with the ingratiating.

And in describing the secret of writing a good sonata, Quantz emphasizes the importance of a *Vermischung* (mixture) of the singing and the lively, and of the pleasing and the brilliant. In other contexts, we have seen, he spoke of the *Abwechselung* of the singing and the brilliant.[77] If we bear in mind, then, Quantz's comparable usage of these two terms, we can see that *Abwechselung*, or *Vermischung*, emerges as an essential ingredient not only of the sonata, but of all music, all good taste, and even of all musical wisdom:

> Die Gemüthsneigungen eines jeden Zuhörers [muss] darinne ihre Nahrung finden. Es muss weder durchgehends pur cantabel, noch pur lebhaft seyn. So wie sich jeder Satz von dem andern sehr unterscheiden muss; so muss auch ein jeder Satz, in sich selbst, eine gute Vermischung von gefälligen und brillanten Gedanken haben. Denn der schönste Gesang kann, wenn vom Anfange

bis zum Ende nichts anders vorkommt, endlich einschläfern; und eine beständige Lebhaftigkeit, oder lauter Schwierigkeit, machen zwar Verwunderung, sie rühren aber nicht sonderlich. Dergleichen Vermischung unterschiedener Gedanken aber, ist nicht nur beym Solo allen, sondern vielmehr auch bey allen musikalischen Stücken zu beobachten. Wenn ein Componist diese recht zu treffen, und dadurch die Leidenschaften der Zuhörer in Bewegung zu bringen weis: so kann man mit Rechte von ihm sagen, dass er einen hohen Grad des guten Geschmacks erreichet, und, so zu sagen, den musikalischen Stein der Weisen gefunden habe.[78]

The disposition of each listener [must] find nourishment in [the sonata]. Its character throughout must be neither pure songfulness nor pure liveliness. Just as each movement must be very different from the others, each movement must within itself have a good admixture of agreeable and brilliant ideas. For after all, the most beautiful song can put one to sleep if nothing else is to be found from beginning to end; and constant liveliness or sheer difficulty causes wonderment to be sure, but neither one is particularly moving. Rather, the composer should include such an admixture of different ideas, not only in a solo but even more so in all musical pieces. When a composer knows how to hit upon this proper balance and consequently knows how to move the passions of the listener, then one can rightfully say that he has attained a high degree of good taste and that he has found, so to speak, the philosophers' stone of musical wisdom.

Charles Henri de Blainville, whose ideas appeared in Hiller's *Wöchentliche Nachrichten*, saw *Abwechselung* of affective contents as necessary both to keep the listener's attention and to keep his "soul in motion"—in short, as essential to accomplishing music's end of moving. Representation is needed too, but it cannot nearly suffice:

Die Musik ist für die Ohren das, was die Mahlerey für die Augen ist. Sie muss den Zuhörer interessiren, sie muss seine Aufmerksamkeit an sich ziehen, indem sie ihm Bilder vorstellt, die er für bekannt annimmt, und indem sie dabei immer auf Abwechselung siehet. Bald gehet sie von der Empfindung der Leidenschaften zu physikalischen Bildern der Natur über; bald von der erhabenen Schreibart zur gemeinen; vom pathetischen Töne zum muntern; von ernsthaften zum scherzenden; so dass die Seele, die durch diese beständig Abwechselung immer in Bewegung gehalten wird, ihr Vergnügen in einem Zustande findet, wo das Mannichfaltige demselben immer neue Nahrung giebt. Denn wenn sie nur einen Augenblick ruhig gelassen wird, so zerstreuet sich die Seele, der Eckel bemächtigt sich ihrer, das Vergnügen verschwindet; alles stehet still, aus Mangel der Bewegung.[79]

Music is for the ears what painting is for the eyes. It must interest the listener. It must draw the listener's attention to it by means of presenting images which he recognizes, and also by means of providing constant contrast. First the music goes from passionate feeling to physical images of nature, then from a sublime style to a common one, then from a pathetic tone to a cheerful one, then from the serious to the joking; thereby, since the soul is always kept in movement by this constant alternation, does the soul find itself in a condition of constant pleasure, where the multiplicity of stimuli is always providing new nourishment. For if the soul is allowed to rest for only one instant, its attention is dissipated, aversion sets in, and pleasure disappears; everything stagnates from lack of movement.

As early as the beginning of the century Raguenet recognized that the Italians had a special gift for uniting even contrary characters. No other nation, he wrote, had even attempted to unite such things as the soft and the piercing, the tender and the sprightly, as Bononcini had done in the aria from Camilla, "Mai non si vidde ancor più bella fedeltà" and its symphony. Raguenet explicitly recognized the aesthetic success of such a unity: "These different characters they are able to unite so artfully that, far from destroying a contrary by its contrary, they make the one serve to embellish the other."[80] However, most German critics were not so sure of the aesthetic validity of such strong contrasts. For the principle of *Abwechselung*, especially in the extreme formulation which Blainville gave it, blatantly disregarded the frequent objections to contradictory contents, most notably the objections to the juxtaposition of the elevated and the common, and of the serious and the joking. And even in its less extreme versions, like Quantz's, one can still see the conflict of this demand for contrast with demands for unity and a coherent, intelligible succession of ideas. It appears that what was perceived as cognitively clear was sensually, or aurally, boring; and what was sensually pleasant and stimulating was perceived as cognitively confusing.

Another closely related feature seen as typical of instrumental music runs into a quite similar problem. Johann Adolph Scheibe, Mattheson, Leopold Mozart, Quantz, and C. P. E. Bach all point out the pleasurable benefits of playing with the listener's expectations.[81] But how does the unexpected, which can cause such pleasurable surprise, find a place in an aesthetic ideology demanding intelligibility, coherence, and the expression of *an* affect? Indeed, what does expectation-play have at all to do with the expression of emotion and the moving of an audience?

For Mattheson, expectation-play was even a very "natural" thing:

Das Gehör hat fast nichts liebers, als dergleichen angenehme Wiederkunfft eines schon vorher vernommenen lieblichen Hauptsatzes: insonderheit wenn derselbe auf eine gescheute Art versetzet wird, und an solchen Orte zum Vorschein kommt, wo man ihn fast nicht vermuthet. Das heisst Natur: und all empfindliche Ergetzlichkeiten haben natürlicher Weise fast eben diese Beschaffenheit.[82]

The ear likes perhaps nothing more than when a delightful theme, with which it is already acquainted, so pleasantly returns; especially when it has been cleverly displaced and then appears in a spot where one would almost never have expected it. This is nature; and all sensual delights naturally have just about this same quality.

C. P. E. Bach, however, in writing of the free fantasy, had treated the unexpected and the natural as opposites. Both, he advised, were essential ingredients of the fantasy; but one must make only moderate use of the potency of the unexpected. If a composer has enough skill, Bach writes, he should not constantly use only natural harmonies; he should also "betray" the ear from time to time. Too much uniformity tires the ear; however, by making use of the "infinite riches of harmonic variety" and by playing with the listener's expectations, one can "rouse and still the passions."[83] In the Blainville quotation above we also saw that the unexpected was not merely an antidote to boredom, but also an element in keeping the listener's soul "in motion." Indeed, it is difficult at times to distinguish divertissement and emotion—to separate "effect" and "affect."[84] When reading Wolfgang Mozart's letters one frequently encounters his concern for the "effect" produced by a piece. His concern with effect led him at times naturally into the deliberate use of the unexpected, as in the opening of the third movement of his Paris Symphony:

Gleich mitten in Ersten Allegro, war eine Pasage die ich wohl wuste dass sie gefallen müste, alle zuhörer wurden davon hingerissen—und war ein grosses applaudissement—weil ich aber wuste, wie ich sie schriebe, was das für einen Effect machen würde, so brachte ich sie auf die lezt noch einmahl an—da giengs nun Da capo. Das Andante gefiel auch, besonders aber das lezte Allegro —weil ich hörte dass hier alle lezte Allegro wie die Ersten mit allen instrumenten zugleich und meistens unisono anfangen, so fieng ichs mit die 2 violin allein piano nur 8 tact an—daraus kamm gleich ein forte—mit hin machten die zuhörer,/wie ichs erwartete/beym Piano sch—dann kamm gleich das forte—sie das forte hören, und die hände zu klatschen war eins—ich gieng also gleich für freude nach der Sinfonie ins Palais Royale—[und] nahm ein guts gefrornes.[85]

Just in the middle of the first Allegro there was a passage which I felt sure must please. The audience was quite carried away—and there was a tremendous burst of applause. But as I knew, when I wrote it, what effect it would surely produce, I had introduced the passage again at the close—when there were shouts of "Da capo." The Andante also found favor, but particularly the last Allegro, because, having observed that all last as well as first Allegros begin here with all the instruments playing together and generally unisono, I began mine with two violins only, piano for the first eight bars—followed instantly by a forte; the audience, as I expected, said "hush" at the soft beginning, and when they heard the forte, began at once to clap their hands. I was so happy that as soon as the symphony was over, I went off to the Palais Royale, where I had a large ice.

Would we say, in this case, that the audience was moved—emotionally affected— or were they just stimulated to pay attention, or merely preserved from boredom by an "ear-tickling" contrast? Can one always draw the line between "affect" and "effect," or between arousal of emotion and the feelings aroused by expectation-play?

In the eighteenth-century the line was drawn quite distinctly. There was a special "affect" ascribed to the "effect" created by the bold and the unexpected: *Verwunderung* (wonderment, or astonishment). Hiller spoke of the "astonishment" evoked by the unnatural gestures typical of instrumental music.[86] Similarly, Muffat wrote at the beginning of the century that if one properly observes the *Abwechselung* in the Concerti he had written, namely

dieser opposition, oder Gegenhaltung der langsamb-und geschwindigkeit, der Stärke, und Stille; der Volle dess grossen Chors, und der Zärtigkeit des Tertzetl, gleich wie die Augen durch Gegensatz dess Schattens, also wird das Gehör in ein absonderliche Verwunderung verzückt.[87]

this opposition, these contraries, of slow and fast, of power and peace, of the fullness of the ripieno and the delicacy of the concertino—then the ear is enraptured, just as is the eye by the contrast of light and shadow, by a singular wonderment.

But *Verwunderung*, we hear again and again in the eighteenth century, has nothing to do with the true goal of music: to arouse *the* passions (my italics) in whose number *Verwunderung* did not appear. Thus was the line drawn.[88] And what was seen as an essential, even natural, ingredient of music, especially instrumental music, was allotted no role in an aesthetic theory which demanded that music purposely arouse a passion in the listener. Just as the qualities of *Abwechselung* and expectation-play were often treated as elements of musical style proper to instrumental music, and especially Italian instrumental music, so did certain writers recognize the innate "freedom" of instrumental musicians to indulge in musical acts far removed from the simple cantabile style of passionate utterance so widely prescribed in the eighteenth-century for vocal music. This freedom could allow many things not considered appropriate to the heart-to-heart communication of vocal lyricism: elaborate contrapuntal textures and display of virtuosity; a vagueness and indeterminateness of musical content; bold and strikingly novel flights of the imagination; *Abwechselung* and expectation-play; a fecundity of invention seemingly for its own sake; and hence a rich variety of contents embracing at times even contradictory elements. Mattheson and Hiller both wrote of the "freedom" of instrumental music. Burney spoke of the "happy licenses" that were the very soul of Italian music.[89] Mattheson recognized as a matter of fact that since instrumental music was bound neither by the limitations of the human voice nor by the obligation to express the sense of a text, a different kind of music would result; virtuosity and contrapuntal complexity could both find a natural outlet in instrumental music. He writes in bold letters,

dass die Instrumente mehr Kunstwerke zulassen, denn die Singestimmen. Die vielgeschwäntzte Noten, die Arpeggio und all andre gebrochene Sachen, ingleichen die harmonischen Kunststücklein der Contrapunkten, Fugen, Canonen sind auf Instrumenten wohl anzubringen.[90]

that instruments make possible a more elaborately worked out style than do voices. Notes with many flags, arpeggios, and other broken figures, as well as the harmonic artifices of counterpoints, fugues, and canons, all are well suited to performance by instruments.

Elsewhere, he adds that of course instrumental melodies would have more large leaps, and larger ranges, than vocal ones. But, Mattheson warns, this freedom could easily lead to formlessness.[91] The "freedom" of instrumental music

gibt demjenigen, der seinen wilden Einfällen den Zügel lässt, nur desto grössern Anlass zu allerhand Misgeburten und unförmlichen Geklängel.[92]

gives to whoever allows his wild ideas to run riot, only all the more occasion for all kinds of freakish and formless clanging.

For Hiller, writing about 30 years later, this freedom loomed as a most enticing arena in which the composer could exercise his powers of invention; and he even defended the indefiniteness of the affective content which resulted, denying that any cognitive confusion need result:

> Welches sind die Gegenstände, mit denen sich die Musik am meisten beschäfftiget? Die Leidenschaften. . . . Diese Leidenschaften sind ihm entweder vermittelst der Worte vorge-schrieben, oder er kann seinen Gedanken freyen Lauf lassen, und ohne durch Worte einge-schränkt zu werden, Emfindungen wählen, die einer oder andern Leidenschafft untergeordnet werden können, oder auch zu mehr als einer zu gehören scheinen. Und gesetzt, dass man nicht wusste, wohin man diese oder jene Erfindungen eines Componisten rechnen sollte, so hören sie doch deswegen nicht auf, ihren Grund in der menschlichen Seele und den Empfindungen dersel-ben zu haben, und die Schuld liegt bloss daran, dass wir die Grenzen dieser Empfindungen noch nicht ganz übersehen, und öffters viele sich äussern konnen, die wir mit keinem Nahmen zu be-nennen wissen.[93]

> What are the objects with which music mostly concerns itself? The passions. . . . These pas-sions are either prescribed to the composer by words, or he can give his thoughts free rein, and without being restricted by words, he can choose feelings which could be classified under one or the other passions, or even which seem to belong to more than one. And even assuming that one did not know how to classify this or that feeling of a composer, these feelings nevertheless orig-inate in the human soul and its sensations; and the reason for that rests merely on the fact that we have not yet completely surveyed the boundaries of these feelings, and often many things can be expressed, which we do not know how to label with names.

Such defenses of the nonverbalizability of instrumental music's content were rare. Even around 1800 the *Frühromantiker* still felt compelled to answer the charge (apparently quite current in the late eighteenth century) that instrumental music's affective content could not be real unless one could verbally specify it.

Junker was at first cool towards the variety, or principle of contrast, inherent in the "symphonic or modern overture style," as Burney characterized it.[94] In rather discontentedly writing that he could give many precepts for the use of speci-fic instruments in the symphony because it had no *Charakter*, he also recognized its varied essence:

> Sinfonie kan alle Instrumente vertragen, weil sie oft alle musikalische Leidenschaften abwech-selnd erregen kan.[95]

> A symphony can embrace all instruments because it is often able to arouse in turn all musical passions.

The concerto was his favorite; it had action, plot, and thematic unity.[96] (Later, Junker looked more favorably upon the contrasts of the symphony, calling them, in good Sturm und Drang language, "Ströme die alles in sich schliessen.")[97] Scheibe and Quantz also both recognized the naturalness of instrumental music's variety:

when music is not bound by a plot, when the interest is more in the sounds themselves, then more variety is not only natural, it is required.[98]

Of course thematic contrast, the first element of variety that comes to mind in
discussing eighteenth-century instrumental music, and most probably the type of
variety Junker alluded to, is not the only type of variety that could fill this requirement. For just as Mattheson saw counterpoint as a procedure proper to an art of
pure sounds, so did the more *galant* Scheibe, Sulzer, and Quantz.[99] While all three
have strong reservations, in varying degrees, about the value of the contrapuntal
arts in a music which is to be, first of all, lyrical and moving, they all nevertheless
approve of, in fact prescribe, contrapuntal interest and integrity for pieces such as
the trio sonata, the concerto, and the chamber symphony. Sulzer explains that
since chamber music is for connoisseurs and amateurs who listen attentively, each
voice must be carefully considered, and the music must exhibit the uttermost purity
of voice leading, as well as a subtle expression and more artful turns. Even for
Sulzer, the moralist, the composer's craftsmanship was central to the success of
these chamber pieces intended for attentive, practiced ears.[100] Again, a musical
element is recognized as appropriate to important genres of instrumental music;
and yet its function within the prevailing aesthetic ideologies is left in question.

There is another quality which practitioners such as Mattheson, Quantz and
C. P. E. Bach point to as not only characteristic of much instrumental music, but as
one area in which it surpasses the more ''expressive'' style of vocal music. Quantz
calls it ''Fertigkeit und Feuer'' (deftness and fire).[101] C. P. E. Bach, similarly and
with a slightly different twist, says that instrumental music excels vocal music in
''surprise and fire.''[102] Quantz suggestively opposes the lively to the cantabile, and
the brilliant to the singing.[103] Both Quantz and Mattheson lament the passing from
popularity of a genre which displayed this fiery quality most prominently—the
French overture. Mattheson wrote that there was nothing more enlivening than the
French *ouverture*.[104] When he writes that vocal music does not have such an ''impetuous and dotted essence'' as does instrumental, he used this genre as an
example.[105] If the liveliness of the French, he writes, could not express itself in
such dotted figures, they would be like cooks without salt. Moreover, this essential
ingredient is a more instrumental than vocal one:

> Gewiss ist es dennoch, dass dergleichen geschärffte und spitzige Klang-Füsse, so schön und
> munter sie auch bey den Instrumenten fallen, im Halse eines Sängers selten eine artige Wirck-
> ung thun, und gewissermassen für Fremdlinge in der Sing-Music zu achten sind.[106]

> It is certain however that such sharp and pointed musical ideas, no matter how beautiful and
> vigorous they sound on instruments, will never make a good effect in the throat of a singer, and
> are to be regarded, so to speak, as foreign to vocal music.

And despite Quantz's allegiance to the widely held view that all music drew its
power from its vocal origins and that all music must sing (as Mattheson had so

emphasized), he wrote that the most beautiful thing in music was "intermingled lyricism". He meant the cantabile as it appears in a context of contrasting brilliant and lively music; that is, when its effect was intensified by virtue of its invigorating contrast of *Abwechselung* with a typically instrumental style.[107] The essence of the French overture gave Mattheson a special thrill, especially due to the succession of the three contrasting parts—when the effect was heightened by *Abwechselung*:

> Höre ich den ersten Theil einer guten Ouvertür, so empfinde ich eine sonderbare Erhebung des Gemüths; bey dem zweiten hergegen breiten sich die Geister mit aller Lust aus; und wenn darauf ein ernsthaffter Schluss erfolget, sammlen und Ziehen sie sich wieder in ihren gewöhnlichen ruhigen Sitz. Mich deucht, das ist eine angenehm abwechselnde Bewegung, die ein Redner schwerlich verursachen könnte.[108]

> When I hear the first part of a good overture, I sense an unusual exaltation of my soul; then with the second part, the vital spirits expand in a fullness of joy; and when then a serious ending follows, the spirits gather themselves back together, to their usual place of rest. I think that is a pleasantly contrasting movement such as could hardly be effected by an orator.

He goes on to describe how certain other kinds of instrumental music arouse *Verwunderung* in him. It was not only the vitality of the French overture to which he was responsive; he also reacted sympathetically to the unspeakable joy of a Hallelujah and to the sheer power of the sounds of the organ. The fire and the liveliness conveyed by celebrative sounds alone obviously had a profound and meaningful emotional effect on him:

> Vernehme ich in der Kirche eine feierliche Symphonie, so überfällt mich ein andächtiger Schauder; arbeitet ein starcker Instrumenten-Chor in die Wette, so bringt mir solches eine hohe Verwunderung zu Wege; fängt das Orgelwerck an zu brausen und zu donnern, so entstehet eine göttliche Furcht in mir; schliesst sich dem alles mit einem freudigen Hallelujah, so hüpfft mir das Hertz im Leibe; wenn ich auch gleich weder die Bedeutung dieses Worts wissen.[109]

> When I hear in church a solemn symphony, I am gripped by a devout awe; when the voices of an instrumental choir vie with each other in energetic counterpoint, a lofty wonderment comes upon me; when the organ begins to roar and thunder, a divine fear arises; and if all that is concluded with an exultant Hallelujah, then my heart leaps for joy—and it would, even if I did not know the meaning of this word.

Most German music lovers seemed to share this receptivity to mere sounds. (We will see later that this sensitivity to music, experienced in the setting of the church, constituted a decisive precedent for German musical thought.) One would ask, after reading the above confession, what more is required of music, if it would pretend to to some significance? However, when it is required (as it indeed was during the eighteenth-century in Germany) that music express and communicate the passions—not merely affect them—then it becomes difficult to construe the celebrative, enlivening essence of these instrumental pieces as having satisfied the goal of music.

We spoke earlier of Hiller's rejection of the unvocal and non-imitative characteristics of concertos and sonatas. They were most often just "unverständliches Mischmasch."[110] However, he was not insensitive to the pleasurable effects of the "Feuer und Fertigkeit" of instrumental music (the runs, the bold leaps, etc.). Just as the *Wunderbar* had an important role to play in literature, so did these unreal, nonrepresentative aspects of music— "das musikalische Wunderbar"—have a role to play:[111]

> [Die Musik] erhebt sich dadurch, wie die Poesie, zu einer fast göttlichen Wurde, weil es uns unbegreiflich scheinet, dass es ein Mensch so hoch habe bringen können. Sie erfüllt uns in diesem Augenblicke mit Erstaunen und Bewunderung.[112]

> Music rises thereby to an almost divine dignity, because it seems incomprehensible to us that a human could accomplish so much. It fills us in that moment with astonishment and wonder.

But, he continues, since man was made for the more gentle emotions, these powerful movements of our hearts, this *Verwunderung*, must not be made the sole object of music.

Sulzer seemed also to recognize that instrumental music was inherently well-suited to serve an enlivening or celebrative function: dances, marches, and other festive compositions were, he wrote, the chief genres of instrumental music.[113] (It seems he deliberately ignored those quite popular genres of instrumental music which he on occasion deemed morally bankrupt and hence aesthetically indefensible: the sonata, the concerto and the symphony.) The mention of dance music presents an interesting case. That mere sounds and the dance belonged together—that dance music was a justifiable form of instrumental music—of course no one questioned; it was part of life. (When Gottsched gives an example of someone's understanding the "meaning" of instrumental music he describes a man who, upon hearing some music, begins to dance!)[114] However, when high-minded, serious German men reflected on the goals of music, they found no meaningful place for the *tanzartig* (dance-like); the light-hearted, dancing, *tändelnd* character of the newest Italian music was rejected. Widespread complaints against the popular and light character of the rondo are a good example.[115] Junker, who characterized the rondo as a "dance-like Allegro," believed that such a piece was not suitable to the serious, epic nature of the concerto. To end a concerto with a rondo would be as nonsensical as reading aloud in one breath first excerpts from *Messias* (Klopstock's high-minded religious epic), and then nothing but comic tales. It would be as if a dramatic poet had made the last act of his tragedy comic. There would be no unity of plot or feeling. But if a composer felt he must use a rondo, Junker adds, than at least he should derive his theme from the manner in which an innocent maiden sings in the springtime—and certainly not from "common" dance music.[116]

One peculiarly instrumental form remains to be discussed: the fantasy. Everyone seemed to agree that the fantasy was an effective, even moving, genre. It broke, however, many of the rules. The fantasy was free—rhythmically, melodically, thematically, formally, representationally, and to a certain extent, harmonically. Expectation-play and the arousal of wonderment, achieved by dramatic affective contrasts as well as by the virtuosity of the performer, were its acknowledged characteristics. The fantasy was a form, wrote C. P. E. Bach, where the clavier player could surpass all other musicians, in that it was the one genre where a musician could exercise a metrically free, rhetorical style of delivery (''das Sprechende'') and ''the quick speedy rushing from one affect to another'' (''das hurtig Ueberraschende von einem Affecte zu andern'').[117] Besides being able to entertain the ear with its unexpected turns, the fantasy had an edge in expressiveness over metrically organized music; for each meter has an element of ''compulsion'' in it—and compulsion of any kind is an obstacle to the accurate portrayal of the passions.[118] One also receives the impression from Bach that the fantasy's freedom from the compulsion of a verbal text, its freedom to indulge in sudden, surprising changes of affective contents—indeed in contrasts and surprises of any kind—was in large part responsible for the fantasy's special ability to ''rouse and still'' the passions.[119]

Mattheson's characterization of the fantasy also emphasizes freedom of form, its strong affective variety, and the arousal of the listener:

Denn dieser [fantastischen] Styl ist die allerfreieste und ungebundenste Setzs- Sing- und Spiel-Art, die man nur erdencken kan, da man bald auf diese bald auf jene Einfälle geräth, da man sich weder an Worte noch Melodie, obwol an Harmonie, bindet, nur damit der Sänger oder Spieler seine Fertigkeit sehen lasse; da allerhand sonst ungewöhnliche Gänge, verstecket Zierrathen, sinnreiche Drehungen und Verbrämungen hervorgebracht werden, ohne eigentliche Beobachtung des Tacts und Tons, unangesehen dieselbe auf dem Papier Platz nehmen; ohne förmlichen Haupt-Satz und Unterwurff, ohne Thema und Subject, das ausgeführet werde; bald hurtig bald zögernd; bald einbald vielstimmig; bald auch auf eine kurtze Zeit nach dem Tacht; ohne Klang-Maasse; doch nicht ohne Absicht zu gefallen, zu übereilen und in Verwunderung zu setzen. Das sind die wesentlichen Abzeichen des fantastischen Styls.[120]

For this style [of the fantasy] is altogether the most free and unconstrained manner of composing, singing and playing, that one could even imagine; for one comes first upon this idea, then upon that idea, and one is bound neither by words nor melody (although by harmony), in order that the singer or player can display his prowess. Here can be engendered all kinds of otherwise unaccustomed passages, obscure ornaments, ingenious turns and embellishments, without any real observation of meter and tonality, in spite of the fact these are found on the music, without proper primary and secondary ideas, without introducing theme and subject—first rushing then hesitating, first with one voice then with many, then even for a short time according to meter, then [without] measured sounds—but not without intent to please, to overcome, and to transport into a state of wonderment. These are the essential features of the fantasy.

Although Mattheson's account is sympathetic to the irregularities of the fantasy, one wonders how he would have reconciled it with his maxim that ''All music must sing.'' The fantasy, although recognized as a viable art form, was nevertheless a theoretical anomaly. Did it effect the understandable communication of a passion? Certainly, it did not use the prescribed vehicle for the representation and arousal of a passion: simple, natural, lyrical utterance.

We come, finally, to a summary of those properties of instrumental music which were recognized in the eighteenth-century and which at the same time did not answer the demands of the music-aesthetic ideology of the time: that music express the passions and move the listener.[121] Obviously not all writers attribute all the following qualities to all instrumental music (indeed, some of the properties are mutually exclusive). And some properties can be seen as applying a priori to any art of pure sound, whereas others obviously apply to specific styles of instrumental music. Also, some comments take the form of complaints, and some appear as part of matter-of-fact descriptions of instrumental music and its specific genres. But, qualifications aside, all these properties were attributed to instrumental music with sufficient frequency that they constituted problems for eighteenth-century music aesthetics; for the apparent success of eighteenth-century instrumental music, which displayed in turn these various recognized qualities, was not accounted for by the prevailing aesthetic theories.

These, then, are the problematic features with which anyone would have to deal, if one wanted to explain the significance of eighteenth-century instrumental music in eighteenth-century German terms:

1. Instrumental music often does not represent any real ''object''; most especially, it frequently does not express the human passions (and these are the most appropriate ''objects'' for musical imitation). Since pure sounds do not refer to objects and passions of the real world, instrumental music has no meaning; bearing no apparent connection to the real world, it has no ''truth'' or ''verisimilitude.'' The instrumental composer does not intend to represent. Instrumental music has no content, it is ''ein blosses Geklingel.''[122]

2. Or, if indeed some extramusical sense of content is apparent, this content lacks sufficient definitude to be ''clearly and distinctly'' understood. Its content cannot be expressed in clear verbal concepts; it is ''nonverbalizable.'' Instrumental music thus fails to occupy the mind. Being inaccessible to the human intellect, most instrumental music is just ''nonsensikalisches Geräusch.''[123]

3. Instrumental music does not specify the subject, object, motivation, or outcome of whatever affect is suggested by the sounds. It leaves the listener in ''Ungewissheit und Verwirrung.''[124]

4. The musical ideas in many instrumental compositions succeed each other in arbitrary, illogical fashion; sudden transitions are the rule.[125] The rich variety and strong contrasts typical of much instrumental music are inexplicable and even at times self-contradictory. There is no order, form, or unity—only incoherence. It is "unverständliches Mischmasch," "unförmliches Geklängel."[126]

5. There is a lack, in much instrumental music, of simple songfulness and touching lyricism. It departs from the true prototype of all music: impassioned vocal utterance. It has a penchant for unvocal and unnatural gestures. Lacking melodies that are "natürlich und singbar," it thus constitutes "das musikalische Wunderbar."[127]

6. The new instrumental music is unable to move the listener, to rouse and still the passions. It is just "das Herz nicht beschäfftigendes Geschwätz"—it fails to occupy the heart.[128]

7. Instrumental music does not produce any salutory moral effect. It cannot teach a moral lesson, nor in any lasting way affect the listener's moral character. It is a waste of time—just "unnützes Zeug."[129]

8. Instrumental music fails to live up to the standards of the other arts; it is no more significant than "papier marbré," or a painting of mere colors and lines.[130]

9. It is boring. Sonatas are mostly "leere einschläfernde Klingeleyen."[131]

10. Or, at best, it is merely aural simulation—a mere pastime. It must rely on sheer sensual diversion, for it only occupies the ear. The new instrumental music is "blos ohrkitzelndes Klingklang."[132]

11. Instrumental music has a natural propensity for the display of "art," or compositional craft and contrapuntal intricacy. It often displays more *Kunstwerk* or *Künstelei* than vocal music.[133]

12. Instrumental music is also an apt vehicle for the display of virtuoso performance skills. Sometimes it is "lauter Blendwerk."[134]

13. Because of its appeal only to the ear, instrumental music relies on novelty, expectation-play and strong contrasts. Unusual and surprising ideas, rather than natural ones, characterize much Italian instrumental music. *Abwechselungen* of all sorts are common. The expression of the music is often violated by the "Bizarrerie" of such elements.[135]

14.   Due to the above three departures from music's true mission, instrumental
       music often arouses only *Verwunderung*—it is more striking than moving.[136]

15.   The new instrumental music displays the characteristics of lowness, mere
       playfulness, childishness, and cuteness; it has a popular, comic tone and
       makes a base appeal. It is offensively simple and frivolous; it is not serious
       and ennobling. It is often like dance music. The harmony is plain and crude,
       not pure and thorough. It is effeminate, lacking force and expression. The
       fashionable new music consists mostly of "niedere Tändeleyen."[137]

16.   Its essence is also often fiery and brilliant; its fullness and liveliness celebrate
       and solemnize. It stimulates and enlivens the listener. Instrumental music
       excels vocal music in "das Ueberraschende und Feurige."[138]

2

French Ideas on German Soil

We turn now to the historical development of our themes. The story that develops is indeed a dramatic one: instrumental music, once the lowly handmaid of poetry, becomes queen of all the arts. As we follow the themes identified in the first chapter, we shall see that this transformation is not sudden and unexplained; rather, there is a complex stream of change. Various themes come in and out of prominence. Relevant discussions occur in unexpected places. Attitudes on some issues change faster than others. And not all the writers we meet speak to the issue of instrumental music's changing status. It is a difficult change to follow. I would like therefore to survey the course of this complex stream before we embark on it. In this way we may more readily grasp the story of instrumental music's changing fortunes.

At the beginning of the eighteenth century instrumental music had its own accepted sphere of activity: whether it was dance music, table music, march music, devotional music, liturgical music, pedagogical music, celebrative music, music for the "allowable recreation of the spirit," or music for sheer divertissement. But as part of the eighteenth-century drive to find fundamental principles underlying the manifold areas of experience, French critics and their German disciples began to explain and judge all the arts on the basis of a common principle and a common corpus of rules. And suddenly, it seemed, instrumental music was faced with the obligation to "imitate nature," as did vocal music and all the other arts. Otherwise it would fail to occupy the attention of the Enlightened listener and would be dismissed as "meaningless noise." The natural "object" that music was most often supposed to imitate was the tone of passionate utterance. Music's content was also supposed to be clearly intelligible, just as the content of vocal music and all the other arts. But given the specific nature of music's materials, which were sensual and nonreferential, instrumental music was going to find it quite difficult to represent the passions intelligibly. In addition, the utterance theory of imitation seemed to reduce music to a kind of recitative which provided little opportunity for such characteristic features of the instrumental idiom as fiery brilliance and contrapuntal richness. Such specifically musical qualities had no role in the new aesthetic, and procedures native to musical art, with no obvious relation to the other arts, were looked upon suspiciously; good taste forbade counterpoint. Moreover, to the burden of *mimesis* was added that of *didaxis*. All the arts were supposed to share the function of serving society by inculcating moral "lessons." But music's specific nature prevented it from doing this very well either. Thus not only did music do a poor job of meeting the new standards, because they were really inappropriate to its specific nature, it seemed the new standards would deprive it of its very character. The aesthetic problem was, how could music be music and fulfill the new requirements for genuine art?

As historical events would have it, the most popular forms of instrumental music in Germany in the latter eighteenth century were the sonatas and symphonies in the new Italian style with no representative or didactic pretense of any sort and no traditionally accepted function. This new music only compounded the problem of instrumental music's aesthetic accountability. Indeed, perhaps it was this frankly sensual and "ear-tickling" music (as most Germans and Frenchmen regarded it) which elicited the critical campaign to bring instrumental music within the domain of the imitative arts in the first place. Whichever was the case, Italian instrumental music constituted a serious challenge to contemporary critical theory: it was an aesthetic anomaly—uniquely bad at fulfilling the new Enlightened standards for all the arts, yet a phenomenal artistic success. How was theory going to explain this practice? In Germany this problem was taken seriously.

Enlightened German music-lovers were torn between an allegiance, on the one hand, to French intellectual culture and the fundamental principle of imitation, and on the other hand, to their long-standing and growing fondness for nonrepresentative instrumental music, including the anomalous new Italian music which encountered such critical hostility in France. Frederick the Great typified the cleavage: although he was one of the most avid Francophiles of eighteenth-century Germany, his taste in music was decidedly German and Italian.[1] Despite the obvious and seemingly irreconcilable clash of mimetic theory and nonrepresentative instrumental music, German music-lovers were willing neither to abandon the principle that human emotions were the proper content of music, nor to constrict the spirit of the specifically musical for the sake of principle. Enlightened German critics were thus confronted with a dilemma: on the one hand, they wanted music to express and communicate the passions, but they also realized that instrumental music, especially Italian instrumental music, was peculiarly inept at fulfilling the new Enlightened standards. But rather than throw up their arms with Fontenelle and say, "Sonata, what do you want of me?" Germans were determined to reconcile theory and practice. German composers infused the sonata with a new seriousness of purpose and German critics demanded, in effect, "Sonata, I want to understand you."

German writers began to find, in some cases perhaps unwittingly, ways in which typical and characteristic traits of a nonrepresentative instrumental music, and of the new Italian instrumental style in particular, could fit in with, even serve, their demands for emotional content and moral utility. And in so doing they provided insights that were to be incorporated into the Romantic view of instrumental music as the highest art. New theories of emotional expression and communication in music arose which called for more specifically musical ''art,'' or compositional craft. German writers amended the utterance theory so as to allow for more musical interest; or they took issue with it altogether and came to speak instead of formal analogues between music and the emotions. This theory of analogues helped show how music as a temporally unfolding art was particularly suited to emotional expression, whereas the utterance theory had made no provision for the successive nature of specifically musical form. Also, theories of the emotions themselves as more dynamic and complex arose, and these theories came to justify the so-called meaningless contrasts of the new music, as well as to give an expressive function to so-called artificial compositional complexities, such as counterpoint and thematic development. Opera debates helped clarify the specific capabilities of the verbal and tonal arts, and helped create an awareness that different standards, different effects, different temporal or formal procedures were appropriate to each. German writers especially defended in these debates the rights of musical art against the encroachments of literary standards. New accounts of the fundamental principle and the moral mission of the arts arose, in which the senses were regarded as an essential channel to the goal of man's spiritual perfection. The sensual appeal of artworks, and especially of music (called the most sensual of the arts), made them especially suited for this. Also, there was a gradual but not total relaxation of the rationalist demand for the clear intelligibility of music's content. German writers were especially sensitive to the inappropriateness of this demand. They emphasized the immediateness of music's affects, and the nonrational, or ''aesthetic,'' moment in musical appreciation. At times they were even willing to construe the sheer affectiveness of music as equivalent to musical expression, or representation.

These efforts on the part of Enlightened German critics helped prepare the way for elements of the Romantic view of instrumental music as the highest art. The Romantics utterly disavowed the notion that music represents emotions by imitating utterances of passion. They pointed rather to the peculiar affinity of the ''grand symphonies with their manifold elements''—the affinity of music crafted after its own specifically musical laws—for suggesting, affecting, and symbolizing the ongoing, ever-changing stream of inner emotional life. Essential to the Romantic view was an account of music's relation to human emotions radically different from the doctrine of the affects, or *Affektenlehre*, of the earlier eighteenth century. The Romantics denied the existence of static emotional entities and instead subscribed to a dynamic doctrine of the soul. They found this new *Seelenlehre* embodied in the highly developed art of contemporary instrumental music: for both the emotional life of the soul and the works of pure instrumental music were seen as ''multifarious streams,'' sharing the same specific nature—ever moving, complex, inscrutable, full of change and contrast. Thus, for the Romantics instrumental music had the potential for carrying on a form of nonintellectual intercourse with man's inner self; and they considered this immediate affective power of music to be of inestimable human worth.

Of course, along with theoretical developments, practice was changing as well. German composers were making their own amendments, revisions, even transformation, of the new Italian style. Certainly composers such as C. P. E. Bach reflected in their instrumental music a desire for an art more serious, significant, and more thoroughly crafted than the Italians'. In other words, the very style of instrumental music in Germany was undergoing significant changes in keeping with German predilections. Thus the very subject of aesthetic controversy was changing. But however more sophisticated the critical understanding of instrumental music became, and however more rich and serious the increasingly popular Italian instrumental idiom became in the hands of German composers, until the time of the early Romantics instrumental music was still almost universally considered to be an inferior art because of a persistent remnant of rationalism: the insistence on a clear, unequivocal, verbally specifiable content. And many of the same aesthetic problems that existed at mid-century still needed definitive solutions. Not until the climax of our story in the nineties—not until the representative demand was dropped altogether, and it was recognized that spiritual significance in music was not dependent on the clear communication of a given emotional content; not until it was realized that this content was itself obscure; and not until the Enlightenment presumption of the ability to explain ran its course—did instrumental music come to be considered an art worthy of comparison with the others. Thus there were some elements of the Romantic view of music which owed little to the ideas gained from the intellectual energy of the Enlightenment.

The strong convictions that lay behind the Romantic view of the 1790's were not, however, without preparation. For contemporaneous with the disputational eddies created by the clash of French ideas and Italian music, there existed in Germany an undercurrent of native faith in the spiritual power of musical art. This faith did not presuppose any intent to infuse content into musical sounds. It depended on neither fundamental principles nor on the canons of good taste. Nor was it to be shaken by the healthy and hardheaded skepticism of the *Aufklärung*. According to this faith, virtually no music was meaningless. Music exerted power over the human soul independently of any representational intent or rational recognition of extramusical content. Music did not need to imitate nature. Music was itself a natural human activity, and by its very specific nature capable of soothing, affecting, moving and enlivening. Its significance was not dependent on the intent to signify. The significance of ordered sounds was a mystery which few were inclined to probe. Along with this faith in music went a great appreciation of musical "art," or compositional craft. Germans traditionally stood in awe before the power inherent in great contrapuntal edifices of sound. They were, in Luther's words, "divine works of wonder." Many Germans were not willing to sacrifice the riches of musical art on the altar of taste. Nor would they offend the majesty inherent in many-voiced polyphony by demanding that it imitate the inflections of monodic utterance. During the period of our study, this German faith in the significance of musical art was seldom announced, although we shall see frequent manifestations of it as a native German outlook towards instrumental music evolves. However, with the coming of the neo-Gothic Romantics came a public reaffirmation of the "wonderful" mystery of music. Only then was it said out loud that the imposition of intelligible content would only prostitute this "divine" art. Given this tradition of respect for and attraction to music, one can perhaps understand why Enlightened German critics seemed determined to explain the appealing new music and to accommodate the new Enlightened demands to its specific nature. Indeed, the Germans' determined attempt to understand and defend instrumental music in the face of inappropriate imported standards may help explain the critical synthesis which is the subject of this study.

The music-critical events of the eighteenth century can be seen as leading to a uniquely German synthesis. There were three currents which in the nineties finally merged, each losing some of its own identity, but each contributing to the new Romantic view of instrumental music as the highest of the arts. One current was that of the French intellectual culture of the Enlightenment. Within this culture the idea had evolved that composers should give their music a clearly intelligible meaning, that music should represent the passions, and that the most natural and reasonable way to do these things was to imitate the tones of passionate utterance. The second current came from Italy and brought with it the new contrast-dominated style of instrumental music, full of aural delight and sheer sensual excitement, full of novelty and variety—but, it would seem, signifying nothing. The third current was that of the native German faith in the innate significance and mystery of music and in the inestimable value of musical art. The German critical genius, nourished on this native faith, was able to reconcile the antitheses posed by the demands of French rationalism on the one hand and by the appeal of Italian music on the other.[2] Thus, elements of all three currents—French meaningfulness and expressiveness, Italian sensuality and imagination, and German craft and spirituality—were combined into a new critical synthesis in tune with contemporary practice. The Romantics freed instrumental music from the yoke of verbally mediated this-worldly representation, but at the same time they elevated it above the other arts in terms of its significance for human life. Instrumental music, by virtue of a new awareness and more sophisticated account of its natural affinity with the inner emotional life, by virtue, that is, of the formal similarities between its current materials and constructive procedures, and the "multifarious stream" of man's inner self, came to be seen as an immaterial embodiment of the ebb and flow of man's inner life and as the unifying symbol of life's irrational contrasts. Instrumental music, the "most Romantic of the arts," was to become a vessel for the transcendance of the mundane and a haven for individual spiritual exercise and regeneration.

In the present chapter we shall examine the influx of French musical ideas into Germany in the earlier eighteenth century. The acceptance of these ideas was of course part of a larger Teutonic desire to capture some of the splendor and grace of Versailles and to rise with France above the barbarism of Europe's Gothic past. For such was the prestige of the speculative outlook of the French, that even practical-minded German musicians would attempt to apply Enlightened theory to an understanding of the art whose mysterious nature they already embraced. From Gottsched to A. W. Schlegel the aesthetic theories of French neoclassicism, whether accepted or rejected, constituted a common point of reference for most aesthetic debate.

In order to make clear the impact of these French ideas on German musical culture, we shall begin by characterizing the tradition of musical thought which was prevalent in Germany in the earlier eighteenth century. As I have suggested, the seemingly indigenous German attitudes toward music were never totally lost. The German adoption of the imitation principle was to be significantly compromised in accordance with these traditional ideas; and indeed, there are some close resemblances between the Romantic view and the pre-Enlightenment German view. Against this essential German backdrop, the central action of the chapter will begin. First, the radically different French neoclassic family of views on music will be characterized, insofar as it plays a central role in our story of the changing aesthetic status of instrumental music in Germany. After painting, perhaps a bit boldly, these two antithetical attitudes, we shall view Gottsched's zealous effort to bring French rationalism and mimetic criticism to Germany, as well as some of the musical implications of his moralistic brand of neoclassicism. Then we shall examine the attempt of his disciple Scheibe to apply Gottsched's light of reason to music criticism. Scheibe's sympathy with traditional German thought and with Italian music prevented him from carrying through the standards of the new criticism into the area of instrumental music. We shall conclude by examining the source of the most prominent wave of French influence, Charles Batteux's *Les beaux arts réduits à un même principe* (1746). This work did more than polarize the partisanship in literary and aesthetic circles in Germany. Batteux's exhortation that "All music must have a sense" was also to occupy German music critics for many decades to come and constituted the real challenge of the century to the aesthetic status of instrumental music.

In the Germany before the *Aufklärung* the science of aesthetics was nonexistent, and music criticism was barely beginning. Religious partisanship and moral concerns dominated all but the most practical considerations. But spiritual commitment did not extend to an ascetic rejection of the pleasures and riches of musical art. A coherent body of belief about music existed, in which music was a highly valued art. Imgard Otto, in her study, *Die deutsche Musikanschauung im 17. Jahrhundert,*[3] has shown that the musical beliefs of the church fathers and of

Luther, especially, were repeated and paraphrased continually in the seventeenth century and that this body of opinion remained current even into the early eighteenth century. We shall see in our study yet a further persistence of these beliefs. Although the cultivation of an elaborate church music and a respect for musical art and science were part of the European Catholic tradition long before the Reformation, the character and force of the German commitment to music seems to stem in large part from Luther, himself an ardent music-lover and the ideological forebear of most of the Germans whose views we shall study. Mattheson, Junker, and Forkel all quote Luther as an authority to back up their own arguments as to the significance of music and musical art. In addition, Nicolai, Ruetz, Hiller, and Krause evince some of the same views as those found in Luther's often enthusiastic writings on music. Thus, these beliefs going back at least as far as to Luther seem to have become the common property of eighteenth-century German musical culture.

The basis for the Germans' high evaluation of music seems to have been its fabulous power to affect the human soul. As Luther said,

> Die edle Musika ist nach Gottes Wort der höchste Schatz auf Erden. Sie regiert alle Gedanken, Sinn, Herz und Mut. Willst du einen Betrübten fröhlich machen, einen frechen, wilden Menschen zäumen, dass er gelinde werde, einem Zaghaftigen einen Mut machen, einen Hoffärtigen demutigen und dergleichen, wass kann besser dazu dienen denn diese hohe, teure, werte und edle Kunst?[4]

> The noble art of music is according to the word of God the greatest treasure on earth. It regulates mind and mood, heart and humor. If you want to make a sad person happy, or tame a wild brazen man so that he becomes gentle, or give a timid person courage, make an arrogant one meek, and the like, what can better serve that end than this sovereign, precious, worthy, and noble art?

This faith in the "peculiar power of music," in the "wonderful effects of music,"[5] goes back, of course, to ancient times and was reinforced in many sermons and books of the day by the credulous retelling of the many age-old stories of healing, soothing, and incitement.[6] Luther liked to recount the Biblical story of David's soothing Saul with his music.[7] And just as Enlightened German music critics were not willing to doubt that music per se was an art of profound human significance, they were not unanimous in dismissing the ancient stories of the "marvelous effects" of music.[8]

There are two aspects to this pre-Enlightenment vision of music's affective power, which I shall call the sacred and the secular. The first has to do with religion and morality, and the second with pleasure and "recreation." As Luther, who valued both, succinctly stated: "Music drives away the Devil and makes people happy."[9] A century later a similar account of music's dual role was given:

> Unter Menschlichen Ergetzungen, so von Göttlicher Güte uns ertheilet werden, sind ja nicht die geringsten die liebe Musica und Poeterey, ... massen sie durch ihre sonderbare Krafft und Be-

wegung, so wol zur Andacht und Lobe Gottes, als auch unterweilen, zum mercklichen Trost unserer angefochtenen Gemüter, Hintertreibung une Verjagung trawiger Gedancken und Erweckung allerhand geziemenden Ehrenfrewden uns gleichsam die Hand bieten.[10]

Among the human delights which Divine Providence has granted us, music and poetry are not indeed the least; . . . for they assist us, through their peculiar affective power, in the contemplation and praise of God, as well as from time to time in the consolation of our troubled spirits, in the expulsion of sad thoughts, and in the awakening of all kinds of noble pleasures.

J. S. Bach evinced the same view. He dedicated his thorough-bass both "to the glory of God and the allowable recreation of the spirit."[11]

Music's religious function was first of all to praise and celebrate God and to inspire awe and reverence in the congregation. All the elaborate resources of musical art were to be used to this end. Also, by virtue of its affective power, music was seen to further virtue and hence serve religious ends. Luther even compared music to theology in its ability to inculcate virtue:

Musika ist eine halbe Disziplin und Zuchtmeisterin, so die Leute gelinder und sanftmütiger, sittsamer und vernünftiger macht.[12]

Music is both discipline and disciplinarian, for it makes man more gentle and meek, more virtuous and temperate.

The manner in which sounds were believed to accomplish such high moral ends, to penetrate to the very soul of man, was generally considered to be a "wonderful" mystery. Augustine, Luther's mentor in many respects, had spoken of the "secret association" ("occulta familiaritas") between sounds and affects of the soul.[13] Similarly, Hiller would say that there were "secret passageways" through which music found its way into the soul.[14] Wackenroder, half a century later, used the term "unexplainable sympathy."[15] The most common account of music's mysterious influence was in the tradition of the *musica humana* of Boethius. Mattheson was to explain this account in the eighteenth century by saying in effect: well-ordered and harmonious sounds produce well-ordered and harmonious souls, and what is virtue but a well-ordered soul?[16] The element of order was especially emphasized by many: "For God is a God of order and He will not lend His power to any disorder or confusion."[17] Mastering the complexities of musical composition and composing music correctly took on an almost metaphysical significance. Some, like Werckmeister, extended this concern with orderliness to include a kind of number mysticism, wherein the proportions of the various intervals were seen to exert unexplainable forces.[18] In the eighteenth century Mattheson and Mizler would attempt to construct a science or mechanics of musical morality, in which the physical properties of sound and the physiological nature of the ear and of the passions were taken into account.[19] But the central point, whatever the color of the attitude towards music's spiritual power, was that the mediation of the mind was not required for music to exert its beneficent influence. Sounds were not signs, and music was not just an instrument for reinforcing the words of a moral lesson. The spiritual power of sound was immediate and was independent of the mediation of a verbal text, or the recognition of a represented content. Music was not to be the handmaid of poetry but the *ancilla theologiae* (handmaid of theology).

Luther's own account of musical morality, as it were, is in some ways the most down to earth, in spite of his reference to the Devil. His account was free of that number mysticism common among the orthodox Lutheran partisans of music in the seventeenth and early eighteenth centuries. It was the elemental, everyday power of music to foster a ''well-adjusted'' disposition that inclined him to rank music next to theology in importance,

> da sie allein nach der Theologie das kann, was sonst nur die Theologie vermag, nämlich das Gemüt ruhig und fröhlich zu machen, zum offenbaren Zeugnis, dass der Teufel, der Urheber der traurigen Sorgen und unruhigen Gedanken, vor der Stimmen der Musik fast ebenso flieht wie vor dem Worte der Theologie.[20]

> since it alone, next to theology, can do that which otherwise only theology can do; namely, it can make the soul peaceful and happy, which is a public testimony that the Devil, the author of all worry and anxiety, flees from the sound of music almost as if from the word of theology.

Music, according to Luther's view, arouses happy, serene thoughts, drives away care, and detracts the mind from vices. Since the Devil is the ''author of all worry and anxiety,'' the Devil cannot stand music, thus he cannot dwell in the soul of the man who is musical and he is driven away. In such a way was music seen to promote religious virtue; for the soul consecrated to God, with complete faith in His grace, was a happy, harmonious and serene soul, as was the soul devoted to music. Thus, for Luther a soul sympathetic to music was doubtless a virtuous soul; he confidently believed that ''There are without a doubt many seeds of priceless virtues in the hearts of those who are attracted to music.''[21] The Turks and the Bavarians could not be all bad, he allowed, because they cultivated the art of music.[22] Conversely, the man who had no relish for music—the unmusical man—was morally suspect.

Given Luther's account of musical morality, it is easy to see why he was enthusiastic about music's secular uses. Indeed, it becomes difficult at times to distinguish the secular from the sacred use. Unlike Augustine, who feared music's direct, sensual power, Luther did not consider the pleasure that men derived from music to be a sinful distraction from the meaning of the words. Nor was the sensual pleasure derived from music considered inconsistent with pure spirituality. Music was called ''a prelude to Heavenly joys'' and ''the greatest treasure on earth.''[23] Many times the view was stated that God gave music as a kindness, to make man's earthly stay more pleasant.[24] Moreover, music's peculiar freedom from earthly reference, from definite representation, made it a ''noble pastime; by virtue of its otherworldly essence it provided a special benefit which Luther saw as superior to the other arts:

> Singen ist die beste Kunst und Übung. Est hat nichts zu tun mit der Welt. . . . Sänger sind nicht sorfaltig, sondern sind fröhlich und schlagen die Sorgen mit Singen aus und hinweg.[25]

> Singing is the best art and exercise. It has nothing to do with the world. . . . Singers are not troubled but are cheerful and drive away cares with singing.

It was this very lack of clear, intelligible reference to the real world that made music such a thorn in the side of neoclassic critics and such a "wonderful mystery" for the Romantics.

It is clear that Luther did not view music as a mere instrument of verbal meaning, or as the handmaid of poetry. To be sure, the music to which he most often referred was vocal music, either the Renaissance counterpoint like that of one of his favorites, Josquin, or more simple songs such as chorale arrangements for congregational singing. And he did of course recommend the use of music to intensify the meaning of a text. But Luther loved counterpoint, he loved the "art" of music even for its own sake. Indeed he held this "artful" music to be an "unspeakable wondrous creation of the Lord''; and people who could not respond to this specifically musical design he considered little better than animals. One gets the impression, in the following description of an elaborate contrapuntal composition, that the words have little to do with Luther's enthusiasm—it is the specifically musical arrangement of sound that he finds so exciting:

> Wo aber . . . die natürliche Musika durch die Kunst geschärft und polieret wird, da sieht und erkennt man erst mit grosser Verwunderung die grosse und vollkommene Weisheit Gottes in seinem wunderbarlichen Werk der Musika, in welcher vor allem das seltsam und wohl zu verwundern ist, dass einer eine schlichte Weise hersinget, neben welcher drei, vier oder fünf andere Stimme auch gesungen werden, die um solche schlichte, einfaltige Weise gleich als mit Jauchzen ringsherum spielen und springen, und mit mancherlei Art und Klang dieselbige Weise wunderbarlich zieren und schmücken und gleichwie einen himmlischen Tanzreigen führen, freundlich einander begegnen und sich gleich herzen und lieblich umfangen.—Wer dem ein wenig nachdenket und es nicht für ein unaussprechliches Wunderwerk des Herrn hält, der mus wahrlich ein grober Klotz sein und ist nicht wert, dass er ein Mensch heisst, und solte nichts anderes hören, denn wie der Esel schreit und die Sau grunzt.[26]

> When . . . natural music is sharpened and polished by art, only then does one see and recognize with great wonderment the great and perfect wisdom of God in his wondrous creation of music. What is most singularly marvelous is the manner in which a simple melody is set against three, four, or five other voices—these play and leap around this simple melody as if in jubilation, and adorn and decorate the same melody with all kinds of art and sound, and perform as it were a heavenly round dance, fondly greeting, soon embracing, and pleasantly surrounding each other.—Whoever ponders such a thing and does not hold it to be an unspeakable wondrous creation of the Lord must truly be a crude boor, and is not worthy of being called a man, and should hear nothing else than a donkey bray and a sow grunt.

Luther seems quite conscious that others with strong religious commitments were wary of the sensual appeal of such polyphonic exuberance. Zwingli, Calvin, and even Luther's mentor Augustine, had strong reservations as to the religious usefulness of music's peculiar excitement. But Luther was undaunted in his enthusiastic defense, claiming that if Augustine "were alive today, he would be on our side."[27] The debate over the role of music in the church continued through the seventeenth and early eighteenth centuries. Orthodox Protestants had to confront the "enemies of music" from within the church (the Pietists) and, later, the new Enlightened opponents. Andreas Werckmeister, echoing Luther's sentiments, denounced passionately those sects that insisted on singing "only those slow, sleepy, and mournful songs with their dragging and putrid harmonies."[28] The use of instruments, and even instrumental music itself, was justified in the same manner as was the elaborate and often exuberant art of counterpoint: through the firm conviction that all the riches of musical art had Divine sanction to be used both for joyful praise and for the regulation and recreation of the soul. (Psalm 150 was often cited as the Biblical authority for this belief.) An orthodox sermon of 1651 claimed that it was nothing but "Calvinistic humbug" to say that

> solch Orgeln und Instrumental Musiciren ein lediges Gethön, so nur die Ohren fülle, und einem darinn wohlthue; mit deren lieblichen anmutigen Hall und Klang aber, vom wahren Gottesdienst ableite, und dessen meistentheil in ein Lauter Klang-und Sangwerck verwandle, dardurch dem Menschen nicht gedienet.[29]

> organ and instrumental music is mere sound, which gives pleasure only insofar as it fills the ears; and moreover its pleasant and charming ring and resonance distract the listener from the church service, which then becomes a mere matter of singing and klinging and thus provides no edification.

Not only the authority of the scriptures, but the daily experience of pious Christians proved the contrary, namely

> dass die Music in gemein, und also auch die Orgeln und Instrumental-Music vor sich besonders, nicht nur einem in die Ohren titillire und wol thue, sondern vielmehr der H. Geist auch durch dieselbige, die Gemühter der Menschen bewege.[30]

> that music in general, and most specifically organ and instrumental music, not only tickles the ears and gives pleasure, but also, the Holy Spirit affects the human soul through such music.

But what was affective power to the orthodox German was to the Enlightened "enemies of music" expressive impotence; harmony for Scheibe was an obstacle to the natural expression of the passions and a relic of past "barbarism."[31] And what was viewed as a "foretaste of heavenly joys" was to the young *Aufklärer* Moses Mendelssohn merely an "idle pastime."[32] But many Germans, even after having undergone the intellectual conversion of the Enlightenment, remained attracted to rich active harmony and to the peculiar pleasures and effects of non-representational instrumental music.

It is apparent that reason played little role in traditional German thinking about music. Luther's enthusiasm for music was based on his own personal experience and on the unquestioned authority of kindred souls before him. Reason, in the form of late medieval scholasticism, had become repugnant to him. Salvation consisted in man's unquestioning faith in the mystery of God's gift of grace. And just as this gift became an article of faith, so did the mysterious affinity of harmonious music for harmonious souls.

But for the Frenchman brought up on Cartesian epistemology and the skepticism of Alexander Bayle, to admit of a mystery was tantamount to an act of intellectual cowardice. The understanding, not the heart or soul, was the only reliable instrument of man's commerce with the real world. For an art to be considered worthy of the attention of the *honnête homme* it had to "occupy the mind"; it could not merely "fill the ear." Instrumental music, especially Italian instrumental music, offered to the Frenchman only sensually distracting sounds with no reference to the real world; such music represented no object and communicated no meaning upon which the mind could fasten. Hence Fontenelle's famous question: "Sonate, que me veux-tu?" ("Sonata, what do you want of me?") For the most radical rationalists of the latter seventeenth and the eighteenth century, an art of sheer sounds was meaningless; it was "empty noise." Less rigid rationalists might admit that some music could have meaning, but only by virtue of "imitating" the inflections of nonmusical human utterance, or by fulfilling a programmatic title, or by functioning within a dramatic context; and even then instrumental music was considered far inferior to vocal music. In the words of Maria Maniates, the French critics of the eighteenth century were never able "to explain the human and spiritual significance of music."[33]

This profoundly different attitude towards music was part of a larger wave, the wave of the Enlightenment, and permeated its empirical as well as its earlier, rationalistic phase. Since, in the eighteenth century, many German intellectuals were anxious to adopt French ideas, these "Enlightened" views of music were to form the basis for the music-aesthetic debate in Germany throughout the period of our study. To be sure, there were whole schools of French thought more sympathetic to the nonrational side of art. Dubos, with his aesthetic based on the natural human desire to be moved, brought a strong emotionalist element into French criticism.[34] Also, there is no doubt that some instrumental music was received in France with considerable relish; one thinks immediately of Couperin and Louis XIV. But on the subject of instrumental music, especially the new Italian instrumental music, there was a broad consensus that transcended divergences of opinion on more prominent issues. The ideas of the emotionalist Dubos, the radical rationalist Pluche, and even the Encyclopedists, all contributed to this consensus.

There was, in short, a prevailing view in French critical literature that was definitely rationalistic and antimusical. This French consensus of opinion on instrumental music, and French rationalism in general, constituted a formidable block of ideas with which many Germans of the latter eighteenth century had to wrestle. Thus we shall be focusing on that mainstream of French critical opinion that had such important consequences for German aesthetic views of instrumental music.

In the France of the latter seventeenth and earlier eighteenth centuries, speculation on the arts was increasing. A school of criticism arose, founded on the authority of the ancients and on faith in reason, which has come to be called "neoclassic." At once the most persistent and the most central element of the neoclassic view of art in general, and music in particular, was an idea going back to the ancient view found in Plato and Aristotle that art was an imitation of nature. What this meant was that art works should represent aspects of the real world and thus possess verisimilitude, or "truth"—a highly prized quality in a culture imbued with the new scientific outlook. Or, as Boileau, the accepted spokesman for the neoclassic view, put it, "Nothing is beautiful but the true." Moreover, in addition to being true, works of art had to contain a moral lesson. They were, in the language of the time, to have a "use". The Ciceronian formula that art was "to please, to move, and to instruct," was strictly adhered to, the first two requirements being frequently seen as instruments of the latter. Thus, since tones possessed neither the power of intelligible reference, nor the ability to teach a moral lesson, music was judged to be inferior by neoclassic standards. The verbal arts stood in the highest esteem.[35]

Indeed, most French reflections on music as an art occur before 1750 in books about art and beauty in general, or in literary criticism where music's role within the *Tragédie lyrique* is touched upon.[36] The tragedy and the epic were considered the highest forms of art; and music, even vocal music, was seen to achieve its highest within the dramatic context of the *tragédie lyrique* (of which Lully's operas were long-revered models). It must be remembered that the French considered their opera primarily a dramatic genre, where music played a supporting role. And as it turned out, music's role within this dramatic genre was to determine, it seems, eighteenth-century French theories of musical expression in general. The meaning of music was to be derived from verbal determinants, such as text or programmatic titles, or from gesture, as in the dance. And musical expression was to be modelled on declamatory accents.

Music's primary function in the *tragédie lyrique* followed from the French notion of opera as chiefly a literary genre. "Music must be made for the poetry, rather than the poetry for the music," wrote Saint-Evremond. In the long recitatives most characteristic of the *tragédie lyrique*, music's role was to heighten the declamation of the words and to reinforce their meaning. Whereas the Italians complained of the boredom of the long French recitatives, the French were proud of their "truth" to the natural inflections of speech and of the clarity with which the words could be understood. Neoclassic critics could not countenance the "excesses" of Italian opera, where the meaning and inflection of the words were sacrificed for sheer musical interest and excitement. Such sensuality (as they characterized the specifically musical charms of Italian opera) was a distraction from the serious moral or dramatic business at hand. In opera, wrote Rémond St. Mard, music should be the "slave of poetry." French opera-goers were chided for being like Germans and viewing opera only as a concert. Some radical rationalists even thought that opera should be banned altogether because its sensual appeal preempted any appeal to reasonable elements.[37]

The vocal portion of the *tragédie lyrique*, in which music served the text, was of course the heart of the opera. When we turn to look at the instrumental portions of the French opera, we can see that here also each instrumental piece had a carefully circumscribed function or meaning determined by the dramatic context. The overture was to get the listener's attention, to hold him in a state of excited anticipation, and prepare him for the drama to follow; it was to celebrate the fact that a drama was about to take place. The function of dance music was obvious. (The French rarely felt called upon to justify its aesthetic significance.) Neoclassic critics pointed to the gestures of the dancers as rendering the meaning of the music concrete and intelligible. The symphonies within the operas were of course programmatic in nature and their meaning was made clear by the dramatic context. They might represent a storm, a pastoral landscape, sleep, or the like. Dubos, not a typical neoclassicist, nevertheless shared a typical French viewpoint towards instrumental music when he expressed a preference for symphonies in their operatic "role":

> Ces morceaux de musique qui nous émeuvent si sensiblement, quand ils sont une partie de l'action théâtrale, plairoient même mediocrement, si l'on les faisoit entendre comme des *Sonates*, de symphonies ou des morceaux détachés, à une personne qui ne les auroit jamais entendues à l'Opera, et qui en jugeroit par conséquent sans connoitre leur plus grand mérite; c'est-à-dire, le rapport qu'elles ont avec l'action, où, pour parler ainsi, elles jouent un rôle.[38]

> These pieces of music, which move us so perceptibly when they are part of the dramatic action, give only indifferent pleasure if they are played as sonatas, symphonies, or independent compositions before an audience which has never heard them at the opera and which consequently judges them without knowing their greatest merit, namely, their relation to the dramatic action; for, in a manner of speaking, they play a role.

Since the "greatest merit" of music was seen to be to serve the dramatic action, it will come as no surprise that, when music is discussed as an artistic genre in its own right, expectations in keeping with its traditional role within the *tragédie lyrique* will be maintained. The French were accustomed to hearing music which imitated the accents of speech, which represented inanimate aspects of the natural world, or which accompanied dance. They expected music to have a meaning.

Thus, when reflection about music left the stage, there was universal agreement that music, just as the other arts, should imitate nature. This mimetic or representative demand upon music was so universal in France of the early eighteenth century that even the emotionalist Dubos could assert:

> Les premiers principes de la Musique, sont donc les mêmes que ceux de la Poësie et de la Peinture. Ainsi que la Poësie et la Peinture, la Musique est une imitation.[39]

> The first principles of music are thus the same as those of poetry and painting. Just as poetry and painting are imitations, so also music in an imitation.

Music could only be good if it conformed to the same rules as the other arts, Dubos continued, mentioning the rule of *vraisemblance*, in particular. He assured his readers that all music, from recitative to symphonie, possessed a "truth," that is, a recognizable correspondence to some aspect of the real world.[40] The neoclassic critic did not tire of insisting upon this truth in music. And the composer Couperin assured his readers that he always had in mind that his instrumental music be an imitation.[41]

Just how, then, was music supposed to imitate nature when deprived of any dramatic context? First of all, we must dismiss the notion that musical imitation of nature had to do only with scenes of nature and such. This type of representation is often called "tonepainting" today; but to the French all music which imitated something, whether passionate or inanimate nature, was said to "paint." And it was "painting the passions" which came to be considered the primany and highest goal of instrumental music. To be sure, musical painting of inanimate nature was discussed and enjoyed; and a theory of representation was developed whereby music represented those things in nature which had "sounds and motions." But the prime concern was with music as an imitation, painting, or expression of the passions. And it was the neoclassic theory of how music imitated or represented the passions which was to have such far-reaching influence in Germany in the latter half of the eighteenth century. This theory, which I call the "passionate utterance theory of musical expression," has its roots in the *tragédie lyrique* and even the ideas of the Florentine camerata (and Vincenzo Galilei in particular).[42] According to this theory, music imitates the inflections of the human voice when expressing a certain passion. French writers took this to be a very truthful and plausible kind of imitation, for they trusted, accepted and often quoted the ancient rhetorical premise that "Every motion of the soul has by nature a certain countenance, sound, and gesture."[43] And since they assumed (with Descartes) that passions were distinct, knowable entities, they believed, quite understandably, that sounds could function as accurate communicators of a definite emotional content.

Dubos's is one of the earliest articulations of the passionate utterance theory of musical expression, which he, however, apparently meant to apply only to vocal music. Significantly, his statement appears in a discussion of how music contributes to the *tragédie lyrique*. He wrote,

Le musicien imite les tons, les accens, les soupirs, les inflexions de voix, enfin tous ces sons, à l'aide desquels la nature même exprime ses sentimens et ses passions.[44]

The musician imitates the tones, the accents, the sighs, the inflections of the voice, by means of which nature herself expresses her sentiments and passions.

Dubos goes on, in his antirationalist way, to call these sounds "natural signs of the passions" and even to imply their superiority to words, which "are merely arbitrary signs."[45] Words were only meaningful by virtue of human institutions, he explained, but the inarticulate language of the passions was intelligible no matter what a person's language. Nature's sounds had a "marvelous force" to move the auditor. Later, Batteux, as well as his opponents, the Encyclopedists, developed Dubos's theory of natural signs further and applied it to the expression of the passions even in instrumental music. Diderot, who went beyond neoclassicism in the strength of passion he felt music should express, still characterized music as an imitation of passionate utterance:

Le chant est une imitation, par les sons, d'une échelle inventée par l'art ou inspirée par la nature, comme il vous plaira, ou par la voix ou par l'instrument, des bruits physiques ou des accents de la passion.[46]

A melody is an imitation, by means of the sounds of a scale (invented by art or inspired by nature, as you please), either by the voice or by an instrument, of physical sounds or of the accents of passion.

Both rationalistic critic and frank emotionalist agreed that music was to be the imitation of a "self-expression" of passion. Thus, when the French in the eighteenth century spoke of musical "expression," they meant the imitation of natural utterances, or expressions, of passion. Musical imitation of the tone of passionate utterance was called, indifferently, the painting, the depiction, the signification, the representation, the imitation, or the expression, of the passions. This account of musical expression was still so viable at the end of the century that Tieck found himself arguing passionately against it.

An important corollary of this view of musical expression was voiced by Rousseau in the well-known statement that harmony was "Gothic" and "barbaric."[47] For harmony, or counterpoint—or, for that matter, interesting accompaniments and inner voices—was seen to obscure the natural expression of the single vocal line, which imitated the tone of passionate utterance. According to neoclassic theory, art was the enemy of nature, and harmony the enemy of expression.

The passionate utterance theory, as I have called it, whereby sounds are taken as natural signs of passions and whereby music is the imitation of these signs, would seem to give music a source of meaning independent of words and hence a significance that might be considered equal to that of the literary arts. But such was the "preparatory set" of the rationalist that he found it difficult to appreciate instrumental music. Even if he granted that music had a powerful emotional effect and could be quite pleasant, and could, in fact, imitate the natural utterances of passion, his faculty of reason demanded exact knowledge of what was being represented in admittedly moving, charming, and sensual garb.[48] And knowledge entailed the application of the standard of clearness and distinctness (for the only truth, according to Descartes, was clear and distinct). In short, reason demanded that it play an active role in the act of aesthetic appreciation, and this called for a determinateness of content that could engage or occupy the speculatively attuned mind.

This demand for an intelligibility certified by reason entailed for the more rigid rationalist the rejection of instrumental music on principle. Words were the organ of reason; sounds, of the emotions (as Batteux, in hailing the latter explained).[49] For Pluche, the mind could only be satisfied when words were present. For him as for the more rationalistic French critics sheer sounds, sounds without meaning, were "boring," an affront to the rational man.[50] Thus Pluche's second rule for music was "to occupy the mind with an object, and to aid the feelings through the ever-affecting agreement of sound and word."[51] The best composers,

> connoissoient trop bien l'homme, et respectoient trop ses inclinations, pour croire qu'on loi plaira longtems, en le traitant comme le bouvreuil ou le sansonnèt qui ne pensent point, et qui passent les jours entiers à entendre ou à repétér de purs sons.[52]

> know man too well, and respect his inclinations too much, to suppose that they could please him for a long time by treating him like a bullfinch or a starling who does not think at all, and who spends the whole day repeating or listening to sheer sounds.

Pluche not only wanted words to occupy him with a meaning; he wanted the words to aid in carrying out his first rule: that music serve society. For, according to neo-classic doctrine, social or moral use was interpreted in the didactic sense of teaching a "lesson." Again, knowledge was to be imparted, since correct action was held to proceed from correct knowledge. And knowledge could only be communicated with words. In short, words were to be the indispensable medium of the moral message of art. For too long, Pluche wrote, music had separated two things which should never be separated; the "instruction of the mind and the pleasure of the ear." Composers who ignored art's moral mission had fallen easily into the latest musical aberration:

> C'est l'usage qui s'est extremement étendu depuis quelques siècles, de se passer de la musique vocale et de s'appliquer uniquement à amuser l'oreille sans présenter à l'esprit aucune pensée; en un mot de pretendre contenter l'homme par une longue suite de sons destitués de sens.[53]

> Namely, the practice which has been extremely widespread for several centuries, of dispensing with vocal music and of applying oneself solely to the amusement of the ear without presenting

any thought to the mind: in short, of pretending to please the listener by a long series of sounds destitute of meaning.

Less rationalistic Frenchmen allowed that some instrumental music could have a meaning and so did not reject it on principle. But the new Italian instrumental music was to arouse complaints from all quarters, from the Encyclopedists as well as the neoclassicists. All French critics of the eighteenth century, with a few exceptions, agreed that instrumental music should have an extramusical content and that the worth of instrumental music was dependent on the clarity of this content. Words, whether providing a model of intelligibility, of dramatic context, a programmatic title, or an interpretation or identification of content, still played an important role in the Frenchman's assessment of the worth of instrumental music. Rameau, himself a musician (and titular head of the faction which defended harmony against typical neoclassic charges that it obscured the melodic imitation of the passions), felt that a composer writing without a text should still find a subject that held him in "the same subjection" as a text.[54] Dubos, as we saw, felt that the symphony was made much more meaningful and enjoyable when its meaning was made determinate by the dramatic context. D'Alembert believed that music in general only attained its full expressiveness when linked with words or actions. Music, he said, was a "language without vowels," which must be "interpreted by word or action."[55] The French would defend their own instrumental music. Though inferior to vocal music in the scope of its expression, it at least had meaning, or "character." The new Italian instrumental music was another matter altogether. As d'Alembert wrote of the "prodigious quantity of sonatas" from the Italians,

Toute cette Musique purement instrumentale, sans dessein et sans object, ne parle ni à l'esprit ni à l âme, et merite qu'on lui demande avec M. le Fontenelle, *Sonate, que me veux-tu?*[56]

All this purely instrumental music without intention or object speaks neither to the mind nor to the soul, and deserves to be asked Fontenelle's question "Sonata, what do you want with me?"

Frenchmen objected not only to the blatantly nonrepresentative character of the new music; they also reacted strongly to its disorderliness, its lack of inner unity and coherence, which was in strong contrast to the homogeneity of their own *pièces charactéristiques*. A sonata, d'Alembert wrote, was "literally a dictionary of words, the collection of which makes no sense."[57] Pluche compared a sonata to a man who for no reason passes from sadness to outbursts of laughter, from jesting to seriousness.[58] Pluche also provides us with a most entertaining description of the "marvelous" incoherence of a contemporary violin sonata, where either nothing is imitated, or (which is just as bad) everything is imitated to no purpose. The violinist plays

d'abord paisible, puis emporté, tout-à-coup il s'arrête. Son archèt va par bonds, par sauts; vien-

nent les soupirs; viennent les tonnerres: viennent les échos. Il semble fuir: on ne l'entend plus. Peu-à-peu il se rapproche, roule, plane, grimpe, tombe et se relève. Il march ensuite frédonnant, gasouillant, sautillant, voletant, pirouettant, papillonnant. S'il quitte les airs brusques et les déchiquetures de la voix des oiseaux; ce sera pour vous livrer des cris de toute une basse cour, le bruit du canon et des bombes ou le raclement des tournebroches, ou le fracas des charrettes. Ainsi ou il n'imite rien, ou il contrefait tout à propos de rien.[59]

at first peacefully, then passionately; all of a sudden he stops. His bow jumps by leaps and bounds. [First] come the sighs, then the thunder, then the echoes. He seems to flee—he isn't heard any more. Little by little he draws near again, rolls, soars, climbs, falls, and gets up again. He then walks humming, chirping, skipping, flitting, twirling, fluttering. He leaves the abrupt airs and screeching sounds of birds behind only to turn to a whole barnyard of noises, guns and bombs or the scraping of a turning spit or the screeching of wheelbarrows. So he either imitates nothing or he mimics everything to no purpose.

It was not only the lack of representative intent, but also the lack of a felt unity of content which rendered the new style particularly unintelligible and intellectually offensive. Its contrasts simply seemed nonsensical.

Thus, neoclassic critics and their successors all insisted on an intelligibility and coherence of content that was modelled on the intelligibility of words and of the verbal arts themselves. It was man's prerogative as a rational being to know, clearly and distinctly, what it was that laid claim to his sensual pleasure or emotional stimulation. Germans later would take issue with this demand for what they interpreted as a namable content. Nevertheless, this rationalistic insistence on the clear intelligibility of music's content was to be, even in Germany, the chief obstacle in the way of granting instrumental music equal status with vocal music until the end of the century. It was to be the most persistent element of French rationalistic aesthetics.

The first considerable wave of French neoclassic influence into Germany arrived with the publication of Johann Christian Gottsched's *Versuch einer critischen Dichtkunst* in 1730.[60] Through the publication of this work, and from his position as Professor of Poetry at the University of Leipzig, Gottsched became for more than a decade the "supreme arbiter of German taste."[61] He initiated a campaign to eliminate the "bombast" and "buffoonery" from the German stage; and through his translations of French classical drama he succeeded in bringing the German theater within the realm of serious literary endeavor. More French than the French, it seems, Gottsched emphasized the rationalistic and moralistic moments of neoclassic thought.[62] He characterized poetry as "the *reasonable* imitation of nature"; good taste as that which "agrees with the rules which were established by reason"; and opera as a "promoter of lust and a corrupter of morals."[63]

Gottsched's twin allegiance to reason and morality is exemplified dramatically in his hierarchical classification of the types of imitation. Many of the themes of later music criticism can be seen in this account. The first and lowest type of imitation is "mere description, or the very vivid depiction of a natural thing which one paints for the eyes of one's readers clearly and distinctly, with all its properties, beauties and faults, perfections and imperfections.''[64] But the Cartesian clarity and neoclassic "truth" of this first type were not sufficient to the highest work of art (although we can see already that music would be hard put to achieve this lowest type). The second type requires far more skill than the first and occurs when the poet assumes the role of author and attributes to himself the words, gestures, and acts which another person would have had in certain circumstances. This is no spontaneous outpouring, Gottsched advises; the poet must obey the principle of verisimilitude. He must study "the innermost recesses of the human heart" and distinguish the "artificial from the unconstrained" by an "exact observation of nature."[65] His knowledge of the emotions was to guide him and assure him, as Sulzer would later say, of the "correct representation of the passions." The artist's fidelity to nature, as scientifically observed, would also preserve the artist from the danger of lapsing into that worst of "mistakes," artificiality. Gottsched, as most neoclassic critics, had a polar view of art and nature. Often this antithesis was expressed as "Gothic" vs. "pleasing," "constrained" vs. "natural," "artificial" vs. "flowing." Thus, in music, any display of artistic skill or harmonic "work" violated nature, "constrained" the realization of music's representative mission through melody, and was thus aesthetically unacceptable. Just as Gottsched used these poles to degrade the "barbaric" poetry of Germany's past (Lohenstein was a favorite target), Scheibe used them in criticizing Bach's music as "turgid and confused."[66]

The third type of imitation is the plot (*die Fabel*). Here we see the real focus of Gottsched's neoclassicism: the moral mission of art. Indeed, preoccupation with the moral dimension of art was to be typical of most eighteenth-century German criticism. Gottsched describes the plot, which represents the "highest achievement of poetry," as

> die Erzählung einer unter gewissen Umständen möglichen, aber nicht wirklich vorgefallenen Begebenheit, darunter eine nützliche moralische Wahrheit liegt.[67]

> the recounting of an event which did not really occur, but which under certain circumstances was possible, and in which lies hidden a useful moral truth.

This isolation of the plot as that which confers moral "use" upon art was typical of neoclassic didacticism; and it is the epic and the tragedy which then naturally emerge as the highest forms of art. Later German critics, though sharing Gottsched's concern for the morality of art, would find themselves espousing different accounts of musical morality to justify music's human significance.

Gottsched turns to a brief consideration of music in discussing the origins of poetry. At first he seems to abandon his neoclassic principles. He claims that poetry grew out of music, which is here seen to originate not at all as an imitation, nor as an aid to poetry, but as a primitive, inarticulate mode of emotional self-expression. Although certainly not original with Gottsched, this account of the origins of poetry is worth examining because it is a classic statement of the passionate utterance theory of musical expression, as well as a typical rationalist's account of why verbal expression is better than musical expression and hence, eventually superceded it. Gottsched begins by describing music not in the neoclassic manner, as the imitation of passionate utterances, but as utterance itself:

> Lehrt uns nicht die Natur, alle unsere Gemüthsbewegungen, durch einen gewissen Ton der Sprache, ausdrücken? Was ist das Weinen der Kinder anders, als ein Klagelied, ein Ausdruck des Schmerzens, den ihnen eine unangenehme Empfindung verursachet? Was ist das Lachen und Frohlocken anders, als eine Art freudiger Gesänge, die einen vergnügten Zustand des Gemüthes ausdrücken? Eine jede Leidenschaft hat ihren eigenen Ton, womit sie sich an den Tag legt. Seufzen, Aechzen, Dräuen, Klagen, Bitten, Schelten, Bewundern, Loben, u.s.w. alles fällt anders ins Ohr.[68]

> Does not Nature teach us to express all our emotions through a certain tone of voice? What is the crying of children if not a song of lamentation, an expression of pain caused by unpleasant feelings? What is laughter or shouting for joy if not a kind of joyful song, which expresses a pleasant condition of the soul? Each passion has its own tone, through which it makes itself known. Sighing, moaning, threatening, complaining, pleading, scolding, admiring, wondering, praising, etc. all make a different sound.

Music, then, was originally a primitive form of emotional expression and communication. But, Gottsched continues, man soon learned to sing, instead of "indistinct tones, understandable syllables and *distinct* words."[69] Although Gottsched makes a gesture of concession to the power of instruments alone, he hastens to add that vocal music, with its "understandable" words, is much more powerful:

> Man hört es freylich auch auf musikalischen Instrumenten schon, ob es munter oder kläglich, trotzig oder zärtlich, rasend oder schläfrig klingen soll: Allein es ist kein Zweifel, dass Worte, die nach einer geschickten Melodie gesungen werden, noch viel kräftiger in die Gemüther wirken.[70]

> To be sure, one can tell even from instruments, whether the music is supposed to sound defiant or tender, angry or sleepy. But there is no doubt that words which are sung to a fitting melody work even more powerfully on the soul.

The understandable power of the "distinct" word is more moving to the reasonable man than the indistinct but direct power of tones. Gottsched implies that sheer tonal communication, with its freedom from the mediation of words, is inaccessible to the intellect and thus inferior. This argument for marking instrumental music as inferior to vocal music for reasons of inferior intelligibility was to persist throughout the eighteenth century. It was part of the legacy of neoclassic thought which remained long after Gottsched's power declined.

Gottsched returns to orthodox neoclassic opinion in his discussion of opera, which he treats in the French manner, as primarily a literary genre. We can learn much about views towards music in general from these debates on operatic issues, which dominated all eighteenth-century musical-critical debate, for they provided a battlefield where the rival claims of the literary arts and the musical arts presented themselves and fought for their own specific prerogatives. Music's subservience to the word, and dependence on verbal determinants, is a central theme of these debates. Many issues relating to instrumental music's status are addressed directly: sensuality vs. morality, truth vs. fantasy, musical "art" vs. musical expression, to name those prominent in Gottsched's discussion of opera. For Gottsched, as for neoclassic critics, the proper role of music in these literary genres was to lend the words more emphasis and appeal and to intensify the "dominant affects" of the text. This recurring view of music's role in opera receives from Gottsched a radical (and it seems deliberately shocking) formulation:

> Das Singen ist . . . nichts, als ein angenehmes und nachdrückliches Lesen eines Verses, welches also der Natur und den Inhalt desselben gemäss seyn muss.[71]

> Singing is . . . nothing but a pleasant and emphatic reading of a verse, which must subsequently be in keeping with the nature and content of the words.

Unfortunately, however, the whole history of opera and cantata had shown, according to Gottsched, a tendency for the musicians to usurp their role and to use these forms as an opportunity to show off their "art" and their clever ideas. The result was that the text was rendered unintelligible by such specifically musical devices as frequent repetitions of words, long melismas, and overbearing accompaniments; and music no longer merely served the poetry. Gottsched characterized music and text as antagonists in the history of opera:

> Jemehr die Musik gewann, desto mehr verlohr die Poesie dabey. Bekam das Ohr dabey veil zu hören, so hatte der Verstand desto weniger dabey zu denken.[72]

> the more music gained by such things, the more the poetry lost. If the ear thereby was given much to hear, then the understanding had all the less to reflect upon.

The battle lines were clearly drawn: ear versus understanding, music versus poetry. It was a battle of the faculties; the senses were winning and reason was losing:

> So ist denn die Oper ein blosses Sinnenwerk: der Verstand und das Herz bekommen nichts davon. Nur die Augen werden geblendet; nur das Gehör wird gekützelt und betäubet: die Vernunft aber muss man zu Hause lassen, wenn man in die Oper geht.[73]

> The opera is then merely a production for the senses: the understanding and the heart get nothing out of it. Only the eyes are blinded; only the ear is tickled and stunned: reason however must be left at home, when one goes to the opera.

The musical and visual arts must subjugate themselves to the reinforcing of verbal meanings, for only such meaning speaks to the higher faculties of man. The specifically musical elements were to have no role to play; they could only distract the mind from more serious and morally uplifting business. In short, opera had to be reformed if it was to meet Enlightened standards.

It was not just the musicians who had ruined opera, Gottsched explained. The very notion of a sung drama violated the rule of verisimilitude: men don't sing in real life; and the characters of opera

> sehen einer Zauberey viel ähnlicher, als die Wahrheit; welch Ordnung und einen zulänglichen Grund in allen stücken erfordert.[74]

> appear more like magic than the truth, which requires order and a sufficient cause in all things.

The plots too had degenerated. Instead of portraying the acts of heroes, instead of arousing fear and pity, plots of romantic love dominated. Obviously, Gottsched writes, those people who regard opera as a "gathering place of all conceivable delights," as the "confluence of all poetic and musical beauties," or as the "masterwork of the human imagination" are not familiar with the true rules of the theater or have not seen them "derived from their first principles."[75] Gottsched's rules left no place for fantasy or sensual delights and little room for "musical beauties." The imagination and the "wonderful" would be left for the Swiss to justify, and sensual delights to Baumgarten. Gottsched merely condemned both, for they had turned the opera into an instrument of immorality, and an "unnatural" offense against reason. He feared that the sheer irresistible sensual appeal of the poetry and gestures, as well as the music, would certainly turn all "masculine Germans" at a young age into "effeminate Italians." Thus, Gottsched concludes his attack on the opera by adopting an almost Lutheran pose and delivering the following patriotic peroration:

> Die Musik an sich selbst ist zwar eine edle Gabe des Himmels: ich gebe es auch zu, dass die Componisten viel Kunst in ihren Opern anzubringen pflegen; wiewohl sie auch oft übel angebracht wird. Aber was die Poeten daran thun, und überhaupt die ganze Verbindung so verschiedener Sachen taugt gar nichts. Ich sehe überdas die Opera so an, wie sie ist; nämlich als eine Beförderung der Wollust, und Verderberinn guter Sitten. Die zärtlichsten Töne, die geilesten Poesien, und die unzüchtigsten Bewegungen der Opernhelden und ihrer verliebten Göttinnen bezaubern die unvorsichtigen Gemüther, und flössen ihnen ein Gift ein, welches ohnedem von sich selbst schon Reizungen genug hat. Denn wie wenige giebt es doch, die allen solchen Versuchungen, die sie auf einmal bestürmen, zugleich widerstehen können? So wird die Weichlichkeit von Jugend auf in die Gemüther der Leute gepflanzet, und wir werden den weibischen Italienern ähnlich, ehe wir es inne geworden, dass wir männliche Deutsche seyn sollten.[76]

> Music in itself is to be sure a noble gift of Heaven. I even allow that composers generally employ much art in their operas, although it is often out of place. But what the poets do to opera, and generally the whole combination of such diverse elements, is good for nothing. Moreover, I recognize the opera for what it is: namely a promoter of lust, and a corrupter of morals. The

most tender tones, the most lascivious poetry, and the most unchaste movements of the opera heroes and their enamored goddesses cast a spell over the unsuspecting audience, and infuse a poison which of itself surely has enough appeal. For how many are there anyway who can withstand so many temptations when they attack all at once? Thus effeminacy is engenered in people's souls from youth on; and we are transformed into effeminate Italians before we realize that we ought to be masculine Germans.

Gottsched's concern for preserving the "masculine" German culture from the sensual, "effeminate" charms of Italian art was a concern shared by many, including Sulzer. (Eighteenth-century Germans were very wary of intrusions by foreign elements.) Moreover, the above quotation, with its reference to music as a "divine gift of Heaven" and its characterization of music as a powerful emotional tool which must be kept in pious hands, shows the debt of even a man with Gottsched's neoclassic principles to pre-Enlightenment Germany. Indeed, the whole moralistic tone of Gottsched's theory of poetics can be seen as part of an ongoing German preoccupation with the morality, or redeeming human value, of art. And this preoccupation remained for some time in Germany an obstacle in the way of a free acceptance of the Italian instrumental style, universally characterized as mere "ear-tickling."

Of course, most Germans did not take Gottsched's views on music and opera seriously. And he was not a musician, nor even a music lover. However, his influence on literary criticism and musical criticism through Scheibe and others was for a time quite strong. His dogmatic brand of neoclassicism, and the challenge to music—especially instrumental music—which it implied, were on the minds of a whole generation of music critics anxious to defend music and to show how the reasonable man could indeed be an ardent music-lover.[77] Gottsched seemed to be the worst if not the most formidable of the rationalistic enemies of music. He provided a foil for the expression of opposing contemporary views (many later writers were in effect speaking to Gottsched), as he provides us a useful foil for most of the remaining views investigated in this study. Although Gottsched was more dogmatic than most Germans and certainly more unsympathetic to music, he successfully transmitted to those following him the central thrust of neoclassic aesthetics: namely, that music's role in art is subject to higher demands—those of the mind, for understanding; and those of the soul, for moral improvement.

The musician Johann Adolph Scheibe (1708–1776) had been a student of Gottsched at the University of Leipzig. It is not surprising then that the preface to his well-known periodical, *Der critische Musicus* (1737–40),[78] contains a manifesto to bring good taste and reason to bear on German music. Scheibe relates that Gottsched had made him view music in a whole new way, "unknown to anyone else." Thanks to Gottsched, he admiringly wrote, *Barbarey* had been banished from poetry and oratory. Music, however, was still languishing in its past. Therefore, Scheibe proposed to use his new periodical to apply his mentor's "rules of criticism'' to music.[79] First among these rules was that the arts were imitations of nature; and Scheibe strongly stated that it was a rule valid even for music:

> Die Nachahmung der Natur ist sonst das wahre Wesen der Musik so wohl, als der Redekunst und der Dichtkunst.[80]

> The imitaion of nature is moreover the true essence of music, just as it is of oratory and poetry.

However, as we shall see, Scheibe's radical program for reform had little bearing on instrumental music. Rather, in discussions involving instrumental genres, Scheibe apparently seems to forget his initial resolve and sanctions conventional compositional procedures which have little relation to art as imitation.

Unlike Gottsched and the so-called neoclassic critics Scheibe was himself a musician. The son of an organ builder and educated in the tradition of Lutheran church music, he pursued a career not only in music journalism but was a conductor and composer as well. From 1742 to1749 he was director of the court opera at Copenhagen. He wrote many church compositions, as well as a fair number of instrumental works in the Italian style: concertos, symphonies, trios, sonatas and the like.[81] But he was not a typical German musician, for he had attended the university and he had been trained to respect and use the powers of reason. Thus in one person, it seems, two elements of German musical culture met which seldom were blended together, but which more often confronted each other—the older cantorial tradition, which had nurtured many of Germany's Protestant musicians, and the Enlightened rationalism, popular among Germany's growing rank of intellectuals. Scheibe's overall ideological allegiances stood of course with the new intellectuals, and the opera reforms for which he fought are in tune with this new aesthetic ideology. But in his views on instrumental music we glimpse a fundamental German receptivity to nonrepresentative music. He seemed quite ready to deal with the Italian instrumental genres on their own ground, rather than on the basis of what reason dictated they should be.

In the course of his periodical Scheibe surveys the field of musical practice in accordance with the neoclassic belief in the purity of genres. He treats each general style and each specific type of composition separately, and in an order dictated, as he explains, by their place in a hierarchy. Accordingly, Scheibe discusses first church style, then theater style, and last, chamber style. The essential attribute of church music was that it praise God and arouse feelings of devotion; this was of course the highest form of music. It was theater music, next in the hierarchy, which stood in closest relation to the imitation of nature principle and to the allied principle of the representation and arousal of the passions:

> Der Endzweck der theatralischen Musik ist vornehmlich, die Zuhörer zu rühren, und in ihnen eben die Gemütsbewegungen und Leidenschaften zu erregen, mit welchem das Werk selbst angefüllt ist.
> Diese Gattung . . . hat vor andern insonderheit mit Gemütsbewegungen und Leiden-

schaften zu thun. Diese erfordern alle einen freyen und ungezwungene Ausdruck, den wir nur allein durch Nachahmung der Natur erhalten werden.[82]

The goal of theater music is primarily to move the listeners and to excite in them the very same emotions and passions with which the work itself is filled.
    This genre . . . especially, has more to do with the emotions and passions than the others. These all require a free and unconstrained expression, which we can only achieve through the imitation of nature.

When seen in this new light, many practices of the contemporary Italian opera seria violated the "rules of criticism." Such "artificial" things as melismas and word repetitions were distortions of the true and natural manner of uttering the passions. The emotions, Scheibe emphasized, must be expressed freely, in an "unconstrained" manner.[83] In addition, the words must be intelligible; hence, "an elaborate and contrapuntal instrumental texture" could be least tolerated in theater music.[84] Like Gottsched, Scheibe saw contrapuntal art or "artifice" as a cloud of compositional arrogance obscuring the clarity of the words and the accurate portrayal of natural passionate utterance. For it was not harmony but melody that communicated emotion. Thus the Enlightened reformer proclaimed that art must not interfere with nature, or in operatic terms, music must not interfere with words, nor sensual diversions obscure intellectual understanding.

    The realm of chamber music, as surveyed by Scheibe, seems curiously free from the dichotomies of art versus nature, words versus music, or sense versus intellect. Nor do we sense here the constraints on music which formed an essential part of Scheibe's Enlightened reforms for the opera. In defining the chamber style, little thought is given to the imitation of nature or the moving of the passions:

Der Endzweck des Kammerstyles ist . . . vornehmlich die Zuhörer zu ergetzen und aufmuntern.[85]

The goal of chamber music is . . . primarily to delight and enliven the listeners.

Emphasizing its functional character, he continues, "It is therefore to be used for celebration, for pleasure, and for fun." Above all, it must be "lively and stimulating" and full of variety:[86]

Bald muss sie die Schreibart erheben, bald mittelmässig, bald auch nur niedrig seyn; in allen aber soll die Annehmlichkeit und die Kunst um den Preis streiten.[87]

At one time the style must be elevated, at another moderate, at still another low. All in all, however, pleasantness and art must vie for dominance.

Significantly, Scheibe did not seem concerned to draw from his mimetic account of music a new view of instrumental chamber music. It would remain for later German writers to impose the demands of the new representative aesthetic more thoroughly. Is the conclusion to be drawn that Scheibe thought some music by its very nature did not partake of the imitative essence of the arts, that the doctrine of mimesis had little bearing on the nature or compostion of instrumental music? Whether we are justified in finding any such revealing inconsistency in Scheibe's account is difficult to determine. He does in any event, have many things to say about the specific nature of the symphony, concerto, overture, and sonata—things which eventually someone would want to incorporate into a more all-encompassing theory of music.

The only reforming impulse one senses in Scheibe's discussions of in-strumental chamber music emerges from a series of dissociated remarks warning the composer to be wary of excessive counterpoint and to take care to write singing lines. In discussing the theater, symphony, or symphony serving as an opera over-ture, he does allow that ''The skillful composer can represent in today's symphony all affects and passions . . . in the most distinct and pleasing manner in the world.''[88] And he explains his emphasis on melody by attesting to its expressive power:

> Sie ist es, welche dieselben schön, rührend, nachdrücklich und erhaben macht. Sie ist es, wodurch wir den Zuhörern ohne Worte und ohne weitere Erklärung dasjenige im Voraus ent-decken und Vorstellen, was sie hernach ausführlicher und deutlicher erblicken. Die Melodie ist es also, wodurch man allerley Affecten und Leidenschaften erregen und ausdrücken kann. Ein wichtiger Beweis, dass die Melodie das Vornehmste und das Trefflichste in der Musik, und also der Harmonie sehr weit vorzuziehen ist.[89]

> It is melody which makes the symphony beautiful, moving, forceful and sublime. It is melody through which we reveal and represent to the listeners, without words and without further ex-planation, what they are about to see more extensively and distinctly. It is melody then whereby all kinds of affects and passions can be aroused and expressed—a substantial proof that melody is the chief and most splendid element of music and therefore that it is to be very much preferred to harmony.

But this plea for melodic expressiveness in the theater symphony comes within the context of a consideration of practical compositional problems such as how coun-terpoint is allowable, and what purpose it serves, how to keep the listener's atten-tion with variety and novelty, and, last but not least, how to please the listener—all real problems for the composer of instrumental music, problems to which the im-itation doctrine provides few answers. Indeed in the case of the theater symphony, Scheibe implies that the crucial benefit of melody is not its expressiveness but its inherently pleasing quality; for it is by virtue of this melodious, pleasing character, he explains, that the new symphonies have advanced beyond the old ones. Where-as earlier composers of symphonies used many contrapuntal devices and ''elabo-rate harmonic work'' to show off their skill and art, today's composers use a lively, flowing, expressive melody, ''whose mother is nature.'' Hence, he observes approvingly, today's symphonies are more pleasing.[90] For Scheibe music could be natural merely by being melodious, it seems.[91]

At the same time, Scheibe wanted to allow for the inclusion of some counterpoint within the theater symphony in the interest of "distinctly" highlighting the melody. He recognized the value of contrast in music when literary critics were preoccupied with unadulterated unity and preferred to exclude counterpoint on principle. Scheibe gives counterpoint a role:

> Und wenn man ja in einigen ernsthaften Synphonien eine stärkere und bündigere Harmonie, oder auch wohl gar eine ziemliche Nachahmung anbringt: so wird doch der Zusammenhang der ganzen Synphonie, und also die Folge aller dieser abwechselnden Stellen ganz deutlich darthun, dass solches vielmehr geschehen sey, die Melodie zu erheben, und ihre natürliche Schönheit, aus dem Gegensatze der Kunst, desto deutlicher und ansehnlicher zu erkennen.[92]

> And if in some serious symphonies one uses a tighter and more contrapuntal texture or even indeed a proper imitation, the context of the whole symphony, as well as the succession of all these contrasting passages, will make it quite clear that this was done mostly to emphasize the melody and to make its beauty more distinct and remarkable due to the contrast of art.

We are reminded of Quantz's *untermischte Kantable*, where the most beautiful cantabile effect was achieved when the brilliant and the singing alternated. Also, Scheibe is willing to justify the contrast provided by novelty and variety on the grounds that it will insure the listener's attention. In the church symphony, for example,

> neue und nachdrückliche Gedanken und Sätze mussen die Aufmerksamkeit beständig vermehren. Diese um desto leichter zu erhalten, muss der Anfang einer solchen Synphonie schon etwas Neues und Unbekanntes zeigen.[93]

> new and energetic ideas and phrases must constantly heighten the attention. To do this most easily, the very beginning of such a symphony must display something novel and unfamiliar.

Such recognitions of the role of contrast, of novelty, and other attention-keeping devices were not to play a significant role in general critical theories until Baumgarten and his new science of "aesthetics." But composers of instrumental music such as Scheibe had been dealing with problems of contrast and attention-keeping all along.

Scheibe's discussion of the independent chamber symphony takes us farther still from questions involving the imitation of nature or the representation of the passions. His prescriptions for this genre revolve around the composer's "fecundity and fire," and his skill in the handling of his materials. A central measure of the composer's success, according to Scheibe, is his ability to use his liveliness and inventiveness in such a way as to engage the listener's attention over a period of time, and to insure his involvement through expectation-play and contrast:

Das Feuer des Componisten ist es fast ganz allein, was diese Synphonien erhebet. . . . Seine Lebhaftigkeit und seine Geschicktlichkeit, eine Melodie zu erfinden, vorzutragen und zu beseelen, sind es ganz allein, denen er folgen muss. Nur einer Gewissen Ordnung des Vortrags, die zu allen Melodien nöthig ist, und ohne welche kein einziges musikalisches Stück schön seyn kann, und die zugleich das Mittel ist, eine wahre und edle Lebhaftigkeit zu zeigen, muss er nachgehen.[94]

It is almost exclusively the fire of the composer which distinguishes this type of symphony. His liveliness and his skill in creating, presenting, and animating a melody are the only guides he must follow. But he must observe a certain order of presentation which is necessary for all melodies and without which no musical piece can be beautiful, and which at the same time is the very means of manifesting a true and noble liveliness.

This identification of a lively, fiery essence as the distinguishing feature of the chamber symphony is quite in keeping with Scheibe's announced purpose of the chamber style: to delight and enliven. It is also consonant with a widespread conception of the character of the instrumental idiom. And we shall see Mattheson even ascribe a superiority to instrumental music insofar as it is more capable of displaying fire and liveliness.

Especially noteworthy in Scheibe's description of the chamber symphony is his recognition that the excellence of the symphony resides chiefly in its form. For he continues his above description with a long account of that "order of presentation" which constitutes the necessary vehicle for the composer's manifestation of liveliness. This account is in part a description of a well-developed binary form: the composer begins with the main idea and proceeds with related or contrasting secondary ideas until he cadences "distinctly" and "naturally" in the new key; in the second half the composer has more freedom to modulate and go farther afield, but he must see to it that he returns to the original key in a "lively and unconstrained" manner.[95] But there is more to the character of the symphony than this basic form. Its success depends on how the skillful and imaginative composer manages to integrate diverse and unexpected elements so that the listener is continually stimulated over a period of time and so that a satisfying unity is also achieved; and if successful the composer has realized the "very excellence of a symphony":

Man muss aber endlich den Zusammenhang so einrichten, dass man zuletzt auf eine lebhafte und ungezwungene Art in die Haupttonart wieder zurückkehrt. . . . Jemehr man aber geschickte und unerwartete Fälle und Gedanken anbringt, desto lebhafter und angenehmer wird auch eine solche Synphonie. Es gehöret aber eine grosse Uebung, eine tiefe Einsicht in die Melodie, und keine gemeine Geschicktlichkeit darzu, alles wohl und natürlich mit einander zu verbinden, und auch die fremdsten Gedanken und Einfälle auf das ordentlichste wieder mit der Haupterfindung zu vergleichen. So müssen dahero ganz unerwartete Einfälle die Zuhörer gleichsam unvermuthet überraschen. Bevor sie aber darüber ihre Beurtheilung anstellen können, muss so fort alles wieder mit der Haupterfindung vereinbaret und verknüpfet werden. Was ich allhier angemerket habe, ist insgemein das Vortrefflichste einer Synphonie: weil es bloss allein auf das natürliche Feuer des Verfassers und auf seine Erfahrung in der musikalischen Setzkunst ankommt.[96]

Last but not least, one must design the sequence of events so that one returns again to the tonic key in a most lively and unconstrained manner. . . . The more one introduces clever and unexpected ideas and thoughts, the more pleasant and lively such a symphony will be. But much experience, a deep insight into melody, and no ordinary skill is required in order to bind everything together skillfully and naturally, and in order to integrate the main theme with even the most foreign ideas in a most proper manner. Accordingly, the composer must surprise the rather unsuspecting listeners with quite unexpected events. But before they can make any judgement as to what has happened, everything must suddenly once again become linked and united with the main theme. What I have here noted is in sum the very excellence of a symphony; for it depends solely on the natural fire of the composer and his experience in musical composition.

What is the nature of the act of aesthetic appreciation described here? Certainly it is not one of recognizing the accuracy and felicity of a certain musical imitation. And neither is this the description of the passive, enervating enjoyment of ear-tickling tidbits. Rather the listener's attention and active involvement in the temporal sequence of musical events have been engaged, and the listener experiences feelings of surprise at the unexpected, and relief at the moment of final integration. The listener is indeed affected; but one would not say that the composer has expressed an emotion or roused and stilled the passions. On two occasions in the above excerpt Scheibe advises the composer unexpectedly to surprise the listener, to play with the listener's expectations. "The more one introduces clever and unexpected ideas and thoughts," he wrote, "the more pleasant and lively will be such a symphony"—that is, the more it will realize chamber music's goal of delighting and enlivening. The liveliness and fire of the composer, that essential ingredient of the symphony, is in effect transmitted to the listener by the rousing and stilling of his expectations, in short, by constructing an interesting and engaging form—and therein resides the "Vortrefflichste einer Synphonie."

Just as in the case of the symphony, Scheibe appears disinclined to apply the new aesthetic rules to the genres of the concerto, the French overture, and the sonata. In the case of the concerto, he even sanctioned a considerable admixture of counterpoint, which was the accepted antithesis of musical imitation of nature. Indeed, the "key to the composition of a concerto" is that all the voices should have "very skillful contrapuntal elaboration"; only of course, "a mere contrapuntal texture does not at all suffice," he warns.[97] Concerti must also be free, lively, pleasant, flowing and fiery "in spite of all their art and painstaking work,"[98] But there is no mention of affect, or of melody as expression. The French overture Scheibe values especially highly, as did Mattheson; he mentions its "perpetual fire," its "natural cheerfulness," its "noble liveliness." It stimulates the listener; unexpected things, such as a deceptive cadence before the return of the opening section, are especially pleasant; they surprise the listener and arouse *Verwunderung*.[99] But there is no mention of the representation of the affects. Rather there is a tacit recognition of that same affective, enlivening, stimulating, engaging essence which we saw in the case of the chamber symphony and which seems to be the peculiar property of certain genres of instrumental music.

The sonata, as the concerto, is characterized by "imitative counterpoint," especially in the upper voices.[100] In discussing the individual movements Scheibe does pay special attention to the affective moment. For example, the last movement should arouse either repose or joy; but there is no suggestion that it is by virtue of emotional representation that the listener is so affected.[101] The charm and pleasantness of the first movement is seen to reside in the successful cultivation of the listener's attention:

> Diese Anmuth muss sich immer vermehren; sie muss uns immer auf neue Art einnehmen, und uns, so lange der Satz dauert, in einer ununterbrochene Aufmerksamkeit erhalten.[102]

> This charm must constantly increase; it must in ever new ways continually involve us, and as long as the movement lasts, maintain us in an uninterrupted state of attentiveness.

Again, the basic elements are those of engaging the listener's attention, of sheer affectiveness, and of compositional craft.

In Scheibe's discussion of instrumental music we are not aware of the typical neoclassic disdain for "meaningless" sounds; rather we sense an appreciation of musical craft, a German musician's receptivity to the engaging and specifically musical qualities of current contemporary instrumental music. Scheibe's recognition of the importance of the skill of the composer in the invention, ordering, and treatment of his musical materials is also not what one would ordinarily expect of a normal neoclassic critic. For neoclassic critics and expression theorists in general spoke little about musical forms, or technical musical problems. Indeed, what does the temporal unfolding of music's form, or the sheer affectiveness of instrumental fire, surprise, and liveliness, or the interest inherent in musical craft, or the engaging of the listener's expectations through contrast and the unexpected, have to do with the musical representation of the passions? Scheibe was not concerned with this question. All the musical elements Scheibe mentions as essential to instrumental genres are given no role in his mimetic theory. It does not even seem to have occurred to him to reconcile his two sets of standards, the one having to do with the imitation of nature and the other with instrumental music.

Thus the first person we have seen attempt to apply the French neoclassic doctrine of imitation to music in fact seems to have ignored its application to instrumental music, as if to say that the demands of this doctrine were inapplicable. And certainly he did say that instrumental music was quite acceptable as it then functioned: to delight and enliven—but not to imitate nature.

Neoclassic influence on German criticism and aesthetics was not to end with Gottsched and Scheibe and their generation. If Scheibe had not applied neoclassic aesthetics to instrumental music, the matter was not to rest there. For a larger wave was yet to come, that of Batteux. Scheibe's *Der critischer Musicus* may have implied the conclusion that instrumental music did not fit into neoclassic theory, but other critics would not accept this violation of fundamental principle. Charles Batteux (1713–1780) was one of those who was determined to subject all art, including instrumental music, to the imitation doctrine. Batteux's primary message, so far as German music critics were concerned, was his emphatic principle, "all music must have a meaning," by which he meant, all music must imitate nature.

Batteux's *Les beaux arts réduits à un même principe* (1746)[103] was to be the chief bearer of neoclassic doctrine into Germany. For Batteux's was the version of this doctrine that most mid-century Germans read. Indeed, this work, which was translated into German numerous times, was more influential in Germany than in France, where the Encyclopedist viewpoint was soon to prevail.[104] Translations appeared in 1751, 1754, and 1756.[105] While it is not true, as we shall see in subsequent chapters, that after Batteux the French dominated German music aesthetics (as Schering contended),[106] the work did attract such a large following in both the literary and Enlightened musical circles of Germany that it defined the terms of the aesthetic debate for the succeeding decades. The strongest challenge yet to instrumental music seemed to be posed by Batteux's insistence that all music and all parts of musical compositions must have an intelligible meaning, a "sens net, sans obscurité." Indeed Gottsched was to use his translation and commentary on Batteux as a platform from which to launch the bitterest attack against instrumental music of the whole century. The time seemed to be ripe for a debate over the increasingly popular instrumental music; and Batteux's views were to figure prominently in the opinions of its detractors.

Batteux's work was essentially a proof, both inductive and deductive, that the imitation of nature was the fundamental principle of all the arts. Optimistically attempting to "imitate the true physicians," Batteux hoped to legislate for all the arts on grounds as unshakable as those of Newtonian mechanics.[107] A professor of rhetoric at the College of Navarre until 1750, he candidly admitted that his original intent was merely the study of poetry, and that he was only later inspired to do for all the arts what Newton had done for physics.[108] Accordingly, his approach to music is typically neoclassic in that he brings to bear on music standards which were originally derived by induction from the literary arts. But although his work can be seen as a kind of culmination or final rationalization of neoclassic principles, it was as well a forward-looking, original and sentimentalist revision of the neoclassic imitation doctrine.[109] Nevertheless Batteux's image in Germany remained that of a rationalist who had made a compelling argument that all the arts were imitations of nature.[110] And Gottsched, who perhaps misunderstood him the most, was to be one of his chief promoters.

Batteux's ideas on music were based on his theory of music as a natural language of the passions. This theory was the same as the "passionate utterance" theory of musical expression we encountered earlier among neoclassic views; only

Batteux articulates it with such emphasis and enthusiasm that it seems his own. And indeed, his German readers were to identify this "rhetorical," or "declamatory," account of musical expression with his name. Like Dubos, he cited ancient rhetorical authority: "Every feeling, according to Cicero, is announced by its own tone and gesture."[111] Since sounds bespoke their utterer's emotional state, sounds were for Batteux "natural signs" of the passions. And just as men use words, or "arbitrary signs," to communicate their ideas, they use the language of sheer sound, the language of passionate tones, to communicate their feelings. This account of tones as natural signs of the passions stems of course from Dubos's own account; the operatic recitative was a series of such signs, whose "truth" derived from

l'imitation des tons, des accens, des soupirs, et des sons qui sont propres naturellement aux sentiments contenus dans les paroles.[112]

the imitation of those tones, accents, sighs, and sounds which are natural properties of the feel-, ings contained in the words.

However Batteux, though agreeing with Dubos's explanation of the recitative, seems ready to leave past tradition and view the meaning of sounds as less derivative from the accents and inflections of verbal utterance. He spoke of the power of music to express "sorrow and joy independently of words," whereas Dubos limited his utterance theory to vocal music.[113] And Batteux waxes rhapsodic in describing the peculiar "advantages" of this language of the heart, as compared to the verbal language which spoke the language of reason:

Les tons de la voix et les gestes, ont sur elle [la parole] plusieurs avantages: ils sont d'un usage plus naturel; nous y avons recours quand les mots nous manquent: plus étendu, c'est un interprete universel qui nous suit jusqu'aux extrémités du monde, qui nous rend intelligibles aux Nations les plus barbares, et mêmes aux animaux. Enfin ils sont consacrés d'une maniere spéciale au sentiment. La parole nous instruit, nous convainc, c'est l'organe de la raison: mais le ton et le geste sont ceux du coeur: ils nous emeuvent, nous gagnent, nous persuadent. La parole n'exprime la passion que par le moyen des idées auxquelles les sentimens sont liés, et comme par réflexion. Le ton et le geste arrivent au coeur directement et sans aucun détour.[114]

The tones of the voice and gestures have several advantages over it [the word]: they are part of a more natural usage, to which we have recourse when words fail us; moreover, this language is a universal interpreter which follows us to the ends of the earth and makes us intelligible to the most barbarous nations and even to animals. Finally, they have a timeless and peculiar association with the feelings. The word instructs us, convinces us, it is the organ of reason; but tone and gesture are organs of the heart: they move us, overcome us, persuade us. The word can only express passion by means of ideas associated with feelings and by means of reflection. Tone and gesture penetrate to the heart directly with no detour.

But dispite the considerable power given above to sheer tones, and despite Batteux's assertion that these tones retained their meaning when arranged into music,

Batteux, as we shall see, did not intend to sanction an art of pure sounds.

The apparent corollary of Batteux's belief in the natural "signification" of passionate tones was that music imitates nature by imitating these natural tones of passionate utterance. In other words, for Batteux the "object" of musical imitation was the natural expressions of the sentiments or passions. Music becomes the imitation of self-expressions. (The ability of music to imitate aspects of inanimate nature is recognized by Batteux, but relegated to a secondary position.) These passionate signs, which are the essence of music and which the artist does not create but finds already existing in nature, are then intensified, decorated, and ordered by the resources of musical art, by rhythm, harmony, and melody. But the "signification" or meaning of the tones remains their essential feature, and the meaning of these passionate tones is the primary content of the music.[115] Thus, when Batteux writes, "All music must signify, must have a meaning," he means that music should represent the passions by imitating the tones of passionate utterance.[116]

The force of Batteux's insistence on representation is matched only by his insistence on the clear intelligibility of this required meaning. Batteux wants "a distinct meaning, without obscurity, without equivocation."[117] He likens the intelligibility of music to the intelligibility of a painting. Both are judged in the same manner: by reference to the object of imitation in the real world. Both should partake of the same denotative distinctness in the representation of natural objects. The musician is no more "free" than the painter.[118] Instrumental music without a clear sense, no matter how "géometrique," is as absurd as a painting would be if it consisted only of lines and colors, with no recognizable object:

> Que diroit-on d'un Peintre, qui se contenteroit de jetter sur la toile des traits hardis, et des masses de couleurs les plus vives, sans aucune resemblance avec quelque objet connu? L'application se fait d'elle-même à la Musique.[119]

> What would one say of a painter who was content to throw onto the canvas bold strokes and masses of the most vivid colors with no resemblance to a known object? The application to music speaks for itself.

An even more pervasive model for music was that of verbal language. Every sound in a work of music has its model in nature and every sound must seem to be "at least a beginning of a thought, as is a letter or a syllable in verbal language."[120] Just as we are not satisfied by a discourse which we do not understand, we are not satisfied with music whose meaning is vague. "Music speaks to me through tones: its language is natural to me: if I do not at all understand it, art has corrupted, rather than perfected, nature."[121] Batteux speaks of music which has this "sens net, sans obscurité" as "parlantes."[122] And these "speaking" tones the composer can find in the natural inflections of speech: "Tones are partly formed by the words."[123] In sum, the same standards of intelligibility apply to music as to oratorical discourse.

Furthermore, the principles of ordering these significant tones, and the rules with regard to unity, variety, and coherence are the same as those of verbal discourse. The succession of musical expressions must form a "discours suivi," so that each expression is explained or prepared by those that follow or precede it:[124]

> S'il y a des expressions qui m'embarassent, faute d'être préparées ou expliquées par celles qui précèdent ou qui suivent s'il y en a qui me détournent, qui se contredisent; je ne puis être satisfait.[125]

> If there are expressions which perplex me because they are not prepared, or explained by those that precede or those that follow, if there are those which mislead me, which contradict each other, I cannot be satisfied.

And just as all the words of a discourse have a meaning relating to the subject (and a single tone relating to it), so all the tones of a musical composition must have a meaning, and a meaning in keeping with it. If joy is the subject then all the modulations must be laughing. Just as all the words of a discourse have meaning, "every tone, every gesture, must lead us to an opinion, or state one."[126] Furthermore, just as it would be redundant or meaningless to repeat the same statement in a verbal discourse, so should all musical expressions be "new"—repetition was useless.[127] Batteux has left little room for such typical musical devices as repetition and contrast. The conventions of musical form must yield, it appears, to the superior intelligibility of Batteux's "coherent discourse."

One final consequence of Batteux's insistence on a clear and easy intelligibility was the limitation on the composers' choice of the very subject for musical imitation. Since subtle or refined meanings could not be clearly communicated with tones, they must be avoided.[128] For why, Batteux asks, does the composer "choose certain objects, certain passions rather than others; is it not because they are easier to express, and that the listeners will grasp the expression more easily?"[129] Thus not all the riches of nature are accessible to the composer:

> Et quelque riche que soit la nature pour les Musiciens, si nous ne pouvions comprendre les sens des expressions qu'elle renferme, ce ne seroit plus des richesses pour nous. Ce seroit un idiome inconnu, et par conséquent inutile.[130]

> No matter how rich nature may be for the musicians, if we are not able to understand the expressions which nature contains, these expressions would cease to be riches for us. They would form an unknown and consequently useless language.

Later German writers would object to this limitation of music's content to what could be easily understood. It seemed to later German critics that Batteux's emphasis on intelligibility would rule out the traditional riches of musical art, and would deny music its peculiar ability to reflect subtle and unnamable shadings of feelings.[131]

In reviewing all Batteux's demands for meaning, intelligibility, and coherence, it seems clear that instrumental music, especially that in the new Italian style, would find little sanction. It is difficult to see how instrumental music could live up to Batteux's demands for representation and intelligibility; especially difficult to achieve would be the assignment of a meaning to every sound, the denotative distinctness of a painting, and the clarity and coherence of verbal discourse. To be sure, Batteux's belief in the natural signification of sounds and his extension of this signification to music "independent of words" would seem to promise greater acceptance of instrumental music as a serious art, one worthy and capable of representing and arousing emotions. And he does make one self-conscious exception to the rationalistic tenor of his insistence on clear intelligibility:

> Il suffit qu'on le [l'objet] sente, il n'est pas nécessaire de le nommer. Le coeur a son intelligence indépendante des mots; et quand il est touché, il a tout compris.[132]

> It is enough if one senses it [the object of imitation]; it is not necessary to name it. The heart has its own understanding, independent of words; and when it is moved, it has understood completely.

But for all Batteux's attempts to reconcile the rival demands of sentiment and reason, in the final analysis feeling yields to reason.[133] The "heart's understanding" and the "distinct sense, without obscurity, without equivocation" remain unreconciled. Batteux was unequivocal about wanting the words, the "organ of reason," to accompany sound: just as words and tones occurred together in real life, so should they in art.[134] Words hold the "first place." People pay more attention to words.[135] And though he seems to avoid explicitly condemning instrumental music on rationalist grounds, one senses in Batteux's final papagraphs on music an antipathy to absolute, or "geometric," music which is well rooted in rationalistic refexes: like Pluche, Batteux believed that the mind must participate in the aesthetic experience by means of a clear comprehension of the object of imitation. Otherwise, although the senses might be amused, the mind would surely be bored. This is the essence of his most explicit objection to absolute music, seemingly directed toward the instrumental music of his day:

> Concluons donc que la Musique la mieux calculée dans tous ses tons, la plus géométrique dans ses accords, s'il arrivoit, qu'avec ces qualités elle n'eût aucune signification; on ne pourroit la comparer qu' à un Prisme, qui présente le plus beau coloris, et ne ne fait point de tableau. Ce seroit une espèce de clavecin chromatique, qui offriroit des couleurs et des passages, pour amuser peut-être les yeux, et ennuyer sûrement l'esprit.[136]

> Therefore let us conclude that even though a musical composition be the most correctly calculated in all its sounds and the most geometric in its harmony, if it has no signification to accompany these qualities, it can only be compared to a prism which yields the most beautiful colors but which produces not the least image. It would be like a color-harpsichord which produced colors and arrangements in order to amuse perhaps the eyes, but which certainly would bore the mind.

Thus did Batteux conclude his chapter entitled ''Toute musique et toute Danse doit avoir une signification, un sens.'' The Germans' interpretation of Batteux as essentially rationalistic, at least so far as instrumental music is concerned, appears not altogether inaccurate.

3

Independent German Currents of Thought: Mattheson—Baumgarten—Krause

The traditional German attitude towards music was not to be totally eclipsed by the influx of French neoclassic criticism. Although almost all German writers on music after Batteux paid at least some terminological allegiance to the mimetic theory of art, and all were obliged to deal with it, certain native traditions were maintained, it seems, which prevented any wholehearted or widespread acceptance on the part of musicians and music critics of neoclassicism's central tenets. These native traditions furthered the ongoing development of an independent intellectual and musical viewpoint which was to prove most favorable for a greater appreciation of instrumental music. As we focus in this chapter on three significant manifestations of independent German thinking, we shall see evidence of the persistence of two native currents, one musical and the other philosophical, one reaching back to Luther and the other to Leibnitz.

Mattheson, writing in 1739 at the end of many years of critical activity, hardly needed to take notice of neoclassic doctrine. He was reacting more against the sterile academicism of the Lutheran *Cantorei*. He does, however, insist that all genres of music express the passions and have moral effect—an insistence, it would seem, totally in tune with Batteux. However, Mattheson had his own individual prescriptions for the musical realization of this ideal. His account of musical morality is closer to Luther's than to any Frenchman's; and his theory of musical expression is totally different from the passionate utterance theory. Mattheson's theory allows for a large admixture of musical craft, and at times interprets sheer effectiveness as an acceptable goal of musical ''expression.'' Also, Mattheson displayed a great receptivity to the peculiar traits of instrumental music and insisted it could express the passions just as well as vocal music. But in the final analysis his preference for vocal lyricism and singing melody brought him to place instrumental music below vocal music.

Baumgarten hardly spoke of music, but he took it upon himself to give a fundamental account of art that deliberately took issue with the Cartesian rationalism associated with the neoclassic account. In so doing he drew upon the German philosophical tradition of Leibnitzian rationalism. Baumgarten's account of art as essentially sensual and hence requiring a large admixture of variety, contrast, and imagination served to justify, within an academically respectable theoretical framework, elements of instrumental music previously considered objectionable or left unaccounted for in terms of critical theory.

Both Lutheran and Leibnitzian currents flow through Krause's thinking. He used Baumgarten's new aesthetic theory, as well as traditional German musical ideas, to defend music against the encroachments of literary and rationalistic standards. He argued that music had its own nature, meaning, and effects with which any verbally specified content must be in accord. He constructed a theory of musical expression which allowed for such typical musical devices and procedures as melismas, counterpoint, repetition, variation, and contrast. And at the same time that he provided for specifically "musical beauties," he provided for the musical representation of the passions.

Johann Mattheson (1681-1764) began his famous musical compendium, *Der vollkommene Capellmeister* (1739), in a way which would have won approval even in France: by announcing the "fundamental principle of music."[1] Mattheson shared with Batteux and the new science a concern for establishing the underlying principle of a family of phenomena. But unlike the typical neoclassic critic who saw music's fundamental principle as the imitation of nature—a principle shared by all the arts—Mattheson's "first principle" was specifically musical:

Alles muss gehörig singen.

All music must sing.

Mattheson was himself a musician, and his *Capellmeister* was designed as a handbook for practicing musicians. Yet his speculative bent was so strong, his allegiance to Enlightened principles and Italian opera so firm, and the German resistance to new music and ideas so ingrained, that he felt he must provide a theoretical justification for the forward-looking practice of his day. This theoretical understanding, he argued, was a necessary part of the reasonable composer's professional equipment. Thus, not only does Mattheson's handbook have an encyclopedic array of information, extending from the physics of sound to the correct performance of ornaments—it has a sense of mission. Indeed, the work can be viewed as a critical manifesto for hidebound German musicians to adopt the expressive cantabile idiom of the Italian aria, the clear "character" of French music, and the new critical awareness of aesthetic ends and means: to view music less as sounding number and more as "heart-moving song."[2]

Instrumental music was one of Mattheson's particular concerns. He repeatedly emphasized that instrumental music was subject to the same standards as vocal music. Like Scheibe and the neoclassic critics, he demanded that all music must

express, or represent, the passions. But Mattheson's demand for musical expression was part of a general theory quite different from neoclassic theory. Mattheson
managed to combine his insistence on representation with profound respect for the
qualities of specifically musical art. Indeed, Mattheson was very sympathetic to
instrumental music.

Mattheson's critical stance was a wide one. His fundamental attitude towards
the spiritual significance of music and the value of musical art was in complete
sympathy with traditional German views. His insistence that all music express the
passions was in tune with the representative insistence of neoclassic criticism. His
musical preferences ran toward the Italian operatic idiom of Keiser. And in trying
to justify his views he put to use the latest scientific findings which were pouring
out of the French academies. Mattheson seems also to have absorbed a healthy
dose of English empiricism: his defense of the cantabile principle against the
rationalistic *musicus* of the old guard takes the form of the sense versus reason
debate. Thus his view of music emerges as a synthesis of German faith in the
"wonderful effects of music," Newtonian mechanics, Cartesian pathology,
Lockean empiricism, neoclassic demands for musical content, a taste for Italian
music, and a thorough knowledge and respect for the art of musical composition.

The course of Mattheson's life helps explain the eclecticism of his critical
outlook. His career was as diverse as the sources of his critical views. His earliest
musical training was through private teachers in Hamburg and at the Johanneum,
where he received the typical preparation in Lutheran church music. Although he
never attended a university, as did Scheibe, he referred to the Hamburg opera,
where he was active for some nine years as singer, composer, and director, as a
"musical university." Under Kusser and Keiser he witnessed the introduction of
the "Italian manner of singing" into Germany and even played a role in Handel's
initiation into this style, then so foreign to north German soil. He retired from the
Hamburg opera in 1705, a cultivated man of the world, proficient in languages,
dance, fencing, as well as organ-playing. His versatility and broad-ranging interests are apparent if we consider that in 1703 he contemplated accepting Buxte-
hude's position in Lübeck, but chose instead of this traditional church position a
position divorced from music altogether. He entered the employ of the English
envoy to lower Saxony first as tutor, then as secretary; and this was to be his permanent source of livelihood. Nevertheless, he continued to be active as composer,
critic and performer, both in the world of opera and in the world of Lutheran church
music. In 1715 he was appointed cantor and canon of the Hamburg Cathedral.
From 1713 on he was engaged in a critical duel of his own making with the adherents of the old musical theory and the opponents of the new music. And after becoming deaf in 1728 his musical energies were directed more and more to writing
and musical journalism. The *Capellmeister* represents a kind of summary of a life-
time of critical reflection and debate.[3] We see in Mattheson a breadth of musical
experience uncommon for his time. He was active in the older, more traditional

world of Lutheran church music, as well as in the progressive worldly arena of Italian opera. In his person the practical and the speculative met.

Mattheson began his encyclopedic handbook by constructing a general theory of music which he hoped would guide the composer in his everyday work. One of the premises of this theory was, as we have seen, the fundamental principle that all music must sing. Another was his definition of music. (Mattheson builds his theory so thoroughly that he even ventures a definition of a definition before giving one.) This definition bespeaks the eclecticism of his approach, for (as Mattheson was to say of the sonata) it seemed to have something for everybody:

> Die Music sey eine Wissenschaft und Kunst, geschickte und angenehme Klänge, klüglich zu stellen, richtig an einander zu fügen, und lieblich heraus zu bringen, damit durch ihren Wollaut Gottes Ehre und alle Tugenden befördert werden.[4]

> Music is the science and the art of cleverly arranging, correctly combining, and delightfully performing both artful and pleasant sounds, so that the glory of God and all virtues are furthered through their euphony.

It had elements seemingly designed to satisfy the older school with its emphasis on the *ars combinatoria*, as well as the newer school which shunned excessive counterpoint in favor of natural, flowing, and pleasing melody. That music should be both a science and an art, that its sounds should both demonstrate skill and provide pleasure, that composition should be ''clever'' and ''correct'' and at the same time ''delightful'' is more of a diplomatic statement than an informative one. And yet it was not altogether empty political rhetoric. Mattheson was serious: he did intend to show how music could both provide pleasure and further virtue. He intended to maintain a respect for musical science, to preserve his predilection for musical art at the same time that he advocated that all music must express and arouse the passions. He could ambitiously attempt to do all these things, which to the French neoclassic critic seemed ridiculous, if not impossible, because his accounts of musical morality and musical expression were radically different from theirs. Furthermore, he applied his Enlightened faculty of reason to show that music's effects were achieved mechanically and immediately, rather than through the mediation of the mind. And as a German musician he inherited a different view of that essence of music for which any such theory must account.

Perhaps the most significant way in which Mattheson's views differ from those of the French neoclassicists, as indeed from the views of the German *Cantorei*, is in his emphasis on the sensual element as essential to the art and effects of music, and his de-emphasis of the role of the intellect. Indeed, Mattheson seems to have seen himself as defending the primacy of the ear in the musical experience. The neoclassic critic was imbued with Cartesian epistemology, wherein the senses were suspect as sources of knowledge; he asked of sounds what they meant that his mind could grasp, not what they offered that his senses could perceive and enjoy.

But Mattheson had had enough of the ill effects of rationalism on music. In an acrimonious struggle with the *musicus* of the old school over the status of the interval of the fourth and other things, he attempted to establish the fact that music was fundamentally beautiful sound, not sounding number.[5] Mattheson dismissed the rationalism of the *Cantorei* by quoting an old empiricist maxim that does not leave room for the rationalism of any school: "For there is nothing at all in the mind which has not first entered through the senses"—certainly not a precept of Cartesian epistemology.[6] Thus he explicitly states at the outset that his treatise of music will have nothing to do with *musica mundana* or *musica humana* because neither of these is addressed to the human ear. All speculation in which he will indulge will be limited to what is necessary

> bloss zeigen und lehren, wie eine solche Music zu verfertigen, und in die Ausübungs-Wege zu richten sey, die dem Sinn des Gehörs, das in der Seelen wohnet, durch die Werckzeuge der Ohren gefalle, und das Hertz oder Gemüth tüchtig bewege oder rühre.[7]

> simply to show and to teach how to compose and perform music which will by means of the aural mechanism please the sense of hearing that resides in the soul, and which will thoroughly touch or move the heart or spirit.

And, as this statement suggests, it was to be the ear through which music was to penetrate into the human soul. For the ear "resides in the soul." Not the rationally mediated cognition of a represented content, but the immediate perception of sounds is to be the essential means to music's moral end.

It is evident that Mattheson shared with his forbears a belief in the "resounding powers" of music.[8] His belief that the ear resides in the soul derived from the traditional German faith in the immediate affectiveness of music. The ear he held to be a special sense (as did Luther); the other senses serve only the body; "but the . . . sense of hearing is intended and reserved for our moral good."[9] Thus he partook of the traditional German view that there was a "secret affinity" whereby well-ordered sounds would impart their harmony to the sympathetic human soul; but he roundly rejected the number mysticism frequently associated with this view.

Mattheson could not rest content with the traditional Lutheran faith in the effects of music. He wanted to ground his theory in science, not in a mystical faith of any sort. He intended to provide an account which the Enlightened man could accept. He felt that the traditional German account needed updating in keeping with the latest findings of the new science. To this end he marshalled together all the relevant facts about acoustics, the physiology of the ear, and the physiological nature of the passions that he could find. He united these into a large chapter on the "Science of Sounds."[10] In this chapter he seems to be searching for an actual mechanism that will account for the immediacy of music's spiritual and moral force. Thus he touches on the anatomy and physiology of the ear, the properties of sounding bodies, sympathetic vibrations, overtones, and even the medical uses of music. The final and most important department of the ''Science of Sounds'' has to do with ''the effects which well-ordered sounds have on the emotions and passions of the soul.''[11] Mattheson does not call into question these immediate physical effects of tones on the soul. Indeed he goes one step further and asserts that since virtue consists in a well-ordered disposition, the science of sounds—since sounds necessarily affect the human soul—is actually of one piece with the morality of music.[12] Or, as Mattheson said, *Naturlehre* and *Sittenlehre* play a musical duet.[13]

That Mattheson united in one theory both music's fundamental nature as a sensual construct—its sensual or aural appeal— and its moral or spiritual significance is especially important for the history of the aesthetics of instrumental music. By maintaining the immediacy of music's beneficial effects he freed instrumental music from the necessity to occupy the mind with an object of representation in order to be significant. To accomplish this fusion of sensuality and morality, Mattheson depended on views of virtue, moral utility, and the passions which were quite different from neoclassic views. For the French neoclassic critic, as for Plato, Descartes, and many others, moral action was based on correct knowledge of what was good and what was evil; given this correct knowledge, virtuous action would presumably follow. Thus the moral utility of the arts consisted in inculcating moral wisdom which could guide the mind in choosing correct behavior. The epic and the drama were accordingly the ideal vehicles for art as an instrument of morality. Music could be morally useful by intensifying and making more appealing a verbal didactic message. But instrumental music, with its non-referential, sensual character, was without redeeming moral or spiritual value; at best it was mere divertissement. The passions, logically, played little role in the neoclassic account of art's moral usefulness, except insofar as their consequences for good and evil had to be known, and as they must be subjugated by the mind; the passions were seen as perturbations of the soul, as potential spoilers of virtue. Mattheson, however, had a different account of virtue, and therefore also a different view of the role of the passions and of music in furthering virtue. For Mattheson the virtuous soul was the well-balanced soul, not the soul with certain knowledge of right and wrong. ''Virtue,'' wrote Mattheson, is nothing other than a ''well-ordered and wisely moderated disposition.''[14] Moreover, the passions had a positive role to play. They must not be stoically suppressed:

> Wo keine Leidenschaft, kein Affect zu finden, da ist auch keine Tugend. Sind unsere Passiones kranck, so muss man sie heilen, nicht ermorden.[15]

> Where there is no passion, no affect to be found, there is also no virtue. If our passions are sick, then they must be healed, not murdered.

The passions were the ''wahre Materie der Tugend''—the very stuff of virtue. And the passions, morality, and sounds, by virtue of their immediate effect on the soul, were all intimately and necessarily connected.

Thus a theory of the passions was to be an essential part of Mattheson's theory of musical expression. Ironically, Mattheson turned to Descartes for an account of the passions. We have not seen so far that Mattheson wanted to have much to do with elements of Cartesian rationalism, or with one of its offshoots, neoclassic criticism; indeed he has been defending the passions as well as the senses from their rationalistic detractors. But Descartes's physiological and mechanistic description of the various passions fit nicely into Mattheson's physical and mechanistic account of the immediate affectiveness of music. And Mattheson was intent upon providing a scientific account of the "wonderful effects of music." In Descartes's pathology each passion was assumed to be an identifiable state of mind with certain characteristic physiological causes or concomitants. Each affective state was described separately and had its own manifestations with respect to the state of the blood, the "animal spirits," and the pulse. The passions were then separable, knowable, in part physical, and more or less static inner entities.[16] Mattheson accepted Descartes's theory as scientifically irrefutable, it seems, and proceeded to base his doctrine of musical expression upon it. Given the proper knowledge of the nature of the passions, the composer could aspire to express or represent these correctly or quasi-scientifically in music. For, Mattheson pointed out—and this is the foundation of his theory of musical expression (frequently called his "Affektenlehre")—there are "isomorphic relationships of sounds," or musical analogues, to the inner physiological causes and concomitants of the passions.[17] For example, since

die Freude durch Ausbreitung unsrer Lebens-Geister empfunden wird, so folget vernünfftiger und natürlicher Weise, dass ich diesen Affect am besten durch weite und erweiterte Intervalle ausdrücken könne.[18]

joy is felt through the dilation of our animal spirits, it reasonably and naturally follows that I could best express this affect through large and expanded intervals.

Similarly, using sounds and rhythms of music one could make a "sensual concept" of all the emotions, and thus express them quite naturally.[19] The physical effects of these rhythms and emotions would then in turn arouse the corresponding affect in the listener. It is almost as if the composer is to function as a musical mechanic, in the best Newtonian sense. One could simply dismiss this account as a latter day rationalization of the traditional *Figurenlehre,* and indeed it is that. But it is important to recognize that by virtue of giving this theory a scientific basis (no matter how naive it might seem to us today), Mattheson was providing an Enlightened alternative to the very different passionate utterance theory of musical expression formulated by the neoclassic critics. Mattheson's theory called for the representation and arousal of *inner* emotional states through the organization of specifically musical resources into conformations analogous to the physical nature of the emotions themselves. The passionate utterance theory, on the other hand, prescribed the musical imitation of *outer* signs or utterances of the passions. If all music in order to be expressive were to imitate these monodic vocal inflections, it would accordingly be limited to a recitative-like idiom with a single-minded emphasis on sheer melody. Indeed, the utterance or ''declamatory'' theory of musical expression was to be rejected by German musicians, as we shall see, as an insult to the riches of musical art. But Mattheson's theory allows for a much broader range of expressive musical idioms; even the peculiarities of the instrumental idiom might serve a representative function. Paradoxically, despite all Mattheson's use of rhetorical devices (especially the aids to invention, the *loci topici*), it was the neoclassic theory, not Mattheson's, that unquestioningly rested on the ancient rhetorical premise that for each affect there is a corresponding tone and gesture by which it makes itself known. Moreover, in neoclassic theory the reason played a large role in recognizing the moving content denoted by these signs; but Mattheson's theory, though using the pathology of the rationalistic Descartes, provided for an immediate affectiveness of music which bypassed the faculty of reason altogether.

Mattheson concludes his large introductory exposition of the science of sounds with a passionate appeal that all music be designed to move the listener. As for the neoclassic critics, merely pleasant, ear-tickling music is not enough; merely clever music is not enough. The composer must intend to represent and move the passions. Indeed if the composer has followed Mattheson's demonstration of how sounds, the ear, the passions, and virtue are all inseparably linked, he can intend no other result. Mattheson's appeal is of course very similar to Batteux's injunction that all music have a sense, and no doubt reinforced the impetus of the neoclassic mimetic demand. And though Mattheson's theory departs in definite ways from neoclassic musical views, as we have seen, it also bears some striking resemblances. In the chapter on musical invention, Mattheson singles out the *locus descriptionis* as ''the most certain and most fundamental guide to invention,''

> indem hieher das unergründliche genannte Meer von den menschlichen Gemüths-Neigungen gehöret, wenn diese in Noten beschrieben oder abgemahlet werden sollen.[20]

> in that here belongs the so-called unfathomable sea of human feelings which are to be described or painted with notes.

Also, Mattheson frequently refers to music as a ''sound-speech'' or ''tone-language,'' and compares music to language.[21] The ideas of ''painting'' the passions and the suggestion of language as a model for music are of course very consonant with neoclassic ideas.[22] But even within Mattheson's appeal for expression, which is so like the mimetic demand, we see evidence of traditional German attitudes which clash with neoclassic doctrine. Throughout the *Capellmeister* Mattheson emphasizes the sheer affective outcome of music, often to the neglect of any mimetic cause. His pleas for musical significance often take the form that music must move, with no mention made of expression or representation. One of his frequent reminders to his readers as to the "goal" of music reads:

> Der Endzweck unsrer musicalischen Arbeit ist, nächst Gottes Ehre, das Vergnügen und die Bewegung du Zuhörer.[23]

> The goal of our musical craft is, besides the glory of God, the pleasing and moving of the listener.

Another reminder states that the aim of melody is nothing else than to provide "such aural pleasure, that the passions of the soul are moved."[24] And whereas for Batteux speaking tones would mean tones whose clear meaning is derived from an imitation of a passionate utterance, Mattheson called the powerfully affecting music of the organ "speaking sounds" with no imitation of passionate utterance in mind.[25] To be sure, Mattheson feels that by representing passions music arouses them, but it is not clear that he sees representation, and certainly not intelligible representation, as a necessary precondition of moving music. Nor is it clear that representation is a sine qua non. Indeed, on many occasions he accepts music on the basis of its affective power alone and does not demand an intelligible content. And certainly he does not use any "speculative" rigor in questioning the verifiability of music's contents; he seems to assume that if the listener is moved then the music has content, it has "die rechte Gestalt."

However, despite the many elements of Mattheson's general theory which are friendly to instrumental music, Mattheson's formal position on the status of instrumental music was that it is an imitation of vocal music, and by implication inferior.[26] We would have expected nothing else, given his fundamental principle that all music must sing. But he has ambivalent feelings about instrumental music; on another occasion he implies that it is just as good as vocal music.[27] Indeed we shall see that in Mattheson's treatment of specific styles, genres, and characteristics of instrumental music he rationalizes, and is moved by, style features peculiar to the instrumental idiom and certain instrumental genres. And despite his reiterations of the principle that instrumental music imitates vocal music, he is equally emphatic that instrumental music must, and indeed can, represent and move the passions as well as vocal music. Mattheson clearly has a high opinion of instrumental music.

Mattheson is one of the first writers to consider seriously the appropriate aesthetic standards for instrumental music, and the relation of instrumental music to vocal music. Discussions focusing on instrumental music are found in his description of the instrumental style within each of the broad style divisions of church, theater, and chamber; in his discussion of the characteristic affects of the various genres of music; and in a whole chapter devoted to the differences between instrumental music and vocal music.[28] Whereas Scheibe had only left us to draw the conclusion that instrumental music had peculiar features that did not fit well within a representative aesthetic, Mattheson is fully aware of instrumental music's characteristics, and feels a definite need to elucidate the problems of instrumental music's status relative to that of vocal music.

In discussing the nature of the instrumental style as it forms a part of church style, Mattheson reiterates most clearly that "All playing is merely an imitation and accompaniment of singing."[29] Instrumental music is explicitly held to the same goal as vocal music, namely the arousal of emotions:

> Weil nun die Instrumental-Music nichts anders ist, als eine Ton-Sprache oder Klang-Rede, so muss sie ihre eigentliche Absicht allemahl auf eine gewisse Gemüths-Bewegung richten, welche zu erregen, der Nachdruck in den Intervallen, die gescheute Abtheilung der Sätze, die gemessene Fortshcreitung u.d.g. wol in Acht genommen werden müssen.[30]

> Since then instrumental music is nothing other than a "tone-language" or "sound-speech," its real intention must be to arouse a certain emotion, to which end careful attention must be given to the proper emphasis in the choice of intervals, intelligent articulation of phrases, measured progression, and so on.

But since, Mattheson points out, the instrumental composer has no "distinct words" upon which to rely, it requires all the more skill to accomplish music's end. Mattheson believed though that instrumental music could nevertheless express "just as much" as vocal music.[31] In order to attain this expressive goal, Mattheson advises the instrumental composer to avoid all "formless clanging" by forming his ideas through singing. For it is in song that "the well-formed and proper essence of melody resides."[32] (Most probably Mattheson had in mind the Italian vocal style for which he had such great admiration.) In other words, Mattheson implies that the singing style is the one true expressive, moving, and well-formed style; in short, expressive form is singing form. But despite Mattheson's relegation of instrumental music to a secondary position, he does not detract from its aesthetic potential. The instrumental composer could and should aspire to the same affective goal as vocal music.

For Mattheson, as for Scheibe, the function of music determines in part the standards applied to it. The function of church music is to praise God; theater music's essence is the "lively expression of emotions."[33] Accordingly, the instrumental style within each style category will be different. In instrumental church music all the parts must be equal but free of "compulsion and artifice"; whereas in theater music the upper part must prevail "as in a monarchy"; instrumental theater music is cheerful, appealing, and pleasant.[34] The function of chamber music is yet again different; hence instrumental chamber music acquires yet again a third character. Whereas instrumental music in the church or theater style usually functions to accompany and intensify the effect of the human voice, in chamber style instrumental music can realize its own potential and display its peculiar virtues. Thus instrumental chamber music will possess qualities for which one would search in vain in the church or theater.[35] Mattheson recognizes that independent instrumental genres have their own specific character. And he is willing to sanction that character even if the melody, the cantabile element, must occasionally suffer, as he admits it will. Instrumental chamber music, according to Mattheson requires more "diligence and development," and "clearer and purer middle voices which constantly and pleasantly compete with the upper voice." Further,

> Bindungen, Rückungen, gebrochene Harmonien, Abwechselungen mit tutti und solo, mit adagio und allegro etc. sind ihm solche wesentliche und eigene Dinge, dass man sie meistentheils in Kirchen und auf dem Schau-Platz vergeblich sucht: weil es daselbst immer mehr auf die Hervorragung der Menschen-Stimmen ankommt, und der Instrument-Styl nur ihnen zu Gefallen und zur Begleitung oder Verstärckung da ist; wogegen es in der Kammer schier die Herrschafft behauptet; ja, wenn auch gleich die Melodie bisweilen ein wenig darunter leiden sollte, will er doch daselbst allemahl aufgeputzt, verbrämt und sprudelnd erscheinen. Das ist sein Abzeichen.[36]

> ties, suspensions, broken chords, alternations of tutti and solo, of adagio and allegro and so on are so essential and particular to it [the chamber style] that one usually seeks them in vain in churches and on the stage: for there it is always more a question of the dominance of the voice, and the instrumental style is merely there to please and to accompany or intensify; whereas in the chamber it clearly maintains dominion; indeed, if once in a while the melody should suffer at the hands of it, it nevertheless always wants to appear brilliant, ornamented, and exuberant. That is its distinguishing characteristic.

Here we can see that in the case of independent instrumental chamber music genres Mattheson has relaxed his insistence that *all* music must sing. And he has controlled his fear that contrapuntal compositional techniques will violate the cantabile principle. Unlike Scheibe, who also applied different standards to vocal and instrumental music, Mattheson explicitly recognizes that he is granting different goals and procedures to independent instrumental music. He seems to have grasped the idea that an art dealing exclusively with sounds will naturally have a different essence from that of vocal music, and he has accepted this idea. Indeed, he is most enthusiastic about the chamber music of Corelli, whose skill in contrapuntal writing gave him "much pleasure," when he heard it in the churches in Holland.[37]

When Mattheson moves from a consideration of the general characteristics of each of the three styles to a detailed accounting of each specific genre of music, we see how he further relaxed his general aesthetic principles to provide for such specific nonrepresentative genres as the sonata, and the concerto. In the chapter entitled "The various kinds of melodies and their distinguishing characteristics" he describes everything from a Lutheran chorale to an Italian aria, and from a menuet to a trio sonata.[38] Each type of music is assigned its "distinguishing mark" (*Abzeichen*), or as Mattheson uses the concept, its characteristic affect. That is, each genre supposedly expresses a certain typical affect. The menuet for example expresses "moderate gaiety," while the gavotte expresses "exultant joy."[39] Mattheson, as we shall see, remains undismayed in his determination to carry out his program that even instrumental music is to express and arouse emotion; yet he is quite willing to stretch his notion of what expressing an affect amounts to, so as to make provision for supposedly nonrepresentative genres. It often turns out that a genre's characteristic affect is obviously not depicted by that genre, but is one which the music merely evokes, or is a human trait associated in some other way with that genre. For example, the characteristic affect of the aria with variations is affectation, or mannerism, since variations are often used by the composer to show off his virtuosity. Fantasies, Mattheson observes, have so little order that one can hardly call them anything other than good ideas. Their characteristic affect is then *Einbildung,* or imagination. The chaconne and passacaglia, since they are so re- petitive, cause satiety; therefore that is their distinguishing mark. Similarly, since the intrada arouses a desire for more, desire is its characteristic affect.[40]

Mattheson gives the sonata an especially detailed treatment; it has a more "prominent status" among instrumental music, he explains. As if to answer Fontenelle's query, "Sonate, que me veux-tu?" Mattheson makes a virtue out of the contrasts inherent in its lack of unified character. The sonata, according to Mattheson, aims chiefly

> auf eine Willfährig-oder Gefälligkeit . . . weil in den Sonaten eine gewisse Complaisance herr- schen muss, die sich zu allen bequemet, und womit einem ieden Zuhörer gedienet ist. Ein Trauriger wird was klägliches und mitleidiges, ein Wollüstiger was niedliches, ein Zorniger was hefftiges u.s.w. in verschiedenen Abwechselungen der Sonaten antreffen.[41]

> to gratify and to win favor, . . . for in sonatas a certain complaisance must prevail whereby ev- ery listener is served. In the variety and contrasts of a sonata a sad person will meet with some- thing plaintive, a sensualist with something pretty, an angry person with something furious, and so on.

If the composer is sensitive to the reactions of the listeners, the sonata is capable of being interpreted so as to suit each listener. Thus it does not have a single charac- teristic affect unless one calls it "complaisance." If not a precise representative vehicle with a determinate content, the sonata is nevertheless an affective one well worth cultivating; and Mattheson lets his representative insistence rest with that. It is only the newfangled solo keyboard sonatas in the Italian style that don't come up to his critical standards. They are a mere "patchwork of stuck-together ideas";[42] they are not natural. Worst of all, they do not have "die rechte Gestalt"; they seem designed only for moving the fingers rather than for moving hearts. Nevertheless, as if to wish to include all music in his encyclopedic survey, Mattheson reminds the reader,

> Doch ist die Verwunderrung über eine ungewöhnliche Fertigkeit auch eine Art der Gemütsbewegung.[43]

Wonder at an unusual dexterity is indeed a kind of emotion.

Thus even virtuosity has an affective power. And even the new Italian instrumental sonata has a characteristic affect: *Verwunderung*. Mattheson is not inclined to belittle any affect if music arouses it.

Mattheson describes the concerto grosso, like the sonata, as having many and contrasting affects. The concerto resembles a festive banquet table; so rich is the contrapuntal texture that its affective characteristic is "sensual pleasure" *(die Wollust)*. In addition, the opposing activity of various counterpoints often can suggest rage, jealousy, envy, and hate.[44] The symphony Mattheson discusses only as an overture. It should express the passions of the work it introduces.

Finally, Mattheson mentions the French overture, apparently his favorite. Its characteristic affect is "nobility" *(Edelmuth)*.[45] He refers the reader to his discussion in the *Neu-Eröffnete Orchestre* (1713), where he calls it the highest form of instrumental music. In 1713 Mattheson did not speak in terms of a characteristic affective content at all. He simply said that there is nothing more "enlivening" *(ermunternd)* than the French overture.[46] (It is tempting to speculate as to why in 1739 he felt the need to assign each genre a characteristic affective content. Perhaps he thought that musical art needed more defense against its Enlightened critics; or perhaps the popularity of the newer nonrepresentative genres led him to a defensive insistence that all music must express and move the passions.)

In none of these instrumental genres—variations, fantasies, chaconne, intrada, sonata, concerto, French overture—does Mattheson claim that an affect is represented. But he seems satisfied to have shown that indeed all genres of music have a connection with the emotions. And, if an emotion can be identified as the cause or the result of the composition, Mattheson is content to imply that this is their affective content. Neoclassic standards of clear intelligibility and accusations of meaninglessness are nowhere in evidence; nor does Mattheson point to a model in nature upon which pieces in these genres were based. Clearly Mattheson wanted to make room in his theory for that practice within his musical culture which was generally accepted and with which he was himself in tune. Or perhaps he consciously wanted to imply that neither emotional content nor spiritual significance had to be achieved through rationally verifiable representation as most French critics believed it did. But we get no reasoned argument as to the emotional significance of these instrumental genres—only a set of claims to counter the neoclassic position that instrumental music had small claim to significance of any kind.

Mattheson's third and most interesting body of opinion about instrumental music could not be more to the point. He devotes a whole chapter of the *Capellmeister* to a discussion "Of the Difference between Sung and Played Melodies."[47] By so doing he seems to be one of the first writers to attempt to set down in a deliberate and thorough fashion the peculiar potentialities of instrumental music versus vocal music, and their relative artistic merits. He is not speaking, he explains, to those who have already determined that the difference consists only in the difference in instrument, nor to those who contend that a melody is a melody, whether played or sung. It is for those who sense that there must be a more profound difference that his chapter is written. And in seeking the grounds of such a difference, Mattheson feels he is touching on some "kind of science" which perhaps others will carry further.[48] In this chapter Mattheson displays and transmits to his fellow German readers several viewpoints which were to survive in spite of the wave of popularity of neoclassic standards. A peculiar sensitivity and attachment to instrumental music, strengthened by its use in the church, forms a dramatic contrast to the hostility towards instrumental music found among French critics.

Mattheson lists, in all, 17 differences between instrumental music and vocal music. In an effort to satisfy his encyclopedic vision Mattheson includes some differences which seem rather obvious and uninteresting. These have to do with differences in range, lung capacity, endurance, different requirements as to meter, phrase lengths, and balance, different ranges of available keys and the different styles and genres appropriate to each type of music.[49] Other differences touch on the relative worth of the two types and on the peculiar capabilities of instrumental music.

In listing the first two "differences" he reiterates his previously stated belief that vocal music is the model and instrumental music the imitator:

Nun ja ist alles gespielte eine blosse Nachahmung des Singens.[50]

Indeed all that is played is merely an imitation of singing.

Vocal music, he writes, is the "mother" of instrumental; instrumental melodies not imitating their mother are like illegitimate children (but at the same time it is only natural that instrumental music should be more "cheerful and childish" than its parent). Thus, since vocal music takes precedence over instrumental, composers should learn to write in the "true singing style" by learning first to write vocal music. Besides, it is more difficult for composers to write moving instrumental melodies, and the "great freedom" of instrumental music often leads composers to write "formless" melodies:[51]

Denn, dass ein Geräusche und auch eine Harmonie gehöret werde, daraus kein Mensch schliessen könne, ob es Fische oder Fleisch sey, das macht die Sache nicht aus.[52]

For it does not suffice if a noise or even a harmony is heard if no one can determine whether it is fish or fowl.

Mattheson commends to the instrumental composer the flowing contours and phrase structure of vocal music; for only by imitating vocal music can true expressiveness be attained. Only the singing style moves. But while making the point that instrumental music must imitate vocal, Mattheson does take note of peculiarities of instrumental music—its cheerful, childlike nature, and its freedom—and repeats his insistence that even an instrumental *Tonsprache* can move the listener just as well as vocal music. Mattheson does not conclude that instrumental music is an aesthetically inferior medium.

Other differences point explicitly to traits peculiar to instrumental music, which Mattheson nevertheless finds worthwhile, even though they are not well suited to vocal performance, hence not imitations of the "true singing style." Mattheson does not seem interested in developing the notion that instrumental music has some independent prowess, and therefore is not merely an imitation of vocal music. But he clearly relishes certain features specific to instrumental music and would not consider banning them in the interests of theoretical purity. One such quality which Mattheson describes as especially typical of violin music is that of "fire and freedom." Indeed this is almost a necessary part of such music, because it could not sustain a vocal melody without becoming "sleepy."[53] (That it was in the nature of instrumental music not to imitate vocal music, that it had a standard specific to itself which could not be borrowed, Mattheson did not choose to emphasize, but he clearly recognizes here something to that effect.) Also typical of instrumental music, but not suited to vocal, are the large leaps possible in instrumental music. (Mattheson mentions Vivaldi's *L'estro Armonico* as an example.[54]) Similarly, the "impetuous and dotted essence" so essential to the French overture would not sound effective if sung. At the same time Mattheson would not think of doing without these "beautiful and vigorous," "sharp and pointed musical ideas."[55] It is certainly significant that the French overture was his favorite form of instrumental music, yet that its essence was a quality actually unsuited to vocal performance.

Finally, Mattheson lists one more "difference," which revolves around a characteristic of instrumental music not shared by the cantabile idiom. Displays of virtuosity and skill—whether in performing or composing—Mattheson sees as more befitting the instrumental idiom (and Mattheson clearly appreciated these skills, when not indulged in excessively):

> Die Instrumente mehr Kunstwercke zulassen, denn die Singe-Stimmen. Die vielgeschwäntzte Noten, die Arpeggie und alle andre gebrochene Sachen, ingleichen die harmonicalische Kunststücklein der Contrapuncten, Fugen, Canonen u.s.w. sind auf Instrumenten wol anzubringen; erfordern aber grosse Behutsamkeit, wenn man sie mit Menschen-Stimmen aufführen will.[56]

> Instruments make possible more artful composition than voices. Notes with many flags, arpeggios and all other figuration, as well as the artful devices of harmony, including counterpoint, fugue, canon and so on, all can be realized well on instruments; but require the greatest care if performed by voices.

Even the most obvious difference does not escape the meticulous Mattheson: namely, that instrumental music has no words, whereas vocal music does. In the eyes of many of the subjects of our study this was indeed the crucial distinction: it was the determinate meaning of the word which made vocal music superior to instrumental music. But whereas most later German writers use this distinction to brand instrumental music as inferior, to relegate instrumental music to a lower aesthetic status, Mattheson uses this distinction as an occasion for expressing all his positive, if not enthusiastic, feelings about instrumental music. He does not even consider the question of determinateness of meaning, nor does he even imply that vocal music is better. In fact, he says that the presence or lack of words is immaterial. He seems anxious to show that instrumental music can be just as good as vocal music, and to exhort composers to make it so. What really matters, Mattheson writes, is that although instrumental music can do well without words, it cannot do without the emotions. Mattheson makes a point of sharing with his readers something which is "very unknown," namely, that even instrumental music must express and move the passions—

> dass die Spiel-Melodie zwar der eigentliche Worte, aber nicht der Gemütsbewegungen entbehren kann.[57]

> that instrumental melodies can indeed do without words as such, but not without the emotions.

Accordingly, he launches into a reaffirmation of the necessity for the composer to intend to move and express all the emotions using just sounds and no words:

> Weil inzwischen das rechte Ziel aller Melodie nichts anderes seyn kan, als eine solche Vergnügung des Gehörs, dadurch die Leidenschafften der Seele rege werden: so wird mir ja niemand dieses Ziel treffen, der keine Absicht darauf hat, selber keine Bewegung spüret, ja kaum an irgend eine Leidenschaft gedenckt. Wird er auch andre mit der Harmonie rühren, so muss er wahrhafftig alle Neigungen des Herzens, durch blosse ausgesuchte Klänge und deren geschickte Zusammenfügung, ohne Worte dergestalt auszudrücken wissen, dass der Zuhörer daraus, als ob es eine wirckliche Rede wäre, den Trieb, den Sinn, die Meinung und den Nachdruck, völlig begreiffen und deutlich verstehen möge. Alsdenn ist es eine Lust! dazu gehöret viel mehr Kunst und eine stärckere Einbildungs-Krafft,wenns einer ohne Worte, als mit derselben Hülffe, zu Wege bringen soll.[58]

> While the proper goal of all melodies can only be to give so much aural pleasure that the passions of the soul are aroused, no one can in fact attain this goal unless he has that intention, unless he himself feels moved, indeed unless he focuses his attention on some passion. If he wants to move others with harmony, then he must truly know how to express without words all the movements of the heart by means of well-chosen and skillfully combined sounds in such a way that the listener can completely comprehend and distinctly understand the motive, direction, meaning, and emphasis as if it were a real speech. Then what a pleasure! If one is to accomplish this, much more art and a stronger imagination is required when no words are used than when the words help out.

Mattheson clearly is enthusiastic about the challenge and potential of the instrumental idiom. He even went so far as to say that the listener can "completely comprehend and distinctly understand'' these purely tonal expressions. Such bold claims were soon to vanish from the German critical scene.

But more importantly, Mattheson manifests a crucial attitude which was never destroyed by French rationalistic dogma: a responsiveness to instrumental music independent of any cognition of represented content—a trust in the affective power of music. In describing his reactions to the French overture he points out that even a speech by the best orator could not move him more. The immediate and physical affective power of these artfully combined sounds is graphically described:

Höre ich dem ersten Theil einer guten Ouvertür, so empfinde ich eine sonderbare Erhebung des Gemüths; bey dem zweiten hergegen breiten sich die Geister mit aller Lust aus; und wenn darauf ein ernsthaffter Schluss erfolget, sammeln und ziehen sie sich wieder in ihren gewöhnlichen ruhigen Sitz. Mich deucht, das ist eine angenehm abwechselnde Bewegung, die ein Redner schwerlich besser verursachen könnte.[59]

When I hear the first part of a good overture, I sense an unusual exhaltation of my soul; then with the second part, the vital spirits expand in a fullness of joy; and when then a serious ending follows, the spirits gather themselves back together, to their usual place of rest. I think that is a pleasantly contrasting movement such as could hardly be effected by an orator.

Perhaps his most vivid description of being powerfully affected by music comes, significantly, in an account of what he experiences listening to music in the church—the very cradle of traditional German attitudes toward music. Again, the emphasis is on the affective power of the music itself; and Mattheson is careful to point out that this power is independent of words. Indeed, we sense it is independent of any recognition of represented content whatsoever: the sounds themselves are the active force, and are clearly not functioning as parts of a language which the composer uses to communicate a predetermined content:

Vernehme ich in der Kirche ein feierliche Symphonie, so überfällt mich ein andächtiger Schauder; arbeitet ein starcker Instrumenten-Chor in die Wette, so bringt mir solches eine hohe Verwunderung zu Wege; fängt das Orgelwerck an zu brausen und zu donnern, so entstehet eine göttliche Furcht in mir; schliesst sich denn alles mit einem freudigen Hallelujah, so hüpfft mir das Hertz im Leibe; wenn ich auch gleich weder die Bedeutung dieses Worts wissen, noch sonst ein anders, der Entfernung oder andrer Ursachen halber verstehen sollte: ja, wenn auch gar keine Worte dabey wären, bloss durch Zuthun der Instrumente und redenden Klänge.[60]

When I hear in church a solemn symphony, I am gripped by a devout awe; when the voices of an instrumental choir vie with each other in energetic counterpoint, a lofty wonderment comes upon me; when the organ begins to roar and thunder, a divine fear arises; and if all that is concluded with an exultant Hallelujah, then my heart leaps for joy—and it would, even if I did not know the meaning of this word, even if I could not understand the meaning of any other word because of distance or some other reason: indeed, even if there were no words—if there were only instruments and speaking sounds.

Thus Mattheson has not used the "words versus no words" distinction to mark instrumental music as inferior. He himself summarizes his extended treatment of this distinction by claiming that instrumental melodies differ from vocal melodies principally in that the former "aspire to say just as much without the aid of words and voices as these do with words."[61] But even if we take it as his ultimate judgement that instrumental music was inferior to vocal music, it is important to recognize that it is not on grounds of intelligibility that instrumental music is faulted—rather it is the primacy of the cantabile idiom.

There is a basic inconsistency in Mattheson's position vis-a-vis instrumental music. On the one hand he insisted that instrumental music was only an imitation of vocal music, and on the other he recognized the affective potential of certain of the instrumental genres. On the one hand he insisted that all music represent and express the emotions; but he gave no account of how in fact such instrumental genres as the sonata and the concerto and the French overture could do this. To be sure, Mattheson attempts to incorporate and integrate the characteristic properties of instrumental music into his overall view. But he blurs together moving and representing, and he gives no scientific account of how instrumental music can be just as intelligible and distinct as vocal music, as he claims.

The impact of Mattheson's *Capellmeister* on the changing aesthetic status of instrumental music is difficult to assess. By rationalizing the traditional German belief in the immediate affectiveness of sounds, and by keeping alive the traditional German appreciation of compositional skill, while at the same time providing a theory of musical expression which allowed for more musical interest than the utterance theory, Mattheson provided good soil for the acceptance of instrumental music as a significant art. Of course both Mattheson and the neoclassicists insisted that even instrumental music must express the passions, and their convergence at this point should not be underestimated. But since Mattheson took as his starting point specific qualities of music, rather than a theory of literary criticism, the total impact of his expression theory was much more acceptable to German musicians, and made much more allowance for the "specific nature" of music. But Mattheson never delved into the "science" he dimly felt he had touched upon in discussing all the differences between vocal music and instrumental music. If he had, we might have gotten a more coherent account of instrumental music's essence and worth.

Perhaps the "science" Mattheson had in mind was that which Alexander Gottlieb Baumgarten (1714-1762) was to christen with the name "aesthetics." Just as Mattheson wanted to defend music against the rationalism of the *Cantorei*, Baumgarten wanted to defend the arts in general from the inappropriate rationalistic standards and speculative rigor associated with French neoclassicism.

In the first volume of his *Aesthetica* (1750)[62] Baumgarten defined the arts as a sphere of human activity fundamentally distinct from that of intellectual inquiry but equally worthy of human pursuit and study. The arts, according to Baumgarten, spoke to man on the level of his feelings and sensations, his "lower cognitive powers"; the sciences and philosophy spoke to his reason or intellect, his "higher cognitive powers." Thus Baumgarten named his new science "aesthetics," after the Greek word, αισθησις, meaning "perception by the senses." Given these two distinct forms of knowledge, one based on the intellect and the other on the senses and feelings, there must then be a different set of standards or rules—"a science"—specific to the arts. The task of this new philosophical discipline was to formulate the type of perfection peculiar to the arts, and to derive from their fundamental nature a set of standards or rules of truth, coherence, and ordering appropriate to them. There was to be a "logic of the lower cognitive powers" (as Baumgarten sometimes referred to aesthetics), as well as a logic appropriate to the rigors of philosophical inquiry. For, contrary to the assumptions of rationalistic neoclassic theory, the rule of reason could not preside over the arts. Higher cognition would destroy the phenomenon of the aesthetic experience itself. Thus Baumgarten argued that aesthetic truth was different from scientific truth, and aesthetic method different from scientific method.[63]

To be sure, others before him had emphasized the importance of the nonrational element in works of art.[64] But Baumgarten, professor of philosophy at the University of Frankfurt am Oder, was a professional philosopher of the old school standing in the solid rationalist tradition of Leibnitz and Christian Wolff. As Herder was to recognize, he was unique, "a rare, strange phenomenon." For he combined in his person two things which Herder saw as previously separated: "taste" and "philosophic reflection." Never before, observed Herder, had anyone attempted to apply the standards of philosophical rigor and thoroughness to an understanding and appreciation of beauty.[65]

The significance of Baumgarten's ideas cannot be viewed apart from the contemporary critical confrontation of Gottsched and the Swiss critics, Bodmer and Breitinger, over the rival claims of reason and the imagination. Gottsched, as we have seen, championed the rules of neoclassic criticism regarding the "reasonable imitation of nature" and the role of the artist as a faithful reproducer of truth. "The Swiss" championed the role of the imagination and the role of the artist as creator. The anti-Gottsched party preferred the "disorderly" but original Shakespeare to the "correct" Corneille, the religious fervor of Milton and Klopstock to the cool rationality of Boileau. It was a battle between *vraisemblance* and *das Wunderbar*, between reason and the imagination. Ironically, almost, the ideas of the Wolffian rationalist Baumgarten supported the forces of the antirationalists; for Baumgarten's rigorously applied powers of reason told him that the rules of rationalistic criticism violated the fundamental nature of the arts as he knew them.[66] Thus the ideas of Baumgarten were to form a new native German philosophical framework within which the literary works of Shakespeare, Milton, and Klopstock could find justification, and within which instrumental music might achieve a higher status.

Baumgarten, however, was not the chief popularizer of his own ideas. His *Aesthetica* was written in Latin, and its audience limited to the academic community. His ideas were spread mostly through his teaching.[67] A student, Georg Friedrich Meier, is generally credited with effecting the most direct translation of Baumgarten's ideas into the general German culture. Meier's widely read *Anfangsgründe der Schönen Künste und Wissenschaften*[68] exposited and elaborated Baumgarten's theories. Other popularizers, each of course with his own revisions or emendations, included Moses Mendelssohn and J. G. Sulzer. Most importantly, Baumgarten's ideas had repercussions in contemporary discussions of musical issues. Nicolai, Krause, Hiller, and Sulzer all use concepts borrowed from Baumgarten to defend the specific beauties of music against the inappropriate strictures of neoclassic criticism.

Baumgarten and Meier themselves spoke only slightly of music. Although they emphasized that the new aesthetic theory was to cover all the arts, they drew most of their examples from literature. Nevertheless, it seems that many of the same principles that were to justify the new appreciation of Shakespeare were to help as well in the forming of a new understanding of instrumental music. Indeed, when Baumgarten's ideas are viewed in the light of the complaints against the new Italian instrumental style, they seem all the more significant. Baumgarten was to provide, as we shall see, a theoretical sanction for some of the very things that were considered problematic aspects of the new Italian style. Variety and contrast were central elements of Baumgarten's aesthetic rules, just as they were widely recognized features of the new Italian style. Lack of clear and distinct meaning, even lack of "truth," incomprehensible contrasts, fantasy, novelty, sheer creative genius and originality, expectation-play, the "wonderful," and the evocation of *Verwunderung*—all these were to have a useful function in Baumgarten's aesthetic. Also, Baumgarten based many of his rules on the necessity of cultivating the audience's attention; and this emphasis on engaging and stimulating the lower powers of cognition is quite in tune with Scheibe's and Mattheson's emphasis on the lively, stimulating power inherent in the best instrumental music. Baumgarten in effect answered the problem of boredom (posed by the question "Sonate, que me veux-tu?") with provisions for "liveliness" and for bringing the listener's expectations into play. The temporal unfolding of an artwork was a particular concern to Meier, just as music's progression over a period of time—its form—was of central concern to composers of instrumental music; the neoclassic passionate utterance theory had had little to say on this fundamental topic.[69] Positions regarding music's role in morality are also affected by Baumgarten's ideas, in that his account of art's moral use departs from the didactic, content-based model of neoclassic aesthetics. Finally, Baumgarten's very emphasis on the sensual[70] essence of art would seem to promise a greater understanding of instrumental music.

Baumgarten built his new science of art around the definition of beauty as the "perfection of sensual cognition." A poem was accordingly defined as a "perfect sensual discourse.'' And the science of ''aesthetics'' was alternatively called the ''logic of the lower cognitive forces,'' or the ''logic of sensual cognition.''[71] For it was the senses and feelings that were the foundation of this new science; indeed Meier seems to view the ''inherent nature'' *(Inbegriff)* of the lower cognitive powers as comparable to gravitation in the field of physics, in its explanatory value.[72] In order to distinguish this distinct type of cognition proper to the arts Baumgarten relied upon the well-established Leibnitzian distinction between the ''higher'' cognitive powers of reason and the ''lower'' cognitive powers of the senses and feelings. Through man's higher powers of reflection and logical analysis he had access to the clear and distinct truths of mathematics and science. To the Cartesians this was the only certain knowledge, and these higher powers were the only ones worth cultivating. The senses, as the passions, were regarded suspiciously as potential sources of error. Whereas truth was timeless, they thought, sense impressions were fleeting and changeable. But Leibnitz and Baumgarten recognized the importance of a lower order of truth as well as a higher. This lower type of knowledge was acquired through the exterior senses and through the knowledge of one's own feelings. Since this knowledge was an intuitive one, not involving any knowledge of causes, nor sharp discriminations or distinctions, it could not be both clear and distinct. It was at best clear and ''confused.''[73] Indeed, Baumgarten held that distinctness, or cognition in a scientific mode, would destroy art. Thus the artist is not obligated to concern himself with ''strict truth and reason.''[74] Nevertheless there still could be an aesthetic truth, a truth proper to lower cognition, but of a different order from that of scientific truth (founded on clear and distinct cognition). Baumgarten illustrated the difference between these two types of truth with the example of the setting sun. For the scientist the sun did not set into the sea; rather the earth rotated and the sun remained stationary. But for the artist the sun indeed sets into the sea.[75] Thus clarity only, not clarity and distinctness, emerged as art's prime positive epistomological attribute.

Baumgarten was quite concerned to establish the usefulness and intellectual respectability of his new science as well as that of the arts themselves. He realized that many held the ''confusion'' of aesthetic experience to be the mother of error. It was indeed a radical position for a professional philosopher to hold that anything ''confused'' could lay claim to man's nobler impulses. But rather than purify the aesthetic experience of any such disquieting confusion, Baumgarten used his philosophical acumen to argue that aesthetic experience, no matter how confused, was an essential ingredient in the harmonious functioning of all human powers. Baumgarten's defense takes a definite empirical tack, and reduces logic to a position coordinate with aesthetics in the development of human knowledge:

> Wenn man bei den Alten von der Verbesserung des Verstandes redete, so schlug man die Logik als das allgemeine Hilfsmittel vor, das den ganzen Verstand verbessern sollte. Wir wissen jetzt, dass die sinnlich Erkenntnis der Grund der deutlichen ist; soll also der ganze Verstand gebessert werden, so muss die Aesthetik der Logik zu Hilfe kommen.[76]

When the ancients discussed the improvement of the mind, logic was recommended as the universal aid for the improvement of the whole mind. Today we know that sensual cognition is the basis for distinct cognition; thus if the whole mind is to be improved, aesthetics must come to the aid of logic.

Meier delights in derogatory remarks about pedants and Stoics. What was needed in the human order, Baumgarten believed, was not more ascetic pedants, but well-rounded, red-blooded, harmonious human beings. There was more to life than the application of reason to the quest for certain truths. A philosopher should be a "man among men," he said.[77] Besides, only a small portion of human knowledge was clearly and distinctly known, whereas sensual knowledge was far more prevalent. Since sensual cognition had to do with pleasure and displeasure and hence with desire, it was the most powerful and common determinant of our moral behavior. Thus the arts spoke to that part of man that was moral. Reason, in fact, did not govern most men's actions. For sensual cognitions were stronger than clear and distinct ones, and often had more power to convince.[78] The arts, all told, "animate the whole man."[79] Herder was to recognize in Baumgarten's design for the cultivation of all man's powers "a new ideal of humanity."[80]

Baumgarten constructs then, following Leibnitz, a new morality and significance for art. This new account of art's usefulness was independent of the didacticism inherent in the belief that correct behavior proceeded from correct knowledge and that works of art should therefore teach moral truths, or precepts, as Gottsched's ideal plot was expected to do. Again, Leibnitz is at the source of Baumgarten's ideas. Leibnitz, to be sure, had accorded the higher status to the "higher" type of knowledge; and Baumgarten as well would no doubt have admitted that man's reason had access to greater certainty than did his senses. But already with Leibnitz we see an account of human psychology and perfection, as well as an account of the very substance of being, which is significantly different from the French rationalist tradition.[81] For Leibnitz the substance of the units of being, the monads, was an active, dynamic, ever-changing essence. "The monad 'is' only in so far as it is active, and its activity consists in a continuous transition from one new state to another."[82] In Leibnitz's words, "The nature of the monad consists in being fruitful, and in giving birth to an ever new variety."[83] Accordingly, the mind (as the chief monad) was the locus of active energy and restless spontaneous "forces"—it was not merely a locus of ideas. And the perfection of the soul or ego corresponded to the intensity of this activity. The focus was on the process rather than the content of the mind.

"All intensification of being I call perfection. . . . Perfection consists in the power to act. Indeed, all being consists in a certain force, and the greater this force, the higher and freer the being. Furthermore, the greater the force, the more we see *multiplicity from unity and in unity.*"[84] This unity in multiplicity is then nothing but harmony, Leibnitz explains, and it is out of this harmony that joy arises and from this joy in turn arises virtue. Virtue then flows from the harmonious soul, just as it did for Mattheson. Accordingly art becomes of profound significance for Leibnitz, for he saw the aesthetic experience as an "animation and intensification of the powers of the mind," an "exaltation of being."[85] Leibnitz did not develop an extensive theory of the arts. But his disciple, Baumgarten, inherited and promulgated his attitude in arguing for the great worth of aesthetic experience:

> Die schönen Wissenschaften beleben den ganzen Menschen. Sie hindern die Gelehrsamkeit nicht, sondern machen sie menschlicher. Sie durchweichen das Herz, und machen den Geist beugsamer, gelenker, and reitzender.[86]

> The fine arts animate the whole man. They do not hinder learning, rather they make it more human. They penetrate the heart, and make the mind more pliant, agile, and more active.

As Sulzer was to say, the arts stimulate the "Seelenkräfte," and this "inner activity" is the basis of all moral action. Baumgarten's views even anticipate those of Schiller, who saw in art the essential mediating influence between man's sensual and intellectual natures.[87] Thus the arts were to stimulate a process, not to instill knowledge. The enlivening essence long attributed to instrumental music and its lack of conceptual content are not at all out of tune with this new conception of art's moral or spiritual function. The traditional view that harmonious sounds create harmonious souls is also reinforced by Baumgarten's theory. For perfection of sensual cognition, or beauty, Baumgarten and Meier believed, had the power to lead to the perfection of man's humanity.[88]

How then was art to attain this perfection? What were the rules specific to this new science, what were its unique standards? First, let us look more closely at Baumgarten's account of aesthetic perfection itself, and then at that specific kind of clarity proper to artistic expression. We shall see that in both accounts the emphasis is on variety, richness, and diversity of content. Just as the rules of neoclassic criticism focused on the unities and on homogeneity of style, Baumgarten's rules, based as they are on the *Inbegriff* of the lower cognitive powers, emphasize richness, variety, and contrasts, for these he saw were necessary for the engagement of man's lower cognitive powers. The traditional definition of perfection meant unity within variety; but Baumgarten's conception of artistic perfection called for the maximum variety that could be grasped as a whole.[89] The more variety, the more perfect:

> Da nun die Menge und Mannigfaltigkeit der Theile, die Vollkommenheit des Ganzen vermehrt so ist eine Vorstellung um so viel volkommener, ie mehrere Sachen sie uns miteinemmale vorstelt.[90]

> Since then the quantity and variety of parts leads to the perfection of the whole, a representation is all the more perfect the more things it represents to us at the same time.

A similar emphasis on the variety and quantity of representations in an artwork is found in Baumgarten's distinction between intensive and extensive clarity. Only representations which were distinct (and hence by definition not aesthetic) possessed intensive clarity; this was an analytical clarity—an interior orderliness of all the parts and subparts into a well-articulated hierarchy. Intensive clarity was proper to the sciences only. Extensive clarity, on the other hand, proceeds from viewing an object on "many sides," from endowing an aesthetic object with a quantity of specific, concrete attributes, a richness of sensual representations, a "rushing fullness of detail."[91]

> Die Merkmale sind der Grund der Klarheit. Damit nun, bey der Fortsetzung der Aufmerksamkeit auf eine Vorstellung, dieselbe entweder immer klärer oder doch nicht merklich dünkeler werde so muss man, die vornehmsten Stücke des Gegenstandes, immer durch neue und neue Merkmale denken.[92]

> Specific attributes are the basis of clarity. In order to insure that with the continuing attention on an idea, the idea becomes either ever more clear or at least not noticeably more obscure, one must conceive ever new attributes for the main parts of the subject.

This extensive clarity alone made possible that most valued of ingredients: "sinnliches Leben," or the ability to move, the ability to bring into play the faculty of desire.[93] This clarity was not Batteux's clarity, but an engaging, exemplifying richness wholly out of phase with the rationalistic and universalizing tendencies of neoclassic thought.

The key to attaining this specifically aesthetic clarity was the artist's ability to get and keep the audience's attention. Thus it is the attention, and not the intellect, that is at the source of Baumgarten's rules:

> Die Aufmerksamkeit ist das einzige Vermögen, wodurch die Begriffe klar werden, und der Grad der Klarheit ist jederzeit dem Grade der Aufmerksamkeit proportionirt.[94]

> The attention is the only faculty by means of which ideas become clear, and the degree of clarity is proportionate to the degree of attentiveness.

It is apparent then that Baumgarten's fundamental principle of art as perfection of sensual cognition will entail new rules for the arts. For the attention, this "highest of the lower cognitive powers," must be occupied if an artwork is to have the desired effect. Indeed, the necessity for the continuing engagement of the attention over a period of time would sanction many procedures not used at the "higher" level of philosophical communication.

The very necessity of unity and variety within an artwork are explained by reference to the demands of occupying the attention. It was not for the sake of clarity of meaning or purity of genre, but rather for the sake of the attention, that unity was necessary. The attention is distracted, Baumgarten writes, if one doesn't know what is happening.[95] But Baumgarten's main emphasis is on variety and contrast: "Variety is necessary, so that the attention will be kept."[96] He explicitly warns that in the aesthetic realm order or unity is not sufficient, that "richness, diversity, and alternation" are also necessary if the attention is to be kept and if the passions are to be aroused.[97]

Some of the most revealing discussions of the attention and of contrast, as well as other subjects with bearing on instrumental music's problem of aesthetic accountability, occur when Baumgarten and Meier discuss "aesthetic method," or the principles of temporal ordering. Of course Baumgarten and Meier were dealing mostly with the problem of coherence and ordering within literary works, and were especially concerned to scrutinize the neoclassic insistence on the unities and on homogeneity of style and content. But insofar as the problem of coherence was central to the debate over the new instrumental music, many principles of aesthetic ordering were to have significance for music as well. Meier devotes a long chapter to aesthetic method, to what is in effect the temporal form of artworks.[98] He derives his rules from the fundamental nature of art as perfection of sensual cognition and from the "inherent nature" of the lower or "sensual" powers themselves, especially the attention and the passions. Accordingly Meier makes it clear that the attention and the imagination have their own rules; that the ordering principles in an artwork are different from those of logic; and that different standards of coherence are applicable. For whereas the sciences are concerned with truth, the arts are concerned with affecting man's lower powers. The highest beauty, Meier emphasized, was the moving of the passions.[99] If mathematical minds find an artwork disorderly it might simply be because they are accustomed only to the philosophical method and do not understand the principles of aesthetic ordering.[100] For example, a philosopher and poet would each treat the theme of the perfections of God differently. The philosopher would prove the proposition, and place his conclusion as to God's perfections last. The poet might put it first and then develop it through many examples and through its consequences.[101] The philosopher would use only one method; but the poet would vary his methods to preserve "entertaining variety."[102]

Baumgarten and Meier were quite aware that their emphasis on the temporal aspect of aesthetic method was a result of the "inherent nature" of the attention and the passions themselves—the very faculties artworks addressed.[103] For whereas the mere statement of truth required little time (scientific truth was immutable and timeless), the audience could only be moved to a certain passion (and this was the highest beauty) over a period of time. It inhered in the very nature of the passions that they could only be aroused gradually:

Eine Leidenschaft . . . ensteht nur nach und nach, und das Gemüth mus durch die gehörige Vorbereitung stufenweise, bis zur Erschütterung geführt werden.[104]

A passion . . . arises but gradually, and the soul must be led by degrees through the appropriate preparation until it is shaken with emotion.

Accordingly in his presentation of aesthetic form Meier speaks of achieving an apex of beauty; this is called the "general assault on the soul of the listener." All the thoughts must be moving, even the introduction, but gradually the power of the ideas must be increased to the point where the listener is completely won over.[105] It also inhered in the very nature of the attention that it could not be maintained at the same level over a period of time; nor could it focus on one thing for very long.[106] Thus it followed from the nature of art, and from the nature of the attention (as the highest of these lower, cognitive powers), that variety and contrast of attributes were essential if an artwork was to achieve the desired effect:

> Wenn man also den anhaltenden Gebrauch der Aufmerksamkeit auf ein Gegenstand erhalten will, so muss man immer mehr und mehr neue und andere Merkmale entdecken. Diese Neuigkeit und Abwechselung der Merkmale belustigt und reitzt die Aufmerksamkeit, und erhält also ihrer Gebrauch, so lange sie fortdauert.[107]

> In order to insure the continuing focus of the attention on an object, one must reveal ever more and more new and different attributes. This novelty and variety of attributes pleases and stimulates the attention, and sustains its application as long as it lasts.

Similarly, not only quantity and variety of *Merkmale,* but the *Abwechselung* of intense and less intense clarity was necessary. The attention would be overwhelmed and would tire if all the representations were equally vivid. Also, if all parts of an artwork were equally vivid, no part could appear especially so.[108] Baumgarten called this contrast the alternation of "light and shadow." He argued that such alternation was not only in keeping with the nature of the attention, it was typical of nature herself, thus turning one of the opposition's own arguments against them:

> Die Aufmerksamkeit würde, durch gar zu viele Schönheit, überladen werden, und unter der Last zu Boden sincken. Einer solchen Abhandlung würde es an der belustigenden Abänderung fehlen, und sie würde unnatürlich seyn. In einer paradiesischen Gegend findet man, die gröste Abwechselung der lichtern und dünklern Farben.[109]

> The attention would be overwhelmed by too much beauty and would sink under the burden. Such a work would lack entertaining variety and would be unnatural. In a utopian landscape one finds the greatest contrast of lighter and darker colors.

For many reasons, then, a chief rule of aesthetic ordering was that "Light and shadow must alternate."[110] "Charming and changing multiplicity" was then an essential ingredient of art, seen as a communication over a period of time with the lower cognitive powers, especially the attention and the passions.[111]

Other qualities, which were recognized as proper to much eighteenth-century instrumental music, were also justified by reference to the necessity for aesthetic clarity in an art which depended on the "logic of the lower cognitive powers." Baumgarten's delectation of variety and contrast even extended to suggesting a useful function for the juxtaposition of contraries; such extreme contrasts could elucidate an idea by forcing the audience to compare it with something quite different:

> Alle Verschiedenheiten, Unähnlichkeiten und Ungleichheiten sind Verhältnisse. Wenn man demnach zwey einander entgegengesetzte Dinge zugleich denkt, so denkt man nicht nur ein jedes derselben vor sich, sondern auch zugleich mit seinen Verhältnissen. Folglich wird dadurch der Gedanke sehr klar, und kan demnach auch lebhaft werden.[112]

> All differences, dissimilarities, and inequalities are relations. Accordingly, if one thinks at the same time of two things opposite to each other, he thinks not merely of each one in itself, but also at the same time of the relations of a thing. Consequently the thought becomes thereby very clear and can accordingly become also vivid.

He called this use of strong contrast "elucidation by the contrary." The novel also served the end of increased clarity and heightened attentiveness. Old ideas would bore the attention; new ideas would stimulate it:

> Wenn aber ein Gedanke neu ist, so ist er verschieden von allen meinen Gedanken, die ich jemals gehabt habe, folglich wird er selbst durch diese Verschiedenheit klar. Ja weil ein jeder eine Begierde besitzt, seine Erkenntnis zu vermehren, so wird durch die Neuigkeit die Begierde erregt, diesen neuen Begrif zu erobern, wir strengen also unsre Aufmerksamkeit gewaltig an, folglich wird der Begrif klar und lebhaft. Also ist die Neuigkeit ganz unentbehrlich, wenn man die aesthetische Lebhaftigkeit erlangen wil.[113]

> When however a thought is new, it is then different from all the thoughts I have ever had, consequently the thought becomes clear by virtue of this very difference. For since everyone possesses the desire to increase his knowledge, novelty arouses the desire to gain this new idea, and we exert our attention energetically. Thus the idea becomes clear and vivid. Thus novelty is absolutely essential if one wants to obtain aesthetic liveliness.

The "surest means" for the artist to arrive at new thoughts would be to create them out of his own original feelings and consciousness. Thus, whereas Batteux had said "In the arts, to invent is not at all to bring an object into existence; it is to recognize where it exists, and how it exists," Baumgarten gave as one of his rules, "One must seek to be an original, if one wants to think something new."[114] Baumgarten spoke often of the artist as creating "another world."[115] And as if in answer to Batteux's insistence on a "coherent discourse" Baumgarten argued that the unexpected could contribute to the clarity of an artwork because it stimulates our curiosity and attention.[116] Dark or obscure ideas in particular often play a useful role as a foil to the vividness of the more aesthetically acceptable clear ideas. They stimulate the expectations and the curiosity; and the more unexpectedly the vivid follows the obscure, the greater is the liveliness or clarity of the following idea.[117] Baumgarten also could see that the "wonderful" (the opposite of verisimilitudinous, a necessary quality of all art on the neoclassic model) possessed great potential for stimulating man's lower cognitive powers—his feelings and passions. Since art was not supposed to deal in truth anyway, Baumgarten left the door wide open to wonderful poetic inventions; for often they made a "greater impression on us than the truths of this world."[118]

All of these qualities—the new, the wonderful, the dark, and the unexpected — were viewed together by Baumgarten and Meier because they all evoked a similar reaction: *Verwunderung*. Whereas other writers implied a distaste for this emotion, saying that certain instrumental music evoked only *Verwunderung,* and did not rouse or still "*the* passions," Baumgarten and Meier clearly valued it as a kind of heightened attentiveness brought on by the perception of "the unexpected, the wonderful, and the pleasantly surprising."[119] It was the intuitive reaction to the most intense aesthetic color—novelty.[120] In his own empirical way Baumgarten accepted *Verwunderung* as one of the typical pleasurable emotions evoked by art. In the following description of the engaging, surprising, and at times bewildering effects of digressions we are reminded of Scheibe's description of the fire and liveliness created through the composer's playing with the audience's expectations (although Meier no doubt had a literary work in mind):

> Sie müssen . . . in eine ganz genaue Verbindung mit der Hauptvorstellung, besetzt werden, und es ist um so viel besser, wenn man den Leser und Zuhörer erst in Sorgen setzt, man werde ihn von der Hauptvorstellung ganz ableiten. Sieht er aber nachgehends auf eine unerwartete und unvermuthete Art, dass man ihn nur durch einen anmuthigen Umweg wiederum auf die rechte Strasse geführt, so wird sein Vergnügen durch die Verwunderung noch mehr erhöhet.[121]

> They (digressions) . . . must be placed in an exact connection with the main idea; and it is all the better if one first makes the reader and listener worry that he is being led far away from the main idea. But then if he later sees in an unexpected and unanticipated way that he has only been brought back to the correct place by a pleasant detour, his pleasure is all the more intensified because of his wonderment.

In sum, Baumgarten seems to have valued anything which would engage the lower cognitive powers. But unlike Dubos, who valued this stimulation for its own sake, Baumgarten suggested a moral or humanizing benefit of aesthetic activity. By emphasizing process rather than precepts, Baumgarten provided a base from which could be built a surer theoretical defense of instrumental music.

Just as Baumgarten defended the special domain of aesthetic activity from the inappropriate rationalistic rules of science, Christian Gottfried Krause (1719-1770) was to defend the rights of musical art against the constraints of "universal" aesthetic principles derived from the practice of other arts. In fact, Krause had been a student of Baumgarten, and used this philosopher's new aesthetic concepts in his defense of music's peculiar virtues and practices. Krause was also a German Protestant and a musician; thus he complemented his Baumgartnian views by drawing on another, much older but compatible, native German source. Like Mattheson, he evinces a belief in music's innate significance, which is part of the heritage of Luther himself. Both Mattheson and Krause saw themselves as defenders of music, and both were drawn to the Italian style of opera. But Krause, writing fourteen years after Mattheson, addressed himself directly to the neoclassic challenge to musical art. Batteux's influential book was just beginning its wide circulation in Germany, and Krause even accepted some of its ideas which did not offend against his own inherited view of music's specific nature. Thus traditional German attitudes, the ideas of a unique German philosopher, and even elements of the mimetic aesthetic, come together in Krause to justify and account for music as an independent and meaningful art. Krause provides as well some original intuitions which adumbrate Wackenroder's *Seelenlehre,* where the dynamic and temporal character of the emotions is seen to be most naturally embodied in music. We see then in Krause the beginnings of the German critical synthesis which prepared the way for Romantic views.

Krause was a lawyer by profession, as well as a composer important in the early development of the German *Lied.* In 1741 he matriculated at the University of Frankfurt am Oder, where he came under the influence of Baumgarten, then professor of philosophy there. Employed in Berlin from 1746 until his death, he took an active part in the intellectual and artistic development referred to as the ''Berlin Enlightenment.'' He came into contact with many of the leading figures of Berlin's burgeoning culture, including the poets Gleim and Ramler, the musician Quantz, and the future encyclopedist of the arts, Sulzer. No mere amateur, his musical activities were as extensive and serious as those of a professional. Krause reputedly maintained one of the finest music salons in Berlin.[122]

In his central essay into music criticism, *Von der musicalischen Poesie* (1753),[123] Krause made a very conscious and considered rebuttal to literary critics who presumed to legislate rules for all the arts. Whereas Scheibe, Mattheson, Baumgarten and Batteux had not seemed concerned that the application of the new Enlightened principles might create special problems for musical art as it was then practiced and appreciated, Krause dealt directly with this problem. Indeed, Krause virtually mentions Gottsched by name. To answer a ''certain critic's'' demand that in vocal music no word can be repeated, Krause replied, emphasizing music's ''peculiar precepts and beauties'':

> Alle Künste und Wissenschaften haben gewisse Regeln mit einander gemein. Eine jede aber hat wiederum ihre besondre Vorschriften und Schönheiten, die man nicht nach den Regeln der andern Künste beurtheilen muss. . . . Man urtheile hieraus, ob einem gewissen Criticus schlechterdings beyzufallen ist, wenn er verlängt, dass man im Singen kein Wort wiederholen solle, welches nicht der Poet auch im Text ohne Uebelstand hatte wiederholen können.[124]

> All the arts and sciences have certain rules in common. At the same time however each one has its own peculiar precepts and beauties, which must not be judged according to the rules of the other arts . . . . Let one judge accordingly whether a certain critic is to meet complete agree-

ment when he demands that no word of a song should be repeated which the poet could not have repeated in the text itself without bad consequences.

Krause proudly proclaims, as if to answer his own question, "Music has become an independent art."[125] . . . And to counter what we know to be Gottsched's assertion that "Singing is nothing but a pleasant reading or delivery of a verse," Krause writes, opposing Gottsched's "rhetorical" rules to Baumgarten's "aesthetic" rules:

> Singen ist also nicht Sprechen. Manches lässt sich gut sagen, aber nicht gut singen, und umgekehrt. Der Gesang hat daher seine besondern Vorrechte und Gründe, die wir aus seiner Natur und der Vernunft, nicht aus der Rede holen mussen. Die blossen Klänge reden auch, und sind verständlich. Stellt der Componist, nach Veranlassung der Worte, seinen Gegenstand mit vielerley Nachdruck und auf vielen Seiten vor, so müssen seine aesthetischen und nicht bloss rhetorischen Regeln, und seine musikalische Erfahrungen ausmachen, wie oft und wie lange er solches thun könne, und wenn er aufhören solle. Es ist dem Affect im Singen viel erlaubt, was im Reden nicht angehet.[126]

> But singing is not speech. Many things can be said well, but not sung well, and vice versa. Song has its own peculiar privileges and principles, which we must not derive from speech but from reason and from the nature of song. Even mere sounds speak and are understandable. If the composer presents his object with various emphases and on many sides, in accordance with the words, then his aesthetic rules, not merely rhetorical rules, and his musical experiences, must determine how often and how long he can do that, and when he ought to stop. Much is allowed in singing which is not permitted in speaking.

This is no mere self-serving musician's argument based on a credulous acceptance of old-fashioned beliefs. Krause answers one professor's demands with another's counterdemands. Although he never mentions Baumgarten by name, Krause is clearly relying in his defense of music on Baumgarten's assertion of the need for presenting an object "on many sides," and on the necessity for the passage of time in the arousal of an emotion. Krause then goes on to oppose Gottsched's rules with one of his own:

> Man lasse also die Componisten immer ihre Worte öfterer wiederholen und zergliedern, als in der Rede und in der Poesie geschehen könnte, wofern sie dadurch nur ihrer Zweck, das Ergötzen und die Erregung des Affects erreichen.[127]

> Let the composers therefore repeat and fragment their words more often than could occur in speech or poetry, for only thereby can they achieve their goal—delight and the arousal of affect.

Krause casts tones, not words, in the leading role in the delightful and moving production of opera. Accordingly, melismas, ritornellos, word repetitions, and da capo form would all find theoretical justification in Krause's essay.

But Krause was no mere Italian opera enthusiast. We have already seen evidence that he was as well a serious student of the new philosophical discipline of aesthetics. Thus not only does Krause's work answer the literary strictures and anti-opera sentiments of Gottsched's party; it constitutes an application of Baumgarten's ideas to music. It is a justification of traditional and prevailing musical practice within the framework of "aesthetic" theory. Baumgarten's definition of art as "sinnlich vollkommene Erkenntnis" is the very foundation of Krause's defense of music's peculiar prerogatives. For example, Krause used Baumgarten's identification of aesthetic representations as clear but not distinct to characterize the nonrational, and justifiable, reaction to music which was typical even of the most highly educated music-lovers. Just as the inexperienced music listener

> vernimmt die Töne, ohne weiter etwas davon sagen zu können, als dass sie ihm gefallen. Die grössten Musikverständigen gedenken bey recht rührenden Stücken oft an sonst nichts. Sie sind sich der darinn enthaltenen Vorstellungen wohl bewust; ihr Gemüth wird aber damit so überhaufet, dass sie sie nicht deutlich machen können, sondern nur klar empfinden.[128]

> perceives the sounds, without being able to say anything besides that they please him. The greatest connoisseurs of music think often of nothing else, when hearing genuinely moving pieces. They are to be sure well aware of the ideas presented; but their mind is so overwhelmed with them that they cannot make the ideas distinct, but can only feel them clearly.

Once then it was accepted that music dealt, could deal, only with "sensual" and not "distinct" cognition, no one could reasonably fault it for its amoral character, nor charge it with immoral effects. It was simply inappropriate to expect music to teach a moral lesson, and unfair to blame it for not doing so. Moreover, once it was recognized that artworks do not address the understanding, as Baumgarten and Krause repeatedly emphasized, and that the sensual impressions of tones were stronger than the intellectual impressions of words, new rules could be formulated which would actually require the use of music's "peculiar beauties." Krause realized that it was important to establish the nonrationality of music's nature and effects if current musical practice, with which he was wholly in tune, was to be defended. And he sensed the value of Baumgarten's carefully worked-out system in answering the intellectually compelling rationalism of the opposition.

Not only Baumgarten's ideas, but, surprisingly, also those of Batteux and other neoclassic critics find tacit acknowledgment in Krause's essay. The parentage of such recurring turns of phrase as "geschickte Nachahmung der Natur," "Inhalt malen," "Natur verschönert dargestellt," and "instrumentalisches Abmahlung der Affecten," is unmistakable.[129] Krause even asserts at one point, "In all of the arts it is a matter of the imitation of nature."[130] Krause is quick to make it clear that imitation of nature, in the sense of depicting brooks and thunderstorms, is not the real and proper goal of music. As Batteux, he sees the passions as the prime subject of music. But Krause denies that imitation is a sine qua non of music. He repeatedly asserts that music's primary function is independent of any representative agency. To be sure, the composer can delight by means of imitation;

aber ausser denselben wirkt er, vermittelst geschickter Rührung unserer Ohrennerven, auch
annoch solche Bewegungen in der Seele, die sich nicht bloss auf die wahrgenommene Überein-
stimmung mit einem cörperlichen Urbilde gründen, sondern wodurch unser Geist zu heftigen
Leidenschaften fortgerissen wird. Und diess ist der wahre und höchste Zweck der Musik.[131]

but besides this, he is able to produce, by means of a skillful stimulation of our aural nerves,
motions of the soul which are based not on the mere perceived agreement with the physical object (of imitation), but which arouse in our soul powerful passions. And this is the true and highest goal of music.

In short, the fundamental principle of music is not the imitation of nature but the
moving and delighting of the listener. For, he writes, musical imitations are not the
chief accomplishment of music; imitations are "only musical insofar as they contribute to the arousal of an affect or to a certain pleasure."[132] Krause's vision of
music's proper function rests on empirical observation of his own musical culture,
and not on ancient authority or on the common practice in the appreciation of other
arts:

Bey Anhörung eines musikalischen Stückes bekümmert man sich nicht, ob es eine Bewegung in
der Cörperwelt nachahme, sondern nur, ob es schön sey, gefalle und rühre: Unser Inneres, unsere ganze Seele will daran Theil haben.[133]

When listening to a piece of music one is not concerned whether it imitates a movement in the
physical world, rather only whether it is beautiful, whether it pleases and moves. Our innermost,
our whole soul wants to partake of it.

Moreover, music achieves its pleasant and moving effects independently of the
powers of distinct cognition, independently of any rational recognition of content;
and this independence is not seen as a hindrance, but as natural and desirable:

Die Musik . . . rühret unmittelbar, und übertrift darinn die Mahlerey unendlich.
Die Musik ergötzet also ganz ausnehmend, ja sie rühret, ob wir gleich ihren Gegenstand mehr-
mals nicht deutlich erkennen.[134]

Music moves the listener immediately, and therein it surpasses painting infinitely.
Music can be quite exceptionally delightful, indeed it can move us even though we never distinctly recognize its object (of imitation).

As Baumgarten had said, the arts arouse only pleasure and pain, not distinct cognitions. Music's effects therefore are immediate, and bypass the understanding, in
which neoclassic critics put so much trust. Like Mattheson, Krause suggests a
mechanism involving the physical phenomena of sounds and the physiological nature of the senses and emotions to explain music's direct effects. According to
Krause's account we are moved by music due to the "complete correspondence"
that obtains between the proportions of musical vibrations and the natural tension
in the veins of the ear. Since the movements of the soul stand in the "exactest

relation'' with the ''state of our blood and veins,'' the passions can be aroused by direct physical, sensual, and physiological means.[135] Thus, although Krause accepts the neoclassic idea that music represents nature, he does not accept imitation as the essential goal of music and he rejects the idea that the mind of the listener must have an ''object of imitation'' upon which to fasten. He reasserts the traditional view of music as a nonrational affective force but with a new corroborative authority, that of Baumgarten.

The announced purpose of Krause's essay is to show how poetry should be written if it is to be set to music. The essay also constitutes a vindication (as the author himself reveals) of the Italianate opera style of Karl Heinrich Graun, opera composer in residence at the court of Frederick the Great. Krause's central and fundamental point is that music has its own nature, its own virtues, and if musical poetry is to be effective it must work in conjunction with the power that belongs to tones per se. Since the sense impressions of tones are stronger than intellectual impressions, the sense of the words must fit with the innate sense, or nature, of music. Thus Krause's ideas on the relations of words and music spring from a strong conviction as to the nature of music itself. This notion bears the marks both of traditional religious German attitudes and of the new Baumgartnian science of ''aesthetics.''

What was then the essence of music for Krause? Apparently reflecting the function of music in the culture around him, Krause held that music's essence was to be pleasant, delightful, and moving. He characterized music as a naturally sought source of pleasure, of excitement, and of affective movement. ''We use music,'' Krause observed, ''for pleasure''; and also, ''One seeks to pass time and lift one's spirits through singing.'' Music was seen not only as a natural manifestation of pleasant states of mind, but even as a form of positive self-expression, a celebration of certain healthy states of mind. Only pleasant emotions (among which he includes not only joy, hope, love, but also sadness, heartache, and desire) led to singing and music making—not emotions such as fear, despair, cowardice, stinginess, anger, and envy. Music arose initially out of a feeling of joy.[136] Thus, going back to the very origins of the musical impulse Krause asserts,

Die Freude . . . ist die erste Quell der Musik. . . . Die ersten Menschen haben die Zufriedenheit und Beruhigung über sich selbst gar bald in reinen und anmuthigen Melodien ausgedrückt.[137]

Joy . . . is the primal source of music. . . . The first men expressed quite early their happiness and tranquility regarding themselves in pure and pleasing melodies.

Moreover, Krause seems intent on making the point that this primal function of music had to do with pure melody ''without words and poetry'':

Aber nicht nur in den ältesten Zeiten, drückte man seine Gemüthsbeschaffenheit ohne Worte und Poesie, bloss mit der Stimme und musikalischen Instrumenten aus; sondern wir werden auch noch täglich der Rührungen inne, so die Musik erreget.[138]

But not only in the oldest times did man express his inner condition with instruments and voice, without words and poetry; but we are still daily witness to the moving qualities of music.

Krause's view of music as a nonrepresentative and purely tonal manifestation and determinant of pleasant, joyful states of mind obviously bears a strong resemblance to traditional German views. Indeed, Krause saw clearly the potential conflict of these views with the neoclassic view of music as imitation and with the utterance theory of musical expression. He deliberately tried to answer the neoclassic challenge to the traditional German view by positing a new kind of alliance between poetry and music (and, in so doing, he puts to rest the declamatory theory of musical expression favored by neoclassic critics):

Wenn es seyn müsste, so könnte man zu jeder Rede eine Melodie machen. Man spricht ja alle Wörter mit gewissen Lauten aus, und diese Laute müssen auch bey Singestücken keinesweges aus der Act gelassen werden. Man sagt vom Lulli, dass er den Klang der Rede bey seinen Compositionen sehr zu Rathe gezogen, und die Worte vorher zum öftern hergesaget und ausgesprochen, ehe er componiret habe. Es scheinet also, als wenn sich die Musik mit allen und jeden durch Worte ausgedrückten Gedanken verbinden liesse. Da aber ihr Wesen hauptsächlich in dem ergötzlichen, und rührenden bestehet, und sie keine andere als diese Vorstellungen erreget, so wird auch nicht eine jegliche Rede, sondern es werden nur rührende Worte, der Verbindung mit der Musik fähig seyn.[139]

If it had to be, one could make a melody for every spoken utterance. It is true that one utters all words with certain sounds, and these sounds must not in any way be ignored in vocal pieces. One says of Lully that he was very much influenced by the sound of speech in his compositions, and that he repeatedly pronounced and declaimed the words before he composed. Thus it would seem that music could be linked with each and every verbally expressed thought. But since the essence of music consists primarily of the delightful and the moving, and since it only arouses such ideas, it follows that not just any verbal utterance, but only moving words are qualified to be set to music.

In other words, the musician and the poet do not impose meanings on tones, nor enlist tones toward certain predetermined ends. Rather they work with the innate "essence" of music; words set to music must be consonant with music's specific nature, natural content, and natural effects. Words and music work independently and equally toward the same end.

Krause is very intent upon establishing the proper content of music. He is concerned that ignorant people not attempt to impose a clearly and distinctly intelligible content on music. Like Baumgarten, he doesn't want art faulted for a lack of distinct cognitive content. Since music's effects are sensual, and hence stronger than the intellectual impressions of words, the real objects of musical representation can only be the pleasing and the moving—those things which affect us with desire or revulsion:

Singen und musiciren wir also nur alsdenn, wenn gewisse Vorstellungen und Empfindungen eine Lust oder Unlust in uns erwecken, und wenn gewisse Bewegungsgründe uns eine Begierde oder einen Abscheu vor etwas verursachen; sagt man, dass wir, wenn dies in uns vorgehet, beweget, und gerühret sind: so folget hieraus, dass auch nur solche Gedanken, und nicht weiter von unserer Begehrungskraft entfernte Vorstellungen, eigentliche Objecte der Musik sind, und Materien zu musikalischen Gedichten abgeben können.[140]

We sing and play instruments only when certain ideas and sensations awaken pleasure or pain in us, and when certain stirrings cause in us a desire or a revulsion. If one can say that we are affected and moved when such things occur within us, then it follows that only such thoughts, and not ideas any further removed from our faculty of desire, provide the true objects (or content) of music, as well as the content for musical poems.

Krause realized that he could preserve and propagate his faith in the immediate affects of music while at the same time giving it an emotional content which would accommodate mimetic demands.

In his explanation of music's ability to represent emotions, Krause went further than just asserting that music naturally expresses or arouses certain affects. He put forth a theory of musical expression based on the "isomorphism" *(Gleichförmigkeit)* of music and the emotions. He was in effect concerned to show congruences between temporal unfoldings of music and of the emotions. Chief among the kinds of movement common to music and the emotions were contrasts and alternations of various sorts *(Abwechselungen)*. He made a point of reminding his reader that the emotions in fact possessed such variety:

Keine Leidenschaft kann bey einerley Umständen lange aushalten. Sie wird gar bald schwächer, muss also etwas von neuem angeflammet werden.[141]

No passion can remain in the same state for very long. It will soon become weaker and must be rekindled anew by something.

Krause was also careful to provide for the variety inherent in music's pleasing nature in his theory of *Gleichförmigkeit*. Only by taking into account music's dynamic nature could a successful congruence be achieved:

Die Musik bestehet aus Bewegungen. Was also darinn nachgeahmet werden muss auch eine Bewegung haben.[142]

Music consists of movements. Therefore whatever it imitates must also have movement.

Given then this moving and changing character of both music and the emotions, various prescriptions could be made as to which emotions could be represented in music and how they could be represented. One of the most difficult emotions to set in music was "an immoderate love of rest," because music by nature consisted of movement.[143] On the other hand, Krause was even willing to use the potent adjective "deutlich" to describe the accuracy with which music could imitate an emotion whose prime characteristic, he said, was *Abwechselung*—namely, inconstancy:

> In der Wankelmütigkeit wechseln Vergnügungen, Hofnung, und Ungeduld mit einander ab, und es lässt sich diese Gemüthesbeschaffenheit in Tönen deutlich schildern.[144]

> In inconstancy, pleasures, hope, and impatience alternate with each other and this state can be distinctly depicted in tones.

Krause recognizes the ability of music, as an art of change, to reflect not only these extremes of repose and ambivalence, but also the patterns of repetition and contrast typical of a given emotional state. For example, the musical expression of joy can tolerate many repetitions because "Man can never express his joy enough."[145] On the other hand, jealousy is expressed by contrasts of various sorts:

> In wankenden und bald leisen, bald stärkeren, verwegenern, scheltenden, bald wieder beweglichen und seufzenden Tönen, bey nicht einerley Zeitmass wird man den Zustand eines Eyfersüchtigen nachbilden können.[146]

> The state of jealousy can be portrayed in tones which are first wavering, then gentle, then stronger and more daring and scolding, and then again touching and sighing, and by more than one tempo.

The emotion that offered perhaps the most congruences between its form and that of music was love. In expressing this complex emotion, wrote Krause, almost every "musical beauty" can be brought into play; it is clear that among these beauties *Abwechselung* occupies a central position:

> Bey den Stufen der verschiedenen Arten der Liebe eräugnen sich verschiedenen Wallungen im Geblüte, und wir bemerken an einem Verliebten, bald muntere und lustige, bald ruhige und stille, bald ungeduldige und klagende Bewegungen des Cörpers, der Glieder und sonderlich der Stimme. Der Musikus kann dabey helle und angenehme, sanfte und liebliche, abwechselnd langsame und geschwinde Töne brauchen. Bald bittet der Liebende auf das beweglichste, bald entzündet sich sein Verlangen auf das heftigste, und die Stimme ist bald gezogen, bald bebend, bald unterbrochen. Mit einem Worte, es ist fast keine musikalische Schönheit, welche nicht bey dem Ausdrück der verschiedenen Arten und Wirkungen der Liebe vorkommen könnte.[147]

> With the degrees of various types of love there occur various agitations of the blood, and we notice various qualities in the movements of the body, the limbs, and especially the voice: first cheerful and happy, at times peaceful and quiet, at times impatient and complaining. The composer can accordingly use bright and pleasant, gentle and graceful, alternating slow and fast tones. At times the lover.pleads most touchingly, at times his desire is inflamed to the utmost, the voice is sometimes trembling, sometimes broken. In short, there is almost no musical beauty which could not arise with the expression of the various types and effects of love.

In all of this discussion as to how music represents the passions Krause is clearly expanding the classical and rather static *Affektenlehre* with its correspondences of key, tempo, intervals, and the like, to include something quite new: the "isomorphism" of music and the emotions over a period of time, that is, correspondences of musical form and emotional form. A newer more dynamic *Affektenlehre* results—one more suited to the music of Krause's day and anticipating the *Seelenlehre* of the Romantics.

At one point Krause explains that music can represent other emotions than just pleasant, noble, and variable ones (music's "natural" content), but only in the manner described by the neoclassicists: music can imitate the outward tones and gestures of certain emotions. With these emotions the listener would have to enjoy the music in a more intellectual way (rather than in an immediate way), by a conscious awareness of "the felicitous imitation." Clearly Krause preferred that music adhere mostly to the noble and pleasant emotions for its *Materie*, its content, for these it expresses most naturally and best.[148]

Music's specific nature could serve moral ends as well as mimetic ends, Krause believed. As if by some pre-established harmony, the very emotions which music most naturally expressed were the same emotions which made man a noble and virtuous creature; and a lover of music will naturally love virtue:

> Nun sind aber die Schönheiten der Tonkunst, und die Affecten so sich darinn am besten und wohlgefälligsten ausdrücken lassen, hauptsächlich in den edlen Empfindungen gegründet, welche die Natur in uns geleget hat, nämlich in der Liebe, Güte, Dankbarkeit, Wohlgefällen an Uebereinstimmung u.d.g. Diese Neigungen haben zum Zweck, uns glücklich zu machen, und eben dieselben sind auch gleichsam dasjenige, was die Tonfolgen und ihren Inhalt begreifet und verstehet. Wer also dieselben zu schätzen weiss, der wird auch das Vergnügen hochhalten, so und die Musik gewehret.[149]

> Now the beauties of music and the affects which it can best and most pleasingly express originate for the most part in the noble feelings, which nature has given us: namely, love, generosity, gratitude, pleasure in agreement, etc. These tendencies have the goal to make us happy, and these are the very tendencies implied and understood in patterns of tones and their content. Thus whoever knows how to treasure these tendencies will also respect the pleasure which music gives.

On more than one occasion he reaffirms his faith in the "powerful effects of music." Also reminiscent of traditional views is Krause's attribution of moral power to music insofar as it possessed so much "order and proportion"—more in fact than any other art. Krause virtually paraphrases Mattheson when he writes

> Die Gemüthsneigungen sind die wahre Materie der Tugend und der Lasterhaftigkeit der Menschen. Die Tugend selbst ist nichts anders als ein wohleingerichtete und klüglich gemässigte Gemüthsneigung.[150]

> The dispositions are the true stuff of human virtue and vice. Virtue itself is nothing other than a well-ordered and intelligently moderated disposition.

Krause also insists (calling upon Shaftesbury for support) that even merely delightful music can *engender* in man a love for order and proportion in all things—and he
goes on to point out that "love of order and beauty in society" is the foundation of
virtue.[151]

Krause's account of music's moral use is quite different from the didactic
account of neoclassic criticism. He admits on one occasion that music can't teach a
moral lesson, and even allows that this detracts a bit from music's significance
relative to the other arts.[152] But he is clearly also determined to defend music
against those "enemies" who would label it as a useless pastime. Echoing Baumgarten, Krause writes that moral behavior isn't based only on "deep insight into
truths; genuine reason actually affects very little in the real world."[153] Virtues are
rather founded on certain tendencies and desires. These tendencies are furthered by
the pleasures of music and vice versa; for since the pleasures of virtuous living are
like the pleasures of music, one makes us more susceptible to the other:

> Die Verwandschaftsliebe, die Sorge für die Nachkommen, die Liebe zum Umgänge, das Mit-
> leiden, die Hülfsbeigierde, alle diese Tugenden kommen von den natürlichen Neigungen her,
> welche wir um deswillen gerne befriedigen, weil wir dabey ein so sanftes Vergnügen
> empfinden; und dieses Vergnügens macht uns die Musik fähiger, und trägt also zur Tugend auch
> das Ihrige bey.[154]

> Familial affection, concern for posterity, close personal relationships, sympathy, helpfulness—
> all these virtues arise from natural tendencies which we so willingly satisfy because we then ex-
> perience such a gentle pleasure; and this pleasure makes us more susceptible to music, and
> moreover contributes its share to the furtherance of virtue.

It is as if Krause wants to say that the virtuous man and the musical man are by
nature the same—an opinion which could have been uttered by Luther himself. An
almost explicit rebuff is delivered to Gottsched when Krause singles out love as not
only that emotion which allowed for the most musical beauties in its expression but
also as the "most important among the virtues, natural inclinations, and
passions."[155] Whereas Gottsched had condemned the opera as immoral because of
its plots of romantic love, Krause called love the foundation of all social virtues.
Thus Krause in effect answers the typical neoclassic complaint that music, especially music qua pleasant sound, is of no moral use. Like his Lutheran forebears,
he believed in the innate spiritual significance of music and in its marvellous
effects.

Certainly the real focus of Krause's essay is the defense and justification of
traditional musical devices which certain Enlightened reformers, including Gottsched and Scheibe, condemned as unreasonable and unnatural. Some of these,
such as counterpoint, were features of the older German, so-called Gothic style.
Most others, including word repetitions, melismas, and da capo form, were essential characteristics of the Neapolitan opera style, then so favored at the Berlin
court. Also, Krause defends the elements of contrast and variety, which proved so

enigmatic to those still partial to the more affectively unified music of previous generations. Perhaps opponents of these commonly accepted musical procedures could previously have made plausible their arguments that the employment and enjoyment of such things proceeded from a *Handwerk* mentality, superstition, intellectual callousness, or a mere desire for sensual stimulation. But Krause, who condoned none of these reputed causes, provided a new and intellectually respectable defense by relying heavily on concepts of the new philosophical discipline of aesthetics.

Word repetitions were explained by Krause, as we have seen, as essential to the complete arousal of a given affect. This arousal, as Meier had said, could only take place over a period of time. Hence the words of an aria must be repeated in order for the desired affect to be aroused. But of course the composer cannot just keep repeating the same words with the same music: it would be disagreeable to have the same image presented so many times from one standpoint only. Calling upon Baumgarten's concept of extensive clarity, Krause explains that it is the repetitions of words with different music which makes possible that viewing of an object "on many sides," which in turn is necessary to aesthetic liveliness and to the moving of the passions:

> Hiernächst aber kann kein Affect in so wenig Worten, als eine Arie enthält, völlig abgebildet werden; und die Worte sind nur dazu, dass der Componist Gelegenheit habe, das rührende Bild auf so viel Seiten vorzustellen, als nöthig ist, den ganzen Affect zu erregen, weshalb die Stücke und Commata einer Arie, zum Wiederholen und Zergliedern bequem seyn müssen.[156]

> But besides, no affect can be fully depicted in so few words as an aria contains; and the words are only there so that the composer has the opportunity to present the moving image on as many sides as necessary in order to arouse the whole affect, to which end the sentences and phrases of an aria must be well suited to repetition and fragmentation.

In the case of a fugue the music has so much power, and the listener is so taken by the arrangement of the tones that he doesn't even think about the fact that the same words are repeated over and over.[157] As Baumgarten had said, sensual impressions are stronger than intellectual ones. Thus in any piece of vocal music, the listener reacts more to the beauty and force of the music than to the cognitive content of the words.

Krause also answered Enlightened objections to the da capo form common to Italian opera arias. Critics had objected that its symmetrical *ABA* structure distorted dramatic reality, and that the form only existed in order to provide the singer with an opportunity to show off his skill in virtuoso ornamentation in the repeat of the "A" section. Krause, however, defends the contrasting middle section and the return to the original feeling because such changes reflect the natural temporal course of many real emotions. Anticipating views common towards the end of the century, Krause asserted that changeableness was natural to all emotions, and that musical form reflected this variability:

> Keine Leidenschaft kann bey einerley Umständen lange aushalten. Sie wird gar bald schwächer, muss also durch etwas von neuem angeflammet werden; and die Wirkung davon ist, in den Arien, dass man wieder auf den ersten Theil zurück fällt.[158]

> No passion can sustain itself for very long in the same state. It will become soon weaker and must therefore be kindled anew by something; and the realization of this, in the case of the aria, is that the first part returns.

In order to impress this point effectively on his reader Krause gives an extensive and vivid description of the emotions as changing, inconstant entities which are subject even to quite definite contrasts; and again he relates these changes explicitly to musical form:

> Wenn wir im Affect sind, und denselben durch Worte und Handlungen an den Tag legen, so reichet die eingeschränkte Kraft unsrer Seele nicht zu, dessen Wuth in einem gleich starken Zuge hintereinander unszuhalten. Sein Sturm brauset durch abgesezte und wiederholte Stösse. Er scheint sich in den Zwischenzeiten zu erholen, um mit erneuerter Kraft wüten zu können. Bald machen wir uns Zweifel, ob die Leidenschaft auch statt habe. Bald stellen wir uns ihre Ursachen und Würkungen naher vor Augen. Bald betrachten wir den Gegenstand derselben auf einer und minder rührenden Seite. Wir wünschen, dass die Leidenschaft nicht so gross wäre; allein dieser Wunsch ist vergeben. Die Vorstellung des rührenden Gegenstandes erneuert sich, und reisst uns desto stärker mit sich fort. Bald vergleichen wir die Beschaffenheit unsers Herzens mit einer andern Sache. Zuweilen wird unsere Leidenschaft durch eine andre Gemüthsbewegung unterbrochen, aber nur deswegen, damit jene über sie siegen könne. Alle diese und dergleichen Empfindungen und Vorstellungen werden sehr natürlich in die zweyte Periode, in den zweyten Theil einer Arie gebracht, und alsedenn lässt sich der erste sehr bequem wiederholen.[159]

> When we are in a state of emotion and are expressing our feelings through words and actions, the limited power of our souls is not able to sustain its frenzy in an even progression. The storm of emotion blusters in separate and repeated gusts. It seems in the meantime to recoup, so that it can rage with renewed energy. At times we doubt whether the passion even exists. At times we observe the object of the passion from another and less moving side. We wish that the passion was not so great; but, alas, this wish is in vain. The idea of the moving object recurs and transports us even more powerfully. At times we compare the state of our heart to something else. Sometimes our passion will be interrupted by another emotion, but only so that the former can triumph over the latter. All these as well as similar ideas and feelings can be brought in quite naturally in the second part of an aria, and then can the first part be quite effectively repeated.

Even if it is accepted that Krause's view of the emotions was not original, he was breaking new ground when he attempted to explain the ongoing temporal patterns of contrast, variety and repetition in music on the basis of analogous, or "isomorphic," aspects of the emotions. We see here a happy alliance of accepted musical practice, aesthetic principles, and a newer more dynamic psychology of the emotions.

Counterpoint is also defended by Krause. Although, as any Enlightened critic, he is concerned lest composers get carried away with displaying their skill and accomplishments in ''harmonic work,'' Krause manifests the traditional German predilection for polyphonic activity and intensity. As for Mattheson, such rich displays aroused in him ''wonderment'' and ''joy'' independently of any representation of the real world. We can see this deep attachment to counterpoint in his description of how counterpoint developed in accordance with the pleasure and excitement man derived from it:

> Man sahe, dass manche Gänge der Melodie sich auch im Basse anbringen lassen. Man wurde gewahr, dass es wohl klingt, wenn etliche Stimmen ein gewisses Thema nehmen, und durch des sen Widerhohlung, und Zertheilung, einen Wettstreit darüber unter sich anstellen. Man merkte, wenn alle Stimmen arbeiten, wie die Tonkünstler reden, dass solches eine Pracht, eine Bewunderung, eine allgemeine Freude, einen grossen Eyfer ausdrückt, und dass das Herz davon mit gewissen hohen und starken Empfindungen erfüllt wird.[160]

> One saw that many melodies could also be put in the bass. One realized that it sounded good when a few voices take a theme and through repetition and fragmentation carry on a competition. One noticed that when all the voices ''worked,'' as the composers say, that such events expressed a majesty, a wonderment, a universal joy, and a great fervor, and that the heart thereby was filled with certain intense and elevated emotions.

Indeed, Krause saw that what the neoclassicists viewed as the most inexpressive and meaningless of musical procedures actually expressed and aroused strong and elevated feelings. But Krause was not content to let his defense rest with his own subjective testimony. He took and altered Baumgarten's concept of intensive clarity to explain the role of counterpoint. Baumgarten had held that intensive clarity only applied to the realm of science, and that only extensive clarity was proper to artworks. But Krause used the concept of intensive clarity to apply to the increased clarity of the parts of an idea as they are developed contrapuntally. This increased clarity, leading to increased ''knowledge,'' occurs

> bey einem musikalischen Stück, dass über eine Thema von einigen Tacten sehr ausgearbeitet ist. Anfangs begreifen wir nur überhaupt, wie in dem Thema die Folge der Töne beschaffen ist. Bey Wiederholung desselben aber, ob gleich in andern Verbindungen, wird uns die Melodie bekanter, klärer; wir lernen sie mehr einsehen, und wohl gar auswendig.[161]

> in a musical composition which develops very thoroughly a subject of a few measures. At first we understand only vaguely how the succession of tones is made from the subject. But by its repetition, even in various contexts, the subject becomes more familiar, clearer; we learn to recognize it, we even learn it by heart.

But, adds Krause, this theme cannot always be repeated in the same context, for the theme would then become distinct and the charm of the new and unexpected would be lost. And, as Baumgarten had shown, distinctness and too much unity destroy aesthetic effectiveness. Krause goes on to say, clearly recognizing the success of Baumgartnian concepts in justifying music's special rules, "Musicians too forbid such uniformity in their rules of composition."[162]

Thus, counterpoint was one way of avoiding boring uniformity while still impressing a certain theme upon the listener's consciousness through varied repetition. But the intensive clarity of polyphony didn't move the listener; only extensive clarity, with its variety of representations, could do that, as Baumgarten had stated. Thus Krause counseled the association of as many other ideas with the main theme as were necessary to achieve the desired effect:

> Es kommen alsdann zu dem Thema, als der Hauptvorstellung immer neue rührende Merkmale die sich aber doch so dazu schicken, dass unsere Empfindung keinen Wiederspruch unter ihnen bemerket; das heist, die Klarheit wird der Ausdehnung nach stärker; und das Gemüth dadurch sehr beweget.[163]

> Ever new and moving attributes become associated with the theme, which fit with the theme insofar as our feelings notice no contradiction among them, that is clarity becomes extensively greater; and one is thereby very moved.

Krause concluded his discussion of the two types of musical clarity by recommending the use of both intensive and extensive clarity. The one was pleasing in itself, as well as in keeping with the respected compositional traditions:

> Durch eine fleissige Ausarbeitung des Thematis thun sie ihren musikalischen Regeln ein Genüge, und es ergötzet den Zuhörer ungemein, wenn er bey öfterer unvermutheter Anbringung des Hauptsatzes gewahr wird, wie aus wenigem so viel gemacht wird.[164]

> Through a diligent development of the theme they do justice to their rules of composition, and it delights the listener exceedingly when, with the unanticipated return of the main theme, so much is made of so little.

But since intensive clarity, though providing compositional interest and pleasure, did not move the listener, the "knowledge and experience" of composers told them to use the other form of clarity as well:

> Daher verbinden sie mit dem Thema so viel andere Vorstellungen, biss sie ihrer Absicht moralisch gewiss sind. Gesetzt, dass ihrer Geschicklichkeit, die Intension der Hauptvorstellung fortzusetzen, noch viel übrig bliebe, so wollen sie lieber gefällige als gelehrte Musici seyn. So lange also eine Musik noch Rührung oder doch Lust gebiehret, so lange finden auch die harmonischen Künsten darin statt.[165]

> Therefore they join with their theme as many other ideas as are necessary to make them certain of realizing their moral intent. Even though their ability to develop the main idea left much to be desired, they would nevertheless rather be pleasing than learned musicians. As long as music offers movement, or indeed pleasure, the art of harmony will have a place.

In sum, although it was better to sacrifice the learned quality of counterpoint for the pleasing and moving effects of variety, there would always be a place for counterpoint.

Melismas also played a positive role in Krause's theory. The typical neoclassic view was that such displays of vocal skill were merely sensually appealing distractions from the morally uplifting content of the opera; that they were inconsistent with the imitation of the natural utterances of passion and that they prevented the clear understanding of the words. Krause answered this latter objection by suggesting that one merely look in the libretto to get the words.[166] And he defended the simple pleasure that such musical ornaments afforded by saying that music would be too boring without them.[167] As for the relation of melismas to the expression of music's content, Krause argued that if one could express emotions on instruments, without words (and this he assumed his reader would not doubt), then why not with a melisma:

> Kann durch Instrumente, ohne Worte, eine Gemüthsbewegung vorgestellt werden, warum solches dem vortreflichsten Werkzeuge harmonischer Klänge nicht möglich und erlaubt seyn?[168]

> If emotions can be represented by instruments, without words, why shouldn't the same thing be possible and permitted for the most excellent instrument of agreeable sounds?

He realized that the age-old Hallelujah was an expression more tonal than verbal, for men had long used it "in order thereby to express the enduring and inexpressible joy of the heavenly hosts."[169]

Krause's essay on musical poetry has great relevance for the history of instrumental music's changing status. Already we have seen that Krause felt that music had moral and expressive significance independently of words, as part of its innate character. That a prominent figure of the Berlin Enlightenment would so emphatically make this assertion, which both reinforced traditional German attitudes and which brought into prominence the implications of the new discipline of aesthetics, was in itself a contribution to the future appreciation of instrumental music. Moreover, Krause did concern himself, if only briefly, with the issue of instrumental music's status. As an Enlightened German he found it quite worthwhile indeed.

In order to evaluate instrumental music Krause used three traditional standards: music's ability to move the listener, music's moral use, and the degree of cognitive communication achieved by music. If one only evaluated music in terms of its ability to move, it would be clear that

> eine gut gesetzte und wohl aufgeführte Musik, auch nur von Instrumenten, eben solche [sinnliche] Eindrücke und noch wohl stärkere macht, als manche Rede oder manches Gedicht.[170]

> a well-composed and well-performed musical composition, even when played only by instruments, makes just as much an emotional impression, indeed a much stronger one, than many a speech or poem.

The view that music is the most powerfully moving art is of course an old one, but it is significant that Krause goes on to propound it at some length. Indeed, Krause confesses that he does not doubt the ''marvellous effects of ancient music,'' and that it was a piece of instrumental music, a harp fantasy, that converted him to this belief.[171]

   Krause is perhaps most earnest in defending music per se, and hence instrumental music, on grounds of its moral use. Krause is the first to admit that instrumental music does not make one more intelligent and that it is utterly incapable of expressing moral precepts.[172] But acutely sensing the charge of the opposition that music is merely an idle pastime and that it is of no permanent redeeming moral value, Krause goes to great lengths, as we have seen, to defend the innate ability of music to cultivate harmonious souls and noble inclinations. In so doing he attacks the naive notion held by the opposition that poetry indeed functions primarily to occupy the mind and to communicate moral truths. Whoever is willing to grant that indeed reason does not govern all our moral behavior, and that in fact most people are not as affected by the truths contained in poetry as they are by certain feelings it arouses, and, furthermore that the sensations of music accustom us to feelings advantageous to humanity in general (love, for example) and occupy our understanding ''by the inner relationships among tones, and by their exterior, beautiful organization''—anyone who grants these points (which Krause has drawn from the authority of philosophical aesthetics, experience, English criticism and his own thoroughly conditioned inner convictions), will not be too inclined to rank music below poetry and oratory.[173]

   But no matter how much power we may grant to music without poetry, Krause writes, the fact remains that it will be even more powerful with the addition of words. For words make music's imitations more ''intelligible''; they give the ''why and wherefore'' of the general emotions expressed; and they are sometimes even needed to confer ''distinctness.''[174] For all their talk about sensual cognition, it must be remembered that people such as Baumgarten and Krause still possessed a strong inclination towards clarity and determinateness of thought; and they were not at all insensitive to the pleasures of intellectual activity. Thus, Krause relates, in spite of the fact that music can be exceptionally moving when we do not recognize any object of representation, ''our understanding always wants to have a part in the movements of the soul.''[175] That is why, for example, one puts fiery words to fiery music. But in his final negative verdict as to the relative worth of instrumental and vocal music, Krause focuses on what the music does for the words rather than on what the words do for the music:

> Lehrreiche, feurige Worte, durch eine einnehmende Melodie noch mehr erhoben, sind von grossem Nutzen, und von unvergleichbarer Würkung. . . . Die Musik arbeitet, so wohl als die Worte, zur Ermunterung der Gedanken und zur Überzeugung und Bewegung der Zuhörer, und sie verleihet Worten, vor denen viel Herzen verschlossen sind, solche Annehmlichkeiten, die die Herzen eröfnen, und den Wahrheiten Eingang verschaffen. Hierin bestehet auch der gröste Vorzug, den die Vocal-vor der Instrumentalmusik hat.[176]

Instructive, fiery words, intensified by a persuasive melody, have the greatest use and incomparable effects. . . . The music, as well as the words, contributes to the animation of the ideas and the persuasion and moving of the listeners; and it confers such pleasantness on words, to which many hearts are closed, that hearts open and truths find entrance. Herein consists the greatest advantage that vocal music has over instrumental music.

The fact remains, however, that instrumental music is considered inferior because it cannot communicate a moral message as effectively as words and tones combined. Although Krause has broadened his readers' visions as to the independence and significance of musical art, he has not abandoned this vestige of verbally-mediated didacticism.

4

Debate in the Wake of Batteux:
Gottsched—Nicolai—Ruetz—Hiller—Ramler—Lessing

Batteux's injunction that all music must have a meaning was a challenge to instrumental music which could not be ignored. All of the writers surveyed in this
chapter are concerned with one aspect or another of this challenge. The intention of
Gottsched, Hiller, and Ramler is to propagate and interpret Batteux. But whereas
Gottsched distorts Batteux to the point of saying that instrumental music is necessarily meaningless, Hiller and Ramler both make significant amendments to Batteux's theory in order not to violate their own vision of the specific nature of music.
Hiller calls instrumental music with no representative character the "wonderful"
in music and sanctions its limited use. Ramler substitutes for nature as music's
model, the composer's own musical experience.

To answer Gottsched's attack on instrumental music Nicolai constructs a defense based on empirical observations of the musical culture around him and on the
new aesthetic theory of Baumgarten; and in so doing he manifests a sympathy with
musical attitudes of pre-Enlightenment Germany. Ruetz takes issue with Batteux's
insistence on representation and clear intelligibility of every sound, because such a
demand would rob music of its riches, would only give ammunition to "the enemies of music," and indeed would lead the amateur to a complete misunderstanding of music. Lessing, though he argued against the neoclassic rules of unity in
literary works, held that unity in instrumental music was essential; for contrast
without verbal explanation was incoherent and unintelligible. Nevertheless, he rejected the notion that words were necessary to make music's meaning definite;
unlike Batteux he confessed to enjoying music's vague meaning.

Thus, Batteux's challenge hit upon a native strain of resistance in all but Gottsched. Nicolai, Ruetz, Hiller, Ramler, and Lessing all resisted neoclassicism in
some way. But all followed neoclassic tradition in deprecating instrumental music
on grounds of its lack of intelligibility.

Eight years after the publication of *Les beaux arts réduits à un même principe* Gottsched published a translation of selections from Batteux's book along with his own

lengthy commentary for the use of his students at the University of Leipzig.[1] Gottsched took this occasion to transform Batteux's treatment of music and dance into a direct attack on the art of instrumental music. Gottsched translated Batteux's reasoned arguments into vitriolic rhetoric. He even contradicted Batteux's fundamental assumption that tones have a meaning, preferring instead to call sheer sounds "soulless and unintelligible":

> Die Musik allein aber ist unbeseelet und unverständlich, wenn sie nicht an Worte hält, die gleichsam für sie reden müssen, damit man wisse, was sie haben will.[2]

> Music by itself is soulless and unintelligible when it doesn't cling to words, which must speak for it, so that one know what it means.

Not even the beckoning gesture or the inarticulate cry of pain had any significance for the rationalistic Gottsched. Even worms gesticulate and children cry, he explained; but only fully developed man uses words.[3] With such rhetoric did he seek to perpetuate Batteux's preference for vocal music.

Italian instrumental music was Gottsched's real target. To back up Batteux's statement that "the very worst music is that which has no character at all," Gottsched launched into a tirade against the meaninglessness of compositions that go by names such as Largo, Adagio, Andante, and Allegro. These pieces express "absolutely nothing" and represent a "mere jangle that makes one neither cold nor warm."[4] A sonata is described as an unaffecting chaos,

> ein Labyrinth von Tönen, die weder lustig noch traurig, weder beweglich noch rührend klingen.[5]

> a labyrinth of tones, which sound neither happy nor sad, neither touching nor moving.

Most puzzling and ridiculous to Gottsched was the indication "a tempo giusto"; neither male nor female, Gottsched observes, pieces so called can only be compared to hermaphrodites.[6]

The base tone of this commentary on instrumental music disappears, however, when Gottsched discusses French characteristic pieces. In condemning the composition of instrumental music in the Italian manner, Gottsched had chastised musicians for being "ashamed" of writing suites of dances, such as sarabandes, gavottes, and allemands.[7] He wished composers had not gotten caught up in the latest meaningless fashion. Indeed, when Gottsched wants to give an example of an instrumental piece whose meaning is as easy to judge as a painting (as Batteux had said musical meanings should be) he tells the story of some princes who upon hearing a new menuet immediately began to dance—that is, they "understood" what was played![8] Such dance music did of course have a clearly defined and unified character and a socially accepted function (some, after the ancients, valued it for its character-building effects). But certainly Gottsched did not regard dance music as the imitation of passionate utterance, which was Batteux's model of musical significance. Apparently Gottsched was making more of a personal than a theoretical statement. Dance suites were French, as were Gottsched's intellectual allegiances, and they were being pushed out of favor in Germany by a new culture with which Gottsched was wholly out of tune.

Gottsched, unlike Batteux, attributed the superiority of vocal music to the power of words to "explain distinctly" the meaning of the music. Despite Gottsched's singular hostility to music and his rationalistic narrow-mindedness, which must have offended anyone with any sympathy for instrumental music, the essence of his view—that instrumental music was inferior because its content was not distinctly intelligible—remained a common opinion. Batteux had raved about the "signification" of the inarticulate tones of passionate utterance, and, while preferring vocal music, had not rejected instrumental music because its meaning was by nature indistinct. Gottsched however makes it clear that words, or even gestures, are necessary if the listener is to fully understand what the tones are trying to say:

> Wir hören, dass eine Musik, ohne Text, oder Tanz, nur ein todtes Ding, nur ein Körper, ohne Geist ist. Warum? Man versteht oder erräth es vielmehr nur halb, was gespielet wird; wenn nicht entweder Gebärden, oder Worte dazu kommen, die das deutlicher erklären, was die Töne sagen sollen.[9]

> We hear that music without a text or dance is a dead thing, is only a body without a soul. Why? One can understand or guess only halfway at the most what is being played, if neither gestures nor words are joined which explain more distinctly what the tones are supposed to be saying.

If only composers had the good sense to accompany their notes with words, Gottsched suggests, then their audience and they themselves would know better what "their grab-bag full of notes is supposed to mean."[10]

What Gottsched really wants is a plot. We recall that in his *Critische Dichtkunst* the plot was characterized as the pinnacle of poetic imitation. But of course a plot could not be made understandable without words. To illustrate the necessity for a plot Gottsched proposes an experiment. What if, Gottsched suggested, the singers and hence the poetry were omitted from an opera performance. "How would the music without the poetry fare?" How could

> die ganze Instrumentalmusik, auch von den besten Virtuosen, die Zuschauer vier fünf Stunden lang beschäfftigen? . . . Wer würde sich aber aus den besten Compositionen etwas nehmen können, das verständlich wäre, und die Seele beschäfftigen könnte: wenn keine Schauspieler eine Fabel voller Gesinnungen und Leidenschaften vorstelleten; welches doch von der Poesie herrühret?[11]

> any piece of instrumental music, even if played by the best virtuosos, occupy an audience for four or five hours? . . . Who could find something from the best instrumental compositions which was intelligible, and which could occupy the soul, if there are no actors to represent a plot full of opinions and passions—which only comes from the poetry?

Gottsched was confident that when the plot and the intelligible content of the opera were taken away nothing interesting or moving would be left.

Virtuosity, compositional complexity, and lack of unity were all singled out by Gottsched as deplorable aspects of musical practice in that they frustrated the listener's need to understand distinctly. Like Batteux, Gottsched was preoccupied with meaning and with the intelligibility of this meaning. Musicians and composers, he complained, forget that the aim of music is to imitate, and want either to show off the incredible speed of their throat or fingers, or their skill at crowding a lot of notes together, with the result that no one knows whether he should laugh or cry.[12] Composers seem to be imitating the poets of the day who prefer "unintelligible riddles" to "distinct words and phrases." They get lost in "wonderful combinations of tones" and even the melody becomes imperceptible.[13] Intelligibility for Gottsched entailed obeying the rule of unity. For example a *Passionmusik* must never degenerate into happy melodies.[14] A composer must never mix his colors and create ambiguity. Colors must be kept distinct from each other so that they can be clearly recognized:

> Was gelb seyn soll, muss recht gelb, und nicht nur gilblich; was dunkelblau seyn soll, nicht half mit weiss gemischet, oder lichtblau ausgemalet werden. So muss auch das Lustige, Traurige, Zornige, Muthige, allezeit mit richtigen vollgültigen Tönen ausgedrücket werden; dass es ein jeder daran erkennen kann.[15]

> What is supposed to be yellow must be quite yellow, not just yellowish; what should be dark blue, not half-mixed with white or printed light blue. Similarly the happy, the sad, the angry, the courageous, must always be expressed with conclusive tones, so that they can be recognized by everyone.

As with Batteux, only the most obvious subjects must be chosen so that everyone can understand distinctly. Gottsched obviously had not been convinced by the new science of aesthetics that intellectual cognition was not central to the function of art and that distinctness destroyed art. Gottsched used the term "distinct" with Baumgartnian precision. He was aware of Baumgarten's ideas and heartily disagreed with them. As he had fought against the superstitious credulity of the past, he resisted the empiricism and sentimentality of the future. His views on the issue of an independent art of music have demonstrated this most clearly.

Christoph Friedrich Nicolai (1733-1811), long-time editor of Germany's central cultural and literary forum, the *Bibliothek der freyen Wissenschaften und schönen Künste* and "the most influential author and publisher of the Berlin Enlightenment," felt called upon to defend instrumental music from Gottsched's attack.[16] Nicolai's defense is decidedly partisan and patriotic in tone, often relying on clever arguments or enthusiastic poetry. He resents the way Gottsched treats Germans like children by trying to establish a French critic as the lawgiver for German artists. Nicolai is proud that the Germans have already surpassed their French models. He characterizes Gottsched as a narrow-minded deductive pedant who presumes to judge and to prescribe rules for music on the basis of his poetic theory alone:

> Kan man wohl zu bitter über ein Mann spotten, der bis auf die Kunstwörter der Kunst unwissend ist, über die er mit der grösten Dreistigkeit urtheilet; der mit einer pedantischen Ernsthaftigkeit alle Künste zu Dienerinnen einer einzigen machen will, . . . der sowohl die Regeln als die Wirkungen einer Kunst in der andern suchet und fordert, und mit dictatorischen Amtsmine, von Dingen, die er nicht versteht, spricht, als wann er sie verstünd![17]

> Indeed can one too severely ridicule a man who doesn't even know the technical terms of the very art which he judges with such harshness; who with pedantic self-righteousness wants to make all the arts into servants of one . . . who seeks and demands the rules and the effects of one art in another, and who with bureaucratic dictatorship speaks of things he doesn't understand!

Ignorance and conceit are not Gottsched's only faults; playing on the Lutheran suspicion of the unmusical man, Nicolai several times makes the damning observation that Gottsched is not even able to feel the beauties of music. How can a critic presume to be a critic of any art, Nicolai wants to know, when he lacks an "empfindsames Herz?[18]

Nocolai's basic strategy is to counter the deductive theory of Gottsched with the actual practice of German music-lovers. He calls not only upon his own inner experience but upon the manifest preferences of the concertgoers of Berlin and of Frederick the Great himself. Whereas Gottsched treated sheer sounds as an insult to his rationality, Nicolai experienced no inconsistency in being both Enlightened and responsive to music. No reasonable man who has actually heard a good piece of instrumental music (and who is not on guard against any perception of musical beauties), Nicolai wrote, would assert, as had Gottsched, that music without words "expresses absolutely nothing and is unintelligible . . . consequently is incapable of all the effects which one once attributed to it."[19] The "superior effects of music" were for Nicolai a fact of daily experience. Shepherd and prince alike cultivated music. Only Gottsched, intent upon his own "chimeras," could not see

> dass wir von den vortrefflichen Wirkungen der Musik täglich die deutlichsten Beispiele haben, und dass sich ihre Eindrükke vorzüglich für allen andern schönen Künsten, auf alle Arten von Menschen erstrekken.[20]

> that we have daily the most distinct examples of the superior effects of music, and that its impressions, foremost among the arts, extend to all kinds of men.

Here Nicolai has cleverly turned the tables and has classified Gottsched's ideas as chimerical and his own inner conviction of the peculiarly powerful effects of music as certain. Nicolai then proceeds to address a short poem to his opponent, the moral of which is that if Gottsched could see, and let himself be moved by, the charm of Frederick's flute, or could observe how the King freed himself from the "cares of ruling" through the soothing pleasure of playing, then Gottsched too would be freed of his hatred of music and would see "that music is indeed divine!"[21] Nicolai is not only calling upon the authority of experience but is reflecting the traditional German attitudes prevalent in his own culture. It was the very musical culture of Berlin which provided Nicolai with the evidence he needed to answer Gottsched's claim that if the words were taken away from opera and a four or five hour concert of instrumental music was all that remained, people would stop attending because no mere instrumental concert (even if played by the best virtuosos) could occupy an audience for so long. This claim, Nicolai observed, was contradicted almost daily by the heavy attendance at instrumental concerts in Berlin (and they weren't even played by the best virtuosos).[22]

The whole issue of the role of music versus poetry in opera brings into focus the antithetical positions of Gottsched and Nicolai—one the champion of words, the other of tones. Gottsched had attempted to illuminate the issue by proposing the experiment whereby the music of opera was taken away leaving only the poetry. He had maintained that the only thing that was lost was a mere decoration which only made the text unintelligible and irritated the listeners with the "eternal repetitions of the aria." For the libretto of an opera could stand on its own feet as a self-sufficient drama; the libretto provided the real interest. (Gottsched's other experiment—to take away the words and leave the sounds—was also intended to demonstrate that the words were central to opera's success). But, Nicolai replied, how can the popularity of the opera be attributed to the text as Gottsched seemed to claim; how can the text keep people in their seats for four or five hours, when people don't even understand the words? Indeed, the texts of most Italian and German operas are so bad that if one persisted in claiming that words were the cause of opera's delight, one could only conclude that the composer was trying to delight his audience with the absurdity of the librettist.[23] The only conclusion, then, that a reasonable man could make was that "the pleasure arises solely from the music, and has absolutely nothing to do with the miserable libretto of the poet."[24] Nicolai reminds Gottsched that people are more moved by arias, where music is the main interest, than by recitatives; and that in accompanied recitatives the tones actually explain the words.[25] Attacking from another angle, Nicolai cites a particularly devastating fact of experience:

> Was ist denn die Oper für den grösten Theil der Zuschauer anders, als eine schöne Instrumentalmusik?[26]

> What is the opera anyway for most of the audience besides a beautiful instrumental composition?

By calling opera in effect instrumental music Nicolai pulled Gottsched's supports right out from under him; for hadn't Gottsched claimed that opera was so much more well-attended because it wasn't boring like instrumental music?

Nicolai then turns Gottsched's experiment around: what is "lost" when music is added back to the opera? Nicolai answers (again reflecting the quality of the librettos in actual use): only dull thoughts, unnatural metaphors and long, boring descriptions, all of which music can transform into interesting, pleasant, and artful sounds. Furthermore, if the libretto of an opera were declaimed, it would be the art of the actor with which we would be taken, not the words; the words themselves would have little effect. But in an opera aria much affective power is gained by the music itself, due to those very repetitions which Gottsched attacked:

> Hier hat der Dichter mit Fleiss die mächtigste Leidenschaft in einer Arie, so zu sagen, gepresst, damit bei den Wiederholungen, die die Leidenschaft natürlich macht, der Musikus seine Kunst anbringen, und das Ergözzen der Zuhörer verdoppeln könne; über diese ist der Schauspieler genöthiget ruhig hinwegzugehen, ohne den grösten Theil der Empfindungen erregen zu können, zu denen wiederholte Töne geschikkt gewesen sein wurden.[27]

> Here the poet has so to speak compressed the most powerful passion into an aria so that, with the repetitions which make the passion natural, the composer can apply his art, and the delight of the listener can be doubled. The actor is obliged to pass over these things, without being able to arouse the greatest part of the feelings, which the repeated tones of music are suited to do.

The repetitions, so natural to music (and, Nicolai is careful to add, to emotions), although cognitively redundant, are necessary for the communication and arousal of most feelings. As Baumgarten and Meier had said, the means and rules for intellectual communication were not the same as those for artistic or sensual communication. The only problem was that Gottsched's "preparatory set" was such that he only sensed the redundancy, and not the affective power, of the music. Nicolai wanted to show that people like Gottsched had the wrong expectations.

Nicolai's next move is to reconstruct Gottsched's other experiment and to take away the words of the opera and leave the music. This time Nicolai gives his own account of what would happen. Nicolai admits the music would of course be less perfect, because it was really vocal music in the first place. But wouldn't the music still be interesting and moving and indeed more so than words or gestures by themselves, Nicolai asks rhetorically (and then gives the redundant but enthusiastic answer):

> Aber wird sie für sich allein auch ein schönes Ganze ausmachen? Ein Ganzes, das zu Ausdrükken, zu Erregung der Empfindungen, der Leidenschaften, eben so geschikkt, ia weit geschikkter ist, als die von ihr getrennten Worte und Gebärden für sich allein? Ja![28]

> Now will it even by itself make a beautiful unity? A unity that is just as capable of arousing the feelings and passions, indeed is even more capable than just words or gestures when separated from music? Yes indeed!

At this point Nicolai leaves all clever reasoning behind. He answers the contentious and base rhetoric of Gottsched with equally extreme enthusiasm as he describes his instrumental opera:

> —Man fängt mit einer frölichen Symphonie an;—alles horcht!—eine zufriedene Langsamkeit
> folgt auf die rauschende Freude, die Stimmen scheinen miteinander zu sprechen, sie
> wiederholen sich,—doch verändert; sie scheinen endlich in einer melancholischen Pause zu
> sterben,—schnell erheben, überraschen die freudigsten Töne die Zuhörer, die in eine Art von
> Erstaunen gerathen,—Die Symphonie schweigt: Die Recitativstimmen sind unter die In-
> strumentisten vertheilt, ein Benda, ein Czarth, ein Seiffart, ein Ried, ein v.S.*** sprechen weit
> declamatorischer, als so viele frostige Schauspieler, das ernsthafte Hautbois und die scherzende
> Flöte machen die Arien: verliehren wir wohl viel an der Stimme und den Worten des Sängers?—
> Jede willige Leidenschaft folgt dem Griffe des Spielers.[29]

> A gay symphony begins—everyone listens! A soothing slowness follows upon the exuberant
> joy. The voices seem to speak with each other. They repeat themselves, but in a varied manner.
> Finally they seem to die in a melancholy pause—suddenly they arise and surprise the listener
> with the most joyful sounds and the listener is put into a kind of astonishment. The symphony is
> over. The recitatives are divided among the instruments—a Benda, a Czarth, a Seiffart, a Ried,
> a v. S.*** speak much more eloquently than so many frigid actors. The serious oboe and the
> playful flute do the arias. Do we really lose so much in the voices and words of the singers? Each
> willing passion responds to the musician's touch.

This vivid description of the opera without words has the sounds cast in the active role. The sounds themselves are the actors. The tones themselves are soothing or exuberant; the tones themselves awaken and die. The tones are neither decorating verbal meanings nor passively signifying. As Hiller and Ruetz were to say, tones don't imitate feeling, tone *is* feeling. Clearly, to a person such as Nicolai, arguments were beside the point. If experience taught that people were in fact moved by the immediate force of music, then that was enough.

Thus Nicolai doesn't venture any explanation of music's affective power, its ability to arouse the emotions. He is not explaining practice really; he is only reporting and reflecting it. But he does venture into the realm of theory long enough to entertain and answer one objection to his enthusiastic claims for instrumental music, the objection namely that tones are not words and cannot do what words can do. Nicolai quickly grants the objection. But at the same time he points out that the distinct cognition made possible by words is out of place is a realm of sensual cognition. He draws upon Baumgarten, as did Krause, to rationalize his view of music as innately moving and morally potent:

> Es ist ausgemacht, dass die Musik, nach der philosophischen Sprache zu reden, nicht deutliche,
> sondern nur klare Vorstellungen verursache, dass sie unmittelbar nur auf die untern Seelen-
> kräfte, und nur mittelbar auf die obern Kräfte wirke; aber indem man dieses zugiebt, so öffnet
> man der Musik das ganze Feld der Gemüthsbewegungen dieser Seile, wodurch alle menschliche
> Handlungen regieret werden, und bekennet, dass sie zu ihren Absichten keiner fremden Hülfe
> benöthigt ist.[30]

It is obvious, to speak in philosophical language, that music causes not distinct, but rather only clear ideas, that it directly affects only the lower faculties and only indirectly the higher ones. But at the same time that one concedes this, one opens to music the whole field of such emotions, which are the very determinants of all human actions, and one also recognizes the fact that music does not of necessity require any foreign aid to achieve her purposes.

Nicolai recognized that the Baumgartnian aesthetics left room for a moving and significant instrumental music, that it freed instrumental music from the demand that it be both clear and distinct, and that it gave a significant role to indistinct cognition, which was all instrumental music had to offer.

Gottsched had objected to such common features of music as counterpoint and the light and shade created by contrasts and transitions. He wanted the melody to be heard distinctly and the character of a piece to be unified, decisively colored and distinct. Nicolai ridicules Gottsched's objection to that basic compositional ingredient especially favored by composers of counterpoint, the dissonance and its resolution (most probably it is the suspension that is at issue). Dissonances, said Gottsched, were "unbearable." He had known a dog, who had begun to howl at all musical dissonances. What can possibly be beautiful, Gottsched asked, that has to be resolved or made right? Nicolai sarcastically observed that it was an honor for the "harmonic part of music, and especially the artful weaving together of dissonances, which are necessary to the expression of most emotions" to be so disagreeable to Gottsched.[31] It is remarkable that a leader of the Berlin Enlightenment should engage his wits to defend the "harmonic part of music" and to imply that it was even necessary for expressing some emotions. Such opinions were at some variance with the negative orthodox Enlightened view as to the usefulness of harmony and compositional craft in musical expression.

Nicolai doesn't reply to Gottsched's insistence on the "rule of unity" directly. But following upon his description of the opera without words he allows himself to be carried away in a raptuous poetic description of his own personal reactions to the affecting and engaging events of a piece of instrumental music full of sudden and gradual changes. We see in Nicolai's poem, as we did in the description of the symphony without singing above, his own empirical testimony that variety, contrast, changingness, and expectation-play are all vital elements in the moving art of sheer tones. He ends by emphasizing, for the benefit of Gottsched, who has a masculine disdain for this pleasant but meaningless idiom, that the music did not bring on a state of passive, effeminate sensuality, but rather (as Baumgarten might have preferred) that he was full of attentiveness—"nicht zärtlich sondern ganz Gehör." "Zärtlich" stood for the quality Gottsched had condemned in contemporary opera. Nicolai seems to be implying in his final question "Who is the magician?" not only that music has more power than poetry but that even Gottsched should see instrumental music's superiority to poetry. For at least the pleasure in music was morally pure (as Luther had said).

Schon bebt die Angst auf seinen Saiten,
Gram, Unruh und Verzweiflung streiten,
Schwachzitternd folgt der matte Ton;
Ich fühl, ich fühl in Brust und Herzen
Halb ängstlich unbekannte Schmerzen;
Ein edles Mitleid rührt mich schon.
Zuletzt hör ich die Unschuld siegen,
Die Freude stürmt in iedem Strich,
Und ieder Ton schallt von Vergnügen,
Und ieder Ton begeistert mich.

Berauschet von Annelmlichkeiten,
Hör ich, wie er die hellen Saiten
Nachlässig und nur leicht berührt;
Jedoch, indem er scheint zu schweigen,
Entzükkt er durch ein schnelles Steigen,
Bis sterbend sich der Ton verliehrt:
Izt bleibt er schwebend zärtlich liegen,
Macht falsche Gänge; doch mit Fleiss,
Die er, den Hörer, zu betrügen,
Schnell, reizend zu verändern weiss.

Izt spielt er weit gelindre Triebe,
Die Zärtlichkeit, die reinste Liebe,
Die Furcht dehnt den langsamen Klang;
Die Töne wechseln, die bald beben,
Bald auf geschwinden Griffen schweben,
Bald ziehet sie der Zweifel lang:
Ich werde, ieden Ton zu fühlen,
Nicht zärtlich—sondern ganz Gehör.
Wer ist der Zaub'rer!—[32]

All these varied and suggestive musical events that so delighted Nicolai must have delighted many of his like-minded compatriots as well. Nicolai has given us a vivid and even unassailable testimony to the meaningfulness of the instrumental idiom. But he has been blind to the fact that these effects were premised on a conditioning process surely involving much listening to music with a verbally-defined content. He has given few theoretical reasons why instrumental music is so worthwhile. Nevertheless, by setting an example for attentive and impressionable listening he helped prepare another generation of music lovers and showed that, at least in practice, one could be both reasonable and musically attuned.

The reactions of Ruetz, Hiller and Ramler to Batteux's ideas on music appeared on the pages of Marpurg's *Historisch-Kritische Beyträge zur Aufnahme der Musik* (1754-1760). Marpurg was quite partial to French music and to French ideas, and an energetic musical journalist as well. An Enlightened man, he believed that knowledge about and reflection upon music could only work to the advantage of composer and listener alike. Thus he brought many intellectual debates into the field of musical journalism. In spite of Marpurg's French allegiances, however, the first of the three reactions, that of Ruetz, takes issue with Batteux in strong language. Hiller and Ramler, on the other hand, support Batteux.

Caspar Ruetz (1708-1755), cantor of the Katharineum in Lübeck from 1737 until his death, was an articulate, university-educated church musician. His "Sendschreiben eines Freundes an den andern über einige Ausdrücke des Herrn Batteux von der Musik," which appeared in Marpurg's journal in 1755, articulates the reaction of most German church musicians to the French neoclassic doctrine.[33] Ruetz feared that the neoclassic rules would provide dangerous ammunition to the "enemies of music" and characterized Batteux's ideas as essentially antimusical. Indeed Ruetz's defense of the "divine art" of music constitutes an attack on the whole body of neoclassic music criticism: on the insistence on representation and the imitation of nature, on the impassioned utterance theory of musical expression, on the hegemony of reason, on the preference for a unified and clear-cut content equally accessible and understandable to all, and on the verbal model for musical intelligibility. While his attack on neoclassicism can be viewed as progressive in that it clears the way for Romantic ideas, his ideas remind us as much of past attitudes as they do of new ones.

Ruetz agrees with Batteux that "all music must have a meaning" if that principle is interpreted to mean that the feelings and passions are the proper content of music.[34] But he disagrees with Batteux's theory that the emotional content of music necessarily derives from an act of imitation. For music itself is a natural form of utterance:

(Musik) ist nicht allein eine Nachahmerin der Natur, sondern die Natur selbst; indem es so wohl in der Natur gegründet ist, durch singende und harmonische Töne zu reden, als durch Worte, rednerischen Votrag und Gebärden.[35]

(Music) is not only an imitator of nature, rather it is nature itself; for it is just as much a natural act to express oneself through singing and harmonious tones, as through oratorical delivery and gesture.

Thus, since music proceeds naturally from man's inner being, it has by its very nature meaning. How can Batteux even speak of a music with no meaning, Ruetz asks. Even in the absence of an identifiable content, there is no such thing as meaningless music:

Eine solche Musik habe ich noch nie gehöret. Denn ein jeder musikalischer Ausdrück hat eine Empfindung oder Leidenschaft zum Grunde; wenn sie auch sonsten keinen Vorwürf für die Einbildungskraft vorstellet; und das ist ihre Bedeutung. Sind nun in einer jeden Musik musikalische Ausdrücke, so hat sie auch ihre gemässe Empfindung, das ist, ihre Bedeutung. Man könte endlich wohl sagen, dass eine Musik, die allerley widersprechende Dinge bedeutet, nichts bedeute.[36]

I have never heard that kind of music. For every musical expression is based on a feeling or passion, even if no other content is presented for the imagination; and that is its meaning. Since then there are musical expressions in every piece of music, then each piece has its corresponding feeling, that is, its meaning. One could of course say that a musical composition with all kinds of contradictory things meant nothing.

In rejecting Batteux's insistence on imitation and on a recognizable object of imitation Ruetz is clearly deriving support from the traditional German faith in the innate significance of music. He does however adopt the more modern notion that music is the natural utterance of passion, and hence he agrees with Batteux enough to say that the content of music is emotional utterance.

But Ruetz goes on to use his inherited respect for music's peculiar nature and its mysterious workings to undermine completely Batteux's theory that music is an intelligible representation of the tones of passionate utterance. For Ruetz calls into question the very intelligibility or determinateness of music's content itself. Batteux's theory (as Ruetz understood it), and neoclassic theory in general, assumed that music imitated something in the real world which one could identify with a verbal label such as "joy" or "anguish"—that music's content came from the same pool of objects for artistic imitation as did the content of, for example, a literary art. But Ruetz, invoking Augustine's *occulta familiaritas*, argues that music not only arouses and communicates feeling in mysterious ways, but that the very nature of the affects aroused by music are sui generis and are knowable only by souls sympathetic to music. Again Ruetz has reason to reject Batteux's doctrine of imitation, though he retains the notion of music as a natural language of the passions. Not only is it true, Ruetz writes, that music depicts feelings,

sie macht uns eben das Empfinden; und tausend andere Empfindungen, deren ein musikalisches Herze fähig ist, und die kein Redner, noch Poet durch seine Worte und bewegliche Declamation erwecken kann, sind ihr Eigenthum. In diesen lezten ist die Musik keine Copie der Natur, sondern das Original selbsten. Sie ist eine allgemeine Sprache der Natur, die nur den harmonischen Seelen verständlich ist. Und ihre eigenthümliche Ausdrücke, welche sie nicht von andern Dingen entlehnet, haben ein geheimes Verständniss mit diesen Seelen. Nicht allein die Gemüthsbewegungen und Leidenschaften, welche zugleich Vorwürfe der Beredsamkeit sind, sind der Musik unterworfen. Deren Seelen mit solcher geheimen Sympathie begabt sind, die erfahren dieses mit innigstem Vergnügen. Die Seele des H. Augustini war so beschaffen, daher schrieb er aus eigener Erfahrung, "dass alle Gemüthsbewegungen vermöge der angenehmen Mannigfaltigkeit ihre eigene Melodien in der Stimme und Gesang haben, durch deren, ich weiss nicht, was für eine geheime Vertraulichkeit der Bekantschaft sie erwecket werden."[37]

it actually causes feelings in us; and music has as its own peculiar property thousands of other feelings to which a musical heart is susceptible, but which no orator or poet can awaken through words or moving delivery. In this latter case music is not a copy of nature, but the original itself. Music is a universal language of nature which is only intelligible to harmonious souls. And its peculiar expressions, which it does not borrow from anywhere else, have a secret understanding with these souls. Not only the emotions and passions which form the content of poetry and oratory, but a thousand other feelings, are subject to musical expression, which however cannot be named or described because they are not subjects of oratory. Whoever's soul is gifted with such a secret sympathy experiences this most inner pleasure. The soul of Augustine was such a soul, therefore he wrote out of his own experience that "all emotions, by virtue of their pleasant variety, have their own melodies in the voice and in song, through which they can be aroused by means of some kind of secret affinity."

What Ruetz is really intent upon attacking is Batteux's insistence on the clear intelligibility of music's content. He fears that Batteux will lead some "young fop" to expect music to be as intelligible as an "understandable speech." (Batteux had demanded as much.) But since music has only to do with the "faculty that has to do with feeling and desire," it cannot fulfill neoclassic expectations. Hence, these expectations only provide ammunition for the "enemies of music." Music must be felt, not understood, Ruetz insists. (One wonders if he had been reading Baumgarten or Meier.)[38]

A misguided determination to translate sounds into intelligible or verbalizable meanings would destroy, Ruetz argues, the genuine act of appreciative listening itself:

> Dies ist die schlechteste Art der Zuhörer, die man nur immer haben kann, welche an statt sich den Empfindungen zu überlassen, alles erkläret haben wollen. Was soll denn dieser Satz bedeuten? Was will dieser Lauf, dieser Harfensprung vorstellen? Was für eine Leidenschaft enthält diese Figur? Was bedeutet dieser Gang? Wer eine gute Musik nicht fühlen kann, noch will, dem kann es gleich viel seyn, was dieser oder jener Satz bedeute. Man erfinde zuvor eine Sprache, dadurch man eine jedwede Empfindung benennen, und von andern unterscheiden kann.[39]

> That is the worst kind of listener there could ever be, who instead of abandoning himself to feelings, wants to have everything explained. Now what does this phrase mean? What does this run, this leap represent? What kind of a passion is contained in this figure? What does this passage mean? It makes no difference what this or that phrase means, if a person cannot feel good music, or is not willing to. First, let somebody invent a language which can name each and every feeling, and which can distinguish each one from the others.

Ruetz's closing remark must not be overlooked. On two other occasions in his short essay he made the same point: not only is it impossible to specify music's content verbally (for which music might reasonably be faulted), but that content itself—the very stuff of man's emotional life—is untranslatable into words. "No language," wrote Ruetz, "is able to give every specific emotion contained in music its own name."[40]

The neoclassic passionate utterance theory of musical expression was singled out by Ruetz as especially inimical to the practice of musical art as he knew it. Recalling Batteux's insistence that music should be as understandable as a speech, and perhaps focusing on Batteux's statement that "the tones of music are half-formed in the words," Ruetz conceived of Batteux's theory as a "declamatory" utterance theory where music imitated the inflections of oratorical or theatrical delivery. Thus he attacked Batteux's account of musical expression by showing the

poverty of declamation as an object for musical representation. Ruetz characterized the utterance theory as an inhibition of music's peculiar riches and beauties:

> Soll die Declamation eines Redners diejenige Schönheit seyn, die ihm zum Urbilde dienen soll:
> so kann er damit nicht weiter kommen, als zum Recitativ; zu einer Arie wirds nimmer
> zureichen. Und warum soll die Musik sich nur mit geringern Schönheiten behelfen, da sie selbst
> die grösste Schönheit der Natur in Tönen und im Klange ist?[41]

> If the declamation of an orator is supposed to be that beauty which serves as (the composer's)
> model, then he will never get any farther than the recitative; an aria will never be attained. And
> why should music help itself only to lesser beauties, when it is itself the greatest singing and
> sounding beauty in nature?

Batteux had so construed nature that it stood in opposition to the riches of musical
art, to which Reutz was attached by affinity and profession:

> Heisst Natur hier so viel nur als die Art der näturlichen Ausprache eines Affects, so stehet diese
> Meinung dem Reichthum der Musik entgegen, als welche weit mehr Töne und Zusammenfü-
> gungen in sich enthält, als alle Arten der Modulation der Stimme, womit eine Leidenschaft im-
> mer in einer ordentlichen Rede mag ausgesprochen werden.[42]

> If nature here means no more than the natural utterance of an affect, then this opinion stands in
> opposition to the riches of music, which contains more tones and combinations than does any
> kind of vocal inflection whereby a passion is expressed in ordinary speech.

To limit music's expressions to representations of the language of the everyday
world and the pulpit was for Ruetz to destroy the very beauty of music, to bury
treasure.[43] Like Luther, he treasured music's otherworldly nature. But a man of his
times, he also characterized music's peculiar special riches as themselves part of
nature; they were, indeed, ''the greatest beauty of nature.'' Clearly Batteux's
account of nature was amiss; if nature violated musical art, then nature must have
been misconstrued.

Batteux's insistence that music should be just as intelligible as a coherent discourse entailed several specific demands in addition to the overall demand for clear
intelligibility. Ruetz rejected each in turn. One was that each and every sound
should have a meaning. Why must we vainly attempt, Ruetz asked, to name a
''specific object'' for all the musical ideas, events, and ornaments that form part of
a normal piece of music? It is enough, Ruetz asserted, that the main character of the
piece was communicated.[44] Indeed Ruetz felt that if the identifiable content of
music was limited to the four emotions of love, joy, sadness, and ill will, then that
was enough.[45] For music's peculiar prowess was in communicating the subtle and
the unnamable.

Another demand of Batteux's was that the meaning of each sound should reinforce the meaning of the whole, that is that unity of content is essential. Ruetz
interpreted this neoclassic ''rule of unity'' to mean in the case of music that all the

musical ideas contained in an aria had to have been first stated in the opening ritornello. But Ruetz wanted to defend the usefulness of transitional and contrasting passages, typical features of much of the music he knew. He felt that such passages could be just as moving as the clearly-defined main idea, which they could actually heighten or clarify (as Baumgarten would have said) by means of contrast:

> Kann man denn die kleinen Zwischensätze, die zur Ausfüllung, Verbindung, Abwechselung dienen, nicht mit eben der Leidenschaft empfinden, als die Hauptsätze, denen sie doch nicht widersprechen dürfen, sondern ihnen Raum zum neuen und veränderlichen Eintritt geben?[46]

> Can't one react to the little transitional ideas which function as filling, binding, and contrast with just as much passion as to the main idea, though to be sure they must not contradict it; rather they should provide room for its new and varied appearance.

Ruetz also thought that varied, contrasting, and novel ideas should be allowed just for the sake of ''beliebter Abwechselung,'' in that they conferred a ''flowing, pleasing'' quality on the music.[47] (In each of his defenses of *Abwechselung* Ruetz is careful to add that none of these contrasting ideas should contradict the main theme nor undermine its dominance. His tolerance for contrast would certainly not have extended to the fully developed classical style.)

Finally, Batteux had said that no statement should be or needed to be repeated, because literal repetitions were cognitively redundant, hence boring. But Ruetz answered the demand that all expressions must be ''new,'' with the simple statement, ''That goes against experience.''[48] Like Nicolai, Ruetz appeals to the actual reaction of listeners and to the nature of music as pleasant:

> Wir habens ja gerne, wenn wir in einer Musik einen Satz gehöret, der uns sonderlich gefällt, und besondere Aufmerksamkeit und Vergnügen machet, dass er abermal wieder vorkomme und sich hören lasse.[49]

> We like for a particularly pleasing musical idea which is engaging and enjoyable to return and to be heard again.

Moreover, Ruetz continues, how would the great composers produce great music without repetition of certain subjects or ideas, without imitations, fugal and canonic passages?[50] If Batteux's rules left no room for the hallowed traditions of musical ''art'', then the implication was clear: Batteux was wrong.

In sum Batteux's whole concept of music as a *discours suivi,* and all that it entailed in terms of musical form and intelligibility, was incompatible with the practice of musical art as Ruetz knew it. ''Beliebter Abwechselung'' and ''harmonische Fülle'' were of the very essence of music, and no acceptable theory could proscribe them.

Batteux, as Ruetz was quick to point out, had simply had so little musical experience that he really was manifestly unqualified to prescribe aesthetic goals for music. He had deduced the universal law for all the arts without having sufficient experience in, or knowledge of, music; and then he had turned around and used this deduction with a lopsided base as a prescriptive law for all the arts.[51] Music was being put to unfair tests, and failing; or worse, being distorted so as to pass them.

Johann Adam Hiller (1728-1812), leader of Leipzig's concert life for 30 years, and an important early composer of *Lieder* and *Singspiele,* wanted to promulgate Batteux's ideas in order to improve musical practice. In his essay of 1754, "Ueber die Nachahmung der Natur in der Musik,"[52] he firmly asserts that "Batteux is right," that all music is indeed an imitation of nature and that all music must represent the affects. However, by emphasizing some of Batteux's themes more than others and by putting his own German musician's interpretation on specific points, Hiller comes up with a view of music that is significantly different from the neoclassic doctrine, of which Batteux was the acknowledged representative. Hiller ends his essay by coming to the conclusion that an independent and worthwhile instrumental music could in fact be reconciled with Batteux's theory of imitation, and that instrumental music does not have to imitate vocal music in order to achieve aesthetically respectable status, as many critics from Mattheson to Koch[53] were to announce.

Hiller begins his essay by strongly affirming the basic role of imitation of nature in the generation and production of works of the fine arts.[54] But already here we sense Hiller's revisionism with regard to neoclassic doctrine. For Hiller interpreted Batteux's account of man's natural drive to imitate to include the strange, the unnatural, and the novel, qualities not readily reconciled with neoclassic standards. Hiller explained that nature herself was too boring to satisfy man's natural drive for constant pleasure; all men respond to the inner command, "Amuse thyself!"[55] Something strange and foreign would answer our needs—something between the natural and the unnatural. Thus, while recognizing that nature was the model for man's creations, Hiller identifies the unnatural and the novel as the potent elements in these creations. He saw that man was proud of his creative capacity and took pleasure in it. He really characterizes not a pleasure in imitation, but a pleasure in novel creations. But Batteux was against creating: "Inventer dans les Arts, c'est ne point donner l'être à un objet, c'est le reconnoitre où il est et comme il est."[56]

Hiller subscribes on the whole to Batteux's passionate utterance theory of musical expression. But like Ruetz he seems quite uncomfortable with the idea that music merely imitates utterances. Rather, Hiller prefers to say "A tone is feeling itself," and that music *is* an utterance.[57] Music did not originate in the imitation of anything; music is a fundamental human expression which really requires no object.

> Liegt nicht der Grund der Musik nicht in den Menschen selbst? Woraus besteht die Musik? Aus Tönen. Wo sind die Töne her? Sind sie dem Menschen nicht so natürlich, dass er sie verschie-

den, wenn er will, hervor bringen kann, ohne sich lange nach einem Muster zur Nachahmung um zu sehen?[58]

Doesn't the basis of music reside in man himself? What does music consist of? Tones. Where do the tones come from? Are they not so natural to man that he can produce a variety of them without having to look around for a model to imitate?

In other words, the first principle of music is not imitation, but the feelings as they are naturally expressed through inarticulate utterances of passion.[59] Hiller has not abandoned Batteux altogether. Their difference is mostly one of emphasis. A more serious divergence occurs though when Batteux calls into question the appropriateness of the impassioned utterance theory itself

Es ist wahr, die Sprache des Herzens ist entweder nicht sonderbar reich, oder auch nicht bestimmt genug. Es sind etliche Töne, und immer dieselben wieder. Da hingegen die Musik zu unendlichen Veränderungen geschickt ist. Sie würde ausgelacht werden, wenn sie beständig aus einem Tone gehen wollte.[60]

It is true, the language of the heart is not especially rich, nor are the tones musical pitches. There are a few tones, and always the same ones again. Music however is capable of infinite variations. It would be ridiculed if it constantly based itself on one tone.

Hiller did not share Batteux's intense concern for intelligibility. For he gives an impassioned description of music's effects which bypasses any mediation of the powers of intellectual cognition, and which omits any reference to the significance of man's natural utterances. Music's power to move the listener's heart is viewed independently of its power to represent namable, even knowable affects, and independently of the need for rational recognition of the affect represented:

Die Musik wird Natur seyn, wenn dieses von ihr eingenommen wird: Sie wird es aber nicht seyn, wenn das Herz dadurch zum Eckel gebracht wird. Die Musik hat geheime Zugänge zu dem Herzen, die wir noch nicht entdecket haben, und die wir vor ihr zu beschützen nicht im Stande sind.[61]

Music is nature when the heart is swayed by it. But music is not nature when it is repugnant to the heart. Music has secret avenues to the soul which we have not yet discovered, and which we cannot protect against music's entry.

It appears that Hiller is going to keep only Batteux's words but abandon his meaning altogether. For Hiller's "geheime Zugänge" are part of that tradition reaching back to Augustine's *occulta familiaritas*. He shared with Ruetz, who was on the other side of the imitation debate, a common heritage which no allegiance to French aesthetic dogma could apparently erase. For both, music's affective power was accepted without dependence on the cognition of a represented content. Also, both men shared a perception of man's emotional life, and music's ability to affect it, which made Batteux's and Gottsched's insistence on clearly intelligible content seem absurd. Hiller explains that music has a special ability to suggest subtle and refined aspects of feeling which would get lost in the heavy tumult of powerful emotions. Not only are these feelings more easily felt than labelled, they are almost unknown, Hiller writes, verging on Romantic agnosticism and even on the Freudian concept of the subconscious. Like Nicolai, Krause, and Ruetz, he appeals to experience. If one actually observed one's own or someone else's reactions to music, wouldn't it be apparent that we experience feelings for which there is no name? For one could only say for sure that one was attentive and that one was pleased:

> Man gebe Achtung, auf das, was in dem Herzen bey Anhörung mancher Musiken vorgehet. Man ist aufmerksam, sie gefällt. Sie suchet weder Traurigkeit noch Freude, weder Mittleiden noch Wuth zu erregen, und doch werden wir von ihr gerühret. Wir werden so unvermerkt, so sanft von ihr gerührt dass wir nicht wissen, was wir empfinden; oder besser, dass wir unsrer Empfindung keinen Namen geben können. Dieses Gefühl der Töne ist uns unbekannt, aber es erwecket uns Vergnügen, und das ist uns genug.[62]

> Let one observe what happens in the heart when most music is played. One is attentive, the music pleases. It seeks to arouse neither sadness nor joy, neither compassion nor rage, and yet we are moved by the music. We are moved so unconsciously and gently that we do not know what we feel; or better, we cannot give our feeling a name. We do not recognize this feeling brought on by tones, but it gives us pleasure, and that is enough.

Here Hiller touches on the problem of using words as indicators of our knowledge of the emotions, and on the relation of this problem to the rightful demands which could be put on music. This was a rather novel insight in 1755, and was to become part of the Romantic view.

It is interesting to note that Hiller used Batteux's authority to buttress his own feeling that it was enough that the heart be moved. He virtually paraphrased Batteux's "La coeur a son intelligence indépendamment des mots." But in contrast to Batteux's strongly qualified use of this statement (he had said that one still sensed the object of representation even if one could not name it), Hiller uses it to sanction an extended and impassioned account of how music arouses unnamable, and even unknown, feelings in the soul with no reference to an object of imitation whatsoever. And nowhere does Hiller emphasize the balance of Batteux's dogma, namely that music must have a "distinct sense, without obscurity."

Hiller comes to discuss instrumental music only at the end of his essay. After having explained that church and theater music must represent the passions, and after having advised composers on the intricacies and pitfalls of *Tonmalerei*, Hiller writes that he could almost conclude his treatise except for the fact that there is still one other type of music which he hasn't considered because it really can't be easily subsumed under the doctrine of imitation:

Die Melodie des Solo oder Concerts, wenn man es allemal eine nennen kann, ist nicht so wohl ein nachgeahmter Gesang der Leidenschaften und des Herzens, als vielmehr eine nach der Beschaffenheit des Instruments, worauf gespielt wird, eingerichtete künstliche Verbindung der Töne, von deren Richtigkeit man mehr die Kunst als die Natur muss urtheilen lassen.[63]

The melody of a solo or concerto, if one can call it such, is not so much an imitation of the song of the passions and of the heart, as it is an artful combination of tones arranged according to the nature of the instruments that are played and judged as correct more in accordance with art than with nature.

Hiller seems here to have established a good basis on which to reject instrumental music, but he soon finds himself trying to find a niche within the imitation doctrine for this musical anomaly.

Hiller had ambivalent feelings about instrumental music. In an extended discussion of the qualities of contemporary instrumental compositions he uses such negative epithets as "sheer jugglery," "irregularity and bombast," "artificial nonsense," "meaningless masterpieces," "serious-seeming child's play," and "unintelligible mishmash." He objected particularly to its unvocal and virtuosic character.[64] And in marking instrumental music as more artificial than natural he places it in a category which was the acknowledged opposite of the verisimilitudinous (the quality possessed by all accurate imitations of nature): instrumental music for Hiller constituted "das musikalische Wunderbar." Hiller concurred with the neoclassic critics that the wonderful was "a dangerous cliff" for the arts, and that for some time the arts had been lost in a night of "bombast and barbarity."[65] And he disapproved of musicians who sought not so much to move as to arouse wonder and astonishment. But he does not want to condemn "the wonderful in music" absolutely, in spite of the fact that its use has led to abuses.

As we recall, *das Wunderbare* was a concept used by the Swiss and by Baumgarten and Meier in opposition to *das Wahrscheinliche,* that is, to oppose the process of fantasy and invention to that of truth and imitation, to oppose the world of gods and heroes to the real world. It is significant that Hiller used the same concept to label the prevailing characteristic of the instrumental music of his time. It was nonrepresentative, and placed great emphasis on inventiveness and art at the expense of imitation and the natural tone of passion. It contained many style features unknown to vocal music, wedded by nature to man's natural vocal utterances. By implication Hiller has said that instrumental music doesn't fit under the imitation of nature doctrine. Thus, that Hiller would adopt this concept of the wonderful and apply it to instrumental music, and that he would give it a positive, though carefully qualified, role to play, represents a compromise, a loosening of the bonds of strict neoclassic theory. Certainly he wouldn't have agreed with Gottsched's hostile condemnaion of instrumental music with its "wonderful arrangements of tones," or with his rejection of opera because it violated the rule of verisimilitude. Hiller clearly had sympathies with the Swiss. For in spite of the limits he put on the use of the wonderful Hiller was quite enthusiastic about its use in music:

Das Wunderbare ist in der Poesie von grosser Wichtigkeit. Es gehet mit Göttern und Helden um, und erhebt sie bey nahe über den Rang menschlicher Künste. Man muss also auch das Wunderbare der Musik nicht ganz nehmen. Man muss es nur gehörig zu bestimmen und einzuschränken suchen. Sie erhebt sich dadurch, wie die Poesie, zu einer fast göttlichen Würde, weil es uns ubegreiflich scheinet, dass es ein Mensch so hoch habe bringen können. Sie erfüllt uns in diesem Augenblicke mit Erstaunen und Bewunderung.[66]

The wonderful in poetry is of great importance. It has to do with gods and heroes and virtually soars above the level of the human arts. One must not therefore completely reject the wonderful in music. One must only try to define it and control it. It then rises, as does poetry, to an almost divine dignity, because it seems incomprehensible to us, that a man could have achieved so much. It fills us in this moment with astonishment and wonderment.

Hiller is referring to both the heights of compositional skill and the heights of performing ability. Both arouse *Bewunderung* and astonishment. But since these are strong emotions, and man is more drawn to the gentler feelings, the composer must return at times from the supernatural and wonderful to the natural and moving. Only this combination of the natural and the wonderful will obtain ''both the wonderment of the ears and the approval of the heart.''[67]

One aspect of Hiller's qualified defense of instrumental music is his explicit rejection of the rule, which he says he has always heard, that instrumental music must imitate vocal music, and that the idiom of the concerto or solo is limited to what can be sung by the human voice.[68] Hiller makes the point that vocal music is already an imitation of the ''natural tone of passion,'' and that it makes more sense for instrumental music to take the natural tone of passion itself as its model than some other artistic imitation of that tone. Moreover, by freeing instrumental music from a vocal model it can exercise its peculiar ''advantages'' and ''freedom'':

Warum verweiset man die Instrumente nicht eben so wohl, wie die menschliche Stimme auf den natürlichen Ton der Leidenschaft? Es ist wahr, sie werden hier weniger nachzuahmen finden; sie werden aber desto mehr Freyheit in der Nachahmung selbst erhalten. . . . Man hat alles heraus werfen wollen, was nicht dem menschlichen künstlichen Gesange ähnlich war. Dieses heisst in der That zu weit gegangen. Man hat diese musikalischen Stücke dadurch eines Vorzuges beraubet, dessen Verlust der Musik selbst gleich nachtheilig ist.[69]

Why are not instruments directed to the natural tone of passion, as is the voice? To be sure, they will find less to imitate; but they will also gain all the more freedom in imitation itself. . . . One has wanted to discard everything that wasn't like a composed human song. But that was going too far. One has thereby robbed instrumental music of an advantage the loss of which is detrimental to music itself.

Hiller clearly wants to bring instrumental music, an accepted form of art, under the jurisdiction of the imitation rule, but he is not willing to constrict the art of instrumental music any more than is necessary.

Hiller concludes his treatise with a prescription for the composition of concertos and solos (a common name for what we today call sonatas) which he believes will provide both for the imitation of nature as well as for those unvocal qualities peculiar to instrumental music which cannot easily be construed as representative:

> Den Plan der Concerte und Solo entwerfe demnach, wie zu andern musikalischen Stücken, allemal die Natur. Er sey allemal ein Gesang, der die Empfindungen des Herzens künstlich auszedrücken bemüht ist. Man schliesse aber das Wunderbare nicht davon aus. Man bringe wohlgewahlte Sprünge, Läufer, Brechungen und dergleichen, an gehörigen Orten, und in gehöriger Maasse an; so wird der ohnfehlbare Beyfall aller Zuhörer, so wohl der Kunstverständigen, als derer die sie nicht verstehen, der Musik unter dem Künstler zugleich Ehre machen.[70]

> Let one design the plan of concerto just as other musical compositions, in accordance with nature. Let it always be a song which endeavors to express artfully the feelings of the heart. But do not exclude the wonderful. Let one use, in the appropriate place, at the appropriate time, well-chosen leaps, runs, arpeggios and the like; then will the unfailing applause of all listeners, not only connoisseurs but also those who do not understand music, bring both the composition and the composer fame.

Notice that despite Hiller's comments above to the effect that instrumental music does not have merely to imitate vocal music, he still thinks of truly expressive music as a ''song which artfully expresses the feelings of the heart.'' He has not really altogether abandoned Batteux's passionate utterance theory.

It is only to be expected, despite the allowances in his thinking for a purely musical art of special significance, that Hiller should give, in keeping with his contemporaries, vocal music the higher aesthetic status. And his reasons stand well within the neoclassic tradition, and are clearly reinforced by Hiller's proclaimed allegiance to the ideas of Batteux. In short, neither Batteux nor Hiller denies to tones a significance, an expressive power (this was accepted by all except those of Pluche's and Gottsched's persuasion); but words were considered necessary to explain the affects, their motivations and other specifications, in order to make the content of music clear and intelligible. Therefore instrumental music is inferior to vocal music:

> Worte also und Töne, zu einem Zwecke genau vereinigt, sind der Charakter der Vocalmusik, und hierinnen übertrift sie alle Instrumente. . . .
> Die Instrumentalmusik erhält von der Vocalmusik eine bestimmtere und gewissere Bedeutung, wenn diese wieder von jener Zierde und Nachdruck zugleich erhält. Wie schön ist diese Vereinigung und wie viel vermag sie nicht über unsere Herzen![71]

> The uniting of words and tones towards one goal is the character of vocal music, and herein it excels all instrumental music. . . .
> Instrumental music gains from vocal music a more determinate and certain meaning, while the latter gains from the former ornament and emphasis. How beautiful is this union, and how it can rule our hearts!

Before rendering his judgement Hiller admits that in fact one tone can express a passion and that instruments can indeed imitate this passionate tone as well as the voice, and, accordingly, that vocal music and instrumental music are equal in this respect. This is perfectly in keeping with Batteux's belief in the meaningfulness of sheer tones. But Hiller explains that man has a need to explain himself when he is deeply moved and that he therefore naturally prefers to use language to explain himself more extensively. Batteux had not really explained his preference for vocal music, nor had he really treated the aesthetic problem of instrumental music's status. We have Hiller then to thank for sympathetically attempting to explain instrumental music within a mimetic framework. Not all partisans of instrumental music held Gottsched's extreme views of instrumental music, which were also supposedly based on Batteux's theory. But despite Hiller's attempt, there remained many unanswered questions about instrumental music as an art with emotional content and import.

Carl Wilhelm Ramler (1725-1798) translated Batteux's complete *Cours de belles lettres,* which included his famous work of 1746. Ramler's translation of 1756-58 appeared in many editions, one appearing as late as 1802.[72] A poet active in the Berlin of the fifties, his name came to be identified with Batteux's. In 1760 Marpurg published Ramler's translation of that part of Batteux having to do with music along with Ramler's commentary.[73]

Ramler agrees with Batteux in most respects. For example, Ramler asserts with Batteux that only depictions can move us. And Ramler warns his readers that music is in danger of being led into excesses, into ''wondrous inventions where the tones bump against each other, without purpose and without meaning'' and that music must return to an ''artful depiction of human passions.''[74] But Ramler is led, in the problematic case of music, to make a few alterations in Batteux's account.

Ramler defends the capriccio, a musical genre which many, he admits, might have rejected as meaningless. He writes that if these pieces are found pleasing then one cannot simply say that they are without meaning. Ramler's defense is very reminiscent of Mattheson. For capriccios arouse wonderment and curiosity and these are indeed affects:

> Denn auch die Verwunderung und die Neubegierde sind Affecten, und selbige werden durch gute Capriccios sehr erreget, und befriediget. Das Wahrnehmen mehrerer Dinge, die uns noch nicht vorgekommen sind, und die Befriedigung des Triebes, den wir haben, immer mehr Sachen zu erkennen, können unsere ganze Seele erschüttern und einnehmen.[75]

> For even wonderment and curiosity are affects, and are aroused by good capriccios. The perception of a multitude of things which have never occurred to us before, and the satisfaction of the drive which we have to be always encountering new things, can shake up our whole soul.

It seems that Ramler, just like Hiller and Ruetz, has blurred together music's affective and representative roles. And, like Hiller, he is describing more a pleasure in novelty and inventiveness than one in imitation of reality.

An even more important exception is taken to Batteux when Ramler inquires as to the source of music's content and as to the whereabouts of its model in nature. Batteux had said that nature provided all the qualities necessary for all the most beautiful imitations. But Ramler observes that there are few occasions when we naturally sing or play, whereas the other arts can indeed find their models in nature:

> Allein für den Musikus scheint keine solche Natur vorhanden zu seyn. Bloss seine Erfahrung in musikalischen Ausdrücken vertritt derselben Stelle.[76]

> But there seems to be no such nature for the composer. Solely his experience with musical expressions must take its place.

Ramler spoke of the composer's memory of "eloquent gestures" as his most important resource.[77] Thus even Ramler saw that the nature of music suggested certain alterations in the imitation theory; indeed Ramler's substitution of musical experience for nature seems to undercut Batteux's most fundamental point about music. But, predictably, Ramler did not draw any further conclusions from this.

Another important literary figure, Gotthold Ephraim Lessing (1729-1781), recorded a few thoughts on music which are important for our study. Lessing was a central figure in eighteenth-century German literary culture; he is credited with steering Germany away from French literary models and the neoclassic rule-bound formulations of Aristotle, and onto a newer road: Shakespeare, not Corneille—genius, not the rules—became the new guides. In his *Laokoön: oder über die Grenzen der Mahlerey und Poesie* (1766), one of the most important works of eighteenth-century German criticism, Lessing successfully challenged the traditional maxim *ut pictura poesis* by showing that the literary arts and the plastic arts have their own peculiar means of expression, which determine in part the very content a given art can successfully communicate. For example, painting is limited to the portrayal of physical bodies, and poetry is more suited to the portrayal of actions. Each art has its own natural "limits" and its own peculiar problems of expression.

It is unfortunate that such an important figure in the history of criticism as Lessing did not examine music's specific strengths and weaknesses in the *Laokoön,* for they constitute one of the themes of our study. But on one occasion he did suggest the nature of music's peculiar problem: unmotivated affective variety and contrast. This occasion was his review of Agricola's music to Voltaire's *Semiaramis* in the *Hamburgische Dramaturgie.*[78]

He begins his review with a long verbatim quotation from Scheibe as to how the symphony must conform to the dramatic action that follows. (Lessing explains his lengthy borrowing by saying that since musicians were always complaining that literary men demanded too much of music, it would be best to have a musician express these "rules.") Then he is led into a discussion of musical expression, lamenting that no philosopher has come along to derive the "universal principles" of musical expression. While musical expression depends in the final analysis on genius and not the rules, Lessing still finds tantalizing the idea that valid generalizations could be made from practice. It is from theatrical instrumental music, he suggests, that such generalizations could best be made, since in vocal music the words are a crutch for the composer and the most ambiguous expressions are made definite only by the words; whereas in instrumental music the meaning is of necessity more distinct:

> Der Künstler wird also hier seine äusserste Stärke anwenden müssen; er wird unter den verschiedenen Folgen von Tönen, die eine Empfindung ausdrücken können, nur immer diejenige wählen, die sie am deutlichsten ausdrücken.[79]

> The artist must in this case apply his utmost skill and diligence; he will choose from among the various successions of tones which can express a feeling only those which express it most distinctly.

Lessing was clearly responsive to instrumental music, going so far as to say that it could express its content distinctly; indeed he put high value on intelligibility. He held moreover that the secrets of this intelligibility could be generalized from the empirical observation of the best examples. Rejection of rationalistic neoclassic prescriptions did not mean for men like Lessing a complete abandonment of the intellectualism of Enlightenment.

In the long quotation from Scheibe, which Lessing included to provide a musician's support for his own ideas, a typical trait of instrumental music is mentioned, one with which we shall be more and more concerned—the trait of variety:

> Da übrigens die Musik zu den Schauspielen bloss allein aus Instrumenten bestehet, so ist eine Veränderung derselben sehr nötig, damit die Zuhörer desto gewisser in der Aufmerksamkeit erhalten werden, die sie vielleicht verlieren möchten, wenn sie immer einerlei Instrumente hören solten.[80]

> Since moreover the music for plays consists only of instruments, a change in the instrumentation is very necessary so that the attention of the listeners will be maintained, for they might lose it if they should always hear the same kind of instruments.

It is significant that Scheibe, the musician, mentioned the need for a certain degree of variety as following upon the very nature of the symphony as sheer sound. For it is this very question of variety that Lessing isolates as music's peculiar problem. But unlike the remark by Scheibe (which is to be sure more suggestive of broader claims than important in itself) which justifies variety, Lessing views variety and especially contrast as elements which are difficult to justify in a music composed of sounds alone.

Lessing begins the body of his review by attempting to explain why Agricola's music between the acts is so satisfactory. It consists of just one movement, which is related only to the closing dramatic situation of the act just ended. The alternative for the composer would have been to include a second contrasting movement which would have anticipated the act to come. But this would not work, for one reason because it would rob the dramatist of the unexpected and the surprising. The second reason, which follows from what Lessing called the "boundaries of music," was that such a change from one affect into an opposing one could not be understandably accomplished by means of tones alone, for music lacks the means, namely distinct concepts, to bind together and provide the motivating explanations for these "disorderly," "contradictory" feelings.[81] Words, on the other hand, can make clear not only the "what" but also the "why" of such sudden transitions. They can also take us most gradually, with no unpleasant leaps, through transitions from one feeling to an opposing one. Music presents however another case:

> Itzt zerschmelzen wir in Wehmut, und auf einmal sollen wir rasen. Wie? warum? wider wen? wider eben den, für den unsere Seele ganz mitleidiges Gefühl war? oder wider einen andern? Alles das kann die Musik nicht bestimmen; sie lässt uns in Ungewissheit und Verwirrung; wir empfinden, ohne eine richtige Folge unserer Empfindungen wahrzunehmen; wir empfinden wie im Traume; und alle diese unordentliche Empfindungen sind mehr abmattend als ergötzend.[82]

> Now we are melting with woefulness, and all of a sudden we are supposed to rage. How so? Why? Against whom? Against the very one for whom our soul was just full of sympathy? Or against another? All these things music cannot specify; it leaves us in uncertainty and confusion; we have feelings, but without perceiving in them a correct sequence; we feel as in a dream; and all these disorderly feelings are more exhausting than delightful.

Here in a nutshell is expressed the confusion caused by the new contrast-dominated style of instrumental music. If music is to be the expression of the emotions, and Lessing clearly heard it that way, how can such contrast make sense; how can the listener perceive a "correct sequence of feelings"? Just as for Gottsched (Lessing's archenemy), who could appreciate the "inanimate sounds" of a French characteristic dance but not those of an Italian sonata, it was the illogic in the sequence of events which was for Lessing the main barrier to intelligibility. For there were many, and Lessing is one example, who could accept the limited specificity of a given musical expression, but who could only perceive the affective contrasts and sudden transitions of the new style as chaos. Also, at least in Lessing's case, it seems that he was attached by profession to the dramatic determinants of plot, motive, subject and object. To him emotional expression without these things was simply not meaningful or effective, as Sulzer was later to agree.

From these observations on variety and contrast in music follow a few remarks on the aesthetic status of instrumental music. Unlike the rationalistic neoclassic critics, Lessing did not fault instrumental music for indeterminateness of its meanings. Lessing takes care to make this point clear:

> Denn es ist bei weitem nicht so notwendig die allgemeinen unbestimmten Empfindungen der Musik, z.E. der Freude, durch Worte auf einen gewissen einzeln Gegenstand der Freude einzuschränken, weil auch jene dunkeln schwanken Empfindungen noch immer sehr angenehm sind.[83]

> For it is not at all necessary to restrict with words the general, indeterminate feelings of music, such as joy, to a certain single object of joy, because even those obscure, uncertain feelings are still very pleasant.

Lessing even admits, at the risk of contradicting his strong emphasis on distinct intelligibility, that he finds these vague general meanings pleasant. However when contrasting or contradictory feelings were to be expressed, words were necessary and this was the greatest service which words rendered music:

> In der Tat ist diese Motivierung der plötzlichen Übergänge einer der grössten Vorteile, den die Musik aus der Vereinigung mit der Poesie ziehet; ja vielleicht der allergrösste.[84]

> Indeed this motivation of sudden transitions is one of the greatest advantages which music derives from the union with poetry—perhaps even the very greatest.

Lessing felt, then, that music by virtue of its specific nature could not intelligibly express contrasting emotions. Accordingly, the expressive potential of music had limits: instrumental music was not free to express sudden transitions and bold contrasts, because these would be unintelligible. And intelligibility was very important to the Enlightened Lessing. He concluded his review with the principle that the more intelligibly a composer expresses the content of his piece, the more praiseworthy he is.

Lessing made a significant contribution to music criticism when he identified the new music's widely experienced problems of intelligibility as stemming from its characteristics of unbridled variety and strong contrasts. For some time people had been saying that words were needed to make the content of instrumental music clearer, when often, as in Gottsched's case (and he objected to indistinct meanings as much as anyone), it was the incoherence, and not the indeterminateness, of music's content which made the Italian pieces so unintelligible. But Lessing is not inclined to find a respectable rationale for the new instrumental style, so his critical insight is limited to defining a problem. Rather than attempt to explain the new practice, he condemned it.

Since Lessing is purportedly writing a review of a symphony, he uses the occasion to express his concerns about contemporary symphonic compositions. In keeping with his principle that contrast is unintelligible in instrumental music, he laments the growing custom of including contrasting affects. Although he rejects the rules of unity in the theater, he demands unity in the symphony; and notice that this demand for unity applies not only to individual movements but to the symphony as a whole:

> Eine Symphonie, die in ihren verschiednen Sätzen verschiedne, sich widersprechende Leidenschaften ausdrückt, ist ein muskalisches Ungeheuer; in *einer* Symphonie muss nur *eine* Leidenschaft herrschen, und jeder besondere Satz muss nur eine Leidenschaft, bloss mit verschiednen Abänderungen, es sei nun nach den Graden ihrer Stärke und Lebhaftigkeit oder nach den mancherlei Vermischungen mit andern verwandten Leidenschaften, ertönen lassen und in uns zu erwecken suchen.[85]

> A symphony which expresses in its various movements different, self-contradictory passions, is a musical monster; in *one* symphony must only *one* passion prevail. And each individual movement must give voice to and arouse in us only one passion, varying it only according to the degrees of its strength and liveliness or according to various mixtures with other related passions.

Lessing's "monster" is reminiscent of Gottsched's "hermaphrodite"; both epithets apply to the new Italian instrumental style. Lessing goes on then to praise Agricola's symphony for its unity. He concludes his discussion of the symphony with a plea for coherence, within as well as between movements. A composer who creates a work where he suddenly breaks off the first affect, to introduce another totally different one, only to launch into a third yet again different one, can perhaps "surprise, deafen, and tickle" the listener but he will never move him. Coherence *(Zusammenhang)*, Lessing insists, as did Batteux, is just as important in speaking to a person's heart as it is in speaking to his understanding. Without coherence the best music is a "vain sandpile", incapable of any lasting impression.[86]

It was, then, Lessing's concern with contrast as music's peculiar problem that led him to reject the contrast-dominated style of the newer symphonies. Certainly many of Lessing's contemporaries found these new instrumental works quite acceptable and not in the least confusing. But few were the critics who could show that contrast might have a nobler and more meaningful aesthetic role than mere ear-tickling. The following chapter will examine the ideas of three such critics.

5

Contrast, Change, and the Worth of Instrumental Music: Sulzer—Junker—Forkel

The three men to be discussed in this chapter all still believed that music should represent and communicate emotion to the listener. All believed music was a "language of the emotions." But they went beyond previous thinkers in trying to account for the temporally changing character of musical art, and in justifying aspects of the new "contrast-dominated style." They realized that an engaging, interesting piece of music could hardly be explained as the mere imitation of passionate utterance, although all three still bore some allegiance to the utterance theory. They realized too that the traditional utterance theory of musical expression as such had little to say about musical form, and they all sought to see elements of musical form as possessing expressive significance. In the process they were brought to new understandings of the function of instrumental music.

Newer, more dynamic theories of the emotions and new, less didactic theories of musical morality played important roles in bringing about this new understanding. It was these theories which were to provide the basis for a new appreciation of the previously perplexing variety and contrast of the new Italian instrumental style, and to help build an understanding of the art of instrumental music in general. What was Lessing's "confusion" became transmuted into Sulzer's "sublimity," Junker's "magnificent middle-thing," and Forkel's representation of the "manifold modifications of the emotions." Also, with the new theories came a recognition that music had an ability to do certain things and not others, and that music had a significance worthy of but different from the verbal or pictorial arts. The yoke of inappropriate verbal standards began to be lifted. Sulzer, Junker, and Forkel all intimated certain aesthetic attitudes which played a role in the Romantic attachment to instrumental music. Nevertheless, all three believed that instrumental music was inferior to vocal music because it lacked the specificity and intelligibility of content which only words could bring.

For Sulzer instrumental music failed the canons of beauty because it could not specify the affect of a piece precisely; but this recognition led him to classify the symphony in a perhaps more appropriate aesthetic category—that of the sublime.

Junker faulted music for similar reasons, but recognized that music's strength lay in portraying the transitions between emotional states. Then Forkel, who saw the emotions not as a collection of entities but as a continuum of constant change or transition, vindicated the whole of musical art by declaring it the best vehicle for the depiction of this complex emotional continuum. With this new emotional theory, which adumbrates the *Seelenlehre* of Wackenroder, the demand for namable emotional content was undercut by the recognition that life itself did not provide such known quantities. None of the three men, however, was prepared to relinquish his representational requirement; and as a result vocal music was still considered superior. This relinquishing came only in the nineties with new aesthetic theories elevating the importance of form above that of content.

Of all the arts, wrote Johann Georg Sulzer (1720–1779) in his monumental encyclopedia of the arts, only the graphic arts originated as imitations of nature. Rhetoric, poetry, music and dance, however,

> sind offenbar aus der Fülle lebhafter Empfindungen entstanden, und der Begierde, sie zu äussern, sich selbst und andere darin zu unterhalten.[1]

> clearly arose out of the fullness of lively feelings, and the desire to utter them in order to maintain oneself and others in this state of feeling.

Quite aware of his opposition to neoclassic premises, Sulzer explained that the first poets, singers, and dancers had "expressed real feelings which they found in themselves, not imitated feelings."[2] The suggestion was clear: the literary and musical arts were not imitations but expressions. But whereas we might have expected this new premise and this new awareness of the limitations of the imitation doctrine to lead to a more sympathetic account of music's aesthetic role, Sulzer in fact imposed the same inappropriate and problematic standards on music as had the earlier French critics: it must represent, and it must do so in a clearly intelligible manner. A negative evaluation of instrumental music followed from these demands; nevertheless, Sulzer adumbrated certain developments which eventually proved favorable to positive evaluation of instrumental music. In the first place, although the utterance theory played a central role in his account of musical expression, he recognized the severe limitations of the passionate utterance theory when it came to explaining the temporal dimension of music. To fill in the breach, he called upon the Baumgartnian elements in his background, and explained music not only as an art which expressed passion, but also as an art whose function was to engage the lower cognitive powers. Secondly, he took a few halting steps in the direction of evolving a less static, more dynamic *Affektenlehre* and anticipated Wackenroder's *Seelenlehre*; in so doing he made some suggestions as to the relation of musical form to musical expression. Most significantly of all, he took that aesthetic anomaly, the symphony, and by in effect subsuming it under the category of the sublime rather than the beautiful, he suggested a whole new way of viewing this blatantly nonrepresentative art form, a way which he still felt was perfectly in keeping with his other premise: that the arts must contribute to the moral good of society.

Sulzer spent eighteen years preparing his *Allgemeine Theorie der schönen Künste* (1771, 1774).[3] And although it is said that his opinions never progressed from the Berlin of the 50's, the views he put forth in his first German encyclopedia of the arts were read, discussed, and cited as authoritative for several decades after their initial publication in the early seventies. His views seem to have summed up, articulated, and even strengthened the anti-French, anti-imitation, but also very moralistic, strain in German thinking about the arts in the latter half of the eighteenth century. Sulzer received academic training at the Zürich gymnasium in theology, mathematics, and philosophy. His career as a teacher in Berlin, first at the Joachimsthalische Gymnasium and then at the Ritterakademie, as well as his membership in the Akademie der Wissenschaften from 1763 to 1773, brought him into contact with Lessing, Krause, and other prominent intellectuals of the *Aufklärung*.[4] Seldom original or even consistent in his thinking, his encyclopedia nevertheless provides us with revealing and useful syntheses of various views current in the Germany of the latter eighteenth century which bore upon the aesthetic function and status of instrumental music and the other arts.

Sulzer's "universal theory" is difficult to classify. For one thing, he relied to an unknown extent upon the advice and even editing and authorship of others with more specialized knowledge in certain areas. We do know that in the case of musical articles Johann Phillip Kirnberger and J. A. P. Schultz were his assistants. Nevertheless, it is generally agreed that the aesthetic viewpoint expressed must be held to be Sulzer's own.[5] And even allowing for the inconsistency of viewpoint possibly attributable to the work of a plethora of pens, Sulzer's thought can only be described as incorrigibly eclectic, if not altogether self-contradictory at times.

Certainly Sulzer would have classified himself as standing in the tradition of Baumgarten, and as a member of the anti-French, anti-imitation forces of Germany's eighteenth century artistic awakening. Like Baumgarten he saw the arts as addressing the powers of indistinct rather than distinct cognition. The arts, they both held, were for the feeling, willing, "moral" man, not the "thinking man." The form of the good must be felt, not merely known; for the arts must make man active for the good.[6] Sulzer also puts special emphasis on the cultivation of the attention, on the ongoing temporal aspects of form, on vivid and specific imagery, and on variety and *Abwechselung* as they help to engage the lower powers of feeling and willing. But unlike Baumgarten, Sulzer places strong emphasis on the didactic element of art; in other words, he uses Baumgarten's notion of "sensual power" as a tool to condition men to love the good and abhor evil.

Sulzer possessed a strong allegiance to the notion of art as spontaneous outpouring; but this allegiance was conditioned by his moralistic and even mimetic inclinations. For at the same time as the artist was to engage in the spontaneous outpouring of feelings he was to exert moral leadership, to "impart the good" and to "spread abroad important truths."[7] And while Sulzer adamantly rejected the notion that the literary and musical arts were imitative, on one occasion he reminds his readers that even a musical composition is judged according to its representation of a model (*Urbild*).[8] Art is described both as an outpouring "out of the fullness of lively feelings," and in other places as the "representation of morals."[9] And although in one article Sulzer sentimentally identifies the best content for music as that which proceeds from an "aufgeschwollenes Herz," he says elsewhere that artistic invention is the work of the understanding, that the artist in moving the passions must be led by *Verstand* and *Weisheit* if not to appear frivolous, and that the diligent and discerning *Studium* of the passions and of nature is necessary to compensate for the excessive tendencies of *Feuer*.[10] Thus the vision of art as essentially an outpouring is severely circumscribed by the boundaries of the real, the reasonable, and especially the good. For the one element which runs consistently through Sulzer's work is that the arts are to carry out a moral mission.

Sulzer's account of the moral end of art takes two very different forms. The more predominant one resembles the older, neoclassic view in which the arts were seen as "thinly veiled moral lessons";[11] according to this view the arts are to instill moral wisdom. The other view of art's moral use stems from the Leibnitzian and Baumgartnian account of art as an activator of man's nobler energies, a stimulus to inner spiritual and mental activity. Thus Sulzer spoke both of a "culture of morals," and an "inner culture."[12] It is impossible to make sense of Sulzer's ambivalent views towards the worth of instrumental music without distinguishing these two views.

Sulzer's predominant interpretation of art's moral mission can only be characterized as didactic. (It was on the grounds of its didacticism that his encyclopedia was bitterly criticized by Goethe and his followers.) For Sulzer the highest works of art were those which imparted the stuff of moral knowledge:

> Den wichtigsten Nutzen haben die Werke der Kunst, die uns Begriffe, Vorstellungen, Wahrheiten, Lehren, Maximen, Empfindungen einprägen, wodurch unser Charakter gewinnt.[13]

> The most important artworks are those which impress upon us those concepts, ideas, truths, doctrines, maxims and feelings whereby our character gains.

Sulzer explained, with a decidedly rationalistic bent, that the instructional element in art must be the highest, because "knowledge or enlightenment is the highest good."[14] The means by which art was to further this "culture of morals," as he called it, was the "representation of the moral life of man." Accordingly, the epic and drama were the highest forms of art, just as they were for the neoclassic critics who shared Sulzer's didacticism and his erstwhile allegiance to the mimetic doctrine of art.[15] By this depiction of a character's whole personality, and not just his separate traits (as in the other arts), the audience learns the objective causes of passions and of their moral cosequences.

In den wichtigsten Dichtungsarten, der Epopee und dem Drama, sind die Charaktere der handelnden Personen die Hauptsache. Wenn sie richtig gezeichnet und wol ausgedrükt sind, so lassen sie uns, jede Würkung der äussern Gegenstände auf sie, vorher zu sehen, die daher entstehenden Empfindungen, die Entschliessungen, jede Triebfeder, woraus die Handlungen entspringen, genau zu erkennen.[16]

In the most important literary genres, the epic and the drama, the character of the central personages is the real center of focus. If they are correctly depicted and well represented, they allow us to anticipate every effect of outer objects on them and to recognize exactly the consequent feelings and decisions—every motive from which action arises.

Thus the depiction of moral character is seen to lead to an understanding of moral character and hence to moral action itself.

Despite this rather rationalistic emphasis on the moral wisdom acquired through art, Sulzer also makes it clear that the mechanism through which man's morals are cultivated is not a rational one, but a sensual one. And here Sulzer dilutes the neoclassic character of his didacticism with a touch of the new science of the senses, "aesthetics." For, like Baumgarten, Sulzer believed that the arts spoke not to man's faculty of knowing, but to his faculty of feeling. Baumgarten's theory could be easily reconciled with Sulzer's insistence on the moral mission of art (which up to now has seemed rather rationalistic), since Baumgartnians generally acknowledged that distinct cognition had no effect on the faculty of desire, and desire for a given object was generally taken as the cause of moral action. In order then to make the truth not merely known, but "active," the character of the good must be *felt*—only by this means could the faculty of desire be affected.[17] Now whereas cognition is clear or obscure, distinct or confused, feelings are only pleasant or unpleasant. Thus we have as Sulzer's most concise statement of his position:

dass die Lenkung des Gemüths, durch angenehmer und unangenehmer Empfindungen, die Hauptabsicht der schönen Künste sey.[18]

that the chief intent of the arts is the steering of the soul by means of pleasant and unpleasant feelings.

What Sulzer's method of steering the soul amounted to was a kind of conditioning. Like nature, the arts used pleasure and pain as "spurs"; by endowing morally desirable objects with pleasant attributes and undesirable objects with replusive features, the arts could work through man's faculty of feeling to make him shun evil and desire virtue.

Und darin besteht der höchste und edelste Zwek der schönen Künste. Sie reizen die Empfindung zwar vermittelst der äussern Sinnen, aber nicht durch blos sinnliche Gegenstände. Sie legen der Vorstellungskraft Gegenstände der klaren Erkenntniss vor, und in diese legen sie den Reiz zu

angenehmen und widrigen Empfindungen, damit der nicht blos thierische, sondern vernünftige
Mensch das Gute and Böse kennen, jenes suchen und dieses vermeiden lerne.[19]

And therein consists the highest and noblest goal of the fine arts. To be sure they charm the feelings by means of the exterior senses, but not by means of merely sensual objects. They present
to the imagination objects of clear cognition, into which they lay the charm of pleasant and unpleasant sensations, so that not only the merely animalian but also the reasonable man can become acquainted with the good and the evil, and learn to seek the former and shun the latter.

Art, the medium of sensual communication, was then to endow the objects of the
good and the true with "sensual power." By this "Zauberkraft" of art, through
this conditioning, men are lead to "know" that virtue, the good, has pleasant consequences, hence is desirable, and that evil has unpleasant consequences, hence is
to be avoided.[20] And since these truths have been impressed upon the lower cognitive faculty, the seat of passions and desires, this sensually-reinforced moral wisdom will make man "active" for the moral life. In the case of the epic or drama,
this meant that by arousing emotion in the audience by the depiction of passionate
objects, and by achieving the sympathetic participation of the audience in the experiences of the characters, they would learn the lessons of the characters themselves. Through vicarious experience they would feel the unpleasant and pleasant
consequences of certain passions and the appealing or abhorrent nature of various
passionate objects (fame, fortune, beautiful women, power, and such); and this
experience would lead man to knowledge as well. Thus despite the sensual means
of moral culture, there can be no doubt that Sulzer envisioned an intellectual har-
vest. He constantly emphasized that works of art should produce knowledge:
"That the knowledge of man which is attained through the accurate representation
of passionate scenes is a most important matter requires no proof."[21] Music, lacking the ability to specify the object of a passion and unable to provide the dramatic
situation wherein the listener could be morally educated through vicarious participation, was bound to suffer under Sulzer's didactic standard of artistic worth. Sulzer called music the most sensual of the arts.

Sulzer's account of the moral mission of art did not rely only on this didactic
element in art, by virtue of which the epic and drama were labelled the "most important" forms of art. Sulzer had an alternate account of the morality of art which
was to form the basis for a whole new way of viewing the worth of nonrepresenta-
tional music such as the "grand symphonies with their manifold elements," so
relished by the Romantics. According to this alternate account, "the most important use" of art was to strengthen, stimulate, and exercise the "active powers of
the soul":[22]

Die würkenden Kräfte der Seele, die, wodurch der Mensch zu einem thätigen Wesen wird, sind
sein vornehmstes Gut. Alles, was diese unterhält, was sie reizet und stärket, muss ihm wichtig
seyn; denn dieses ist die eigentliche Nahrung des Geistes, wodurch er seine Gesundheit erhält
und seine Kräfte immer vermehrt.[23]

The active powers of the soul, through which man becomes an active being, are his prime possession. Everything which occupies them, which stimulates and strengthens them, must be important to him; for herein lies the true nourishment of the mind and spirit, from which his powers constantly increase.

Sulzer called the activity of these inner powers of the soul man's "true inner wealth." It elevated him above a mere animalian existence. And, most importantly, it was this activity which constituted the ground of all moral action and spiritual health. For the moral man was a man of action, and action came from *Seelenkräfte*, not from mere intellectual knowledge, nor from mere refined sensibilities. According to this account, not moral truths but certain well-balanced and active inner tendencies were the foundation of morality.[24] Let us call this account of art's morality Sulzer's "humanizing and activating" account. It bears not a few resemblances to the ideas of Leibnitz and Baumgarten. We recall that Leibnitz saw man's perfection in the power to act; and Baumgarten had argued for the value of the arts because they "animated the whole man." Similarly, Sulzer saw the arts as stimulating an increase in the strength of these innate human powers, until man approached a "state of perfection."

One of the primary qualities isolated by Sulzer as contributing to this perfection was *Abwechselung*. "Variety in ideas and feelings" seemed to be a natural need of the reasonable man.[25] This natural drive for activity (which brings to mind Dubos's ideas) he saw as containing the seeds of man's perfection because it stimulated the *Seelenkräfte*:

Dieser Hang zu Abwechselung trägt sehr viel zur allmähligen Vervollkommnung des Menschen bey; denn sie unterhält und vermehret seine Thätigkeit und verursachet eine tägliche Vermehrung seiner Vorstellungen, die eigentlich den wahren innern Reichthum des Menschen ausmachen. . . . Je Mehr man die Lust abgewechselter und mannichfaltiger Vorstellungen genossen hat, je stärker wird das Bedürfniss, folglich das Bestreben die Anzahl derselben zu vermehren. Daher kommt es, dass der Mensch allmählig jedes innere und äussere natürliche Vermögen, jede Fähigkeit brauchen lernt; dass er sich allmählig dem Zustande der Volkommenheit nähert, um alles zu werden, dessen er fähig ist.[26]

This predilection for change contributes very much to the gradual perfection of man. For it sustains and augments his activity and causes a daily increase in his ideas, wherein man's true inner wealth consists. . . . The more one has enjoyed the pleasure of changing and diverse ideas, the stronger will be his need and consequently his striving to increase them. Therefore it happens that man gradually learns to use each inner and outer capacity, each ability, so that in order to become everything he is capable of he gradually approaches the condition of perfection.

It was as if nature herself contained the plan and devised the means for man's nobility and perfection. A man's natural sensitivity and natural desire to be active, to use his inner *Seelenkräfte* was sustained by the beauties of nature. Through our sensing of the varied colors, forms, and voices of nature

wird ein zarteres Gefühl in uns rege, Geist und Herz werden geschäfftiger, und nicht nur die grobern Empfindungen, die wir mit den Thieren gemein haben, sondern auch die sanften Eindrüke werden in uns würksam. Dadurch werden wir zu Menschen; unsere Thätigkeit wird vermehrt, weil wir mehrere Dinge interessant finden; es entsteht eine allgemeine Bestrebung aller in uns liegenden Kräfte; wir heben uns aus dem Staub empor, und nähern uns dem Adel höherer Wesen. [27]

a more gentle feeling is aroused, mind and heart become more active, and not only the coarser feelings which we have in common with the animals but also the gentle impressions are awakened. Thereby we become men; our activity is increased because we find more things interesting; there arises a general exertion of all our powers; we rise out of the dust and approach the nobility of higher being.

Sulzer frequently warned that a state of mere refined sensibility was not in itself sufficient. To be sure sensitivity (*Empfindsamkeit*) is a necessary step towards moral as well as human perfection; and it is a primary task of art to cultivate this sensitivity. But too much *Empfindsamkeit* is a bad thing, it makes a man inactive, "soft, weak, and effeminate." [28] Merely ingratiating and entertaining pleasures such as a cool summer breeze or a landscape painting, and much instrumental music, could not attain the humanizing and activating goal of art.

What aesthetic quality was it then which stimulated most powerfully this drive to inner activity and which raised art above the merely entertaining or sensitizing? Drawing upon the concepts of English criticism, Sulzer calls it "the grand" or " the sublime." This quality alone takes art above the gently ingratiating by providing strong "masculine" spiritual exercise:

Die Werke des Geschmaks, die uns blos zum angenehmen und wollüstigen Genuss reizen, die der Phantasie und dem Herzen sanft schmeicheln, ohne sie jemal zu erschüttern, ohne sie aufzufodern, die würksamen Kräfte zu brauchen, sind Lekerbissen, die keine Nahrung geben, und deren Genuss allmählig alle Lebhaftigkeit, alle Kraft der Seele auslöscht. Nur das Grösse unterhält und stärkt alle Seelenkräfte; es leistet dem Geiste den Dienst, den der Körper von starken, männlichen Leibesübungen hat; wodurch er immer gesunder und stärker wird. Die Kräfte der Seele müssen, wie die Leibeskräfte, in beständiger Uebung unterhalten werden; der stärkste Geist kann in Unthätigkeit versinken, wenn er lange Zeit nichts um sich siehet, das seine Würksamkeit auffodert. [29]

Works of art which stimulate a merely pleasant and sensual enjoyment, which gently flatter the fantasy and the heart without even shaking them up, without inciting them to use the active powers, are like candies, which give no nourishment and the enjoyment of which gradually extinguishes all liveliness and all strength of the soul. Only the grand sustains and strengthens all powers of the soul; it does for the spirit what strong masculine physical exercises do for the body, whereby it becomes healthier and stronger. The powers of the soul must be maintained by constant exercise, just as bodily powers; the most intelligent mind can sink into lassitude if for a long time it sees nothing around which incites its activity.

Although Sulzer treats the two concepts in separate articles, he explains that the difference is only one of degree, and he often uses the two concepts interchange-ably.[30] He defined the grand in art as that which stimulated our *Seelenkräfte* to strong exertion in order to understand it in its entirety. Examples in literature would be the wrath of Achilles or a "boldness which sees no danger." The sub-lime goes even beyond our ability to gråsp; it has an element of incomprehensi-bility. Even apparent contradictoriness is a desirable aesthetic quality when it forms part of the sublime; for the more difficult something is to understand, the more our inner powers exert themselves in trying to understand it.[31] It affects us most powerfully and "shakes us up." The sublime exceeds our expectations and arouses wonderment; it is that which is

> in seiner Art weit grösser und stärker als wir erwartet hatten; weswegen es uns überrascht und Bewunderung erwecket. . . . Das Erhabene würkt mit starken Schlägen, ist hinreissend und ergreift das Gemüth unwiderstehlich.[32]

> in its way far greater and more powerful than we had expected it to be, for which reason it sur-prises us and arouses wonderment. . . . The sublime works with strong blows, transports us, and grips us irresistably.

Accordingly, Sulzer concludes, the sublime must only be used for arousing power-ful reactions—"when one wants to incite the powers of the soul or to hold them back with force."[33] Given then that the activity of these inner powers of the soul is man's greatest treasure, and the foundation of all useful social action, Sulzer calls the sublime and the grand the "highest" in art.[34] This represents some divergence from his position that those arts which taught the most were the highest. Thus one account of art's morality emphasizes precepts and the other process. Sulzer never addressed, or even acknowledged, this inconsistency in his view, and we shall see that this ambivalence carries over into his views on instrumental music.

Sulzer's views on music were determined by his belief in the moral mission of art. Just as a "mere play of the passions," or merely "laughing and dancing pic-tures" were insufficient to Sulzer's view of ennobling art, so in music was the "merely transitory ear-tickling" considered typical of Italian instrumental music.[35] It was Sulzer's didactic account of art's moral function that played the predominant role in determining his evaluation of instrumental music. According to this account, the moral function of music was to arouse the passions, and through this arousal to instill desire for the good and abhorrence of evil. For it was the passions which were the spurs to action.

A passion, according to Sulzer and to contemporary psychology, was a feel-ing of desire for, or revulsion to, a given object. The person suffering the passion was accordingly impelled towards or repelled from some "object," such as a woman, wealth, or death, and would act accordingly.[36] Thus one important way in which the arts could arouse a passion was by depicting one of these so-called pas-sionate objects. An object would be depicted with such "sensual power" that it aroused desire or disgust, and then the intended passion would be aroused, such as love, rage, dread. And a knowledge of what was good and what was bad would result. The more specifically or precisely these passionate objects are depicted, the more knowledge they could impart. However, instrumental music, lacking such precise means of depiction, was considered inferior to the literary arts in that it could not achieve a moral end in such a precise and effective manner.[37] In the article "Instrumentalmusik" Sulzer uses this argument to brand instrumental music as inferior.

Sulzer identified another manner in which music could arouse the emotions: by representing actual utterances of passion. In this case the listener is brought to sympathize with the utterer and is then moved to the same passions himself. At one point Sulzer virtually limits music to this alternative path to moral efficacy:

> Die Musik hat ausser der Schilderung leidenschaftlicher Auesserungen, nur wenige leiden-schaftliche Gegenstände in ihrer Gewalt, weil ihr eigenliches Geschäfft in dem Ausdruck der Empfindung selbst nicht der Schilderung der Gegenstände besteht.[38]

> Music has, besides the depiction of passionate utterances, only a few passionate objects in her power, because its real business consists in the expression of feeling itself, not in the depiction of objects.

But the more details we are given as to the cause and object of this passionate utterance the more it affects the listener and the more the listener learns from his vicarious experience. Thus we react more strongly to an utterance of passion in vocal music than to an emotional utterance in instrumental music.[39] Representation was to move the listener and moving was to improve him. Conversely, in order to improve the listener the artist must move him and in order to move him he must according to Sulzer, depict either passionate objects of passionate utterances. The moral and representational obligations of music were only two sides of the same coin. Thus when Sulzer writes,

> Der richtige Ausdruk der Empfindungen und Leidenschaften in allen ihren besondern Schattir-ungen ist das vornehmste, wo nicht gar das einzige Verdienst eines vollkommenen Tonstükes.[40]

> The correct expression of feelings and passions in all their characteristic shadings is the chief, if not the only, merit of a perfect musical composition.

we must remember that this emotional expression was not to be enjoyed or in-dulged in for its own sake, but that it was to function as a means towards achieving the highest goal of art, the inculcation of moral wisdom. A painting of a beautiful sunset, or a musical work which fills our ears with a series of harmonious tones, had no moral use or significance for Sulzer because it did not arouse the passions by either representing passionate utterances, or by representing passionate objects.[41]

Sulzer's insistence that music express feelings and passions might appear to be a forward-looking pre-Romantic prescription. To be sure, his frequent definition of music as a "Sprache der Empfindungen" ("language of the feelings"), is a very suggestive one. But if we examine Sulzer's statements carefully, it becomes clear that his doctrine of musical "expression" has little to do with the Wordsworthian spontaneous overflow of powerful feelings.[42] As indicated above, Sulzer held that music "expressed" the passions by imitating the tones of passionate utterance. Indeed he subscribes to the passionate utterance theory of musical expression also espoused by Dubos, Batteux, and the Encyclopedists, including Rousseau. "Expression" in music meant for Sulzer not self-expression in the nineteenth-century sense, but the imitation of passionate utterances—the imitation of emotional expression, so to speak. The concepts of both depiction and expression are mingled together in Sulzer's definition of melody:

Das Wesen der Melodie besteht in dem Ausdruck. Sie muss allemal irgend eine leidenschaftliche Empfindung, oder eine Laune schildern. Jeder, der sie hört, muss sich einbilden, er höre die Sprache eines Menschen, der, vor einer gewissen Empfindung durchdrungen, sie dadurch an den Tag leget.[43]

The essence of melody is expression. It must always depict some particular passion or mood. Anyone who hears it must imagine that he is hearing the speech of a man who is immersed in a certain feeling, and that he is making it known.

Like the French critics, he based his expression theory on the wisdom of the ancient rhetoricians, as this paraphrase of Cicero shows:

Jede Leidenschaft hat nicht blos in Absicht auf die Gedanken, sondern auf den Ton der Stimme, auf das Hohe und Tiefe, das Geschwinde und Langsame, den Accent der Rede, ihren besondern Charakter.[44]

Every passion has its peculiar character, not only with regard to its thoughts, but also with regard to the tone of voice, whether high or low, fast or slow, and the inflections of speech.

Given this specific character of each emotion, it is then incumbent upon the composer to investigate the "tone" of all the passions, to "view men only in this light."[45] The composer will then achieve "correctness of expression" if he observes most precisely the facts gained from his study—facts such as the following:

Die Freude spricht in vollen Tönen mit einer nicht übertriebenen Geschwindigkeit, und mässigen Schattirungen des Starken und Schwächern, des Höhern und Tiefen in den Tönen. Die Traurigkeit äussert sich in langsamen Reden, tiefer aus der Brust geholten aber weniger hellen Tönen. Und so hat jede Empfindung in der Sprache etwas eigenes.[46]

Joy speaks in full tones without exaggerated speed and moderate shadings of loud and soft, of high and low. Sadness is uttered in slow speech, in not so bright tones, which are drawn from deep within the breast. Thus every feeling has its characteristic manner of speech.

These tones which arise naturally out of man's emotional states and whose meaning is understandable independently of words are "passionate tones," also called by Sulzer (after Dubos and Batteux) "natural signs of the passions."[47] We understand them just as we can understand the emotional content of a passionate utterance in a foreign language.[48] The meaning of an *Angstgeschrey*, for example, is universally understood. All music is based on the power of these inarticulate tones to express the passions.[49] Melody is defined as "a series of passionate tones";[50] and these tones are utterances:

> Die einzelne Töne, woraus der Gesang gebildet ist, sind Auesserungen lebhafter Empfindungen.[51]

> The individual tones which constitute a melody are utterances of lively feelings.

Thus, all the suggestive but vague terms Sulzer used in speaking of music's significance—"Sprache des Herzens," "empfindungsvolle Rede," "Sprache die uns die Aeusserungen eines fühlender Herzens verräth," "Sprache der Leidenschaften," "empfindungsvolle Rede"—all refer to a single theory of musical expression: the depiction (Batteux would have said "imitation") of the natural, understandable, utterances of passion. It seems only fitting that the eclectic encyclopedist managed to integrate the functions of imitation and expression. The utterance theory, in Sulzer's formulation, served both the traditional representational requirements, and at the same time, by emphasizing emotional expression, it fit the Sturm und Drang view of art as emotional outpouring.

Strong as Sulzer's attachment to the passionate utterance theory was, he recognized that it was insufficient to explain the whole temporal extent or purpose of a musical composition. This was a significant step away from the neoclassic roots of this utterance theory. If music were only the utterance or language of feeling, writes Sulzer, then a few bars would suffice "to express a feeling so definitely and correctly that the listener could recognize quite precisely the mood of the singer."[52] For feeling itself is a simple thing and can express itself with only a few tones. But, Sulzer firmly asserts, this sheer utterance of feeling is "not the intention of music":

> Wenn also ein Tonstück nichts anders zur Absicht hatte, als eine Empfindung bestimmt an den Tag zu legen, so wäre eine solcher kurzer Satz, wenn er glüklich ausgedacht wäre, dazu hinlänglich. Aber dieses ist nicht die Absicht der Musik; sie soll dienen den Zuhörer eine Zeitlang in demselben Gemüthzustande zu unterhalten.[53]

> If therefore a piece of music had no other intention than to make a feeling definitely known, such a short phrase, if it were felicitously conceived, would suffice. But this is not the intention of music; it must serve to maintain the listener for a period of time in the same emotional condition.

But in order to maintain the listener in "the same feeling" one could not simply repeat the same utterance over and over; it would be too boring and the listener's attention would falter.[54] Viewed in another light, simple expression of passion, as it naturally occurs in a temporal series of utterances, is too formless to engage the attention, and to involve the listener. Compared to music it is formless and disorderly:

> Hatte die Musik keinen andern Zwek, als auf einen Augenblik Freude, Furcht, oder Schreken zu erweken, so wäre allerdings jedes von vielen Menschen zugleich angestimmte Freuden- oder Angstgeschrey dazu hinlänglich. Wenn eine grosse zahl Menschen auf einmal frohlokend jauchzen, oder ängstlich schreyen, so werden wir gewaltig dadurch ergriffen, so unregelmässig, so dissonirend, so seltsam und unordentlich gemischt diese Stimmen immer seyn mögen. Da ist weder Grundsatz noch Regel nöthig.
>
> Aber ein solches Gerausche kann nicht anhaltend seyn, und wenn es auch dauerte, so würde es gar bald unkräftig werden, weil die Aufmerksamkeit darauf bald aufhören würde.[55]

> If music had no other aim than to arouse joy, fear or terror in one instant, then certainly any cry of joy or distress from many men at the same time would be sufficient. For when a great number of men rejoice happily at once, or scream with anxiety, that grips us powerfully, no matter how irregular, how dissonant, how strange or how disorderly this mixture of voices may be. For that neither principle nor rule is necessary.
>
> But such a noise does not maintain itself continuously, or if it did continue, it would quite soon lose its power over us, because the attention would cease to he held.

Like Baumgarten and Meier, in their discussions of aesthetic method, Sulzer was concerned to show that the formal poles of chaos and boredom must be avoided if the listener's attention and hence the power of music was to be maintained. Sulzer recognizes clearly the insufficiency of the passionate utterance theory to explain an artfully constructed music composition. He describes music's function not only in terms of the imitation of passionate utterance and of intelligibility, but also in terms of the basic formal elements of unity and variety, as they are manifest over a period of time.

Indeed, Sulzer asserted that musical form is a result of music's goal of entertaining, that is, stimulating the attention and sustaining ''one and the same'' emotion over a period of time. Avoidance of boredom while maintaining unity of affect became a primary task of the composer:

> Also müsste mann ein Art des Gesanges erfinden, in welchem ein und eben dieselbe Empfindung, mit gehöriger Abwechselung und in verschiedenen Modifikationen, so oft könnte wiederholt werden, bis sie den gehörigen Eindruck gemacht haben würde.
>
> Daher ist die Form der meisten in der heutigen Musik üblichen Tonstüke entstanden, der Concerte, der Symphonien, Arien, Duette, Trio, Fugen u. a.[56]

> Thus one had to discover a kind of melody in which one and the same feeling could be repeated with appropriate contrast and with various modifications until the desired impression would have been made.
>
> From thence has arisen the form of most current contemporary music—concertos, symphonies, arias, duets, trios, fugues, etc.

Sulzer also spoke, in a Baumgartnian vein, of the listener's viewing the feeling "from all sides."[57]

Given then that music's task was to sustain a single emotion, entailing a considerable amount of thematic unity, how was the attention to be kept? What was to be the source of music's variety? Evidently for Sulzer a prime source of variety was to proceed from the craft of thematic development. It was just this skill which Sulzer saw was absent from most current Italian instrumental music, and which was needed to provide interest over a period of time and to avoid the boredom of simple-minded harmony, or the confusion caused by a mishmash of contrasting and unrelated, incoherent ideas:

> So sieht man in den Werken einiger Tonsetzer, entweder, dass sie durch ein ganzes Stük denselben Gedanken immer in andern Tönen wiederholen, dass die ganze Harmonie auf zwey oder drey Accorden beruhet; oder im Gegentheil, dass sie eine Menge einzeler, sich gar nicht zusammenpassender Gedanken hinter einander hören lassen. Nur der Tonsetzer, der das zu seiner Kunst nöthige Genie hat, weiss den Hauptgedanken in mannichfaltiger Gestalt, durch abgeänderte Harmonien unterstützt, vorzutragen, und ihn durch mehrere ihm untergeordnete, aber genau damit zusammenhangende Gedanken so zu verändern, dass das Gehör vom Anfang bis zum Ende beständig gereizt wird.[58]

> Thus one sees in the works of many composers either that they always repeat the same idea throughout a whole piece, that the whole harmony rests in two or three chords, or, to the contrary, that they stick a crowd of indivdual thoughts one after the other which do not at all fit together. Only the composer who has the necessary genius for his art knows how to present the main idea in diverse forms, supported by various harmonies, and to vary the main idea by means of several subordinate ideas which nevertheless cohere precisely with it in such a way that the ear is constantly charmed from beginning to end.

The simplicity of modern Italian instrumental music, as well as the trend to mixtures of opposing and highly contrasting ideas (such as the sublime and the trivial) seem to be Sulzer's targets here.

In propounding his theory of emotional expression and maintenance Sulzer said little about the nature of the emotions themselves. Sulzer subscribed rather uncritically to the traditional doctrine of the emotions as static, homogeneous, separable and classifiable entities, or "affects." He subscribed as well to the notion that a given musical piece expressed only one of these "affects." As we have seen, change and variety in a piece did not come from any changes or variety of affective content; rather other types of variety were seen as necessary to maintain the listener in "one and the same feeling." As with Mattheson, a musical piece was viewed as a temporal prolongation of a timeless affective entity. Musical compositions, even instrumental compositions, Sulzer pointed out, must have a "definite character"; and by that he meant a homogeneous, coherent, and intelligible affective content.[59] And since the affects themselves were considered distinct and knowable, Sulzer could require correctness in emotional expression; the justice of this requirement rested on Sulzer's announced faith (a faith he shared with the neoclassic critics) in the Ciceronian maxim that for each passion there is a corresponding tone and gesture through which it is known.

Thus, Sulzer gives many prescriptions as to how to express this emotion and that. He counsels the artist to study diligently how the various affects are expressed. The patterns of temporal unfolding characteristic of emotional experience did not enter into this traditional doctrine of the passions, or *Affektenlehre*. As we saw, Sulzer held that the whole affective content of a piece could be expressed in a few measures, with a few passionate tones. By virtue of these views Sulzer was certainly more of an apologist for the older style than for the newer contrast-dominated one described by Burney. Unlike the theories of Junker and Forkel, Sulzer's basic theory of emotional expression and maintenance did not require the propounding of any novel view of the emotions. His conservative view was hallowed by long use and required no justification.

However, Sulzer, ever the eclectic, was also a man of his time. There is much talk, in keeping with the new, "refined" taste that was becoming prevalent in Germany, and in keeping with the spirit of *Empfindsamkeit*, of the "finest shadings" of the emotions, of the "finest nuances," and of the necessity for "correct" musical expression to reflect these subtleties "precisely."[60] Good performance approaches the character of the "language of the passions." to the degree that these subtle shadings are expressed through dynamic nuance.[61]

Most significantly, we see in Sulzer glimmerings of a newer, more dynamic emotional theory, and an attempt to relate the temporal and changing character of the emotions to musical form. On occasion he describes the form of a musical composition as reflecting, even derived from, the changing nature of the emotions over a period of time. In discussing the appropriateness of the da capo form to the expressions of various emotions, Sulzer observes that frequent repetitions are only suitable to the expression of "certain feelings and passions in which the soul always revolves, so to speak, around only one point."[62] Such repetitions are unnatural in cases

> wo die Vorstellungen sich beständig ändern, nach und nach stärker, oder auch schwächer werden, oder gar allgemach in andere übergehen.[63]

> where the emotional content is constantly changing, becoming gradually more intense, or more delicate, or even changing into something else altogether.

Though not novel (if we recall Krause's attempt to relate emotional form to da capo form), we have at least here a recognition of the relation of musical form to emotional form and to the changeability of some emotions.

Elsewhere Sulzer develops the idea further. He speaks of following the man in a state of passion "through all developments of the affect";[64] and of changing the meter and the harmony when feelings or thoughts take a new turn. And in the article "Leidenschaften" Sulzer emphasizes that the depiction of the passions must be in accord with

> den verschiedenen Graden ihrer Stärke, von den ersten Regungen an, wodurch sie entstehen, bis auf den höchsten Grad ihre vollen Ausbruchs.[65]

> the various degrees of their intensity, form their first stirrings, from which they arise, all the way up to the point of their complete climax.

In short, the artist must tell the whole story of a passion; for a passion has within it a temporal progression, a shape, a form; and in order to depict a passion accurately the artist must take this temporal unfolding into account. But, Sulzer warns, such changeableness in emotional portrayal must not degenerate into a "romantic" "play of passions"; rather it must reflect "the genuine developments and multiple changes which are appropriate to each passion."[66] There is acceptable and unacceptable variety; accuracy of emotional portrayal is the test.

Sulzer becomes most specific in relating musical form to emotional expression when he discusses phrase lengths in the article "Melodie." He begins by giving straightforward correspondences between certain emotions and certain phrase lengths, in the manner of the traditional *Affektenlehre*; for example, longer phrases are appropriate to more serious passions. But he ends by showing how the dynamic shape of certain emotional states can also be reflected:

> Dieses aber muss in Absicht auf den Ausdruk noch gemerkt werden, dass durch Abwechselung längerer und kurzerer Einschnitte sehr merklich könne gemacht werden, wie eine Leidenschaft allmählig heftiger und ungestümer wird, oder wenn sie mit Ungestüm anfängt, nach und nach sinket.[67]

> One more thing must be noted with respect to expression, namely, that it can be made very evident by means of alternation of shorter and longer phrases how a passion becomes gradually more intense and more turbulent, or how it gradually subsides.

Despite Sulzer's use of such non-Romantic aesthetic concepts as "science" and "imitation," Sulzer at one point, in order to describe music's ability to express emotion, invokes the Romantics' favorite metaphor for emotional life—the stream—with its suggestion of fluid movement and temporal progression:

> Es giebt Leidenschaften, in denen die Vorstellungen, wie ein sanfter Bach, einförmig fortfliessen; bey andern ströhmen sie schneller, mit einem mässigen Geräusche und hüpfend, aber ohne Aufhaltung; in einigen gleicht die Folge der Vorstellungen den durch starken Regen aufgeschwollenen wilden Bachen, die ungestüm daher rauschen, und alles mit sich fortreissen, was ihnen im Wege steht. Bisweilen gleicht das Gemüth in seinen Vorstellungen der wilden See, die itzt gewältig gegen das Ufer anschlägt, denn zurüke tritt, um mit neuer Kraft wieder anzupressen.

Die Musik ist vollkommen geschikt, alle diese Arten der Bewegung abzubilden, mithin dem Ohr die Bewegungen der Seele fühlbar zu machen, wenn sie nur dem Tonsetzer hinlänglich bekannt sind, und er Wissenschaft genug besitzt, jede Bewegung durch Harmonie und Gesang nachzuahmen.[68]

There are passions in which the ideas uniformly flow along, as in a gentle brook; in others they stream along faster, with a moderate noise, hopping but without stopping; in some the series of thoughts resembles the wild brook, swollen from heavy rains, which therefore swirls tumultuously and carries everything away with it that stands in the way. Sometimes the soul in its thoughts resembles the wild sea, which at times strikes powerfully against the shore, then recedes, only again to press in with renewed energy.

Music is perfectly able to depict all these kinds of movement, and consequently to make the ear feel the movements of the soul, if only the composer is familiar enough with them and possesses sufficient science to imitate every emotion through harmony and melody.

Unlike the Romantics, Sulzer obviously did not let such fluid notions of the emotions lead him into agnosticism or mysticism with regard to music's content. Musical expression remained something which aspired to total correctness and intelligibility. His writings on music are full of prescriptions for means of expression of this emotion or that. The streams Sulzer describes are for the most part within the various emotional states, not between them. Successful musical compositions resulted from a conscious predetermination of the *Charakter* or *Affect* to be represented.

Sulzer is one of the few writers we have met who attempts to treat extensively the question of instrumental music's aesthetic status. His negative verdict is no surprise, given his predominantly didactic approach to musical morality and his strong allegiance to the impassioned utterance theory of musical expression. Sulzer admits that the whole art of music is based on the power of inarticulate tones to speak the "language of the feelings" without words, and that therefore instrumental music would seem to be the prime manifestation of musical art.[69] But since music and words originated together as passionate utterance and since only by the use of words could music achieve its full power, Sulzer feels instrumental music must in fact be regarded as a secondary manifestation of musical art.[70]

Words make music more powerful because they make it more understandable. It is this understandability which renders vocal music, in Sulzer's view, more moving and hence more morally useful. What words provide is not so much a specification of the passionate tone or of the passion itself (along with Batteux Sulzer attached strong significance to such tones), but an actual dramatic situation, where causes and circumstances of the passion are named. In the article "Instrumentalmusik" Sulzer states this position clearly:

Wir können sehr gerührt werden, wenn wir in einer uns unverständlichen Sprache, Töne der Traurigkeit, des Schmerzens, des Jammers, vernehmen; wenn aber der Klagende zugleich verständlich spricht, wenn er uns die Veranlassung und die nächsten Ursachen seiner Klage entdeket, und die besondern Umstände seines Leidens erkennen lasst, so werden wir weit stärker gerührt.[71]

We can be very moved, when we perceive tones of sadness, pain and suffering in a language unintelligible to us; but when the complaining one speaks understandably at the same time, when he reveals to us the occasion and the immediate causes of his complaint, and makes known the special circumstances of his suffering, then we are moved far more strongly.

Although Sulzer had defined instrumental music as that art which used only inarticulate tones to make its expression "understandable," it seems clear that for Sulzer, as for Lessing, true understandability, hence true affectiveness, entailed knowing of a passion specifically, in Lessing's words, "Why? For what? Towards whom?" It was the dramatic model for emotional expression in the arts that seems to have led both Lessing and Sulzer to demand a musical expression of passions with similar dramatic determinants. Sulzer's interpretation of the moral effect of emotional expression called for vicarious experience, and knowledge gleaned from participation in a dramatic situation where the specificity provided by the dramatic determinants of a subject, cause, motivation, consequence, and especially an object, made the experience more vivid and the resulting lesson more precise.

In the article "Singen," Sulzer focuses particularly on the power of the word to name the passionate "object." It is instrumental music's inability to depict this object that makes it inferior. Sulzer even suggests that words were added to the admittedly expressive tones of music, specifically for their ability to name or depict the passionate object; and the old view that instrumental music is an imitation of vocal music is once again given currency:

Dass das Singen eine weit grössere Kraft habe, uns zu rühren, als jede andere Veranstaltung der schönen Künste, ist unstreitig. Die ganze Kunst der Musik ist eine Nachamung der Singkunst; denn diese hat zuerst Anleitung gegeben, Instrumente zu erfinden, auf denen man die Töne der Stimme nachzuahmen suchte. Hat man es nun auf den Instrumenten so weit gebracht, dass man durch diese blossen Töne so veil Leidenschaftliches ausdrücken kann: wie vielmehr muss nicht durch das Singen ausgedrükt werden können, da es noch die Worte zu Hülfe nimmt, und den Gegenstand nennt, der die leidenschaftlichen Töne verursachet? . . . Denn da das Hülfsmittel der Sprache die Gegenstände der Empfindungen schildern kann, welches die Instrumente allein nicht thun können: so ist das Singen mit der Musik verbunden worden.[72]

Singing is indisputably the most important and essential work of music, in comparison with which everything else which music produces is secondary. That singing has a power to move us far greater than any other form of art is indisputable. The whole art of music is an imitation of the art of singing; for singing originally gave cause for the introduction of instruments, upon which one sought to imitate the tones of the voice. If one has now come so far with instruments, that one can express so much that is passionate through these mere tones, how much more then cannot be expressed through singing since it in addition uses the assistance of words, and names the object that causes the passionate tone? Since the resource of language can depict the objects of the feelings, which instruments cannot do, singing was made a part of music.

The passionate object was important because of its role in the moral functioning of art. The audience was seen to benefit from being conditioned to desire or reject certain passionate "objects." This conditioning process was particularly successful in the case of the *Lied*. Thus of all the genres of music, indeed of all the works of art, Sulzer held the *Lied* to be the most morally efficacious:

> Indem die Künste leidenschaftliche Gegenstände und Leidenschaften selbst kräftig schildern, erweken sie allemal in uns gewisse daher entstehende Empfindungen, und verstärken dadurch allmählig unser Gefühl der Zuneigung, oder Abneigung; denn es ist offenbar, dass wir endlich herrschende Neigung oder Abneigung für solche Gegenstände bekommen, die wir oft mit Vergnügen oder mit Schmerz, Unwillen oder Ekel empfunden haben. Von allen Werken der Kunst scheinen die Lieder in dieser Absicht die grösste Kraft zu haben.[73]

> Insofar as the arts graphically depict passionate objects and passions themselves, they consequently always awaken in us certain feelings, and thereby they gradually strengthen our feeling of inclination or disinclination; for it is obvious that we ultimately receive a prevailing inclination or disinclination for those objects which we have often sensed with pleasure or with pain, displeasure, or disgust. Of all the works of art, *Lieder* seem to have in this respect the greatest power.

Sulzer did not hesitate to draw implications for instrumental music: it was by comparison "artful noise."[74]

Sulzer was willing to admit the self-sufficiency of some instrumental music which expressed emotions, even though sounds alone were incapable of expressing the objects of these passions—but only some:

> Man kann in der That bey Tänzen, bey festlichen Aufzügen und kriegerischen Märschen, die Vocalmusik völlig missen, weil die Instrumente ganz allein hinreichend sind, die bey solchen Gelegenheiten nöthigen Empfindungen zu erweken und zu nähren. Aber wo die Gegenstände der Empfindung selbst müssen geschildert, oder kennbar gemacht werden, da hat die Musik die Unterstützung der Sprache nöthig.[75]

> One can, it is true, completely do without vocal music when it comes to dances, festive pieces, and military marches, because on such occasions instruments all alone are sufficient to awaken and nourish the appropriate feelings. However, when the objects of feeling must themselves be depicted or made recognizable, then music finds the support of words necessary.

Since dances, marches and festive pieces were sufficiently understandable on their own terms and did not require words to perform their function clearly, they were considered by Sulzer instrumental music's "most important genres."[76] And the implication is clear that other forms—Sulzer singles out genres of Italian origin, the solo, concerto, sonata, etc.—are definitely inferior. For whereas dances, marches, and other festive pieces had a clear social function, a definite "use," concertos, trios, sonatas, and such served only the lowly function of practice pieces, or pieces for passing the time. The function of emotional expression in a sonata was problematic in a way that the affective content of dances, marches, and such was not. Whereas dances, marches, and such had by tradition their "well-established character," the Italian genres had "no definite purpose," and their invention was largely a matter of chance.[77] Most of these were nothing other than "a pleasant sounding noise which enters the ear calmly or tempestuously."[78] Thus it was not merely the expression of emotion in music without words, but also the expression of emotion without a traditionally accepted function or character that he found unacceptable.

Although Sulzer lamented the popularity of these new Italian genres, he realized that he could not simply wish them away. He therefore made some suggestions to the composer of these popular forms in the article "Instrumentalmusik." He recommended to the composer of sonatas that before writing he distinctly focus his imagination on the character of a person, a situation, or a passion until he seemed to hear the person in this situation *speak*. A great aid to the composer would be to seek out places in poetry which were "passionate and fiery, or gentle and delicate passages," and to *declaim* them in an appropriate tone.[79] Once again we see the importance of the utterance theory, and of the dramatic determinants found in literary contexts, in conferring significance on music. In the article "Singen," instrumental music is advised to imitate the impassioned vocal utterance which is the essence of music's primary form, vocal music. And in Sulzer's final words of wisdom to the instrumental composer, he holds up understandable impassioned utterance as the one true model of musical representation:

> Er muss nie vergessen, dass die Musik, in der nicht irgend eine Leidenschaft, oder Empfindung sich in einer verständlichen Sprache äussert, nichts als ein blosses Geräusch sey.[80]

> He must never forget that music in which no passion or feeling is uttered in an understandable language is nothing other than mere noise.

We know, of course, from other contexts that Sulzer preferred the meaning of "understandable words" to that of inarticulate, indeterminate passionate utterances.

Sulzer objected to instrumental music not only in principle; he had pointed complaints against the specifically Italian manner of composing specific genres. Even Italian opera displayed the faults of Italian instrumental music. A "meaningless series of tones" resulted from "apathetic variations which only delight the ear" wherein the virtuoso singer displayed his skill. The words were rendered unintelligible, and the "melody itself transformed into an instrumental line." This unaffecting, tasteless style had been taken up in instrumental music as well, and all true and good taste, it was to be feared, would be lost to this utter *Tändeley*. Thus, a vocal form which might have been the highest of all musical forms was being prostituted; and it was the *Lied*, rather than opera, to which Sulzer turned in order to find the realization of music's moral potential.[81]

The Italian forms of the sonata, symphony, and concerto displayed the same degenerate symptoms of meaninglessness and uselessness found in contemporary Italian opera. Although C. P. E. Bach's sonatas aspired to the most profound expressions, most sonatas, and especially those of the modern Italians and their imitators, were nothing but

> ein Geräusch von willkührlich auf einander folgenden Tönen, ohne weitere Absicht, als das Ohr unempfindsamer Liebhaber zu vergnügen, phantastische plötzliche Uebergänge vom Frölichen zum Klagenden, vom Pathetischem zum Tändelnden, ohne dass man begreift, was der Tonsetzer damit haben will.[82]

> a bustling of tones following each other in an arbitrary manner, without further intention than pleasing the ear of insensitive amateurs—fantastic sudden transitions from the happy to the complaining, from the pathetic to the frivolous, without one's being able to know what the composer means by them.

Italian opera overtures—Italian symphonies—are in keeping with the Italians' desire merely to amaze the ear and the eye in their operas: they "merely make euphonious noise" over a drum bass and three chords; and the slow movements are trifles "without force and expression."[83] The concerto, which Sulzer defines as "nothing but an etude for composers and players, and a completely indeterminate, undefined aural delight aiming at nothing more," receives a blanket condemnation from Sulzer. It has "no definite character; for no one can say what it is supposed to represent."[84] If it represents anything, it represents only

> ein lebhaftes und nicht unangenehmes Geräusch, oder ein artiges und unterhaltendes, aber das Herz nicht beschäftigendes Geschwätz.[85]

> a lively and not unpleasant noise, or an artful and entertaining chatter, failing however to occupy the heart.

The only use of the concerto seems to be for amateurs to pass away empty hours among the noise of their instruments, or to abandon themselves to the "freyen Herumirren ihrer Phantasie."[86] In sum, Sulzer felt that the Italian forms and the Italian style were leading Germany away from "the true taste" into a style of mere *Tändeleyen*. In all these complaints Sulzer's insistence on clear affective content and on moral usefulness is the decisive criterion of worth. Italians did not come up to Enlightened standards of artistic "truth," nor did they satisfy the German demand for art with high seriousness of purpose.

Sulzer had kinder words for French instrumental music, and as we saw above, for the forms with a clear and accepted function: dances, marches, and festive pieces. These pieces had *Charakter*—a single, clear, and coherent affective content throughout—hence they had meaning as well as use. Indeed it was the neglect of these overtures and partitas and suites containing dances of diverse character and expression which was leading Germany to the characterless, spineless "Misgebuhrten'' of modern music.[87] Today's performers who were not brought up on these French pieces "perform music in an effeminate, trifling, and mannered style."[88] The French overture, whose character was brilliance and dignity, was one of Sulzer's favorite instrumental forms, as it was of Mattheson. Sulzer lamented the fact that this venerable genre, which displays "almost the ultimate which art can attain through instrumental music," was going out of style because composers no longer had sufficient science, knowledge, and taste;[89] and performers no longer knew how to perform them.[90] Sulzer, like Mattheson, was especially fond of the element of contrast in the French overture, as when in the middle of the "most fiery stream" several soft, ingratiating measures are inserted, "which is very surprising, and as a result the following makes a better effect." It seems inconsistent that Sulzer would relish these properties of contrast and fire for their own sake, this music with no portrayed passions, with no object, subject, or moral lesson. But as with the other French genres, their clear coherent character, their accepted social function, their masculinity or definiteness, the conventional agreement as to their affective content, made them acceptable in Sulzer's eyes.

Sulzer did not deny that in the hands of certain composers the sonata, the symphony, or the genres of chamber music could be worthwhile. In spite of his account of music as the imitation of passionate utterance and in spite of the typical Enlightened disgust with the "barbaric" art of counterpoint, Sulzer realized that since chamber music is written for connoisseurs and is for their express musical delight, it is composed in a more learned and artful style. Musical craft is granted a useful role, and surely it is preferred to the "drum bass" of Italian symphonies. In the article "Solo" the sonata is described as eschewing both lyrical melody and the craft of *reinen Satz*, for the sake of providing the performer with opportunities to show off his instrument and his skill. The characteristic features of such compositions are "unexpected progressions, strange and difficult passages, unnaturally high notes, leaps, runs, double trills and such."[91] Consequently the solo aims more at wonderment than at moving, and Sulzer does not therefore regard this nonrepresentative genre very highly.

Sulzer had insisted that all instrumental music must have a "definite character." But in the article "Sonate" he surprisingly makes a virtue out of the sonata's lack of conventionally accepted character, suggesting that its peculiar virtue was the ability to express many affects:[92]

> Die Instrumentalmusik hat in keiner Form bequemere Gelegenheit, ihr Vermögen, ohne Worte Empfindungen zu schildern, an den Tag zu legen, als in der Sonate. Die Symphonie, die Ouvertüre, haben einen näher bestimmten Charakter . . . . Ausser diesen und den Tänzen, die auch ihren eigenen Charakter haben, giebt es in der Instrumentalmusik nur noch die Form der Sonate, die alle Charaktere und jeden Ausdruck annimmt. Der Tonsetzer kann bey einer Sonate die Absicht haben, in Tönen der Traurigkeit, des Jammers, des Schmerzens, oder der Zärtlichkeit, oder des Vergnügens und der Fröhlichkeit ein Monolog auszudrüken; oder ein empfindsames Gespräch in blos leidenschaftlichen Tönen unter gleichen, oder von einander abstechenden

Charakteren zu unterhalten; oder blos heftige, stürmende, oder contrastirende, oder leicht und sanft fortfliessende ergötzende Gemüthsbewegungen zu schildern.[93]

Instrumental music has in no other form than the sonata a more suitable opportunity to make known her ability to depict feelings without words. Symphonies and overtures have a more closely defined character . . . . Besides these forms and besides dances, which also have their particular character, there remains in instrumental music only the form of the sonata, which can accommodate all characters and every expression. In the sonata a composer can intend to express a monologue in tones of sadness, suffering, pain or tenderness, or in tones of pleasure and happiness; or he can intend to carry on a sentimental conversation in merely passionate tones among similar or contrasting characters; or he can depict merely intense, stormy or contrasting emotions, or delightful emotions flowing along delicately and gently.

For all its freedom the sonata remained a representative vehicle in Sulzer's eyes. He speaks of C. P. E. Bach's sonatas as models, in which the tones seem to speak an "understandable language."[94] He clearly was responsive to the seriousness which the Germans had infused into an admittedly meaningless form, and respected the power of the sonata's inarticulate tones to speak "the language of the passions."

Sulzer seems to have reached a crisis when he came to consider the symphony. It passed none of the tests he had set up for a beautiful and morally useful work of musical art. Unlike the sonata, it did not in Sulzer's view represent various emotions; nor did it seem to speak an "understandable language." And yet he seems to have sensed a powerfully affecting and even spiritual quality in it. One might have expected a diatribe against the symphony: the Italian import which supplanted the "ultimate" in instrumental music—the French overture. However, the symphony emerges from Sulzer's theory as a "sublime" creation, a piece of instrumental music which has unquestionable moral and human worth. Sulzer does not take as his point of departure the Italian symphonies he so deprecatingly dismissed as meaningless trivial noise. Rather his conception of the symphony is a noble and mighty one:

Die Symphonie ist zu dem Ausdrück des Grossen, des Feyerlichen und Erhabenen vorzüglich geschickt. Ihr Endzweck ist, den Zuhörer zu einer wichtigen Musik vorzubereiten, oder in ein Kammerconcert alle Pracht der Instrumentalmusik aufzubieten.[95]

The symphony is most excellently suited to the expression of the grand, the festive and the sublime. Its goal is to prepare the listener for an important musical work or, in a chamber concert, to offer all the brilliance of instrumental music.

Although Sulzer had stated firmly that the significance of instrumental music rested in the power of tones themselves to convey the feelings of their utterer, we shall see no suggestion in Sulzer's description of the symphony that the music is imitating the tone of passionate utterance so natural to vocal music. (He even criticizes Graun's symphonies for being too aria-like.) Rather, he states that the goal of the chamber, or independent, symphony is to "offer all the brilliance of instrumental music." Thus in Sulzer's description we see many of the traits Mattheson identified as peculiar virtues of instrumental music, namely, virtuosity and fire, counterpoint and compositional craft, brilliance, strong rhythms. We see as well the sudden changes and enigmatic contrasts that Lessing and others identified as striking but meaningless and disorderly. These are no mere ear-tickling sounds Sulzer describes: they shake the listener up; they are in effect the musical sublime. Sulzer clearly is enthusiastic about the symphony:

> Die Kammersymphonie, die ein für sich bestehendes Ganzes, das auf keine folgende Musik abziehet, ausmacht, erreicht ihren Endzweck nur durch eine volltönige, glänzende und feurige Schreibart. Die Allegros der besten Kammersymphonien enthalten grosse und kühne Gedanken, freye Behandlung des Satzes, anscheinende Unordnung in der Melodie und Harmonie, stark marquirte Rythmen von verschiedener Art, kräftige Bassmelodien und Unisoni, concertierende Mittelstimmen, freye Nachahmungen, oft ein Thema, das nach Fugenart behandelt wird, plötzliche Uebergänge und Ausschweifungen von einem Ton zum andern, die desto stärker frappiren, je schwächer oft die Verbindung ist, starke Schattirungen des Forte und Piano, und vornehmlich des Crescendo, das, wenn es zugleich bey einer aufsteigenden und an Ausdruck zunehmender Melodie angebracht wird, von der grössten Würkung ist. Hiezu kommt noch die Kunst, alle Stimmen in und miteinander so zu verbinden, dass ihre Zusammentönung nur eine einzige Melodie hören lässt, die keiner Begleitung fähig ist, sondern wozu jede Stimme nur das Ihrige beyträgt. Ein solches Allegro in der Symphonie ist, was eine pindarische Ode in der Poesie ist, es erhebt und erschüttert, wie diese, die Seele des Zuhörers, und erfordert denselben Geist, dieselbe erhabene Einbildungskraft, und dieselbe Kunstwissenschaft, um darin glücklich zu seyn.[96]

> The chamber symphony, which constitutes a self-sufficient whole, which is not related to any following music, achieves its goal only through a full-bodied, brilliant, and fiery style. The allegros of the best chamber symphonies contain grand and bold thoughts, free treatment of compositional rules, apparent disorder in melody and harmony, strongly marked rhythms of various kinds, powerful bass melodies and unisons, obbligato middle voices, free imitations, often a theme which is handled imitatively in a fugue-like manner, sudden transitions from one key to another, which are all the more astonishing, the weaker the connection is, strong shadings of forte and piano, and most especially the crescendo, which when used along with an ascending melody is of the greatest effect. Here also is found the art of weaving all the voices in and out of each other in such a way that only a single melody is heard, which is capable of no accompaniment, but to which each voice contributes its part. Such an allegro in a symphony is what a Pindaric ode is in poetry: it likewise elevates and shakes the soul of the listener, and demands the same spirit, the same sublime imagination and the same knowledge of art in order to be successful.

But how can Sulzer value all of these stirring qualities given his overall aesthetic theory? How can these unvocal, disorderly, strongly contrasting traits which signify nothing, which awaken only wonderment, serve the moral end of art? For these were the very qualities which Sulzer and many of his contemporaries rejected in contemporary instrumental music; they were some of the very qualities which had long been recognized as characteristic of instrumental music, but which had never played an active role in any aesthetic theory of musical significance.

Nevertheless Sulzer did accord the symphony and its characteristic features significance—not a representative, didactic significance, but a "humanizing and activating" significance. For they constituted the "sublime" in music. Sulzer never defined what the sublime in music amounted to, nor did he say that the symphony was of high moral worth because its content was the grand and the sublime. Nor did he seem to realize that he was justifying some of the very traits he and his contemporaries had strongly objected to in instrumental music. But we can see that he did in effect do these things if we only pull together some of the widely scattered pieces of his encyclopedia.

Although he had objected to the "sudden transitions" and the strong contrasts of the Italian sonata, he includes "sudden transitions" in his description of the sublime symphony. And Sulzer wrote in another article that *Abwechselung* furthered the development and perfection of the powers of the soul, and this stimulation was the very ground of the moral significance of the sublime.[97] An "apparent disorder," even contrasts which were difficult to understand, is found in Sulzer's symphony. Lessing had objected to the unintelligibility of the contrasts in the new Italian instrumental style, and even Sulzer had complained of the unintelligibility of the "arbitrary series of tones" in the Italian sonata. But Sulzer had also written that the grand and the sublime required an element of obscurity or unintelligibility in order to stimulate the powers of the soul to understand. In the article on "Bewunderung" (which was the characteristic affect of the sublime), he stated that even "apparent contradictoriness" played a role in stimulating the powers of the soul.[98]

Lastly, whereas Sulzer had condemned music as "mere noise" which did not "utter passions in an understandable language," and had said that all instrumental music was an imitation of vocal music, in his description of the symphony we recognize no such vocal model. Indeed he had said that the role of the symphony was to offer all the "brilliance" of instrumental music. We find Sulzer has justified these unvocal traits elsewhere in his encyclopedia too. In the article on "Feuer" (fire), which Sulzer tells us borders on the sublime because it subjects the power of the soul to strong exertion, Sulzer actually tells us what "fire" in music amounts to:

> In der Musik zeiget sich die Würkung des Feuers in schnellen, fortrauschenden Gängen, in ungewöhnlichen dreisten Accorden und plötzlichen Ausweichungen, in kühnen Figuren, und in grossen Intervallen.[99]

> In music the effect of fire is shown in fast headlong passages, in unusual and daring chords, and in sudden modulations, in bold figures and in large intervals.

These are very similar to the unvocal, inexpressive traits Sulzer wanted to forbid from instrumental music. But when they are viewed as part of the sublime symphony, rather than as part of an art form which purports to represent passionate utterances, their role becomes a significant one.

Thus the unintelligible and the obscure, the strongly contrasting, and the unvocal, brilliant, and virtuosic characteristics of the symphony are all identified by Sulzer as contributing to the aesthetic quality of the sublime. Many others had said that certain instrumental genres typically displayed these traits, but no one had provided the concept under which they could be subsumed as significant, and at the same time suggested how these specific characteristics of instrumental music could in part constitute a new kind of musical and even moral worth. For it must be remembered that Sulzer held the grand and the sublime to be the "highest" elements in art because they stimulated man's inner activity, the origin of all moral action, and his true source of humanity. The symphony in Sulzer's account has become an ennobling and humanizing source of spiritual exercise. The "wonderful" in music has become the musical "sublime."

Karl Ludwig Junker (1748–1797) seems to have been the first to have worked out an aesthetic theory of music based explicitly on the dynamic nature of the feelings and passions. This theory can be seen as an attempt to do for music what Lessing had done for the literary and graphic arts in the *Laokoön*, namely, to define the peculiar limits and peculiar virtues of a given art. Proceeding from the specific nature of music and from that of music's traditionally accepted subject matter, the passions, Junker finds a certain natural congruence between the two, and defines accordingly music's proper aspirations and limits. Though espousing on occasion the passionate utterance theory of musical expression with its conventional correspondence of tonal gesture and definite affect, Junker leaves the traditional *Affektenlehre* far behind in his account of the passions. Junker felt that it was absolutely necessary first to establish the changeable and dynamic nature of the emotions in order to justify music's natural affinity for expressing and affecting them. Junker also weaves into his aesthetic (but with less conscious intent) a third element, in addition to the nature of music and the nature of the emotions; and that is the logic of sensual cognition, as Baumgarten called it. The rules for sensual communication, for the engagement of the powers of sensing and feeling, prove on Junker's account to be quite consonant with the demands that music realize its peculiar beauties and its specific nature, and that music express and affect the emotions. Thus a kind of triple congruence results. But despite the originality of some of Junker's ideas, and despite the fact that some of his ideas anticipate the Romantic *Seelenlehre* and the Romantic conception of the peculiar prowess of instrumental music, Junker is very conservative about the potentialities of an art of pure sound. His reasons take us back to the neoclassic viewpoint: instrumental music is held to be inferior because the intelligibility of its content is inferior to that of vocal music; moreover, due to the necessity of clear emotional communication, Junker limits the content of instrumental music to only four emotions. Junker does recognize, however, music's superiority to words in expressing the transitions between emotions.

Junker was an amateur musician and art critic, and a clergyman by profession. He matriculated at the University at Göttingen in 1769, just nine days later than Forkel. He attended other universities as well, and subsequently held assorted tutorial and clerical positions in many different localities of southern Germany and Switzerland.[100] His principal writings on music[101] reveal him to be a "sentimental music critic."[102] His writing is full of the enthusiastic exclamations and enigmatic effusions typical of the Sturm und Drang. Such terms and expressions as *Ausguss, Glut, originelle Genie,* "inexhaustible imagination," and "outpouring of his autonomous heart" are common. The active, aggressive hero common in Sturm und Drang literature seems to figure prominently in his thinking; he exhorts his readers to be *männlich* and eschew effeminate rondos, preferring the heroic sentiment he sensed in the concerto. His friend Schubart praised his musical writings because Junker had shown how "to view sensually a sensual art."[103] But alongside Junker's emotionalism and anti-intellectualism we shall find some rather hard-nosed speculation on musical topics. An avid aesthetic speculator, he had read his Batteux, Avison, Sulzer, Webb, Moses, and even Sauveur. He was possessed of the desire to explain the sources of musical pleasure, to explain how it is that music expresses what it can in fact express; and he had a keen interest, as did Lessing, in differentiating the capabilities of the various arts.

Junker's theoretical essays into music criticism were based on a common contemporary conception of music's end: the communication of passion from composer to listener, or in Junker's words, the "awakening of passionate sympathy."[104] This entailed more than just a spontaneous overflow of powerful sentiment. For if communication was to occur intelligibility was essential. It is not surprising then to see Junker's ideas on expressing and arousing passion expressed in the neoclassic phrases "imitation of the passions," or "depiction" of passion.[105] Like Sulzer, Junker insists on the "correct expression of the feelings." He suggests passionate utterances as models for musical expression and commends to the composer the "study of passionate tones."[106] The extent to which Junker's theory both includes and goes beyond the idea of music as an outpouring of emotion is shown nicely in his suggestions for how to compose a piece of music. Although Junker speaks of the theme as flowing naturally out of the artist's fantasies, or of figures flowing on their own out of the artist's feeling, he is also concerned that the artist scrutinize these virgin products of the soul to see if they do in fact express the intended passion.

We have here a picture not of mere spontaneous overflowing, but of deliberately induced self-expression with the goal of emotional communication:

Er überlegt, welche Gattung von Musik er nun behandle, welche Empfindung er herfürbringen wolle; er setzt sich selbst in diese Empfindung hinein, denkt sich bey der ersten Fantasie, durchs mentale Bewusstseyn, den Mann dieser Leidenschaft, mit allen Bewegungen, wie er ihn sah, und bestimmt denn, den Charakter seines Stücks.

Er studiert das Verhältniss der Harmonie, zur festgesetzeten Leidenschaft; ob sie voll, oder durchsichtig; [u.s.w.] . . . seyn müsse. . . .

Kurz zuvor sucht er die festgesetzte Leidenschaft, die er erregen will, in Schriften auf, und besonders in solchen, wo ihre ganze Geschichte geschildert ist;—in dramatischen Werken.

Er liesst das Trauerspiel, das die zwey Hauptleidenschaften, Liebe und Zorn, für ihn enthalten muss, *laut*; er declamirt, er verbindet Action damit, um sich tiefer in die Situation seines Helden hinein zu fühlen; er überlasst sich jedem Eindruck, und fängt denn an mit der völligsten Stimmung seiner Seele zu arbeiten. . . .

Wenn er z.B. die Leidenschaft der Liebe behandelt, so sucht er Tafel, wo sie mit allen ihren Ausgussen geschildert ist. . . .

Er spielt lange, er spielt wiederholt, er giebt aber wohl Acht, welche Leidenschafts Arten in dieser, oder jener Modulation enthalten seyn können, denn sucht er möglichst zu concentriren, und setzt sein Thema fest, das natürlich aus dem Gang seiner Fantasien fliessen muss.[107]

[The composer] thinks over what musical genre he is writing in and what feeling he wants to arouse; he immerses himself in this feeling, imagines himself in his first fantasy, by means of mental consciousness, to be the man gripped by this passion, with all the movements that he imagined, and then determines the character of his piece.

He studies the relation of harmony to the predetermined passion, whether it should be full or transparent [etc.] . . . .

Shortly before composing he seeks out the appointed passion, which he wants to arouse, in literature, especially where its whole story is depicted—in dramatic works.

He reads the tragedy aloud which for him must contain the two primary passions of love and anger; he declaims, and adds actions as well, in order to identify more deeply with the situation of the hero; he abandons himself to every impression, and then begins to work, with the most fully-tuned soul. . . .

When, for example, he is treating the passion of love, he finds a picture where love is depicted in all its effusions. . . .

He plays for a long time, he plays repeatedly, he pays special attention to what kind of passion is contained in this or that melodic turn, then he seeks to concentrate it as much as possible and determines his theme, which must flow naturally out of the course of his fantasies.

His mention of portraying ''the whole history of a passion'' looks forward to the dynamic emotional theories espoused by the Romantics. But his suggestion that the composer declaim a poetic text as an aid to musical invention and his suggestion that the composer first view paintings that show how the passion in question is uttered recall the passionate utterance theory of musical representation. Certainly we are not dealing here with any specifically musical content. Junker's view of music as an outpouring is combined with an equally strong opinion that music represents and communicates the passions also depicted in literature and painting.

Junker built his theory of how music communicated the passions, or emotions, around the dynamic nature of the emotions themselves. Frequently, rather than just say that music expressed the emotions, Junker would write that music expressed the ''course,'' the ''story,'' or the ''progression'' of an emotion, as when he writes that in music:

Empfindung wird erregt, oder verstärket, ihre Progression geschildert, bis zur Hohe des leidenschaftlichen fünlens.[108]

Feeling is aroused, or intensified, its progression depicted, up to the peak of passion.

Junker repeatedly reminds his reader that the emotions are not static entities. He
wrote that man's whole emotional life is ebb and flow,[109] and that he could not even
imagine a passion "in an ever even course, without contrast."[110]

Moreover, a feeling could not even be made "sensually comprehensible"
without contrast.[111] For the very means of sensual communication, of giving pleasure and arousing sympathetic emotions require variety and contrast. Junker sup-
plements these Baumgartnian views with those of his English mentor, Daniel
Webb. Junker begins his first chapter of his *Tonkunst* by calling upon the authority
of Webb to support his view that change and variety were essential in order to
please and move the listener:

Natur, Kraft und Endzweck der Tonkunst ist's, das Herz zu rühren, dadurch dass sie Leidenschaften erweckt; denn das Wohlgefallen, sagt Webb, ist nicht die Folge eines beständigen und
fortdauernden Zustandes der Nerven und Lebensgeister.[112]

The nature, power, and purpose of music is to move the heart, so that passion is awakened; for
pleasure, according to Webb, is not a constant and permanent condition of the nerves and vital
spirits.

Junker goes on to emphasize that music does not work on the imagination, as Avi-
sion had claimed, but only on the *senses*.[113] Junker explained that a "sensual" representation was more noble and more effective the faster it rushed by. Thus if the
artist wants to arouse a sympathetic reaction in the listener he must avoid prolonging a single passionate expression, for that becomes boring.[114] Passions, then, can
best be aroused by "transitory" and "fleeting" representations, especially when
these form part of the "story" of an affect:

Nur durchs transitorische können Leidenschaften in der Tonkunst erregt werden,—nur dadurch,
dass eine Empfindung ihren Gang durch verfolgt, und auf ihren höchsten Gipfel gebracht
wird.[115]

Only by means of the transitory can passions be aroused in music—only by following a feeling
through to its climax.

Junker, relying on newer dynamic theories of the emotions and on the science of
"sensual cognition," had found then a natural compatibility between music as the
representation of the emotions and music as pleasant and moving. The same dynamic character which was necessary to express the emotions also served to arouse
them in a most pleasant and effective way.

Moreover, music was naturally suited to reflect this progressively evolving nature of the emotions and to provide the pleasure and affective movement made possible by variety and contrast. Twice Junker reminds his readers that ''Music is a progressive art.''[116] Like Lessing, he is aware of the peculiar signs and limits of the various arts; he pointed out that

Die Tonkunst verhält sich zur Mahlerey wie Fortschritt zum Stillstand.[117]

Melody is related to painting as progress is to standing still.

It is only natural then that music expresses passions in their temporal progression.[118] Accordingly Junker defines melody as ''the progressive, sensual representation of feeling by means of tones.''[119] Thus, music's nature as transitory, sensual, and changing—all qualities for which it had been faulted—makes it an especially apt vehicle for the expression of a sensual content with sensual means. Junker's theory of musical expression combines three things: the specific nature of music, the nature of the emotions, and the nature of sensual pleasure and communication. The variegated, progressively changing forms essential to all three form on Junker's account a felicitous threefold congruence.

Junker's prescriptions for expressing specific emotions in music reflect his new insight into the nature of music as a ''progressive,'' ''sensual,'' art and as an art representative of changing, contrasting, emotional entities. To be sure, he repeats some of the old clichés. Some of his suggestions sound almost as if borrowed from Mattheson; they reveal a view of the emotions as distinct entities, and a faith that there exist corresponding composites of musical characteristics to ''express'' them. Certain meters, tempi, tonalities, and instruments are all suggested as befitting certain emotions.[120] Junker also recommends, as did Batteux, the passionate tone as the fit object of imitation; every passion has its tone, and experience tells us that passionate tones, such as the *Angstgeschrey*, awaken analogous feelings.[121] But some means of musical expression suggested by Junker take us far away from the static entities of the Matthesonian *Affektenlehre* and the formulas of Ciceronian rhetoric. It is here that Junker comes to speak most eloquently of music's special advantages and to suggest a whole new theory of expression based on the emotions as dynamic entities with characteristic degrees and patterns of change within them. Here Junker puts the controversial properties so characteristic of contemporary music—variety and contrast—to good use. He did not approve of contrasts for their own sake.

In Junker's new theory of musical expression, dynamic aspects of certain emotions suggest certain specific means of musical treatment. Junker spoke of an ''analogy'' between the movements of music and the movements of the emotions. Dynamics alone are a useful and essential tool in reflecting the ''progression'' of a passion.

Die Abwechselungen des Piano und Forte werden geformt nach der leidenschaftlichen Progression, und Abnahme.[122]

The contrasts of piano and forte are formed in accordance with the passionate progression and decline.

Dissonance is useful for passions with contrast, and modulation is a good way of moving to another emotion.[123] Since some emotions are more changeable than others, different emotions require different degrees of suddenness in their contrasts and cadences. Sudden contrasts, for example, are fine in expressing happiness, they are *frappant*. At the same time, happiness, being more pleasant and uniform by nature, can tolerate more unity than sadness. Frequent sudden strong contrasts simply don't fit peaceful and gentle emotions, whereas they correspond well to the nature of pride and anger.[124] Patterns of repose and movement also vary from emotion to emotion:

Je stärker die Leidenschaft im Fortschritt wurde, desto natürlicher ist Ferma. Bey der Leidenschaft des Zorns, kan Ferma, urplötzlich den Gang hemmen; bey der Leidenschaft der Traurigkeit darf dieser Ruhepunkt nicht so ohngefehr seyn.[125]

The more intensely a passion progresses the more natural is a fermata. In the case of the passion of anger, a fermata can suddenly arrest the forward course; in the case of sadness this point of repose must not be so arbitrary.

Sudden changes, so common to the Italian instrumental style, were only appropriate for certain emotions; for example, very contrasting and distant modulations would be appropriate to "contrasting, unpleasant passions which quickly change their direction."[126] Junker saw the contrapuntal style, which Enlightened taste had disdained, as useful in expressing "multiple and ambiguous turns of passions."[127] Music thus had peculiar resources for reflecting the inner dynamic characteristics of various emotions.

However, due to the manner in which this communication was effected the number of emotions which music without words could communicate was quite limited. Junker was acutely aware that instrumental music was a sensual art and that its content could only be communicated by sensual means. That is, sounds had no reliable meaning that could be grasped by the mind.[128] Like his German forebears he believed in the immediate affectiveness in music. But rather than rest content with speaking of a "secret association," Junker posited a "mechanical analogy" between the movements, or dynamic shapes of music and the dynamic shapes of the emotions themselves.[129] The movements and intensity of music, which were patterned after the movements of the emotions it expressed, stimulated the nerves directly and aroused what Junker called "isomorphous" movements in the listener; these movements were then associated by the listener with real emotions with the same movements. And thus was emotion communicated. Junker's theory of the immediacy of music's affects maintained a mechanistic rigor. For since only movements were in fact transmitted, and since certain patterns of movement were in fact common to a whole class of emotion, Junker's account provides only for the communication of four classes of emotion by sounds alone.[130] Junker describes these four classes—anger, love, pride, and sadness—which he borrowed rather directly from Webb, as follows:

Zorn.
Plötzliche Uebergänge, gewaltsame Wiederkehr der Töne, die die Nerven mit Gewalt angreifen, und die Lebensgeister in Bewegung setzen.

Liebe.
Ruhige Folge verlängerter Töne, die sanfte, ruhige Vibrationem erwecken.

Stoltz.
Allmählige Zunahme der Töne, die die Lebensgeister erhöht, und ausbreitet.

Traurigkeit.
Abnahme der Töne, die die Lebensgeister nachlässt, und Schlaff macht.[131]

Anger.
Sudden transitions, powerful returns of tones, which powerfully affect the nerves and set the vital spirits in motion.

Love.
Restful series of sustained tones, which awaken gentle, restful vibrations.

Pride.
Gradual increasing of tones, which elevates and expands the vital spirits.

Sadness.
Diminution of tones which relaxes the vital spirits, and makes sleep.

Junker emphasizes that these are only classes of emotions. Music, by imitating the progression of movement and the intensity of an emotion—by awaking physical sensations analogous to those of certain emotions—can, by its very nature, by the nature of its limited representational and affective potentialities, by only so specific. For example, the very movements identified above as those of love are also common to friendship and sympathy.[132] In his *Betrachtungen* Junker even limited the number of emotions music could clearly express to two—pleasure and sadness—on the·basis of the limited possible physiological effects of music. It is doubtful whether even Batteux would have so constricted music's content.[133] Junker rejected Webb's notion that specific objects could be represented by association, as when the composer seeks to arouse in his listener the same movements which the listener would feel if the given object were present. He would have denied the ability of music to represent more than two or four emotions for the same reason: words or gestures were necessary to make the necessary "determination."[134]

While Junker's theory of an analogy between the dynamic characteristics of music and the emotions seems quite forward-looking, his position on the function of instrumental music is more reminiscent of neoclassic attitudes. Not only did Junker severely limit the expressive potential of sounds alone on grounds of precise communication, he even suggested that music should subordinate itself to poetry because only words can "distinctly define" a passion:

> Weil die musikalische Nachahmung der Leidenschaften ohne Poesie schwankend ist, d.h. weil erst Poesie, jede Leidenschaft deutlich bestimmen kan, so muss sich der Setzer, dem Dichter unterwerfen.[135]

> Since without poetry the musical imitation of the passions is ambiguous, i.e. since only poetry can define each passion distinctly, the composer must subordinate himself to the poet.

Junker also believed for reasons of intelligibility that instrumental pieces should possess a unity of affective content. For example, if in a mere instrumental composition whose main idea is the emotion of love a secondary theme were brought in, arousing anger, then this second emotion would occur without preparation. It would be an "indeterminate, unexplainable passion," and the whole piece would lose its "definite meaning."[136] Therefore composer and poet must go "hand in hand,"[137] for only the poet can make meanings clear—both of specific emotional content and of contrasting affects.

But Junker grants one signifying power to sounds alone: the power to depict the "transition from passion to passion":[138]

> Aber den Uebergang von Leidenschaft zu Leidenschaft, desselben Geschlechts, wer schildert ihn? Die Poesie nicht! Bey ihr ist alles Bestimmung seiner Art; höchstens nur der Deklamator, durch Abändrung des Tons, und der Stellung.
>
> Aber die Musik; und darinnen scheint mir einer ihrer Hauptvorzüge zu beruhen.
>
> In der ganzen Leiter der Leidenschaften kettet sie Glied an Glied, durch ein gewisses Mittel, das ich, wenns Farbenkunst war, Mezzo tinto, nennen möchte. Im Ueberschritt, von Glied zu Glied, zieht sie jedem was ab, webts zusammen, daraus entstehet dieses herrliche Mittelding.

> But who depicts the transition from passion to passion of the same genus? Not poetry! Everything in it determines the type of the passion. (Perhaps the orator, by means of vocal inflection and gesture.)
>
> Rather music does. And therein lies, it seems to me, of its chief advantages.
>
> In the whole ladder of passions, it links one member to another through a certain means I would call, if it were painting, *mezzo tinto*. In the transition from one member to another music takes something away from each, weaves them together, and out of that arises this marvelous middle-thing.

Here Junker has identified a peculiar virtue of sheer sounds, one which no other art

shares: the ability to make "conceivable" or "comprehensible" the subtle un-
named shadings and transitional states associated with the emotions.[139] The
Romantics would develop this notion much further. For Junker it was not such an
important virtue, for he placed too much weight on the intelligibility of the namable states themselves. And he had been careful to add to his assessment of music's
"chief advantage" that of ·course poetry would define the two states between
which music expressed the transition.[140]

We noted earlier that Junker recommended unity of affect for instrumental
pieces, including of course sufficient elements of variety to maintain the listener's
interest, and sufficient to characterize the course of the emotion expressed. What
did he think, then, of the symphony, notorious for its bold, meaningless contrasts
and surprises, and apparent incoherence? Junker saw the symphony as an excep-
tional case. After a long section giving precepts for the use of various instruments
in accordance with what feelings they are to express, Junker explains that none of
his precepts applies to the symphony because the symphony

> oft alle musikalische Leidenschaften abwechselnd erregen kan.[141]

> often can arouse all musical passions in turn.

In his *Tonkunst* and *Betrachtungen* he clearly preferred the affective unity of the
concerto to the symphony. The concerto had dramatic unity and dramatic action.
The soloist was the hero, and the theme represented the concentrated feeling. The
symphony had the least character of all musical compositions:

> Verbindung der Poesie mit Musik abgezogen, hat kein musikalisches Stük mehr Handlung, als
> Konzert. Um so nöthiger ist da, Klugheit in Anwendung des Thema.
> In keinem Stük, ist Thema weniger fühlbar, also in der Sinfonie. Denn keine musikalische
> Stück zielt weniger auf die Erregung einer besondern Leidenschaft ab, als sie.[142]

> Except for the combination of poetry and music, no musical form has more plot and action than
> the concerto. Therefore ingenuity in developing the theme is all the more necessary in that form.
> In no other musical form is a theme less perceptible than in the symphony. For no genre of
> music aims less at the arousal of a specific passion.

But Junker also admitted to being drawn to the affective multiplicity of the symphony. Here, using the Romantics' favorite metaphor of the stream, he describes a
symphony by Toeschi:

> Strom in dem sich die Empfindung ergoss,—eine mannigfaltig schattirte Empfindung;—ge-
> schickte Verbindung der Instrumente zu einem Zweck;—sinnliche Melodie, ohne studirt zu
> seyn;—gehöriger Abstand zwischen dem erhabenen und sinnlich schönen; diess alles machte sie
> anziehend.[143]

a stream where all feeling is poured forth—multiply-shaded feeling—skillful combination of instruments to one purpose—sensual melody, not studied—appropriate separation of the sublime and the sensually beautiful: all of these things make it interesting.

Unlike Sulzer, Junker provided no framework of moral significance against which his favorite instrumental genres could be viewed. In a later work, *Ueber den Werth der Tonkunst*, he defends music using traditional German arguments that it makes the soul happy; he sees music more as stimulating than communicating, and he espouses a kind of agnosticism with respect to the emotions. But in his main works of music criticism we are left thinking that music is good or worthwhile only insofar as it communicates passion effectively. It is to Junker's credit, however, that when he showed how music could be a vehicle of emotional communication, he took into account its characteristic limits and its specific nature as sensual and changing.

The ideas of Johann Nikolaus Forkel (1749–1818) provide another interpretation of the essential relationship between the changing and complex nature of the emotions and the procedures and form of music. But whereas the language of instrumental music was a meager one for Junker, for Forkel the language of sheer sounds rivaled the diversity and expressiveness of verbal language. Forkel combined his account of musical expression with a determined defense of the craft of music, and of the necessity of traditional rules and precepts. The fortunes of instrumental music rose as a result. Suddenly all the riches of musical art became meaningful; for it was only music in the highly-developed state it had acquired in eighteenth-century Germany which was able to express the "infinite and diverse modifications of the emotions." Forkel believed that he had assured the spiritual significance of music at the same time that he had held inviolate music's specific nature.

Forkel's career was spent largely at the University of Göttingen where he was active, first as a law student, then as university organist, then as Director of Music. He had received the traditional music education of a German church musician, first under the tutelage of the cantor of his hometown in Thuringia, then as choirboy in Lüneburg, and then as prefect of the cathedral choir in Schwerin. Besides supervising concerts at the University, and working on his monumental *Allgemeine Geschichte der Musik* (1788), he apparently gave lectures in what we now might call "music appreciation." Forkel was active as well as a composer and musical critic. His journal, *Musikalische Kritische Bibliothek* (1778–1779), reflected the growing German interest in English critical and aesthetic views. He remained at Göttingen until his death, his history remaining incomplete and his unused plates for a historical anthology of music having been melted into French imperial cannon balls.[144]

Being a musician himself, Forkel was deeply concerned that music was in danger of regressing from its eighteenth-century pinnacle of progress. A man of the Enlightenment, he believed that the only thing that could save it was good theories—not the old kind of music theory involving mathematics and complicated rules of composition (which had scared so many amateurs away), but a new kind, hardly voiced by any others, he claimed. The trouble was that most amateurs could not recognize good music, and most good composers were not receiving their due recognition. Currently popular music was nothing more than a thrown-together bunch of ideas with no connection one to the other.

The new theory, which Forkel called ''musical rhetoric'' or ''aesthetic,'' would show how the only way music could express and affect the feelings and passions was to use all the accumulated resources of musical art in a coherent and orderly fashion. For the emotions, Forkel emphasized, were themselves complex entities, subject to ongoing ''multiple modifications.'' Forkel's lectures at Göttingen and most of his other writings evince a desire to spread the knowledge of this new kind of theory, so that amateurs would appreciate and demand good music. Forkel's tastes in music were decidedly not progressive. His heroes were J. S. Bach (of whom he wrote one of the earliest biographies), Hasse, Graun, Handel, and C. P. E. Bach. His aesthetic was an inclusive one, displaying the necessity for genius *and* rules, nature *and* art, *Feuer* and *Fleiss*. Just as he repeatedly stated that music was to express the complex phenomena of the emotions, he defended the complexity of musical art itself. He showed that musical expression entailed the highly-developed art of music as found in those composers he revered. Thus he argued passionately against the partisans of Gluck who wanted to make music the handmaid of poetry. The declamatory expressionism of the French ''naturalists'' was insufficient. If sounds were to represent nature, all the resources of musical art were not only necessary but sufficient. In Forkel we see the synthesis of the traditional German view of the nobility of musical art, and newer theories of emotional expression in music—an accommodation of Italian style and French ''truth,'' of English psychology and German musical craft.

Forkel's definition of music is quite traditional: music is the ''depiction and communication of each kind of sentiment.''[145] There is no trace of didacticism in Forkel's view of music's function; he views music more in the manner of an earthly balm. He wrote that the fundamental law of all of aesthetics was

angenehme Leidenschaften und Empfindungen zu schildern, oder mit andern Worten, dem Menschen wohlzuthun und ihn zu ergötzen.[146]

to depict pleasant passions and feelings, in other words to contribute to man's well-being and to delight him.

In another passage Forkel adds the function of mitigating unpleasant emotions.[147] But despite these traditional attitudes we detect a novel element in his pronouncements. Forkel rarely speaks of just the feelings; in the introduction to the first volume of his history, which represents his most mature and most fully worked-out theory of music, he almost invariably adds a qualification such as "with all their connections and modifications." Thus Forkel's complete definition of music takes on new individuality: music becomes the "depiction of a feeling with all its infinite modifications."[148]

Forkel recognized clearly the dependence of his theory of musical expression on a dynamic theory of the emotions. He frequently felt called upon to explain that the feelings were really only stages in an ongoing, ever-changing continuum. For example, if an amateur wonders why a musical piece which begins brilliantly doesn't continue so, if it leaves him cold and unfeeling, he needs to know something about the "aesthetic ordering" of thoughts. He must know that music expresses the "multiple modifications" of feeling through multiple modifications of musical expression.[149] Like Junker, Forkel derived many ideas on human psychology from the English. Forkel most probably got his views from Lord Kames, whom Forkel read and occasionally quoted. Kames had written, "Passions are seldom uniform for any considerable time; they generally fluctuate, swelling and subsiding by turns, often in a quick succession."[150] Kames's ideas go back to those of Hume, who wrote in a similar vein:

> Tis difficult for the mind, when actuated by any passion, to confine itself to that passion alone, without any change or variation. Human nature is too inconstant to admit of any such regularity. Changeableness is essential to it.[151]

Thus, although Forkel defended Mattheson's insights into musical rhetoric and expression against his Enlightened adversaries, the *Affektenlehre* upon which Forkel's theory was to be based was as different from Mattheson's as Hume's epistemology was from Descartes's. Forkel's favorite term for this phenomenon of changeableness was "modification," which he most carefully defines, echoing Kames's observation:

> Keine Empfindung, die anhaltend seyn, oder durch irgend ein Mittel nicht nur geweckt, sondern auch unterhalten werden soll, ist sich, von Anfang ihrer Entstehung as bis ans Ende, gleich. Sie nimmt nach und nach durch unendliche und unbegreifliche Grade von Stärke und Schwäche ab und zu. Dieses Wachsen und Abnehmen der Empfindung nennt man gewöhnlich Modification.[152]

> No feeling which is of any duration, or which must be not only aroused but also maintained, is consistent from beginning to end. It swells and subsides through infinite and incomprehensible degrees of strength and weakness. This waxing and waning of feeling is commonly called modification.

But Forkel went beyond this dynamism within the emotions to focus on the natural continuity between various emotional states. Just as all things in nature develop naturally one out of the other, so do the natural phenomena of the emotions. Just as Hume wrote that

All resembling impressions are connected together, and no sooner one arises than the rest immediately follow. Grief and disappointment give rise to anger, anger to envy, envy to malice, and malice to grief again.[153]

Forkel wrote:

Wenn man bemerkt, dass in der Natur alles einem unaufhörlichen Wechsel unterworfen ist, alles nach und nach entsteht, vergeht, und auf eine ähnliche Art wieder entsteht, so kann der Aesthetiker leicht den Schluss machen, dass Empfindungen eben sowohl als körperliche Dinge diesem nothwendigen Laufe der Natur unterworfen seyn werden. Daraus folgert er das Gesetz der Mannigfaltigkeit in den Schilderungen unserer Gefühle. Wenn z.B. in dem Herzen eines Menschen die Empfindung des Unwillens über etwas entsteht, so wird sie sich nicht lange auf einem Punkte erhalten, sondern entweder zum Zorn, zur Rache oder Wuth empor steigen, oder sich wieder besänftigen, und zur Zufriedenheit zurück gehen.[154]

If it is observed that in nature everything is subject to constant change, that things gradually come into being, then disappear, then similarly arise again, then the aesthetic theorist can easily conclude that even emotions, as well as physical objects, are subject to this necessary course of nature. From this follows the law of multiplicity in the representation of our feelings. When, for example, the feeling of annoyance over something arises in a man's heart, the feeling will not remain for long at a given point, but will swell to wrath, vengeance or madness, or it will diminish and revert to satisfaction.

In short, diversity and changeableness are natural characteristics of the train of psychological events, and therefore music must also display these qualities. Also such was the nature of this continuum, this "coherence of the feelings among themselves," that a passion was only distinct from all other passions at one point in time; all other points within the passion partake of the nature of gther passions.[155] A corollary of this theory of the emotional continuum was that it was not natural to swell immediately from annoyance to wrath, vengeance or madness; sudden transitions were not usually convincing or natural. This was Forkel's defense against the tasteless contemporary music, which was just a "collection of ideas with no order or connection." Forkel only wanted a changeableness congruent with that of the emotions.

Not only did this view of the emotions as a continuum determine his view of musical expression, it brought a slight touch of healthy agnosticism into the soul of this Enlightened German (more than we saw in Sulzer or Junker). Significantly, Forkel makes a most articulate statement as to the inscrutability of the emotional life in a rejoinder to Webb's (hence Junker's) listing of the four classes of affects which could be expressed in music. Webb had argued that music could express only classes of emotions and not specific ones. Forkel replied that he feels no threat to music's abilities in Webb's classification because any expectation that music should express specific feelings assumes that there exists in nature such a "specific passion distinguished from all others." But since such things don't exist, then music is no worse off than all the other arts.[156] Nor could music be faulted if its contents could not be translated into words. Forkel ridiculed Riedel's assertion that a Gluck overture could tell the whole story of the opera if only each sound were translated into words. Forkel would agree that verbal and musical languages have many similarities with respect to their inner structure, but to expect a meaning in music with the distinctness of words was inappropriate and unfair. Music's meanings are beyond words the way religion is beyond reason, Forkel suggested. Musical meanings and verbal meanings were incommensurable, for music

> erst da anfängt, eigentlich Sprache der unendlichen Grade von Empfindungen zu werden, wo andere Sprachen nicht mehr hinreichen, uns wo ihr Vermögen sich auszudrücken ein Ende hat.[157]

> only becomes the real language of the infinite gradations of the feelings at that point where other languages can no longer reach, and where their ability to express ends.

Despite the nonexistence of distinct musical meaning and of specific emotions, Forkel is not deterred from hoping that some day the secrets of musical expression will be solved, just as scientists have solved many mysteries of the material world. He expresses this hope in rushing to the defense of a traditional charge made by Beattie that music was not imitative because one could not name the content of a Corelli concerto grosso. Music has content just as a painting does, Forkel claims. It isn't music's fault that we don't yet have the words for or the knowledge of the ''subtle relations and agreements among dark feelings.''[158] (Forkel goes on to reject the notion of music as imitative, but for other reasons.) In short, it is easier to get at the ''outer'' images of painting or poetry than the ''inner spiritual image'' which is found ''in the most secret corner of our being.[159] Like the Romantics, Forkel has a healthy respect for that thing that music was said to express—the feelings. He frequently opposes the outer form of music to its inner essence, and exterior things to spiritual things.[160] And he speaks of going beyond the physical to the metaphysical, of going to another sphere, of flying up to embrace an ideal.[161] Surely he shared with the Romantics the acute awareness that music's commerce was with an elusive, inscrutable inner reality, which by its very nature could not be depicted with words. He believed inner feelings were communicated from composer to listener intuitively, given the proper musical experience and refinement of feelings. Thus if the ''practiced feelings'' of a listener sensed a represented content, Forkel was not inclined to take issue with him. For every piece was formed by the original, ''inner stamp'' of its composer.[162] Composers wrote intuitively out of themselves, and did not consciously attempt to imitate an utterance or some such. Nevertheless the rules of musical art were valid, because they were formulations of what these geniuses had realized, if only dimly. As Kant was to say, genius gives the rule to art.

For all his similarities with the Romantics regarding the obscure, inner, changing nature of the emotional life and the untranslatability of music's language, the Enlightened Forkel viewed most of these mysteries with intellectual curiosity as well as awe. He wrote in his history that the "inner sanctuary of art" had not been fathomed *yet.*[163] Accordingly his writings attempt to explain how it is that music expresses and communicates the emotions.

Forkel's treatment of just how the "manifold turns" of music express the "manifold modifications" of feeling does not pretend to be extensive, but only to suggest new kinds of connection that will be helpful to the amateur. It differs from previous accounts in that it deals more with the form, or principles of temporal ordering, than did previous theories. We find few prescriptions for how one expresses such and such a feeling with such and such musical means. Forkel did not see this as his mission. But he does talk about such things as contrast, transition, intensification, connection, and diversity and the like. This recognition that the temporal dynamic characteristics of the emotions in nature were to be reflected in musical form led to the theoretical justification of the new Italian style's multiplicity of affective content as well as to the justification of the hallowed procedures of fugue and counterpoint, and even to what we now call "thematic work" (which Forkel treated as part of counterpoint or "harmony"). These elements were all present in the "grand symphonies with their manifold elements," which for the Romantics were the epitome of music.

Forkel attempts in various ways to use his emotional theory to explain such a broad range of musical changes as the succession of contrasting sonata movements and the succession of contrasting themes within a given movement. He is no doubt addressing the problem of many who, like Lessing, found the contrasts of the newer style more confusing than moving. He thought if amateurs could be brought to understand the "aesthetic ordering of thoughts," of the "law of multiplicity in the representation of the feelings," then the confusion would disappear and a deeper understanding of the language of music would result. After explaining, somewhat inconsistently, that musical compositions are "speeches for the feelings" and that the aesthetic arrangement of the thoughts is based "solely on the manner and way in which feelings develop out of each other," Forkel explains the form of such a speech:

> Jeder Gedanke, und jede Empfindung hat eine Veranlassung; diese Veranlassung ist gleichsam die Einleitung, wodurch wir den Zuhörer auf unsere Hauptempfindung, die hier der Hauptsatz, das Thema ist, leiten wollen. Die Hauptempfindung muss vorzüglich genau bestimmt werden; daher bedient man sich (1) der Zergliederung, um sie auf alle möglichen Seiten zu zeigen; (2) passender Nebensätze, um sie damit zu unterstützen; (3) möglicher Zweifel, das heisst im musikalischen Sinn, solcher Sätze, die der Hauptempfindung zu wiedersprechen scheinen, um durch die darauf folgende Widerlegung derselben den Hauptsatz destomehr zu bestimmen; und endlich (4) der Bekräftigung durch Vereinigung, oder nähere Zusammenstellung aller Sätze, die vereint dem Hauptsatz die stärkste Wirkung verschaffen können. Dies sind die gewöhnlichsten Theile eines Tonstücks nach dessen aesthetischen Anordnung.[164]

Each thought, each feeling, has a cause; this cause is, as it were, the introduction, wherein we attempt to lead the listener into our predominant emotion which in this case is the main theme. The predominant emotion must be precisely defined. To that end one makes use of (1) fragmentations in order to show it on all possible sides; (2) appropriate subordinate clauses, in order to support it; (3) plausible doubt, that is, in the musical sense, such ideas or phrases which seem to contradict the predominant idea, in order better to characterize it through contradictions with it, and finally (4) affirmation through unifying or putting closer together all ideas which give the predominant feeling its greatest effect. These then are the most common parts of a musical composition in terms of aesthetic arrangement.

The emphasis here is on achieving a desired effect, on arousing in the listener a sympathetic reaction, just as the orator is able to convince his listener by a careful arrangement of his ideas. One might be tempted to find the sonata-allegro form lurking behind Forkel's rhetorical plan of attack. Certainly he has seen to it that the orator's plan of attack allows room for contrasting themes and techniques of thematic development. Nevertheless, it is difficult to be convinced that the ordering principles inherent in the way feelings develop out of one another are the same as those for a successful speech.

Less problematic is his account of appropriate orderings for contrasting sonata movements. Since the function of music is to arouse or maintain pleasant feelings or to subdue unpleasant ones, the three movements of a sonata can show a significant progression. For example, in C. P. E. Bach's Sonata in F Minor from the third collection "Für Kenner und Liebhaber," the ordering is one where an unpleasant emotion is subdued. The first movement expresses "anger," the second "reflective deliberation," and the third, "melancholy calm."[165] Thus Bach's sonata meets Forkel's standard for a correct and appropriate progression of feelings. Finally, Forkel brings in his emotional theory to recommend the manner in which these contrasting, or differing, diverse elements are combined in natural temporal succession. He praises C. P. E. Bach's transitions, both within movements and between movements, observing that transitions are the stuff out of which the emotions are made, and that every good piece must make much use of this technique. Transitions between movements are also useful in that they do not bruise the feelings by too sudden a change, which is not natural. (In the example given of a C. P. E. Bach transition, motivic development plays a prominent role.)[166]

Forkel came closest to a systematic attempt to show how music expressed emotion when he gave an historical account of the development of these means in the introduction to his history. In order to make accurate judgements as to the worth of other music, Forkel argued, one must have a true concept of the nature of music and the nature of the emotions, and the nature of man. Since, he argued, the emotions are entities as complex as thoughts, and since the powers of thinking and feeling are just two aspects of the same "fundamental power of the soul," music—the language of the emotions—must be just as diverse as the language of ideas, and it must follow the same laws, and have the same inner structure. In fact, the birth of language and music were one, in the single tone of expression, and only gradually did they become separated, as man himself became more sophisticated. Both languages became more refined over time until their present high state of development.[167] The whole introduction can be viewed as a vindication of the necessity of harmony and a discrediting of the utterance theory of musical expression. Forkel wanted to show that music was a "universal language of the feelings . . . whose domain is and can be just as large as the domain of a well-developed language of ideas.[168]

In the first period of music and language there were only single tones and only nouns. Tones, to be sure, can express and awaken feelings, but *Empfindungslaute* alone form a very imperfect language for reflecting the "manifold modifications of feeling." In the second period scales and simple melodies were used and tones were able to express properties and relations of feelings just as the various parts of speech express properties and relations of ideas. Greek music fell into this period. Only with the third period, the modern period, were the means evolved which made it possible for music to exist as an "independent and autonomous art relying on its own powers."[163] Only then did music acquire the determinateness and the quantity of expressions that could reflect man's ever-growing power of discrimination regarding his own emotions. Similarly, language had grown to express the increased precision and scope of man's thoughts. This newfound musical means, this source of determinateness and quantity, was harmony.

"Harmony" was for Forkel and many eighteenth-century writers a broader term than it is today. If referred not only to chords, and homophonic composition (as in "harmonizing" a song); but it also referred to polyphony, or the contrapuntal process (as when Rousseau called harmony a "Gothic and barbaric" invention which obscured the "natural" expression of the melody). In addition, Forkel seems to have included in this designation the processes which today we group under the heading of "thematic development." Indeed, part of the virtue and necessity of harmony centered on this latter technique, which, he has reminded us, is not limited to use in fugal or contrapuntal compositions:

> Die Kenntnis derselben verschafft einem Componisten überall Mannigfaltigkeit und Reichthum an Melodie und Harmonie, weil sie musikalische Gedanke durch mancherley Arten der Nachahmung, nicht nur modificirt, sondern auch noch ausserdem durch Zergliederung und andere contrapunktistische Künste so natürlich aus einander entwickelt, dass es fast einzig und allein durch ihre Hülfe möglich ist, in den Gang eines Tonstücks, es sey von welcher Art es wolle, Zusammenhang, Einheit, und Mannichfaltigkeit der Gedanken zu bringen.[170]

> Knowledge of this [harmonic art] provides a composer with the means for variety and richness of melody and harmony, because it not only modifies musical ideas with various types of imitations, but it develops musical ideas out of each other by means of fragmentation and other contrapuntal devices so naturally that it is only with the aid of this harmonic art that the course of a musical composition, of whatever type, acquires coherence, unity, and variety of expression.

It is clear that in speaking of "harmony" he includes together the older techniques of fugue and the newer freer types of contrapuntal activity associated with thematic development.

Forkel gave three main reasons for harmony's decisive role in the development of a musical language able to express the "infinitely diverse modifications of feeling."[171] In the first place, harmony made music more determinate—not, to be sure, the kind of determinateness demanded by rationalistic tests for the intelligibility of musical content—but a specifically musical kind of determination. Forkel gives as an example a melody that could be harmonized in one of four keys. When it occurs as a melody alone, it suffers from a certain ambiguity and indeterminateness. This ambiguity is removed, however, if it is harmonized in a particular key. Thus harmony is a "Bestimmungsmittel."[172] In the second place, the invention of harmony has provided an amazing multiplication of musical expressions. This increase occurs largely through "the art of combining several melodies," commonly called the polyphonic procedure.[173] The third advantage of harmony is that it led to the creation of a system of temperament whereby one could move among all the keys. And thereby one could express closely and distantly related feelings.

Forkel is most aware of the opposition he is meeting when he asserts that harmony is necessary to a fully developed "language of the feelings." He takes issue with Rousseau's and other "Naturalists' " assertion that harmony is "unnatural" and is an obstacle to the unemcumbered expression of the passions.[174] He puts the nature of the feelings as he has described them to his own use in defending harmony:

> Da nun in der Natur diese Vielartigkeit der Empfindungen statt findet, da die Kunst das Vermögen hat, alle mögliche einfache und zusammengesetzte Empfindungen zu schildern, warum sollte sie sich dieses Vermögens nicht bedienen, warum nicht treu der Natur in allen ihren Modificationen folgen?[175]

> For since there exists in nature this diversity of feelings, and since art has the ability to depict all possible simple and compound feelings, why shouldn't it use this ability, why not be true to nature and follow all their modifications?

Forkel also defended double counterpoint, which many Enlightened critics regarded as an "empty trifle," saying that it too was based on the "manifold modifications of the feelings."[176]

Forkel's most striking defense of the fugue and fugal procedures takes us back, ironically, to the utterance theory of musical expression. If homophony, Forkel argued, is the imitation of the utterance of one person, then could not the fugue be viewed as the emotional utterance of more than one person—even an entire *Volk*?

> Man stelle sich also ein Volk vor, welches durch die Erzählung einer wichtigen Begebenheit in Empfindung gesetzt worden ist, und denke sich nun, dass ein Mitglied desselben, vielleicht

durch die Stärke seiner Empfindung zur Aeusserung derselben zuerst hingerissen, einen kurzen, kraftigen Satz als Ausdruck seines Gefühls anstimmt; wird nicht dieser Ausbruch seiner Empfindung nach und nach die sämmtlichen Glieder dieses Volks ergreifen, wird ihm nicht erst eines, dann mehrere, und zulezt die meisten nachfolgen, und jedes den angestimmten Gesang, zwar nach seiner eigenen individuellen Empfindungsart modificiren, im Ganzen aber dem Hauptgefühl nach mit ihm übereinstimmen? Und wenn ein solcher Auftritt, eine solche nach und nach ausbrechende Aeusserung der Empfindung musikalisch geschildert werden soll, entsteht nicht auf das natürlichste von der Welt erstlich der Führer (*dux*), sodann der Gefährte (*comes*), der Wiederschlag (*repercussio*), kurz, die ganze aussere und innere Form der Fuge? Ist die verschiedene Führung und Verwebung der Stimmen, die zusammen eine angenehme, aber mannichfaltige Harmonie ausmachen, die sämmtlich dem Anscheine nach auf verschiedenen Wegen nach einem und ebendemselben Ziele laufen, und sich, wie Luther sagt, unterwegens einander freundlich begegnen, sich herzen und so lieblich umfangen, dass diejenigen, so solches ein wenig verstehen, sich des heftig verwundern müssen, und meynen, dass nichts seltsamers in der Welt sey, denn ein solcher Gesang mit vielen Stimmen geschmückt, ist sie nicht, diese mannichfaltige und künstliche Verwebung, eine getreue Abbildung der Natur, ist sie nicht der vollkommenste Ausdruck der mannichfaltig modificirten Empfindungen aller Glieder eines Volks, die erst nach und nach entstehen, sodann eber in einen allgemeinen Strom sich ergiessen?[177]

Let us imagine a people which through the narration of a great event is put into emotion, and imagine at first that a single member of this group, perhaps through the intensity of his feelings is driven to make a short powerful statement as the expression of his feeling. Will not this outburst of his feeling gradually grip the collective members of this people, and will he not be followed by first one, then several, then most, and each will sing the same song with him, each, to be sure, modifying it according to his own way of feeling, but on the whole concording with him as to the basic feeling: And if such a scene, such a progressively developing outburst of emotion is to be represented musically, do not first the *dux*, then the *comes*, then the *repercussio* arise in the most natural way in the world—in short, the whole outer and inner form of the fugue? Is not this variegated leading and weaving of voices, which together make a pleasant but manifold harmony, which seem to be going by different routes to one and the same goal, and which as Luther says, en route warmly greet and embrace each other so sweetly that those who have only slight understanding of such music must be quite perplexed and think that nothing in the world is stranger than such a song, embellished with many voices—is this not, this multifarious and artful weaving, an accurate representation of nature, is this not the most perfect expression of the multiply modified feelings of all the members of a people, feelings which first gradually arise, but then pour themselves out in a universal stream.

We see vividly in this interpretation of the fugue as a "universal stream" the meeting of traditional German attitudes, represented here by Luther himself, and the Romantic vision of the "wonderful significance" of the "profundities of musical compositions." Proceeding from his theory of the manifold modifications of the emotions, and perhaps motivated by his own inherited predilection for the contrapuntal idiom, Forkel has managed to reconcile the "accurate representations of nature" demanded by Enlightened criticism with the specifically musical procedures of the fugue in such a way that musical "art" acquires a new significance.

The relation of musical form to emotional form is perhaps most closely shown in Forkel's "figures for the imagination." Although Forkel held that music spoke directly to the feelings, he believed also that the more faculties that were stimulated the better; for, like Herder, he believed that there was really only a single "Grund-kraft der Seele." If all faculties could be stimulated simultaneously and harmoniously then the artwork would be more powerful. Thus the figures were aids for engaging the faculties of the understanding, of the attention, and of the imagination. The figures for the imagination reflected graphically the dynamic, modulating quality of the emotions which Forkel considered so important. Forkel mentions first the figures for the imagination called *Malerei* which imitate visible or sounding objects. But he does not consider these so important.

> Die Tonsprache hat aber auch Mittel, selbst *innere Empfindungen* so zu schildern, dass sie der Einbildungskraft gleichsam sichtbar zu werden scheinen. Die Empfindungen äussern sich auf sehr mannichfaltige Weise. Sie stehen bisweilen auf einmal still, entstehen wieder, steigen immer höher, kehren wieder zurück, u.s.w. und von allen diesen so mannichfaltig modificirten Aeusserungen kann sich die Einbildungskraft ein Bild vorstellen, welches ihr sichtbar zu seyn scheint. Die Uebertragung dieses Bildes in die Form des Ausdrucks geschieht durch die sogenannten Figuren für die Einbildungskraft.[178]

> However, music has other means to depict even *inner feelings* in such a way that they seem, as it were, visible to the imagination. Feelings express themselves in very manifold ways. They sometimes stop all of a sudden, arise again, intensify more and more, then recede, etc., and the imagination can form an image of these so multiply modified utterances which seems to be visible, even. The transmission of this image in the form of expression occurs through the so-called figures for the imagination.

For example, after growing gradually to a high degree of intensity, a feeling may suddenly break off and stand still. The figure for expressing this pattern of change is called "Ellipsis," and can be realized in two ways. A phrase which has grown progressively to a high degree of liveliness can unexpectedly break off and then resume immediately with a new thought. Or a deceptive cadence can accomplish the same effect. Forkel illustrates this figure with an example from a sonata by C. P. E. Bach. He then adds, making allowance for the particular intensity of the emotion in question, "the stronger the emotion is, whose course is to be speedily cut off, the more unusual and strange must be the unexpected cadence."[179] Other figures for the imagination are repetition (applicable to either single notes or whole phrases), suspension (expression of a postponement so that the listener only realizes music's purpose at the end), the epistrophe (where the ending of one phrase recurs later ending another phrase), and dubitation, or doubt. Forkel takes special note of the figure of Gradation or Intensification. He comments that it is one of the most beautiful and effective figures and that it occurs when one climbs, as it were, by steps from weaker phrases to stronger ones and thus expresses a constantly growing passion.

Forkel does not claim his list is exhaustive; he only wants to begin a theory of the figures. He does add that most of the other figures he couldn't list were certain types of repetition, "whereby individual parts of phrases now varied, now unvaried, now augmented, now diminshed, sometimes repeated from the beginning or from the middle, sometimes even repeated from the end, so that the hearer believes that feelings in various ways are transformed and return."[180] What Forkel has described is the technique of thematic development, typical of the mature classical symphony. And like the Romantics he can see that this technique is especially suited for symbolizing the complex, ever-changing character of the emotions.

Forkel was so determined to show how music, "relying on its own powers," could be a language of refinement comparable to that of verbal language, that he in fact showed how instrumental music, displaying its characteristic traits, could be an art as significant as verbal art. His portrayal of the emotions as being subject to continual manifold modifications was the key to his account of how the contrast-dominated symphonic style could be viewed as portraying human emotions. He had accepted the premise that music represents the emotions, and had shown a way in which it could in fact do this, while at the same time allowing, in fact requiring, the exercise of contemporary instrumental music's peculiar proclivities for compositional complexity and for variety and contrast.

Nevertheless, when he considers the question of the relative worth of instrumental and vocal music, if only briefly, he gives vocal music priority. First Forkel rejects as too harsh Sulzer's judgement that most instrumental music was only an "artful and entertaining chatter, which did not occupy the heart."[181] But he admits that even if within the "inner circle of art" a piece can rise to the "most refined and highest ideals," the amateur indeed needs a translator to make music's content comprehensible.[182] Thus, although Forkel displays many Romantic viewpoints, and though he has actually shown how the "grand symphonies with their manifold elements" can represent the inner dynamic stream of emotional life, he still believes—with Batteux, Hiller, Junker, and Sulzer (to name only a few)—that instrumental musican be faulted for its inferior intelligibility.

6

The Romantics' View of Instrumental Music

The climax of our story of the change in instrumental music's aesthetic status is reached in the enthusiastic and effusive ideas of the *Frühromantiker*—most notably Jean Paul, Wilhelm Heinrich Wackenroder, Ludwig Tieck, August Wilhelm Schlegel, and Ernst Theodor Amadeus Hoffmann. These men, beginning in the 1790's, saw in instrumental music a power and significance surpassing not only vocal music but the other arts as well. Instrumental music was, in short, "the most Romantic of all the arts."[1]

Certainly we cannot adopt uncritically the common view that the Romantics thought that music was for expressing the emotions, whereas the rationalistic mind of the eighteenth century delighted in the "absolute" music of the symphony, sonata, and string quartet. Rather, if we compare latter eighteenth-century German views with those of the *Frühromantiker,* something close to the opposite appears to be the case. Not only did the men of Enlightenment Germany labor mightily to fit instrumental music into their representative formulae and condemn any music which did not represent and communicate emotion, but one of the hallmarks of the Romantics' attitude was their absolute distaste for representative music—music compelled to perform the task of reproducing or suggesting some aspect of the real world. Most especially the Romantics ridiculed the attempt to use music as a means of communicating "definite feelings." We even sense below in Tieck's eloquent appeal for the "freedom" of music an indirect attack on C. P. E. Bach, the man most admired in eighteenth-century Germany as a composer of expressive and aesthetically justifiable instrumental music:

> Glaubt man, dass alle menschliche Musik nur Leidenschaften andeuten und ausdrücken soll, so freut man sich, je deutlicher und bestimmter man diese Töne auf den leblosen Instrumenten wiederfindet. Viele Künstler haben ihre ganze Lebenszeit darauf verwandt, diese Deklamation zu erhöhen und zu verschönern, den Ausdruck immer tiefer und gewaltsamer emporzuheben, und man hat sie oft als die einzig wahren und grossen Tonkünstler gerühmt und verehrt. . . . In der Instrumentalmusik aber ist die Kunst unabhängig und frei, sie phantasiert spielend und ohne Zweck, und doch erfüllt und erreicht sie den höchsten, sie folgt ganz ihren dunkeln Trieben, und drückt das Tiefste, das Wunderbärste mit ihren Tändeleien aus.[2]

If one believes that the sole purpose of all man-made music is to signify and express passions, then one is delighted the more distinctly and definitely these passionate tones are reproduced by lifeless instruments. Many artists have spent their whole lives to this end: heightening and beautifying this declamation, making the expression ever more profound and powerful. And they have often been praised and honored as the only true and great composers. . . . However, in instrumental music art is independent and free; here art phantasizes playfully and purposelessly, and nevertheless art attains the ultimate. It follows completely its deep inscrutable instincts, and expresses the most profound, the most wonderful, with its playfulness.

Not only should music be free and not compelled to express the passions; but, as Tieck would have it, music's *Tändelei* alone was somehow capable of expressing profound and wonderful things. And he singles out the symphony as the highest form of instrumental music. In proceeding to discuss the "wonderful and infinite" possibilities of a liberated instrumental music, he mentions enthusiastically many attributes which we saw at the end of the first chapter had once constituted aesthetic problems (only the tone of the language has changed): its lack of verisimilitude (that is, in Tieck's words, its affinity for the *Wunderbar*); its lack of determinate meaning; its confusing and enigmatic contrasts; its juxtaposition of contraries (such as joy and pain); and its brilliant, enlivening grandeur. Thus we get indirectly a picture of that "specific nature" of music which was to figure so prominently in E. T. A. Hoffmann's ideas:

Der Komponist hat hier ein unendliches Feld, seine Gewalt, seinen Tiefsinn zu zeigen; hier kann er die hohe poetische Sprache reden, die das Wunderbarste in uns enthüllt, und alle Tiefen aufdeckt, hier kann er die grössten, die groteskesten Bilder erwecken und ihre verschlossene Grotte öffnen, Freude und Schmerz, Wonne und Wehmut gehn hier neben einander, dazwischen die seltsamsten Ahndungen, Glanz und Funkeln kehrt zurück, und die horchende Seele jauchzt in dieser vollen Herrlichkeit,

Diese Symphonien können ein so buntes, mannigfaltiges, verworrenes und schön entwickeltes Drama darstellen, wie es und der Dichter nimmermehr geben kann; denn sie enthüllen in rätselhafter Sprache das Rätselhafteste, sie hängen von keinen Gesetzen der Wahrscheinlichkeit ab, sie brauchen sich an keine Geschichte und an keine Charakter zu schliessen, sie bleiben in ihrer rein-poetischen Welt.[3]

The composer possesses [in the symphony] an endless field for demonstrating his power, his deep thinking. Here he can speak the elevated poetic language which reveals the most wonderful in us, and which lays bare all depths. Here he can awaken the grandest, the most grotesque images and open their sealed sanctuary. Joy and sorrow, ecstasy and melancholy accompany each other here, and in between appear the strangest intimations. A sparkling brilliance returns, and the attentive soul rejoices in this full magnificence.

These symphonies can produce a drama of greater color, diversity, intricacy, and development, than could any dramatist or poet: for symphonies reveal in enigmatic language the enigmatic; they are dependent on no laws or verisimilitude; they do not need to rely upon any plot or any characters—they remain in their pure poetic world.

The basic, and most radical tenet of the new Romantic attitude, which should emerge clearly from Tieck's words, is that meaning does not have to be conferred upon sounds, especially as these sounds are arranged in the "grand symphonies, with their manifold elements."[4] An insistence on verisimilitude or extramusical content, on referentiality or representation is antagonistic to the very undefined, or "infinite," nature of instrumental music's content. And music, by its very nature, is significant and affective. There need be no requirement that the instrumental composer purport to express or represent. A highly charged drama can be suggested which is independent of any plot or characters.

Moreover, in making these points, Tieck makes explicit use of aspects of the new instrumental music which were previously aesthetic anathema—qualities already recognized as proper to the new Italian instrumental music, but which had found little theoretical sanction: the *Tändeleien,* the rich variety and strong contrasts, and the sheer instrumental brilliance und elaboration. These problematic aspects of instrumental music are no longer problems, but, as we shall see, have a positive, recognized role to play in the new Romantic "theory" of instrumental music.

E. T. A. Hoffmann also emphasized most clearly, in spite of the vague, high-flown nature of many of his phrases, music's freedom from reference to the real, external world of the senses—and again this external world included "definite" feelings.[5] For Hoffmann the demands of previous generations were inapplicable. Definitude, especially that conferred by words, was constraining and abhorrent to him. The infinite was alone the proper subject for pure musical embodiment:

> Sollte, wenn von der Musik als einer selbständigen Kunst die Rede ist, nicht immer nur die Instrumental-Musik gemeint sein, welche, jede Hülfe, jede Beimischung einer andern Kunst (der Poesie) verschmähend, das eigentümliche, nur in ihr zu erkennende Wesen dieser Kunst rein ausspricht?— Sie ist die romantischste aller Künste, beinahe möchte man sagen, allein echt romantisch, denn nur das Unendliche ist ihr Vorwurf.— Orpheus' Lyra öffnete die Tore des Orkus. Die Musik schliesst dem Menschen ein unbekanntes Reich auf, eine Welt, die nichts gemein hat mit der äussern Sinnenwelt, die ihn umgibt, und in der er alle *bestimmten* Gefühle zurücklässt, um sich einer unaussprechlichen Sehnsucht hinzugeben.
>
> Habt ihr dies eigentümliche Wesen auch wohl nur geahnt, ihr armen Instrumentalkomponisten, die ihr euch mühsam abquältet, bestimmte Empfindungen, ja sogar Begebenheiten darzustellen?—Wie könnte es euch denn nur einfallen, die der Plastik geradezu entgegengesetzte Kunst plastisch zu behandeln?[6]

When we speak of music as an independent art, should we not always restrict our meaning to instrumental music, which, scorning every aid, every admixture of another art (the art of poetry), gives pure expression to music's specific nature, recognizable in this form alone?— It is the most romantic of all the arts, one might almost say, the only genuinely romantic one, for its sole subject is the infinite.— The lyre of Orpheus opens the portals of Orcus. Music discloses to man an unknown realm, a world that has nothing in common with the external sensual world that surrounds him, a world in which he leaves behind him all *definite* feelings to surrender himself to an inexpressible longing.

Have you even so much as suspected this specific nature, you miserable composers of instrumental music, you who have laboriously strained yourselves to represent definite emotions, even definite events? How can it ever have occurred to you to treat after the fashion of the plastic arts the art diametrically opposed to plastic?

If we consider these rather enigmatic words of Hoffmann in the light of Tieck's more extensive and suggestive remarks above, we can get a clearer idea as to what Hoffmann may have meant by the "specific nature of music" and by the "infinite" as its "sole subject." This nature derives partly from instrumental music considered merely as an art of sounds, and partly from the nature of the new symphonic style itself. By music's "specific nature" he meant in large part the immateriality and nonreferentiality of its matter, its brilliant interweavings and striking juxtapositions, and the uninformative but suggestive and affecting essence of its multifarious and purely "musical" (in Hoffmann's words) content. By the "infinite" is meant all the "wonderful" things which do not partake of the mundane definitiveness of the external sensual world and of the plastic and verbal arts.

This infinitude of music's content can best be understood in contraposition to the definitude of the word. Indeed, it is clear from the above statements of Tieck and Hoffmann that the Romantics believed that words threatened the prostitution of musical art. Witness as well Wackenroder's intense resentment of the word's threat to tonal wealth, and his corresponding disdain for the paltry certainty revealed by reason:

> Was wollen sie, die zaghaften und zweifelnden Vernünftler, die jedes der hundert und hundert Tonstücke in Worten erklärt verlangen, und sich nicht darin finden können, dass nicht jedes eine nennbare Bedeutung hat wie ein Gemälde? Streben sie die reichere Sprache nach der ärmeren abzumessen, und in Worte aufzulösen, was Worte verachtet? Oder, haben sie nie ohne Worte empfunden? Haben sie ihr hohles Herz nur mit Beschreibungen von Gefühlen ausgefüllt? Haben sie niemals im Innern wahrgenommen das stumme Singen, den vermummten Tanz der unsichtbaren Geister? Oder glauben sie nicht an die Märchen? . . .
>
> Aber, was streb' ich Törichter, die Worte zu Tönen zu zerschmelzen? Es ist immer nicht wie ich's fühle. Kommt, ihr Töne, ziehet daher und errettet mich aus diesem schmerzlichen irdischen Streben nach Worten, wickelt mich ein mit euren tausendfachen Strahlen in eure glänzenden Wolken, und hebt mich hinauf in die alte Umarmung des alliebenden Himmels![7]

> What do they want, the timid and doubting reason-mongers, who demand that each of hundreds of musical compositions be explained in words, and who cannot see that not every piece has a statable meaning as does a painting? Are they striving to measure a rich language by a poorer one, and to resolve into words something which scorns words? Or have they never felt without words? Have they filled up their wooden hearts with nothing but descriptions of feelings? Have they never perceived in their innermost selves the dumb singing, the disguised dance of invisible spirits. Or do they not believe in the *Märchen*?
>
> But why am I, foolish one, striving to melt words into tones? It will never be the way I feel it. Come, you tones, draw me away and save me from this painful earthly striving after words, transform me with your thousandfold beams from your shining clouds, and lift me up into the primeval embrace of all-loving Heaven.

The word was thus tainted with this-worldiness. But what was this *other* world into which the Romantics so yearned to be transported? It was not just something up in the clouds. As is clear from the above quotation, it existed in the immateriality and obscurity of the innermost self. And, although not seeming to partake of the intelligibility of rational concepts, this inner world possessed a truth and immediacy far surpassing the material certitude of the "real world." Given this new view of the ultimate truth, music for the Romantics had no business envying the definiteness of verbal labels; for words do not accurately reflect the "way it feels" in the darkness and deepness of the inner self. Music's own "language," puzzling and obscure as it was, was seen as a positive asset, and not a liability; for it did not threaten to misrepresent the infinite riches of the life of the soul by using crass and definite verbal labels.[8]

The vagueness of music's language was also an asset in that it allowed the listener to bring his own individuality into play. Since the affinities of music for suggesting and stimulating inner events were still recognized (in spite of the Romantics' denial of music's obligation to represent "definite" feelings), and since instrumental music did not specify any subject or object to these inner states or processes, the listener could blend the dynamics of the music with his own, and the music could stimulate his own psychic processes—the "content" of the music could vary, so to speak, with each listener. To be sure, no emotion had been communicated from composer to listener, but the listener could nevertheless be profoundly moved. And, as we see in Wackenroder's description of Joseph Berglinger's reaction to music, the intensity of this catalytic effect of music was in direct proportion to the obscurity of music's language (Joseph has just experienced a powerful musical transition from a happy cheerful melody to loud intense sobbing):

> Alle diese mannigfaltigen Empfindungen nun drängten in seiner Seele immer entsprechende sinnliche Bilder und neue Gedanken hervor: eine wunderbare Gabe der Musik,—welche Kunst wohl überhaupt um so mächtiger auf uns wirkt und alle Kräfte unsers Wesens um so allgemeiner in Aufruhr setzt, je dünkler und geheimnisvoller ihre Sprache ist.[9]

> All these manifold varied sensations brought forth in his soul ever corresponding sensual images and new thoughts: a wonderful gift of music,—an art which affects us all the more powerfully, and which stimulates all the powers of our being all the more fully, the darker and more mysterious its language.

Jean Paul also described music's strength, or "omnipotence," as lying in the listener's ability to make music an "accompaniment to one's own inner melody," to use the sounds to "paint scenes of his own." In *Hesperus* he describes how Victor's "swelling speechless heart absorbed the tones unto itself and took the outer tones for inner ones." To be sure, music, according to Jean Paul, arouses certain feelings or images: but these may—and most fittingly, should—vary with the individual nature of each listener's innermost, "speechless" self. And the fact that music's emotions have no names or specified objects presents no obstacle for Victor; for that feeling of infinite longing—that "great monstrous desire which exalts our spirits"—itself has no name or object.[10]

We have seen that the Romantics felt that both music and our inner life had a dark inscrutable nature and an immediate forcefulness—a potency independent of verbal mediation or communication. And although they spoke out against the attempt to represent definite feelings, they nevertheless saw music as in some way an affective art; for both music and the soul shared this inscrutability and immediacy. In addition, the Romantics recognized another aspect of late eighteenth-century instrumental music as similar to, or even congruent with, their affective lives. The new music's rich variety, constantly evolving over a period of time, and its juxtaposition of strongly contrasting material, took on a symbolic value for the Romantics. And this symbolism, it must be emphasized, did not need to be conferred upon music by some symbol-constructing composer. For A. W. Schlegel this symbolism was inherent in music's very nature, merely by virtue of the temporal continuum which forms the basis of music's existence and the changeability inherent in music's succession of events. He most explicitly points out this congruence of music's nature and life's nature, and hence music's potential for symbolizing the ever fluctuating and changing essence of the inner life:

> Wir haben gesehen, dass der Gegenstand der Musik das Zeiterfüllende, ihr allgemeines Vorbild der innre Sinn ist. . . . Die ursprünglichste Form der Musik ist also die reine Succesion, wo nur nach, *nicht neben* einander ein Mannichfaltiges wahrgenommen wird. In dieser Gestalt ist sie ein Bild des nie ruhenden, beweglichen, ewig wechselnden Lebens.[11]

> We have seen that the object of music is the time-filling, and that its universal archetype is the inner sense. . . . The most original form of music is therefore pure succession, where a manifold is perceived *not next* to each other, but after one another. When viewed in this manner music is a symbol of life—never resting, moving, ever changing.

Other Romantics extended music's symbolic potential to include more specific style features than Schlegel's "ever-changing," "never-resting" essence. Whereas in the first chapter we witnessed many strong complaints against the new Italian instrumental music because of the seeming incoherence and arbitrariness with which the musical ideas were chosen and arranged, such objections were themselves senseless to men like Wackenroder. For him such incoherence and contrasts became a symbol of the multifarious and often capricious ongoing totality of life. A symphony presented to Wackenroder a

> Traumgesicht von allen mannigfaltigen menschlichen Affekten wie sie gestaltlos zu eigener Lust, einen seltsamen, ja fast wahnsinnigen, pantomimischen Tanz zusammen feiern, wie sie mit furchtbarer Willkür, gleich den unbekannten, rätselhaften Zaubergöttinnen des Schicksals, frech und frevelhaft durcheinander tanzen.[12]

> vision of all the manifold human affects, as they celebrate for their own pleasure, a strange, indeed almost insane pantomimic dance, as they boldly and wantonly dance among each other with frightening caprice, as do the unknown, enigmatic mystic goddesses of fate.

Elsewhere Wackenroder calls attention to the symbolic potential inherent in the symphony's ability to embrace and fuse even contradictory contents. Berglinger's constantly fluctuating soul ("ewig bewegliche Seele") was completely aplay with tones ("ganz ein Spiel der Töne") as he listened to a symphony; and the tones effected

> eine wunderbare Mischung von Fröhlichkeit und Traurigkeit in seinem Herzen, so dass Lachen und Weinen ihm gleich nahe war; eine Empfindung, die uns auf unserm Wege durch das Leben so oft begegnet, und die keine Kunst geschickter ist auszudrücken, als die Musik.[13]

> a wonderful mixture of happiness and sadness in his heart, so that he was equally near to laughing and crying—a feeling that we meet so often on our way through life, and which no art is more able to express than music.

And notice that this fusion of contraries is not for Wackenroder a truth-offending contradiction, but an aspect of the real inner world of the soul—an aspect moreover which music is especially able to suggest. Tieck mentions a similar symbolic power which is peculiar to instrumental music, and specifically to the symphony. The unity effected amid music's diverse elements and symbolic richness, even conflict, was itself symbolic:

> So blüht in jeder Kunst eine volle, üppige Pracht, in der alle Lebensfülle, alle einzelnen Empfindungen sich vereinigen und nach allen Seiten streben und drängen, und ein vereinigtes Leben mit bunten Farben, mit verschiedenen Klängen darstellen. Nichts scheint mir in der Musik so diese Stelle auszufüllen, als die grossen, aus mannigfachen Elementen zusammengestzten Symphonien.[14]

> Thus, in every art blooms a full, luxuriant display in which all the fullness of life and all individual feelings unite and struggle and press in all directions and thus depict a united life with bright colors, and diverse sounds. To me, nothing in music fills this role so well as the grand symphonies with their manifold elements.

Thus, we have seen in several instances that certain features long identified with instrumental music—such as its variety, contrasts, even capriciousness, and its "pure" unadulterated, nonrepresentative ("meaningless") successivity—have become for the Romantics grounds for asserting instrumental music's superiority over the other arts. Previously, however, as we saw in the first chapter, these features had occasioned much aesthetic misunderstanding, if not outright complaints.

Perhaps even more significantly, certain newly appreciated features of instrumental music are seen by the Romantics to bestow a kind of spiritual uplift. Tieck characterizes music's unification of contraries as a means of spiritual purification, a release from preoccupation with this-worldly squabbles. All suffering and happiness, all delight and all tears, he feels, are transformed into one thing; and their beauty is heightened by the contrast, so that the listener, in such a moment of intense pleasure no longer "distinguishes and analyzes," as does the intellect so fondly, but he is led away from this world, as if drawn down ever more deeply by a "whirlpool."[15]

Not only this *Meerstrudel* produced by the captivating contrasts of the "grand symphonies with their manifold elements," but the naive, happy, merely pleasant sounds of certain instrumental music were valued highly for their redemptive effect. The simple childlike pleasure taken in pure tones was not degraded into merely frivolous diversion. Rather the innocent view of the world which this child-like state of pleasure fostered was recommended as a kind of balm to men engaged in the "serious business" of this world. Clearly, these "pure tones"—tones liberated from any burden or compulsion to represent—could by their very nature confer a unique moral uplift:

> Wahrlich, es ist ein unschuldiges, rührendes Vergnügen, an Tönen an reinen Tönen sich zu freuen! Eine kindliche Freude!—Wenn andre sich mit unruhiger Geschäftigkeit betäuben, und von verwirrten Gedanken, wie von einem Heer fremder Nachtvögel und böser Insekten umschwirrt, endlich ohnmächtig zu Boden fallen;—oh, so tauche ich mein Haupt in dem heiligen, kühlenden Quell der Töne unter, und die heilende Göttin flösst mir die Unschuld der Kindheit wieder ein, dass ich die Welt mit frischen Augen erblicke, und in allgemeine, freudige Versöhnung zerfliesse.—Wenn andre über selbsterfundene Grillen zanken, oder ein verzweiflungsvolles Spiel des Witzes spielen, oder in der Einsamkeit missgestaltete Ideen brüten, die, wie die geharnischten Männer der Fabel, verzweiflungsvoll sich selber verzehren;—oh, so schliess' ich mein Auge zu vor all dem Kriege der Welt—und ziehe mich still in das Land der Musik, als in das Land des Glaubens, zurück wo alle unsre Zweifel und unsre Leiden sich in ein tönendes Meer verlieren—wo wir alles Gekrächze der Menschen vergessen, wo kein Wort-und Sprachengeschnatter, kein Gewirr von Buchstaben und monströser Hieroglyphen-schrift uns schwindlich macht, sondern alle Angst unseres Herzens durch leise Berührung auf einmal geheilt wird.[16]

> Truly, it is an innocent touching pleasure to find joy in tones, pure tones! A childlike joy!— When others are making themselves dizzy with anxious industriousness and when confused thoughts whiz around them like an army of strange night birds and evil insects, until they finally fall to the ground;—oh, then I dip my head down into the holy, cooling spring of tones, and the holy goddess instills the innocence of childhood in me again, so that I see the world with fresh eyes and I am overcome with a universal, joyful feeling of peace.—When others quarrel over imagined troubles, or play a desperate game of wits, or brood alone over monstrous ideas, who, like the armored men of fable, are consumed with desperation;—oh, then I shut my eyes to all the quarrels of the world and retreat quietly into the land of music, as if into the land of belief, where all our suffering and doubts are lost in a resounding sea of tones—where we forget all the banging and crashing of men, where no jabber of words and language, no maze of letters and monstrous symbols make us dizzy, but where by a gentle touching we are instantly healed of all anxiety.

For Schlegel the purity and immateriality alone of instrumental music—its freedom from reference to objects of any kind—transported the listener away from an "earthly hell" into a pure ethereal realm; the passions were thus "purified" of all "material filth."[17]

Whether whirling eddy, cooling spring, sounding sea, or simple purification, the quasi-aquatic flow of music's intangible sounds is seen as a means of drawing us away from the petty concerns of this world, away from the finitude of mundane existence, and of conveying a yearning for the infinite. And it seems that many of the style features mentioned in connection with this uplifting transport—the fullness and energy, the variety and contrasts, and the *Tändelei*—are the same aspects which were previously considered responsible for instrumental music's sheer ear-tickling sensuality, which was at best an amoral characteristic.

At times the benign effect of this redemptive transport is seen as a temporary release only. But at other times instrumental music is seen as fostering an ongoing tranquillity in the face of the vacuous hustle and bustle of the real world. Thus, even a durable social and moral "use" could be found for instrumental music. Wackenroder, for example, finds the unification of such contrasting affective contents to have a uniquely beneficial, even permanently uplifting quality:

[Musik] ist die einzige Kunst, welche die mannigfältigste und widersprechendste Bewegungen unsers Gemüts auf die *selben* schönen Harmonien zurückführt, die mit Freud' und Leid, mit Verzweiflung und Verehrung in gleichen harmonischen Tönen spielt, daher ist *sie* es auch, die uns die echte *Heiterkeit* der Seele einflösst, welche das schönste Kleinod ist, das der Mensch erlangen kann; jene Heiterkeit meine ich, da alles in der Welt uns natürlich, wahr und gut erscheint, da wir im wildesten Gewühle der Menschen schönen Zusammenhang finden, da wir mit reinem Herzen alle Wesen uns verwandt und nahe fühlen, und gleich den Kindern die Welt wie durch die Dämmerung eines lieblichen Traumes erblicken.[18]

[Music] is the only art which reduces the most manifold and the most contradictory movement of our spirit to the *same* beautiful harmonies, which in the same harmonious tones plays with joy and sorrow, despair and reverence. Therefore music is the *very* art which instills in us that genuine *serenity* of soul, which is the most beautiful jewel man can ever acquire;—I mean that serenity where everything in the world seems to us natural, true, and good, where we find a beautiful coherence in the wildest tumult of men, where we feel with pure hearts that all beings are related and near to us, and where we see the world as through the twilight of a lovely dream.

And whereas earlier writers had derided certain aspects of the new instrumental music by calling them "frivolous," "childish," and "child's play," the Romantics, as can be seen in the last two quotations, relished the childlike. Tieck pointed explicitly to the affinity of instrumental music for the childlike as a ground for music's superiority over the other arts:

Das scheint mir eben das Grösse aller Kunst, absonderlich aber der Musik, zu sein, dass all ihr Beginnen so kindlich und kindisch ist, ihr Streben dem äussern Verstande fast töricht, so dass sie sich schämt, es mit Worten auszudrücken,—und dass in dieser Verschämtheit, in diesem Kinderspiel, das Höchste atmet und den Stoff regiert, was wir nur fühlen oder ahnen können.[19]

To me, the greatness of all art, but especially of music, seems to be that its initial impulse is so utterly childlike and childish, and its aspiration for outer understanding so nearly ridiculous, that it feels abashed to express anything with words,—and that in this bashfulness, in this child's play, it breathes the ultimate and reigns over all the elements which we can only feel or forebode.

Dance-like music also acquired a new respectability as a result of the Romantics' emphasis on music with a simple and pure appeal. Although Junker, not many years before, had rejected the *tanzartig* as too common and undignified to find a place in a piece of truly serious and noble music, Wackenroder took it upon himself to defend dance music.[20] Upon attending an outdoor concert of wind instruments bringing forth the most "cheerful and happy tones of spring," he reflected upon his reactions and those of the variegated audience: his blood filled his veins with exultation; and the listeners, drawn from all ages and from all walks of life, all reacted to the music in their own individual ways, and were transformed into a single "glow of joy." "Clearly," he concluded,

so oft ich Tanzmusik höre, fällt es mir in den Sinn, dass diese Art der Musik offenbar die bedeutendste und bestimmste Sprach führt, und dass sie notwendig die eigentlichste, die älteste und *ursprünglichste* Musik sein muss.[21]

whenever I hear dance music it strikes me that this kind of music obviously speaks the most meaningful and definite language, and that it must necessarily be the oldest, the most genuine, and the most *primal* music.

The verb "dance" is moreover frequently used in describing a certain aspect of the nonrationalizable and nonvocal "content" of instrumental pieces. E. T. A. Hoffmann speaks of the "merry dance" of "strange figures" in a Beethoven symphony in the same breath as the "mysterious premonitions" evoked by music's "unfamiliar language."[22] And we have already seen Wackenroder's likening of a symphony to the celebration of a wild, almost insane, pantomimic dance, and his call to perceive in our innermost selves the "dumb singing, the disguised dance of invisible spirits." Dance was seen as a celebration of life, and of man's inscrutable inner drives, and that alone was significant.

It should be clear from the Romantics' view of instrumental music which we have already seen that we are dealing with more than just new attitudes towards music. Obviously their whole view of life and reality was different; and therein lies the key why they could relish instrumental music's variety, vagueness, incoherence, playfulness, its nonvocal characteristics, and its unsuitability for communicating something statable in clear, verbal concepts. It is not our task here to make a rigorous examination of the sources and elements of this new world view— to study, for example, their fascination with the dance, the dream, the childlike, or the "spirit world." But it is important to understand how certain elements of the Romantics' overall thinking related specifically to their extremely high evaluation and unprecedented appreciation of instrumental music.

One such element, which does, however, bear some extended discussion, be-

cause it had such consequences for the Romantics' understanding of the new instrumental music, is their view of man's emotional life. I cannot speak of their
ideas on *the* emotions or *the* passions, for they acknowledged no boundaries between these commonly recognized affects. Indeed, the verbal labels by which
these "definite" emotional states were known in the real world were totally rejected, as we have already seen. Nor did they believe that the inner states so inadequately represented by these names constituted the whole of man's sensitive existence. How then did they manage to speak of man's emotional life?

One of the most prominent adjectives they used was *innig* (inner). This would
seem like an absurdly redundant qualifier, if we did not realize to what extent pain-
ters, poets, and orators had been instructed to study and imitate the passions on the
basis of their corresponding outer manifestations—facial expressions, bodily
movements, speech patterns, tone of voice, and the like.[23] And even music, if it
was to express a particular passion, was to imitate, as were the other arts, these
"natural signs" of the passions—in the case of music this meant impassioned vocal utterances, or what Rousseau called the "natural accents of passion."[24] Sulzer,
for example, believed that since music's real business consisted in the arousal of
emotion, and since it could not do this through the depiction of passionate objects
(that is, objects arousing passion), music's expressiveness was limited to the "depiction of passionate utterances."[25] And Junker felt that hope could not be depicted
in music because it was not usually uttered—it was not outwardly manifested.[26]
Junker, Sulzer, and others enjoined composers to study these external signs of the
passions so that they might better express them in their music. In such a way, it was
believed, the passions could be clearly communicated from composer to listener,
since these signs were believed to be universally understandable. A corollary of
this impassioned utterance theory of musical expression in its most orthodox form
was that all that was inwardly felt naturally found an outlet in these understandable
outer manifestations.

But for the Romantics, inner reality could not be fathomed by "outer understanding," as Tieck called it in the quotation just above. Or, as Schiller said, "If
the soul *speaks,* then alas, it is no longer the *soul* itself who speaks."[27] And not
only was feeling often "speechless," inner feelings often were kept within their
own mysterious inner realm: many feelings were not in fact uttered in any way.
The introvert Victor, for example, the typical Romantic "hero" of Jean Paul's
Hesperus, preferred to hide the effects the music had on him from "worldly men";
for "when immersed in his feelings he shunned and hated all concern with the
attentions of outsiders."[28]

"Outer" had to do, of course, with the scorned real world of material objects,
of intellectual "truths," sterile certainty, and "definite" feelings. The inner
world of men existed in the uncharted and undefined realm of the intellectually
impenetrable "infinite," which was the ultimate goal of all Romantic transport.[29]
And it was in part the very fact that this other, inner world was inaccessible to

verbal labels, was dark, inscrutable and mysterious, which made it part of this world of the infinite. This dark inner reality was simply not held to be translatable into the clear language of the "outer" understanding. Thus the adjectives "innig" and "dunkel" (meaning "dark" or "obscure," the opposite of "clear" in the rationalistic formula "clear and distinct") are among the Romantics' most frequently used adjectives for describing the "wonder" of man's inner life.[30] And since music had, it was felt, a special ability to affect this inner life, and since its content too was dark and inscrutable, instrumental music possessed a special affinity with this realm of the truly real. As E. T. A. Hoffmann said, music's sole subject is the "infinite"—it is the "most romantic of the arts."

Just as the Romantics refused to acknowledge the demand for clarity and denied the reality of "definite" feelings, by asserting the more profound truth dwelling in man's dark inscrutable inner life, they refused to acknowledge the demand for distinctness and questioned the existence of separable emotional entities, by speaking of man's inner emotional life as an ever-flowing, "ever-changing," dynamic process. In short, there was nothing either clear or distinct about the emotions: their real nature was, on the contrary, dark and confused. This latter aspect of this new view of the emotions—the aspect of dynamism—is especially pregnant with consequences for the Romantics' new appreciation of instrumental music. For there was a new view of the very essence of man's inner emotional life which the adjectives "inner" and "dark" could only qualify. Man's emotional life was no longer seen as a composite of namable static entities, such as sadness, happiness, rage, love, and so on: it was a dynamic process, a "never resting, moving, ever changing" succession over a period of time, as A. W. Schlegel characterized it. And this inner dynamic reality, embracing the "whole quality of our existence" was for Schlegel particularly close to the essence of music:

> So wie die bildenden Künste die klärsten Anschauungen geben, so die Musik die innigsten; jene am nächsten mit der Erkenntniss verwandt, diese mit der Empfindung, das Wort in dem weiteren Sinne genommen, wo es nicht eine Gemüthsbewegung, einen Affect bedeutet, sondern die ganze Qualität unserer Existenz.[31]

> Just as the graphic arts elicit the clearest ideas, so does music arouse the innermost; the former are most nearly related to knowing, the latter to feeling, in the broader sense of the word, where not an emotion or an affect is meant, but the whole quality of our existence.

We can get a good glimpse of what relevance this new view of the emotions had for an appreciation of instrumental music by reading the relatively articulate words of a non-Romantic. Ferdinand Rochlitz becomes an eloquent apologist for the Romantic view that the whole quality of our existence cannot be divided into separate, namable, and "definite" entities, when he defends the indefiniteness of music's content on the grounds that man's emotional life itself is inscrutable and indivisible. Although stopping short of denying the reality of such emotional entities, he points most eloquently to the revealing fact that one cannot say precisely where one entity gives way to another:

> So wahr es auch seyn mag, dass Musik und Poesie nur vereinigt das Höchste und Stärkste würken: so sagen doch die in aller möglichen Form ewig wiederholten Klagen über Unbestimmtheit und Charakterlosigkeit der Musik. . . . Weg mit dem Gedicht, das nicht auch klingt; aber noch weiter weg mit der musikalischen Komposition, die nichts sagt! Wenn Musik Ausdruck der Empfindung ist: so kann ja das, worin keine Empfindung ist, eben darum keine Musik seyn. Nun verlangt man—ich weiss es wohl:—Lieber, so nenne mir einmal die ganze Reihe der Empfindungen, ihrer Uebergänge, Wendungen und Nuäncen, welche z. B. in diesem, im Ganzen freylich wohl erhabenen Sinfoniensatze liegt oder liegen soll—Dies ist aber eine etwas sonderbare Prätension. Lieber, nenne du mir erst einmal die ganze Reihe Deiner Empfindungen, ihrer Uebergänge, Wendungen und Nuäncen, welche z. B. in dieser Stunde, wo Du dich erhaben gerührt fühltest, in Dir lebte! Du wirst dies nicht vermögen: so kann ich jenes auch nicht. Also nicht in der Musik—in Dir selbst suche den Grund davon. . . . Du kannst sagen: in dieser Viertelstunde war ich froh, in der darauf folgenden schwermüthig; Du kannst auch bestimmen, in dieser Minute war ich nicht mehr so froh, es gesellete sich ein gewisses weichmüthiges Gefühl zu meinem Frohsinn, in dieser nahm dies überhand u.s.w.: aber Du kannst die einzelnen Mischungen, Gradationen, Uebergänge, Nuäncen, nicht angeben. So ist es natürlicherweise auch mit dem Ausdruck derselben durch ihnen entsprechende Töne.[32]

> However true it may be that only when united do music and poetry achieve the most intense and most elevated effect: this is said in the eternally repeated complaints about the indefiniteness and characterlessness of music. Away with the poem [they say], with the musical composition, which says nothing. If music is to be the expression of feeling, then that music which contains no feeling must therefore be *no* music. They demand—I know it well— ''name me, my dear fellow, just once the whole series of feelings, their transitions, changes, and nuances, which for example lie, or are supposed to lie, on the whole, in this admittedly quite sublime symphony movement.'' All this is, however, a strange pretension. My dear fellow, name to me just once the whole series of your feelings, their transitions, changes, and nuances, which, for example, lived in you in this hour when you felt sublimely moved! You will not be able to do this: even so I cannot fulfill your request. Seek not then the reason for this in music—seek it in your very self. You can say that in this quarter hour you were happy, in the following one you were melancholy. You can also determine that in one minute you were no longer so happy, a certain melancholy feeling associated itself with your happiness; in another minute the latter took the upper hand, and so on: but you cannot specify the mixtures, gradations, and transitions of these feelings. The same holds true, naturally, with the expression of the same in music.

Rochlitz, of course, separates himself from the orthodox Romantic conception of music in that he is willing to grant to vocal music the higher, more powerfully affecting status. But in giving a model of the inner life as an ongoing, intellectually unanalyzable succession, and in suggesting the relevance of one's recognition of this inner reality to one's appraisal of instrumental music, he articulates most clearly the Romantic view that the indeterminateness, or nonverbalizability, if you will, of music's content is defensible on the grounds that the affective flow of life itself is likewise unsuited to verbal description.

We get another view of the inadequacy of language in representing this flow of the emotional life when Rochlitz takes it upon himself to defend the practice of first writing the music and then adding the words. Not only were words too definite, they were unsuited to mirroring the ever-changing dynamic of the emotions. For, Rochlitz argued, we cannot treat the materials of poetry "freely." Language contains so much that is empty and lifeless for the feelings; its essential articles, auxiliary verbs, particles, and such are merely for the understanding. Thus words often are not conformable to all the "turns, gradations and nuances of feelings." "Tones, however," Rochlitz points out,

> sind bildsamer und gefügiger als das weichste Wachs, in der Hand der wahren Künstlers; sie schmiegen sich in alle Wendungen, Uebergänge und Nüancen der Empfindungen—sind, an sich, allein für die Empfindung. Jene feinen Uebergänge der Empfindungen in einander lassen sich nur fühlen, und in natürlichen, nothwendigen Zeichen *ausdrücken*, nicht *nennen*, und in konventionellen Zeichen *beschreiben*.[33]

> in the hands of a true artist, are more plastic and manageable than the softest wax; they can conform to all the turns, transitions, and nuances of the feelings—they are by nature for the feelings alone. Those subtle transitions of one feeling into another can only be felt, and only *expressed*, in natural, necessary signs; they cannot be *named* and *described* with conventional symbols.

Tones, in short, were more suited for reflecting the ever-changing inner dynamism of the emotional life.[34] And this is the view the Romantics shared—only Rochlitz seems to have explained it more clearly.

The Romantics loved to speak metaphorically. They had a favorite family of images for expressing this progressively changing and unanalyzable nature of both life and music; most of them all had to do with water. These aquatic metaphors did not originate with the Romantics, however. Goethe's lyric poetry of the Sturm und Drang is rich with present participles and verbs of growing and becoming, "as if he could only think of attributes as motion."[35] And Goethe actually compared the "ever-changing" *(ewig wechselnd)* essence of the soul to water:

> Des Menschen Seele
> Gleicht dem Wasser:
> Vom Himmel kommt es,
> Zum Himmel steigt es,
> Und wieder nieder
> Zur Erde muss es,
> Ewig wechselnd.[36]

> The soul of man
> is like unto water:
> From Heaven it comes,
> To Heaven it ascends,
> And then again
> To Earth it must,
> Eternally changing.

But it seems the Romantics were the first to apply this "ever-changing" idea to the understanding of instrumental music. Wackenroder most explicitly asserted and explained the aptness of this aquatic metaphor for both music and the inner life, and music's consequent superiority as an art. We have already seen in this chapter the whirlpool, the cooling spring, and the sounding sea. But the most common metaphor, especially in the case of the "grand symphonies with their manifold elements," was that of the stream—Wackenroder referred to it as a "mannigfaltiger Strom":

Ein fliehender Strom soll mir zum Bilde dienen. Keine menschliche Kunst vermag das Gliessen eines mannigfaltigen Stromes, nach allen den tausend einzelnen, glatten und bergigten, stürmenden und schäumenden Wellen, mit *Worten* fürs Auge hinzuzeichnen,—die Sprache kann die Veränderungen nur dürftig *zählen* und *nennen,* nicht die aneinanderhängenden Verwandlungen der Tropfen uns sichtbar vorbilden. Und ebenso ist es mit dem geheimnisvollen Strome in den Tiefen des menschlichen Gemütes beschaffen, die Sprache zählt und nennt und beschreibt seine Verwandlungen, in fremden Stoff—die Tonkunst strömt ihn uns selber vor. Sie greift beherzt in die geheimnisvolle Harfe, schlagt in der dunkeln Welt bestimmte dunkle Wunderzeichen in bestimmter Folge an—und die Saiten unsers Herzens erklingen, und wir verstehen ihren Klang.[37]

A flowing stream shall serve as my metaphor. No human art is able with *words* to reproduce for the eye the flow of a multifarious stream, according to all the thousand individual, smooth and bumpy, tempestuous and effervescent waves; language can only inadequately *count* and *name* the changes; it cannot represent to us the continual transformations of drops. Thus is it also with the secret stream in the depths of the human spirit: language counts and names and describes its transformations—music makes the stream itself flow before us. Music boldly grips the strings of the secret harp, it causes definite dark portents to ring in definite order in the dark world—and the strings of our heart resound, and we understand their sound.

Wackenroder suggests an intensification of Rochlitz's view. For in the eyes of the Romantic there were often not even any namable states with unnamable transitions. Rather the "secret stream" in the depths of the human spirit was in a state of constant transition, so to speak—in a state of what A. W. Schlegel called "reine Succession."[38] And such was the nature of music's "stream" with its unanalyzable, "formless," nature, and with its suggestion or embodiment of the *ewig wechselnd* nature of the emotional life, that no composer need intend to represent or to express, to symbolize or to evoke.

In den Wellen der Musik . . . strömt recht eigentlich nur das reine, formlose Wesen, der Gang und die Farbe, da ja auch vornehmlich der tausendfältige Übergang der Empfindungen; die idealische, engelreine Kunst weiss in ihrer Unschuld weder den Ursprung noch das Ziel ihrer Regungen, kennt nicht den Zusammenhang ihrer Gefühle mit der wirklichen Welt.[39]

In the waves of music . . . streams forth, strictly speaking, only pure, formless essence, movement and color, but especially the thousandfold transitions of feelings; this ideal and pure angelic art knows in its innocence neither the origin nor the goal of its movements, does not know the connection of its feelings with the real world.

In both the above quotations of Wackenroder we are once again reminded that for the Romantics music did indeed possess some affinity with the inner emotional life, but that music's affective power did not exist by virtue of any representative intent; it existed rather by virtue of music's own "pure," "specific nature." And if this stream, by virtue of a dynamism isomorphic with the "ever-changing" nature of the inner life itself, could not succeed in evoking or suggesting any "definite" feelings, it could do even better: by virtue of the nameless, objectless character of the affective response it elicited, it could convey that very sense of "infinite longing" (itself undefinable and objectless) which was so delicious to the Romantics.[40] The symbolic celebration of the existence and the elemental force of such objectless, ineffable, enigmatic feelings was the celebration of the mystery of life itself—was, for the Romantics, the very essence of instrumental music.

Thus can one see the demise of the rationalistic *Affektenlehre* and in its stead the ascendancy of Wackenroder's *Seelenlehre*—a doctrine of the uncommunicable, mysterious, ever-changing nature of the inner life as found in the most powerful stimulant or symbol of that life: "the grand symphonies with their manifold elements," their fleeting contrasting connotations, their ever-changing streams which the "prepared" listener could sense as analogous to the stresses and strains of his own private existence. That music's freedom need not be compromised by this new doctrine, that music's soul-relatedness need not constrain the sensitive composer's intuitive handling of his specifically musical materials, and that this soul-relatedness was as much a result as a cause of such "wonderful" compositions, is implied by the very title of Wackenroder's central essay on the relation of instrumental music to the emotions: "The specific inner nature of music and the doctrine of the soul found in today's instrumental music."[41] Both the new *Seelenlehre* and the new instrumental music came of age together, and the growth of one, it appears, stimulated that of the other.

The way in which the multifarious stream of music affects the secret stream of the inner life is an important part of the Romantics' view of instrumental music's significance. When Wackenroder spoke of music's evocation of "Wunderzeichen in bestimmter Folge," he used a traditional metaphor to describe the manner in which a musical embodiment of an inner flow could make an impact on the listener—sympathetic vibration.[42] And he emphasized that this sympathy was broad enough to include the very order of musical events or suggestions. The Romantic view is clearly stated in Wackenroder's above account of the metaphor of the stream. Not only is music effective because of its intelligibility as a symbol of something itself unintelligible: the very ordering of its materials, as well as the materials themselves, affect us in a direct, physical way—and it is this effect (in fact an "affective" one) that is then "understood" or recognized. That is, for the symbolism of music to be effective, it does not first have to be recognized on a conscious cognitive level. The mediation of the cognitive powers is not needed. For the effects of tones are immediate.

The Romantics did not attempt to analyze this immediate connection between tonal movements and inner spiritual movements; they accepted it, as they did many mysteries from their German past. They believed, as did their German forefathers many generations earlier, in a "secret association" between the sounds of music and the human soul. But in their characterization of this immediate sympathetic reaction, they went far beyond the Boethian notion that harmonious or disharmonious proportions between tones effect harmonious or disharmonious proportions within the human body and soul. They also went beyond the Cartesian and Matthesonian *Affektenlehre*, whereby definite intervals and tempos were held to correspond to the various states of the blood and vital spirits, all of which were the physical concomitants of the various passions.[43] Nor did they limit themselves to the neoclassic theory whereby music was to imitate the external and understandable accents of a particular passion. Rather, the whole sequence of music's varied events over a period of time possessed a certain congruence or analogy with the patterns of the inner emotional stream such that a series of musical events could set in motion a series of inner events.[44] And since the sequence of musical patterns stimulated this inner reaction directly, even physically, without conscious recognition, on the part of the listener, of an object of representation, the result of the listening experience was the evocation of actual inner events, of emotional states of some sort—and not the communication of ideas of these inner states. It was this affective result which was then consciously recognized; and it was an introspective, rather than a rational, form of recognition. As we have mentioned before, it was part of the Romantic view that the emotions aroused by the music could vary from listener to listener; it was not essential to their view that this immediate effect of music would bring invariable results, although certainly they could have sensed the evocation of some music as quite unequivocal. It is also important to recognize that they did not necessarily believe that the emotive responses aroused by music had to correspond to real-life emotions. Jean Paul's Victor spoke of the "artificial suffering" aroused by music, and Wackenroder tells of the "mirror of tones" which, by arousing new feelings in us, or by bringing to the fore latent emotional potentialities, enables us to know ourselves:

> In dem Spiegel der Töne lernt das menschliche Herz sich selber kennen; sie sind es, wodurch wir das *Gefühl fühlen* lernen; sie gaben vielen in verborgnen Winkeln des Gemüts träumenden Geistern lebendes Bewusstsein, und bereichern mit ganz neuen zauberischen Geistern des Gefühls unser Inneres.[45]

> In the mirror of tones the human heart becomes acquainted with itself; it is they, through which we learn to *feel emotion;* they give living consciousness to many ghosts dreaming in hidden corners of the soul, and they enrich our inner life with wholly new magical spirits.

In the same context Wackenroder spoke of the "completely new and wonderful turns and transformations of feelings" which can be evoked even by the "dry scholarly system" of composition.[46] E. T. A. Hoffmann suggested that in a Beethoven symphony mysterious premonitions are articulated and that a specifically musical (or at least, musically induced) form of self-understanding results.[47] Indeed, so great was the "sensual power" of tones that even the "science" of musical composition, when pursued purposelessly, that is, for its own sake, nevertheless possessed a "wonderful significance":

> Es gibt ganz Tonstücke, deren Töne von ihren Meistern wie Zahlen in einer Rechnung . . .
> bloss regelrecht, aber sinnreich in einer glücklichen Stunde zusammengesetzt wurden. . . . Sie
> reden eine herrliche empfindungsvolle Sprache, obwohl der Meister wenig daran gedacht haben
> mag.[48]

> There are whole pieces whose tones were combined by their masters as if they were numbers in a
> calculation . . . merely according to rule, but with ingenuity, in a felicitous moment. . . .
> They speak a magnificent, sensitive language, although the master may hardly have had that intention.

Although Wackenroder's precise meaning is vague as to how the intricacies of musical composition play a role in music's affectiveness, he is nevertheless explicit in defending musical "art," or "science" such as was rejected by the partisans of Rousseau's extremely homophonic theory of musical expression. It seems that for Wackenroder it is the richness, variety and complexity of content, successfully treated by the new highly developed musical forms (incorporating the intricacies of both counterpoint and motivic development), which can make them so affectively potent. Specifically, he speaks of the "refined multiplicity" *(verfeinerte Mannigfaltigkeit)* which the sensual power of music had gained from the "learned system, the scientific profundities of music."[49] And the uniting of contraries is not the least accomplishment of this "learned system": the highest triumphs of instrumental music are the "grand symphonies,"

> worin nicht eine einzelne Empfindung gezeichnet, sondern eine ganze Welt, ein ganzes Drama
> menschlicher Affekten ausgeströmt ist.[50]

> wherein is depicted not an individual feeling, but a whole world, a complete drama of human
> affect is streamed forth.

Other writers point more specifically to counterpoint as an important means of reflecting or affecting the newly recognized dynamic complexity of the emotional life. Contrapuntal complexity is essential to the "Mahlerey der menschlichen Empfindungen," explains a writer in an early issue of the *Allgemeine musikalische Zeitung,* because

> gedachte Empfindungen nicht minder gemischt, gleich oft mit einander im Kampfe sind, gleich
> oft von einer in die andere übergehn, und überhaupt, wie Licht und Schatten, einander
> wechseln.[51]

aforesaid feelings are not merely mixed with one another, but are equally often in conflict, often change into another, and constantly alternate with each other, like light and shadow.

And Herder himself, at one time an adherent of Rousseau's theory of musical expression, was heard to admit freely, around 1800, a similar enthusiasm for the affective symbolism of counterpoint; and again, this enthusiasm is based on an active, changing, conflicting pattern of emotional reality:

Die Gewalt der Chöre, insonderheit im Augenblick des Einfallens und Wiedereinfallens ist unbeschreibbar. Unbeschreibbar die Anmuth der Stimmen; die einander begleiten; sie sind Eins und nicht Eins: sie verlassen, suchen, verfolgen, widersprechen, bekämpfen, verstärken, vernichten einander, und erwecken und beleben und trösten und schmeicheln und umarmen einander wieder, bis sie zuletzt in Einem Ton ersterben. Es giebt kein süsser Bild des Suchens und Findens, des freundschaftlichen Zwistes und der Versöhnung, des Verlierens und der Sehnsucht, der zweifelnden und ganzen Wiedererkennung, endlich der völligen süssen Vereinigung und Verschmelzung als diese zwei- und mehrstimmige Tongänge, Tonkämpfe, wortlos oder von Worten begleitet.[52]

The power of choruses, especially in the moments when voices enter and re-enter, is indescribable. Indescribable the charm of the voices which accompany each other; they are one and then not one; they leave, seek, pursue, oppose, combat, intensify, destroy and annihilate one another—and awaken and rejuvenate and comfort and compliment and embrace each other again, until they finally die away in One Tone. There is no sweeter symbol of searching and finding, of friendly dispute and reconciliation, or of loss and longing, of doubting and complete recognition, and finally of complete sweet reuniting and coalescence than these two and three voiced tone processions—tone-struggles—wordless or accompanied by words.

Thus, when Wackenroder speaks of "today's instrumental music" as an "abundant and flexible mechanism for the depiction of human feelings,"[53] we must understand that all talk of *Affektenlehre,* or of representing "definite" feelings, is out of the question, in spite of the fact that the words "depiction" and "mechanism" remind us more of rationalistic than of Romantic thought. Rather, Wackenroder has in mind, as he himself told us above, a *mannigfaltiger Strom* as his model for the human feelings—that is a new concept of the inner life as something "never resting, moving, ever changing," a concept which he called *Seelenlehre*. This stream contained changes, turns, transitions, and conflicts, and by its ever progressively changing nature, could not be analyzed into defined emotional states, nor expressed in verbal labels. Thus "depiction" can be no more precisely understood than these states themselves, and can mean no more than "suggest," "symbolize," or "evoke." And the word "mechanism" refers to the immediate sensual power of tones, which operated on a physical or physiological level, and bypassed any form of intellectual cognition, as we have seen. His statement is thus an accurate, if misleading, representation of the Romantic view of the new instrumental music—a view profoundly influenced by this new view of the emotions.

Moreover, the wonder of it all was that in music's specific nature were combined, as if by some fortuitous confluence of phenomena, these three ingredients: compositional "profundity" (even when pursued for its own sake), "sensual power" (the means by which tones affect the "individual fibers of the human heart"), and the symbolism of the human feelings (that is, "significance"):

Das Dunkle und Unbeschreibliche aber, welches in der Wirkung des Tons verborgen liegt, und welches bei keiner andern Kunst zu finden ist, hat durch das System eine wunderbare Bedeutsamkeit gewonnen. Es hat sich zwischen den einzelnen mathematischen Tonverhältnissen und den einzelnen Fibern des menschlichen Herzens eine unerklärliche Sympathie offenbart, wodurch die Tonkunst ein reichhaltiges und bildsames Maschinenwerk zur Abschilderung menschlicher Empfindungen geworden ist.

So hat sich des eigenthümliche Wesen der heutigen Musik gebildet. . . . Keine andre vermag diese Eigenschaften der Tiefsinnigkeit, der sinnlichen Kraft und der dunkeln, phantastischen Bedeutsamkeit auf eine so rätselhafte Weise zu verschmelzen. Diese merkwürdige, enge Vereinigung so Widerstrebend-scheinender Eigenschaften macht den ganzen Stolz ihrer Vorzüglichkeit aus.[54]

The dark and indescribable, which lie hidden in the effect of tones, and which are not to be found in any other art, have acquired a wonderful meaningfulness through the system [of the science of musical composition]. An unexplainable sympathy between the individual mathematical tone relationships and the individual fibers of the human heart has revealed itself, whereby music has become an abundant and flexible mechanism for the depiction of human feelings.

Thus has the specific nature of today's music formed itself. . . . No other art is able to melt together in such an enigmatic way these properties of profundity, sensual power, and dark fantastic significance. In this remarkable, intimate alliance of such seemingly opposing qualities consists the whole glory of music's superiority.

We come, now, to a final elucidation of this new *Seelenlehre* and its relation to the new symphonic style. The strong contrasts of the new style, the compositional techniques of thematic work, even counterpoint, the Beethovenian art of transition, the unity which was achieved amid such profound variety by means of motivic development—all are given metaphysical significance by Hoffmann, in the following account of a Beethoven trio movement:

Ein einfaches aber fruchtbares, zu den verschiedensten kontrapunktischen Wendungen, Abkürzungen u.s.w. taugliches singbare Thema liegt jedem Satze zum Grunde; alle übrigen Nebenthemata und Figuren sind dem Hauptgedanken innig verwandt, so dass sich alles zu höchsten Einheit durch alle Instrumente verschlingt und ordnet. So ist die Struktur des Ganzen; aber in diesem künstlichen Bau wechseln in rastlosen Fluge die wunderbärsten Bilder, in denen Freude und Schmerz, Wehmut und Wonne neben-und ineinander hervortreten. Seltsame Gestalten beginnen einen lustigen Tanz, indem sie bald zu einem Lichtpunkt verschweben, bald funkelnd und blitzend auseinanderfahren und sich in mannigfachen Gruppen jagen und verfolgen; und mitten in diesem aufgeschlossenen Geisterreiche horcht die entzückte Seele der unbekannten Sprache zu und versteht alle die geheimsten Ahnungen, von denen sie ergriffen.

Nur *der* Komponist drang wahrhaft in die Geheimnisse der Harmonie ein, der durch sie auf das Gemüt des Menschen zu wirken vermag.[55]

A simple but fruitful theme, songlike, susceptible to the most varied contrapuntal treatments, curtailments, and so forth, forms the basis of each movement; all remaining subsidiary themes and figures are intimately related to the main idea in such a way that the details all interweave, arranging themselves among the instruments in highest unity. Such is the structure of the whole, yet in this artful structure there alternate in restless flight the most marvellous pictures in which joy and grief, melancholy and ecstasy, come side by side or intermingled to the fore. Strange figures begin a merry dance, now floating off into a point of light, now splitting apart, flashing and sparkling, evading and pursuing one another in various combinations, and at the center of the spirit realm thus disclosed the intoxicated soul gives ear to the unfamiliar language and understands the most mysterious premonitions that have stirred it.

That composer *alone* has truly mastered the secrets of harmony who knows how, by their means, to work upon the human soul.

We see in the above that a form of instrumental music could both arouse affects and suggest or symbolize affects, or at least the dynamic realities of the affective life, without relying on the traditionally recognized means of musical expressiveness: the idiom of vocal music. Like Wackenroder, Hoffmann stresses not the representation of feelings, nor even the self-expression of the composer's feelings, but the composer's ability, through specifically musical compositional techniques, to "work upon the human soul." And a form of understanding results, not of what the composer was intending to express or communicate, but of the listener's own inner workings, as evoked by the music. The process of composition which produces the "grand symphonies with their manifold elements" also produces an embodiment of the dynamism of the inner life which can symbolize, suggest, or evoke the unnamable riches and ineffable intensity of this inner life. Whether in creating a continuous stream, involving the much remarked-upon transitions from one feeling to one quite different, or whether in juxtaposing and uniting the most restless alternations of grief and joy, the composer displays music's specific nature, and the listener experiences some kind of affective regeneration, or revealing spiritual exercise, for which the skilled and knowing composer, by following his specifically musical instincts, provides the vehicle.[56] The emphasis is on the effects of music, not on their cause. The composer is not necessarily consciously trying to express, communicate, or arouse this or that emotion.[57] He is, however, whether by intent or not, adhering to the new *Seelenlehre*, setting the soul into motion, using the art whose specific nature is most like the soul's: "never resting, moving, ever-changing."

7

Conclusion: Romantic Transformations of Enlightened Themes

It is time now to look back over the eighteenth-century critical debate bearing on the aesthetic understanding of instrumental music and to inquire as to the relation of this debate to the Romantic attitude that instrumental music was the highest of the arts. We saw in the previous chapter that the early Romantics, in spite of their anti-speculative and iconoclastic proclivities, dealt with the same themes as those identified in the first chapter as central to eighteenth-century Enlightened critics' opinions of instrumental music: most importantly, the issues of representation, intelligibility, spiritual or moral value, and the role of contrast and counterpoint. At the end of this chapter the opposing "Enlightened" and "Romantic" positions on each individual issue are listed side by side so that the extent of the change in attitude, with all its components, can be readily grasped. It will be clear from this summary listing that the Romantic treatment of these themes constituted a veritable transformation of opinion.

The really interesting question, as we review the opinions surveyed in the preceding chapters, then becomes: Were these transformations prepared or sudden—were Romantic attitudes towards instrumental music part of an evolution or a revolution in musical thought? Thus we shall organize the better part of our review around an inquiry into the nature of the historical developments that made possible the truly unprecedented belief that instrumental music was the highest of the arts. For in the course of the eighteenth century Romantic positions on several crucial issues were already being formulated by German critics concerned to explain the contemporary phenomenon of instrumental music. Still other Romantic attitudes bear close resemblances to the attitudes of pre-Enlightenment Germany. By looking at the various issues of the critical debate in turn we should be able to come to some answers to the evolution versus revolution question.

First let us look at the issue of representation. It was indeed a bold, even revolutionary, assertion on the part of the Romantics to say that instrumental music only prostituted itself when it attempted to represent definite aspects of the "real" world, especially definite emotions. For the insistence on verisimilitude—or a deliberately imposed and definite extramusical meaning—was one of the most persistent neoclassic attitudes in eighteenth-century German music criticism. During most of the latter eighteenth century, music without such a content was considered incapable of moving, if not downright trivial and boring. Even Forkel and Junker, certainly not adherents of French critical principles, clung to the idea that music's task was to represent some aspect of the extramusical world, namely the emotions, and that music moved the listener by virtue of this emotional content, which the skillful composer communicated by means of a "correct" and "determinate" musical representation. However, many earlier Germans, those not yet touched by the skepticism and intellectual rigor of the Enlightenment, had not held that music must represent in order to move. Like the Romantics, they sensed an affective force independent of any consciously recognized emotional representation; they believed that music's meaning was not imposed from without, as a result of the composer's representational intent, but that this meaning was somehow innate and certainly not statable or verifiable using the means of any nonmusical language. Even the Enlightened Scheibe in the forties had not insisted that instrumental chamber music must imitate nature, in order to interest and affect the serious listener. But the impact of French ideas was so strong by mid-century that the idea became firmly entrenched that all music, and most explicitly the Italian instrumental genres, must represent some definite aspect of reality, preferably a passion or feeling.

Few Germans between Batteux and the Romantics would have disagreed with Sulzer's statement that "[The composer] must never forget that music in which no passion or feeling is uttered in an understandable language is nothing other than mere noise." Nevertheless there were in the post-Batteux Germany definite glimmers of the notion that all music need not be construed as a language representing definite, statable aspects of the real world.

Even in the process of adapting Batteux's mimetic theory to music, some Germans showed a strong streak of resistance to the statement that music "imitated nature." Hiller in 1755 held that musical utterances were themselves natural and were a natural act of expression and hence not imitations at all. Ramler, whose translations of Batteux insured the currency of mimetic theory into the nineteenth century, in 1760 explained that the musician's creative model in the real world was the language of other musical compositions! Krause attributed to music an innate essence which the musical poet and the composer with representational intent must not violate with their own attempts to imbue music with meaning and significance. Ruetz, also writing in the fifties, but an open opponent of the Batteux partisans, argued that music was itself an "original," hence did not need to be a mere vehicle of representation, and that there was no such thing as music with no meaning. The notions of the "wonderful" and the "sublime," applied respectively by Hiller and Sulzer, both believers in musical mimesis, to nonrepresentative instrumental music, were in effect early attempts to give aesthetic status to certain characteristic features of the Italian instrumental style obviously not sanctioned by mimetic theory or theories of emotional communication. Finally, Forkel was still arguing against the neoclassic partisans in 1788 when he asserted that music's meanings are beyond words the way religion is beyond reason and that music "only becomes the real language of the infinite gradations of the feelings at that point where other languages can no longer reach, and where their ability to express ends." Both Ruetz in 1755 and Forkel in 1788 agreed that music indeed expressed the emotions in some sense, but they argued against the neoclassic partisans by claiming that this emotional content was inaccessible to other languages, hence incommunicable except by specifically musical means.

As we have seen, the Romantics were loath to speak of music as representation of a given content but rather spoke of music as symbolizing, suggesting, or merely arousing emotional experience. They obviously shared the view that music had in some sense an emotional content, though the Romantics saw this content as innate and specific to music—not as something imposed upon the essentially nonreferential materials of music. The "specific nature" of music became for the Romantics a symbol of man's dark and essentially indescribable inner being, providing unique access to this mysterious inner realm. Thus music was valuable for its own sake and not for its function as a translatable term in a language communicating already known psychological phenomena. And this was the crux of the content issue: whether music's content had to be deliberately imposed upon it by the composer, or whether it was innate to works of true musical genius.

During the course of the eighteenth century, theories of the emotions were of course also changing, so that even though both Enlightened and Romantic minds saw music as in some way embodying and moving the emotions, a considerable change in music's relation to the emotions was inevitable.

The issue of instrumental music's content was very closely related to the issue of the intelligibility and definitude of this content. Although there was, as we have seen, a broad consensus supporting the notion that the emotions were the proper content of music, there was a lively debate as to the manner in which this content made its effect, and as to the degree of intelligibility one could justly expect of a piece of instrumental music which purported to communicate some emotional content. Batteux, Gottsched, and the neoclassic school in general adamantly maintained rigorous standards for music: it was to aspire to the same denotative distinctness and clarity, as well as the same logical coherence (shunning discontinuity and redundance) of the best verbal discourse. It was to address and satisfy the intellect—to "occupy the mind with an object." A corollary view seemed to follow: if the content of music was indeed intellectually recognizable, and if a piece of music possessed an intersubjective truth, then that content should be translatable into a verbal equivalent. The Romantic view, on the other hand, which seemed to be forming earlier in the century, held that verbal or scientific standards of intelligibility could not justly be applied to music and that in fact the content of music, namely the emotional stream, was itself not rationally analyzable, or namable. For the early Romantics the word prostituted the reality it proposed to represent; and intellectual cognition was irrelevant, for music's effects were immediate.

The most prominent development leading away from the neoclassic attitude regarding intelligibility and towards the Romantic one was the theory, voiced by several eighteenth-century critics, that music's content was not communicated through channels of rational cognition, but through physical and physiological ones. They buttressed this view, though reminiscent of medieval theories of *musica humana*, with the new science, and referred to the mechanism of the ear, the constitution of the nervous system, and even to vibrations in the air. Mattheson in 1739 made an early attempt to give a scientific account of the immediate effects of music. Krause in 1753 also put his trust in the direct physiological effects of music's vibrations; and a similarly conceived physical "mechanism" was the cornerstone of Junker's theory of musical communication in 1770. Secondly, with Baumgarten's "aesthetics" in 1750, came a significant loosening of the bonds of misplaced and inappropriate cognitive requirements; the arts were a sphere of human activity fundamentally distinct from rational, intellectual discourse; hence they had their own standards for intelligibility and their own peculiar perfection. Instrumental music, and the specifically musical elements of vocal music, were defended by Nicolai and Krause, who relied explicitly on Baumgarten's definition of art as the perfection of sensual (i.e. nonrational) cognition.

Finally, throughout the eighteenth century, in spite of the desire of most critics to be "enlightened" and skeptical, to shun superstition and probe all mysteries, there was an undercurrent of almost reverential agnosticism towards the emotional content of music itself and of unquestioning faith in the mysterious channels through which this content was transmitted. It is most significant that Hiller and Ruetz, who in the fifties were on opposite sides of the debate over the applicability of Batteux's ideas to music, held similar opinions on this issue. Ruetz explicitly quoted Augustine in pointing to the "secret association" between musical sounds and the human soul; and Hiller, in arguing for a flexible and broad interpretation of Batteux, paraphrased the same church father in speaking of music's "secret passageways" into the soul. Ruetz spoke of the peculiar emotional content of music, that could only be known by "musical souls" and which no language could describe. Hiller, for his part, characterized some of the emotions typically aroused by music as too subtle or refined to be identifiable, or, as he himself interprets, to be named; Hiller saw this as a precious gift of music which must not be taken away in the name of theoretical purity. Forkel, though much farther removed in time from pre-Enlightenment attitudes, defended music from the charge of inferior intelligibility by pointing out that it was easier to get at the "outer" images of painting and poetry than the "inner spiritual image" which is found "in the most secret corner of our being." It isn't music's fault, he wrote, that we don't have words for the "subtle relations and agreements among dark feelings"; for music's peculiar content reflects an aspect of the emotions which other languages can never reach.

Of course, although they did in fact help preserve an attitude that was fundamental to the Romantic view of instrumental music as the highest art, neither Hiller, Ruetz, nor Forkel intended to use their respect for the inscrutability of the emotions as a means of promoting instrumental music to an aesthetic pinnacle (though they were very aware that they were defending music against the challenge of the new rationalistic "enemies of music"). Forkel, who was in some ways the most progressive figure we surveyed, admitted that since amateur music listeners needed a "translator" in order to understand music's meaning (in contrast to true connoisseurs, who of course understood this peculiarly expressive language which reached beyond the realm of limited verbal meanings), vocal music was therefore superior to instrumental.

Thus, despite all the glimmerings we have seen that musical meaning was different from verbal meaning, instrumental music, before the coming of the *Frühromantiker*, was generally considered inferior to vocal music because of the inferior intelligibility of its wordless medium. During most of the eighteenth century words were clearly considered the greatest aid to clear intelligibility, and words of course belonged only to the medium of vocal music. Instrumental music, by virtue of its specific, nonverbal nature was necessarily inferior, even in the eyes of eighteenth-century critics sympathetic to instrumental music's peculiar virtues.

All considerations of verbal meanings aside, vocal music had yet another ground for superiority: the superior expressive and moving qualities of vocal lyrical utterance itself. And this ground seems to have commanded especially widespread acceptance. From Mattheson to Koch, it was frequently considered axiomatic that instrumental music should imitate vocal music. On the issue of instrumental music's expressive dependence on vocal models there was little anticipation of the Romantic viewpoint.

For some, the primacy of the vocal idiom was based simply on the unique beauty and naturally affecting quality of the human instrument itself, and on an aesthetic preference for the smooth lyrical lines designed especially for this instrument. Luther considered the human voice the most beautiful instrument; Mattheson placed a great premium on "heart-moving song"; Quantz and C. P. E. Bach seemed to equate moving music with vocal, singing, cantabile music. (Conversely, some condemned vocal music for imitating instrumental gestures.)

Many others adopted and promulgated the account of the primacy of the vocal idiom which I have called the "passionate utterance theory of musical expression." This theory remained influential long after more rationalistic elements of neoclassic aesthetics had been rejected. In 1788 Forkel, who was actually defending musical "art" or craft against Enlightened French critics such as Rousseau, still explained his figures for the imagination as imitations of the way passions are uttered. And Tieck at the century's end still felt compelled to argue against the meaningfulness obtained by imitating vocal utterances—pointing a finger at the partisans of C. P. E. Bach's strikingly serious and expressive instrumental style.

Sulzer's encyclopedia, first published in 1771–1774, had been especially influential in furthering the currency of this theory. Though he explicitly rejected the French neoclassic doctrine of art as imitation, and though today he is listed on the side of the proponents of expression as opposed to imitation, Sulzer's commitment to the utterance theory of musical expression was whole-hearted, and his reiterated formulations of it bear the marks of intense partisan fervor. Anyone who hears a melody, Sulzer wrote, "must imagine that he is hearing the speech of a man who is immersed in a certain feeling and that he is making it known." Any other melody he called "mere noise." Hiller and Ruetz, who were on opposite sides of the musical debate over the applicability of the imitation doctrine to music, as well as Krause, C. P. E. Bach, and Junker, all viewed musical expression on the model of vocal passionate utterance. This conception of musical expression remained widespread in Germany throughout the eighteenth century. The Romantics finally put the utterance theory to rest by pointing to the higher truth of that essentially incommunicable inner reality—as opposed to the spurious reality communicated by readily graspable, but necessarily falsifying, outer signs.

Despite the long dominance of the passionate utterance theory of musical expression, many eighteenth-century German critics did evince a decided skepticism towards it—even critics who were among the first partisans of the mimetic theory, and even writers who saw a close link between music and passionate utterance. Since the characteristic and idiomatic traits of instrumental music were especially vulnerable to attack by adherents of the utterance theory, German reluctance to embrace this French import whole-heartedly worked to clear the way for the growth of a new and more sympathetic view of instrumental music. Indeed, German writers seemed quick to realize that the utterance theory threatened to render aesthetically unjustifiable certain specifically musical traits and devices which were characteristic of the very nature of music as they knew it, such as melismas, harmony, counterpoint, contrasts, idiomatic instrumental figures, and virtuosic brilliance. There were few Enlightened Germans who were willing to stifle musical art—to violate what the Romantics would call music's "specific nature"—for the sake of abstract aesthetic principles, no matter how reasonable they seemed.

Hiller, in the same 1753 article where he argued that Batteux's mimetic principle was valid for music, expressed the reservation that it was unfair to expect instrumental music to sacrifice certain of its characteristic traits to the principle that all music must imitate the more meaningful vocal idiom of passionate utterance. He called certain features of this characteristically instrumental idiom, such as counterpoint and virtuosic passage-work, "das musikalische Wunderbar," and sanctioned their qualified use. Ruetz's whole attack on Hiller's article and on musical imitation was based on his conviction that the passionate utterance, or "declamatory," model threatened the very "riches" of music; he was especially anxious to defend the riches of harmony, but he also insisted that the specifically musical function of transitional and contrasting passages be recognized. Though he balked at calling music an imitation of an utterance, Ruetz did allow that music constituted a passionate utterance.

Krause, while accepting the idea that music was an imitation of nature, and while viewing music, with Ruetz, as itself a passionate utterance, also sought to meet the threat to accepted musical practice posed by a narrow interpretation of the notion that music was essentially the imitation of meaningful vocal inflections. He pointed to music's "peculiar privileges and principles" and defended devices characteristic of accepted musical practice such as counterpoint, melismas, word repetitions, thematic variety, sudden contrasts—devices which Gottsched and his doctrinaire followers, who saw music as the slave of poetry, regarded as aesthetically reprehensible. Ruetz, Hiller, and Krause all preferred to think of music as itself an utterance of some inner reality—but an utterance sui generis—not the imitation of some audible vocal inflection from the extramusical realm of reality. As Ruetz said, music was itself an "original."

The ideas inherent in this German reserve towards the utterance theory of musical expression can be seen as part of a tradition which included the views of Johann Mattheson. Though he was writing before the publication of Batteux's pivotal work, hence too early to be caught up in the debate over the validity of the utterance theory, Mattheson articulated and strengthened a native tradition of musical thought which helps explain the fact that German critics never accepted the French neoclassic music aesthetic without reservation. Unlike the passionate utterance theory, espoused by Enlightened French critics, in which music was seen to imitate the outer, natural, signs of the passions, Mattheson's theory of musical expression posited an "isomorphic relationship" between the inner nature of the emotions and music. He believed that music spoke to the listener's soul immediately, and independently of any clearly recognizable representation. (Mattheson's dependence on the Cartesian theory of the emotions must not cloud our understanding of how his view of musical expression was in fact fundamentally different from, and independent of, the French rationalist account of musical representation.) To be sure, Mattheson viewed vocal lyricism as the model for expressive music, and he announced more than once the common eighteenth-century principle that "All that is played is merely an imitation of singing." But Mattheson also identified and defended most energetically the peculiar strengths and the expressive potentialities of the instrumental idiom. He cited its affinity for passage work, for fire and brilliance, and for contrapuntal textures—all traits of music to which Mattheson himself responded with great enthusiasm. And though he was adamant that all music must sing, must move, and must communicate an emotional content, he envisioned many other realizations of this ideal than that of a musical composition which modelled itself on the outer signs of the passions.

Towards the end of the century Forkel and Junker were again pointing to music's analogy with the inner nature of the emotions, though they still on occasion mouthed assent to the utterance theory as well. Forkel's and Junker's assessments of the extent of music's ability to communicate this inner reality were, however, quite different. Junker identified music's expressive potentialities on the basis of its ability to create structures analogous to the inner dynamics of the emotions (pardoxically, he still commended to the budding composer the "study of passionate tones"). But Junker concluded that music's ability to represent intelligibly these inner emotional progressions was limited to only a few classes of emotions. Forkel, on the other hand, like Ruetz and Krause, felt keenly the need to preserve and defend musical "art" against those who would limit music's range of expression to that obtainable through melody and lyrical utterance alone. He argued that only by using all the complex resources of musical "art" (among these he meant especially counterpoint and thematic work), could the composer hope to represent the complex reality of man's inner emotional life. One of Forkel's answers to the threat which the utterance theory posed to counterpoint and compositional craft was almost too clever: he characterized a fugue as the representation of the utterance of the emotions of a whole *Volk*.

Finally, Sulzer himself realized that the passionate utterance theory had definite limits. There was more to a piece of music than the imitation of a passionate utterance. Only the first few measures of a piece could be so explained. The remainder of the piece, if not to become boring, had to rely on constructive skill and interest and on contrast and variation appropriate to the given emotion in order to "constantly charm the ear from beginning to end" and hence to maintain the listener for a period of time in the "same emotional state." Sulzer's outspoken commitment to the utterance theory as the only justifiable account of a piece of music was also qualified by his use of the concept of the sublime, although in this case he seems to have been unaware that he was compromising his basic principle. At times Sulzer states that the most important use of art is that it strengthens, stimulates, and exercises the "active powers of the soul," the true source of man's humanity and the very foundation of morality. He recognizes, in effect, that an artwork which does not conform to his sometime principle of communicating a passion or moral truth in "understandable language" can nevertheless be of great spiritual value if, by virtue of some unexpected and incomprehensible power and greatness, or even some apparent contradictoriness, it shakes the listener up, arouses *Verwunderung*, and causes him to exert his inner powers in an effort to comprehend the artwork. Such artworks Sulzer called "sublime." The "instrumental brilliance" and power of the symphonic idiom and the "apparent disorder" of the symphony's contrasts and sudden transitions contributed to just such a sublime artwork, according to Sulzer. But of course these widely recognized, "sublime," characteristics of the classical symphony were a far cry from the imitation of understandable passionate utterances, upon which Sulzer tried to base his whole aesthetic of music, including instrumental music. (The eclectic's inconsistencies no doubt reflect a certain ambivalence in contemporary musical thought as a whole.)

Prominent in both Sulzer's emotional maintenance theory and in his description of the stirring sublimity of the symphony is the element of variety and contrast. Sulzer recognized that the utterance account of a musical composition could not explain the compositional interest and structural variety essential to the whole temporal extent of a musical composition, and that, in short, music conceived as a mere utterance of one and the same feeling would be too unpleasant and boring. Moreover, the utterance theory, with its associated vision of music as an "understandable language of the passions" left no room for the idiomatic instrumental gestures and contrasts of the successful symphonic style. But Sulzer, despite his reservations, clung to the utterance theory as the fundamental explanation of music's significance and worth.

Sulzer's failure to integrate his most fundamental observations into a consistent theory of musical expression and his ambivalence towards instrumental music provide a useful introduction to our inquiry into the widespread critical wrangling with the issue of contrast. In the eighteenth century, contrast was at once the most commonly recognized distinctive trait of the new instrumental style and apparently the most confusing. Moreover, contrast is the one issue around which we today can see substantial and obvious signs of an evolving Romantic attitude. For whereas eighteenth-century German critics, despite all their reservations, were not really ready to give up their commitment, inherited from neoclassic aesthetics, to the clear, intelligible expression of an extramusical content based on the superior expressivity of vocal utterance, they exercised much ingenuity to show that the unity of style which seemed such an integral part of neoclassic prescriptions was not in fact essential to the effective and intelligible communication of an emotional content. As if following the maxim that theory follows practice, or at least that theory will bend to accommodate practice, they tried to show how musical contrasts need not be pointless or confusing even to those music lovers committed to emotional expression in music. They tried to give variety and contrast—so essential to the new Italian style—a positive role, whereas other departures from Enlightened neoclassic norms, such as lack of extramusical content, unintelligibility, and idiomatic instrumental gestures, were hardly ever allotted a central and significant aesthetic role until the Romantics.

To the Romantics contrast was of course no longer an issue or problem to be grappled with. The *Abwechselung* and variety of the Italian symphonic idiom were essential to their definition of instrumental music as the most Romantic art. They saw in the "grand symphonies with their manifold elements" a "vision of all the manifold human affects." However, Enlightened critics, committed to representation and intelligibility in music and to vocally-conceived musical expression, viewed the new contrast-dominated style as an enigma, if not an outright intellectual insult—its contrasts were more confusing than pleasant. Audiences accustomed to the older, more homogeneous music were confused, and critics were faced with problems, because the contrasts between implied affective contents seemed to undermine the new music's integrity and intelligibility as a vehicle of emotional expression.

The accepted norm in the earlier part of the century had been the representation of only one affect within a given composition. This norm rested in part on a psychological norm. Pluche said, for example, that it would be absurd to represent a man who for no obvious reason "passed from sadness to great outbursts of laughter." Lessing, though renowned for his rescue of Germany from the tyranny of French neoclassic dogma, shared much the same view: that the musical representation of contrasting affects in succession was "disorderly" and confusing because the listener could not perceive in them a "correct sequence." Pluche singled out sonatas and Lessing pointed to symphonies as genres which were frequently guilty of such absurdities. Not only did contrasting affects fail to correspond to any recognizable psychological reality, they seemed to cancel each other out like contradictions in an argument. Music expressing only one affect was obviously intelligible to many people in a way music with contrasting affects could not be. Gottsched felt that the contrasts of the newer Italian style rendered it unintelligible and void of any content; neither male nor female, he contended, these new sonatas could only be called hermaphrodites. Lessing more or less concurred, saying that a symphony expressing different, self-contradictory passions, was a "musical monster"; he cited the principle of coherence as essential to all art. Batteux had been the biggest champion of coherence; his likening of music to a "coherent discourse" had set a sense-making standard for music which required that if the piece was sad then all its sounds must be sad. This literary model of coherence clashed hopelessly with the very essence of the new Italian instrumental practice.

The issue of musical contrast was especially critical in the case of instrumental music. As Lessing and Junker recognized, the instrumental medium simply did not have the means, namely words, to make its contrasts intelligible to the eighteenth-century Enlightened listener. Also, because of its lack of words, instrumental music needed more variety, or *Abwechselung*, so as not to be boring. Scheibe, Mattheson, and Quantz all recognized this basic practical principle. Vocal music, on the other hand, could provide a rational basis for its variety of content, and could keep the listener's interest and occupy the listener's mind with the ideas contained in its words. At the same time, since it was bound to a verbal text, vocal music did not have the "freedom" of instrumental music and so was not so liable in the first place to indulge in questionable extremes of variety and contrast. Instrumental music, for its part, was faced with a peculiar dilemma because of its very nature. It seemed that the very things that made it interesting and entertaining made it unintelligible. Lacking words, it could not explain its contrasts; but lacking contrasts it was boring. If it was too unified, it was intelligible but boring; if it had too much variety and contrasts, it was entertaining but unintelligible. If it followed its own natural instincts and exercised its own freedom it was labelled "ear-tickling" and "meaningless."

Of course there were those who accepted the ear-tickling variety, surprises, expectation play, and *Abwechselung*, or contrast, of Italian instrumental music and enjoyed the entertainment provided by its specifically musical elements. For Mattheson the affective variety of the sonata provided its justificatory affective hallmark. Scheibe called the demonstration of the composer's skill in expectation play the "very excellence of the symphony." Quantz, Krause, and even Sulzer, all recognized that a certain amount of variety was as an essential feature of the ingratiating, pleasant, character of the newer galant style (as opposed to the older "learned" style), though they balked at the high levels of contrast in the most modern Italian idiom. And surely many listeners throughout the country who did not allow aesthetic scruples to get in the way of their musical enjoyment accepted and relished the strong stimulation afforded by the famed and ever-bolder Italian penchant for variety and inventiveness.

But the sheer sensual pleasure afforded by the ear-tickling, enlivening sounds of Italian instrumental music was not sufficient to justify them in terms of eighteenth-century aesthetic theory. With the coming of Batteux's insistence on a clear musical intelligibility modeled on coherent verbal discourse, and with the insistence that even instrumental chamber music should imitate the inarticulate vocal utterances of passion, the value of many characteristic features of the new Italian instrumental style, especially contrast, was thrown into doubt. To the many music lovers and music critics anxious to apply the principles of Enlightened criticism to music, the contrasts of the new style presented a serious and challenging intellectual problem. Those German writers who, despite their intellectual quandary, found themselves responsive to the new idiom sought then to employ their Enlightened wits to answer the riddle: how could contrasts of affective content serve the end of an intelligible and effective communication of an emotional content?

Baumgarten's "Aesthetics" provided one sort of theoretical answer to the questions posed by the new instrumental practice. Since, he argued, art speaks not to man's higher, rational faculties, but to his lower, "sensual" ones, art must be constructed in such a way as to engage these lower faculties, that is, to keep the audience's attention. Therefore, the use of generous admixtures of variety, novelty, and contrasts—features which insured against the fundamental danger of boredom—were considered essential and wholly justifiable elements of artistic communication. Scheibe's prescriptions for successful chamber music had also called for the elements of surprise, contrast, and expectation-play as means of engaging the listener's attention and entertaining him; but for Scheibe this was only practical, tried and true, musical advice. Baumgarten's contribution was in part to give a respectable philosophical justification for many of the things music had been doing all the while. Moreover, whereas for Scheibe the entertainment provided by expectation-play was merely a pleasurable end in itself, for Baumgarten the artwork's stimulation of man's lower faculties led to the development and perfection of the noncognitive part of man's soul—a result of far-reaching spiritual and moral benefit to the whole man.

Krause, a student of Baumgarten, used Baumgarten's notion of "extensive clarity" to justify the variety of the newer galant music. (He also felt that even the sensual pleasure afforded by music made man sensitive to harmony and order in society.) Sulzer, another Baumgartnian, realized that variety was necessary to keep the listener's attention over a period of time, and that representations of passionate utterances were not enough (though he rejected the "meaningless contrasts" of Italian instrumental music). He assimilated Baumgarten's ideas about sensual stimulation and spiritual exercise into the concept of the sublime and pointed out that *Abwechselung* was an essential ingredient in works which stimulated the listener's active powers of soul. Even the element of apparent contradictoriness was acceptable in sublime works of art; for the more such artworks forced the listener to exert his inner energies in order to comprehend them, the greater and more profound their emotional effect could be—the more, Sulzer explained, they "shook up" the listener. Junker also drew upon Baumgartnian concepts in asserting that the passions could not be aroused by prolonging a single passionate expression. He explained that a "sensual representation" was more noble and more effective the more it encompassed changing and transitory contents, and that indeed a feeling could not be made "sensually comprehensible" without contrast.

Another answer to the question of the role of variety and contrast in music was provided by a new view of the very content music was supposed to embody. New, more dynamic, theories of the emotions were put to use all through the latter eighteenth century to justify ever higher levels of contrast and variety in instrumental music. This relation of emotional theory to music-aesthetic theory I believe to be at the center of our story of instrumental music's rise in aesthetic status. Baumgarten's theory had had to do only with interesting, or engaging, form. But for many, a justification of contrast on grounds of mere attention-keeping or sensual stimulation was not enough. Variety would have to be justified as well in terms of content. For as long as people expected a single piece of instrumental music to represent understandably "one and the same passion"—and this expectation runs from Mattheson as well as the neoclassic critics, through Lessing, Sulzer, and virtually all the critics surveyed, except Forkel, up to the early Romantics—the contrasts of the emerging classical style stood in the way of its intelligibility, and hence its aesthetic appreciation.

The disagreement between French neoclassic theory and contemporary Italian musical practice on the issue of affective contrast was open and long-lasting. Gottsched and Batteux insisted on complete homogeneity of affective content in the interests of intelligibility, and thereby condemned much contemporary music in the Italian style as aesthetically unacceptable by Enlightened standards. Thus contrast, or *Abwechselung*, was one of the aspects of musical practice which certain German writers felt called upon to defend against the excessive rationalism of the more narrow French school. For example, Ruetz, a musician defending at mid-century older German traditions, was afraid the newly-imported neoclassic criticism would lead some "young fop" to ask of every musical turn what it meant, that is, what affect it represented; he feared it would deny a valid role to transitional and contrasting passages, which he saw as essential to music's pleasing character. Lessing's condemnation of affective contrast in the symphony suggests that in fact—despite the extent to which Italian music was widely enjoyed—contrasts continued to present problems to the Enlightened music-lover who wanted to perceive music in the aesthetically correct and reasonable way, namely, as the representation of a passion or feeling. There were evidently enough such listeners, who still felt with Sulzer that the Italian instrumental style offered only "meaningless" contrasts, that Forkel in 1777 chose to dramatize the rationale of his new discipline of "musical rhetoric" by suggesting that it could remedy precisely such confusion: the amateur who wonders why a musical piece which begins brilliantly doesn't continue so, simply needs to know that music expresses the "multiple modifications" of feeling through multiple modifications of musical expression. Forkel stated most directly that it was his theory of the "manifold modifications of the feelings" which could indeed make sense of music as a "language of the emotions" at the same time as it allowed for, indeed required, the specifically musical elements of affective contrast and compositional interest and variety.

Forkel was not the only one to bring emotional theory to bear on the aesthetic appreciation of the new instrumental music. Over the course of the latter eighteenth century, changing views of the nature of man's emotional life were taken up by successive German writers to justify elements of changing musical practice, especially the increasing amount and degree of contrast. Never wholly content with the utterance theory of musical expression, these writers, it seems, were constantly looking for some other account of the connection between musical structures and man's inner emotional states—a connection they seem to have never questioned. Most often their account was based on the concept of analogy, or "isomorphism," that is, of similarity in temporal dynamic structure. Thus, if the emotions were seen to be full of change, then of course music analogous to the structure of the emotions should also be full of change. The romantics, who spoke of music as a symbol of the emotions, drew upon this eighteenth-century view of the temporal analogy between inner emotional states and music: both, they held, were "never resting, moving, ever changing."

Of course theories of the emotions had played an important role in theories of musical expression throughout the eighteenth century. Even before contrast or the utterance theory became prominent issues, Mattheson asserted that there were "isomorphous relations" between the music and the passions, which he, like the neoclassic critics, regarded on the Cartesian model as clearly differentiated, homogeneous, and rather static entities. Since Mattheson expected a single composition to express a single affect, he naturally expected (as did the contemporary neoclassic critics who viewed music as the imitation of passionate utterance) an expressive musical structure to evince throughout the same affective unity and homogeneous character as the passion to which it was analogous. Later, the theory of the emotions, or *Affektenlehre*, was revised so that each emotional state was seen to have certain characteristic shadings, or developments, within it. Reflecting the mid-century preoccupation with *Empfindsamkeit*, Sulzer said that music must express the "finest shadings" and the "finest nuances" of the emotions. He suggested that by using shorter and longer phrase lengths the composer could make evident "how a passion becomes gradually more intense and more turbulent, or how it gradually subsides." The composer should enable the listener to follow a man's state of passion "through all developments of the affect," "from its first stirrings all the way up to the point of their complete climax."

Krause, writing before Sulzer, spoke of a *Gleichförmigkeit* between music and certain emotions, as had Mattheson. But Krause's conception of the emotional content of music went beyond Mattheson's and possibly even Sulzer's in the degree to which this emotional content embraced strong contrasts. Krause explicitly took a dynamic view of the emotions: "No passion can remain in the same state for very long." He then applied this view to making his own prescriptions for musical expression: the "portrayal" of jealousy would entail "tones which are first wavering, then gentle, then stronger and more daring and scolding, and then again touching and sighing." For Krause, the representation of love could embrace at the same time almost all "musical beauties" and the whole spectrum of affective states characteristic of love, "from cheerful and happy, to peaceful and quiet, to impatient and complaining." The diversity within the emotion of love made it an especially apt object for musical representation. After having observed that the emotions themselves are characterized by "various agitations of the blood and various movements of the body, limbs and voice," Krause explained why such dynamically-conceived emotions were the ideal content of music: "Music consists of movements; therefore whatever it imitates must also have movement." Music's inherent nature and the dynamic nature of the emotions formed a natural alliance.

Junker, writing some 25 years after Krause, also based his doctrine of musical expression on a dynamic view of the emotions. Just as Krause emphasized the "movement" that was essential to both music and the emotions, Junker pointed to the characteristic of "progression" which was common to them both. Junker also used the concept of analogy (or "Analogon") to identify music's relation to its emotional content. However, his insistence on clear intelligibility prevented him from allowing for strong contrasts in the instrumental representation of affect and caused him to limit instrumental music's representational repertoire to only four (at times even two) affective states. There was, though, one notable progressive element in Junker's thought: he recognized music's peculiar affinity for expressing the transitional states in between the commonly recognized emotions as they had been defined in the traditional *Affektenlehre*. He realized that these transitional states constituted an area of emotional experience inaccessible to representation by the other arts, and even called music's expression of these "distinct." (He nevertheless insisted that in order for such representation to be intelligible the emotional points of departure and arrival must be defined verbally.)

With Forkel we approach the view, basic to the Romantic *Seelenlehre*, that man's emotional experience was nothing but a continuum of change—a constant state of transition. Whereas Krause and Junker had reinterpreted the old *Affektenlehre* so as to include more contrast and so as to allow for the dynamic character of given emotional states over a period of time, Forkel questioned the very existence of separable and identifiable emotional states. Since the emotions were "subject to constant change," one could only perceive the existence of a given emotion for an instant; at all other times it bore marks of the one preceding or the one following. Forkel noted, in praising a C. P. E. Bach transition in a rondo, that transitions were indeed the very stuff out of which the emotions were made; and he pointed to the usefulness of thematic development in expressing such a complex phenomenon. When Forkel did speak in terms of definite emotions he most often added the qualification "with all their manifold modifications." These modifications of the emotions encompassed "infinite and incomprehensible" degrees of strength and weakness and even led into wholly different states. From this observed fact of nature Forkel posited "the law of multiplicity in the representation of our feelings." On the basis of this conception of the emotions he could then easily justify the inclusion of contrasting themes, if they corresponded with the way emotions "naturally develop out of one another."

Thus we have seen over the course of the latter eighteenth century an evolution from static theories of the emotions to more and more dynamic ones and a parallel and interrelated growth in the critical acceptance of contrasts in instrumental music. But the Romantic view was not totally anticipated. For the degree and suddenness of many of these musical contrasts constituted a major critical stumbling block for many writers. Even the progressive Forkel felt the listener's feelings should not be bruised by too sudden transitions; he praised C. P. E. Bach's transitions between movements. Earlier in the century Ruetz and Hiller had singled out contradictory affects within a single piece as nonsensical (Haydn's music was attacked by the latter on this score); closely related affects were on the other hand acceptable. Forkel, Junker, and Krause could justify more extreme contrasts of affective content, but only if these extremes corresponded to the way the emotions naturally developed over a period of time. The sudden and "meaningless" contrasts of the new Italian style continued to present a special problem.

It was only with the coming of the Romantics that the seemingly senseless character of the classical style's extreme contrasts came to be viewed in an altogether positive light. They spoke of the "enigmatic," "capricious," "almost insane" character of the symphony's presentation of "manifold human affects." The Romantic *Seelenlehre* was partly behind this new acceptance; it went beyond

˙earlier emotional theories in recognizing the psychological truths contained in sudden juxtapositions and contradictory elements. Feelings were not just seen as blending, or progressing gradually, one into another, but as in frequent conflict. The Romantics could see, for example, that inner struggles could be readily reflected in the contrapuntal "tone struggles" (of which Herder spoke). And they believed that music had a peculiar power to unite "the most manifold and contradictory movements of our spirits." Earlier, it seems Beethoven's teacher Neefe had been aware of the music-critical implications of his own introspection when he wrote, "I am sad and happy . . . both these passions sometimes alternate very quickly in me." Wackenroder's fictional character Joseph Berlinger even spoke of a "wonderful" simultaneity of happiness and sadness, an inclination to both cry and laugh, which is so typical of life and which "no art is more able to express than music."

Changing emotional theories contributed in more than one way to the Romantic glorification of the classical style. Not only did more dynamic theories of the emotions play a major role in sanctioning ever-growing levels of variety and contrast in the evolving instrumental style—a new realization that the complex, constantly changing reality of man's emotional life was by its very nature inaccessible to verbal and rational analysis, and the consequent belief that this inner reality could not be accurately communicated by merely imitating certain outer "natural signs of the passions," led to an acceptance of the inherent indeterminateness of instrumental music's meaning and to a new vision of the expressive potential of such compositional complexities as counterpoint and thematic work.

We have already seen that the issue of intelligibility was a most critical one for instrumental music. Again and again, even among critics quite responsive to the peculiar appeal of symphonies and sonatas, instrumental music had been deemed inferior because its meaning was less determinate than the verbally defined meaning of vocal music. However, with the growing realization that the emotional or spiritual aspect of man with which music dealt was itself essentially obscure and beyond the reach of verbal labels or descriptions, music's failure to satisfy the verbally-conceived neoclassic standards of intelligibility became less and less of a mark against it. Music's mysterious affinity for the dark and obscure became instead an advantage. Moreover, this new acceptance of the essential obscurity and inseparability of the emotions led to a disdain for the presumed intelligibility of the "natural signs of the passions." The idea that "every feeling is announced by its own tone and gesture" was undercut by the new view of the emotional stream as essentially unanalyzable. Distinct signs for an indistinct and obscure reality made no sense. Utterance was of necessity an act of misrepresentation, for the reality of man's dark inner stream was itself unutterable. Instrumental music's obligation to imitate these vocal utterances could be forgotten, and it could feel free to indulge its peculiar proclivities.

Once the complexity of the emotions had been recognized, and once loyalty to the passionate utterance theory of musical expression had been undermined, the Enlightened musical ideal of lyrical melody with simple homophonic accompaniment became harder to justify. Indeed, Forkel believed that if the language of music was truly to reflect the complexity of the emotions, "with all their connections and modifications," then all the resources of a highly-developed musical "art," or "language," would be necessary. The introduction of harmony into music, Forkel explained, had led to an amazing multiplication of musical expressions, especially by virtue of the contrapuntal combining of melodies; and, he argued, should not the diversity natural to the feelings be reflected in the diverse resources of art? Especially significant was the fact that the harmonic techniques of fragmentation and contrapuntal combination enabled the composer to develop ideas out of each other very naturally and thus reflect the way feelings were constantly developing out of one another. Forkel even argued that the art of double counterpoint was based on the "manifold modifications of the feelings."

The early Romantics also extolled the virtues of the more complex techniques of musical composition. Wackenroder, sounding much like Forkel, spoke of the "refined multiplicity" which music had gained for the expression of complex and varied content from "the learned system [of composition], the scientific profundities of music." He felt that the "science" of musical composition, even when pursued for its own sake, possessed a "wonderful significance" and that the "dry scholarly system" of musical composition could evoke "completely new and wonderful turns and transformations of feelings." E. T. A. Hoffman spoke of the "spirit realm" and the "mysterious premonitions" disclosed by the various contrapuntal interweavings and combinations of the themes in a Beethoven trio; the greatest composers, he wrote, know how to use the "secrets of harmony" "to work upon the human soul." Not the least of the achievements of this learned system, which could fuse into a single unity the most diverse contents using the techniques of thematic development, were the "grand symphonies, wherein is depicted not an individual feeling, but a whole world, a complete drama of human affect." Such a uniting of contraries was a feat Enlightened critics such as Lessing would have held to be unattainable by specifically musical means alone.

Of course, the appreciation of "harmony" was not new in Germany, though Forkel seems to have been the first to justify it on the basis of its necessity for emotional expression. Before Enlightened critics such as Scheibe and Rousseau branded harmony (or what we today might call counterpoint) as "gothic" and "barbaric," the art of contrapuntal writing was viewed in orthodox Lutheran circles as a unique and elevated exercise in the contemplation and glorification of the Deity. The harmony and order of God's creation could be mirrored in the harmony of a well-wrought musical composition. Well-ordered music could contribute to a well-ordered soul; an interesting and artfully-crafted contrapuntal composition could contribute to the "allowable recreation of the spirit." "Harmony" and the whole craft of musical composition were enjoyed and valued for their own sake.

Moreover, in spite of the fact that harmony was on the defensive during the *Aufklärung* in Germany, there was during this same time an undercurrent of appreciation for musical "art." Even Enlightened critics had words to say in its defense; for the bland homophonic texture demanded by the aesthetic of imitation of natural passionate utterances and the new "galant" standard of taste did not correspond to many Germans' preconceived notions of what good music should be. The prominent *Aufklärer*, Friedrich Nicolai maintained (against Gottsched's attack on the highly-developed art which taught such unnatural technicalities as the resolution of dissonances) that counterpoint was even necessary for the expression of some emotions. Christian Gottfried Krause, another figure of the Berlin Enlightenment and a spokesman for the galant style of Graun, took it upon himself to defend counterpoint's contribution to the pleasure, movement, and intelligibility which the Enlightened listener expected from music. Relying on Baumgarten's concept of intensive clarity, Krause argued that the intensive contrapuntal development of a single idea contributed to its distinctness and intelligibility. Also, Krause believed that it was a fact of experience that "what the composers call harmonic work" expressed "a majesty, a wonderment, a universal joy, and a great fervor, and that the heart was thereby filled with certain intense and elevated emotions"; this statement shows how Krause even drew upon traditional attitudes towards music to defend the "art" of music. Krause nevertheless fully approved of the composer who, if he was forced to make the choice, would choose to be "pleasant" rather than "learned." Like his contemporaries, Krause felt that the variety and charm of the galant style were preferable to the "uniformity" and esoteric intellectual appeal of the learned style. But Krause did not want composers to feel forced to make this choice. He did not see a necessary conflict between art and nature.

Ruetz, an opponent of Batteux's ideas, defended counterpoint without reservation. A spokesman for the typical German church musician, he saw Batteux's utterance theory as a direct threat to the "riches" of musical art. Hiller, an early musical spokesman for Batteux, and Ruetz's opponent in debate, argued against a narrow interpretation of the utterance theory, since he too feared its emphasis on the natural tones of passion might exclude "artful" combinations of tones, such as were typical of certain instrumental genres. He called the nonimitative elements of compositional and technical virtuosity "the wonderful in music," and in sanctioning their limited use he defended the elevated emotions of "astonishment" and "wonderment" which they aroused.

Not only Mattheson, whose ideas were viewed as hopelessly old-fashioned in the latter eighteenth century, but the Enlightened critics Scheibe and Sulzer saw counterpoint, or "harmonic work," as essential to certain genres of instrumental chamber music. The Enlightened critics, to be sure, rejected counterpoint in the expression of the emotions (only unadorned lyrical utterance would do this); but this rejection did not entail a wholesale doctrinaire rejection of all the riches of musical art. Harmony retained a justifiable, if carefully circumscribed, function.

Sulzer realized that skillful manipulation of musical ideas was essential to maintain the listener's attention once the initial passionate utterance had made itself known; and when music was to be attentively listened to, as in the case of instrumental chamber music, he saw contrapuntal interest as essential. In Germany the skill of interweaving many voices would always have a place.

Our survey of attitudes towards counterpoint and the highly-developed craft of musical composition has revealed more than a striking similarity between Romantic and pre-Enlightened German attitudes. We have seen as well in the latter eighteenth century a continuing undercurrent of appreciation for "harmony" and the "riches" of musical art. This undercurrent persisted despite the inundation of Germany with Enlightened criticism, which demanded that harmony yield to melody and art to nature. But what we have seen revealed is only part of a larger pattern. It was no isolated development that the Romantics arrived at a new appreciation of what they termed the "science of musical composition," which had been so disdained by Enlightened music criticism, and so treasured in earlier German thought. For just as the Romantic movement in general displayed a yearning for Germany's dark distant past, and found a new appreciation for the fantasy of fairy tales and the unreasonable exuberance of Gothic cathedrals, certain fundamental Romantic musical views seem to constitute a return to basic pre-Enlightenment attitudes towards music. The Romantics' whole vision of music's significance and value bears striking similarities to the traditional German viewpoint. To this extent Romantic attitudes which appear revolutionary with respect to Enlightened criticism also contain a certain reactionary element. And just as was the case with the so-called gothic art of counterpoint, we shall see that this reactionary element was in part prepared by the covert persistence of certain pre-Enlightenment musical attitudes. Indeed, this persistence helps account for the uniquely German critical synthesis found in the musical views of the *Frühromantiker*.

The notion that music ministered to man's inner state rather than the good of society as maintained by moral action, the belief that music had a unique power to bring man's soul into immediate contact with a higher spiritual reality, and the conviction that music was therefore of inestimable value, its mysterious effects not replicable by any other art and its peculiar content not translatable into any other medium—all these fundamental attitudes were shared by the Romantics and by those who were part of the church-dominated musical culture of Germany before the *Aufklärung*.

The most elementary instance of this shared attitude is the idea that music soothes and enlivens: that it is a balm in the face of the troubles and pressures of mundance existence, and that it instills and strengthens feelings of happiness and joy. Luther, the seminal figure in what I have termed traditional German musical thought, wrote that music makes the soul peaceful, happy, and free of all worry and anxiety. Similarly, Wackenroder wrote that after immersing himself in the "holy, cooling spring of tones," the pleasure of pure tones healed him of all anxiety and he was overcome with a "universal, joyful, feeling of peace." According to the traditional view, music, because of its calming and enlivening capabilities, was the best means to insure an harmonious inner balance; it could give a timid person courage and make an arrogant one meek; it was a moderator between extremes. Wackenroder recognized a similar power peculiar to music. Music is the "very art," he wrote, which "reduces the most manifold and most contradictory movements of our spirits to the same beautiful harmonies"; consequently music was "the only art which instilled that genuine serenity of soul where everything in the world seems to us natural, true, and good, where we find a beautiful coherence in the wildest tumult of men . . . where we see the world as through the twilight of a lovely dream." Both viewpoints implied that music conferred an invulnerability to the slings and arrows of earthly fortune, though the means envisioned were of course different.

In addition, both views emphasized the value of music's otherworldly, non-referential, nature. Whereas for neoclassic critics music's lack of clear reference to the real world was a violation of the fundamental principle of verisimilitude and rendered music morally impotent (a "useless" rather than a "noble" pastime), according to traditional and Romantic German viewpoints music's freedom from this-worldly reference was a cornerstone of its special value to the human spirit. Luther wrote "singing is the best art and exercise. It has nothing to do with the world. Singers are not troubled but are cheerful and drive away cares with singing." Similarly, the Romantics found in music a "purification of earthly filth." Because music was dependent on no laws of verisimilitude it could remain in its "pure poetic world" and it could transport the listener away from the everyday grind of "anxious industriousness." The pleasure taken in music was seen by both to be pure and "noble" pleasure. It was God's gift to man to make his earthly stay more pleasant and a "foretaste of heavenly joys." Wackenroder spoke of the innocent childlike pleasure he experienced in the land of pure tones, which he likened to the land of belief.

But more important to both views than the belief that music provided a release from earthly concerns was the belief that in so doing music provided a unique and peculiar access to a higher realm of spiritual truth and experience. According to the traditional view, harmonious and orderly music put the soul in harmony with the order of God and the universe. Music's immateriality made it a unique medium for the contemplation and celebration of the Divine. Furthermore, next to theology music was the best route to piety and virtue; for virtue was based on a well-ordered and well-moderated disposition, a gift that only music among the arts could confer. Harmonious sounds, it was believed, created harmonious souls; and only harmonious souls were responsive to the beauty of well-ordered sounds. Just as the Devil dwelled only in the anxious and immoderate soul, God dwelt only in the serene, harmonious soul. Thus a man insensitive to music was morally and spiritually suspect; conversely, there had to be "many seeds of virtue in those attracted to music," or so Luther confidently claimed.

For the Romantics, too, music afforded a unique access to a higher realm of spiritual truth. Only the Romantics were more interested in probing the mysterious depths of the human spirit than in attaining a state of piety and virtue, or in comtemplating divine mysteries. They felt that music alone, of all the arts, could reveal the "secret stream in the depths of the human spirit." Words, the tools of "outer understanding," could not penetrate into this innermost realm; only music could utter the unutterable. As Tieck wrote, "symphonies reveal in enigmatic language the enigmatic." E. T. A. Hoffmann claimed that the peculiar power of musical language gives voice to, and brings the listener into immediate communion with, the dark powerful indescribable forces within his own soul; and that through music we come to understand the "most mysterious premonitions" that have stirred us. Similarly, Tieck wrote that music "reigns over all the elements we can only forebode," that it "lays bare all depths." The "infinite" and mysterious inner realm revealed by the "richer" language of music possessed for the Romantics a profounder truth than that expressed in the "poorer" language of words with its "definite" emotions.

Both views saw in music a peculiar and mysterious power to reach into and affect man's inner being. This affective power functioned independently of verbal texts and required neither the composer's deliberate representation of a certain extramusical reality nor the listener's conscious recognition of a definite content. If indeed music could be said to have a "content," this content was innate and peculiar to it and could not be expressed in words, nor could it be rationally comprehended. Its effects likewise were sui generis and immediate and could not be duplicated by any other art. Music was regarded somewhat reverentially as a mysterious phenomenon, beyond human understanding. Augustine's phrase "occulta familiaritas" ("secret affinity"), which was fundamental to the traditional view of music's relations to the emotions, was also echoed by Wackenroder when he spoke of the "unexplainable sympathy" between tone relationships and the "individual fibers of the human heart." Older writers often referred to the "peculiar power of music" and believed in its "wonderful effects" as if it were an article of faith, a divine mystery; Romantic writers attributed to music a "wonderful significance" not to be found in any other art, and believed that music's power was all the greater, the more mysterious its language. Thus the attitudes behind Luther's description of music as an "unspeakably wondrous creation of the Lord" and the ideas found in Wackenroder's essay, "Die Wonder der Tonkunst," have much in common. Given the prevalence of the neoclassic assumption that music could not move the listener unless the passion which it represented, or expressed, could be rationally apprehended, and given the consequences of this assumption for instrumental music, this commonality is a most significant one for understanding the origins of Romantic musical thought.

Any simple and clear continuity between "traditional" German musical beliefs (i.e., pre-Enlightenment musical ideas) and early Romantic musical thought was of course precluded by the widespread currency in the latter eighteenth-century of their very antithesis: Enlightened music criticism. However, many of the reactionary elements of the Romantic musical revolution against Enlightened principles were already present in the continuing undercurrent of traditional attitudes which persisted in spite of the prevalence of Enlightened criticism. Evidence of this covert persistence of traditional attitudes has appeared earlier, within our selection of eighteenth-century musical writers, most of whom considered themselves reasonable and Enlightened souls.

In 1739, when Mattheson's *Capellmeister* sought to bring the new science to bear on the art of musical expression and composition, we saw evidence of a continuing commitment to the notion that well-ordered sounds create well-ordered dispositions; and since Mattheson still held to the traditional belief that virtue was nothing other than a well-ordered disposition, he confidently concluded that well-ordered sounds were a powerful moral force, and that the "marvelous effects of music" were indeed realizable. Music's effect on the passions, and hence on virtue, was seen to be an immediate and nonrational one, operating through the sense of hearing: the soul "resides in the ear," Mattheson wrote, and "the sense of hearing is intended and reserved [by God] for our moral good." Though these ideas are clearly part of the pre-Enlightenment tradition of musical thought, for Mattheson the "marvelous effects of music" were rendered less wondrous by his physical and physiological rationale for the immediacy of music's power.

Krause, a central figure in the Berlin Enlightenment, also did not doubt the "powerful effects of music"; he too saw a natural connection between music and virtue. The pleasures of music make us susceptible to virtue and vice versa, he explained; moreover, the very emotions music expresses best—hope and love, for example—are the very emotions which form the foundation for all social morality. Krause reasoned that since in no other art is there so much "order and proportion" as there is in music, music is in a special position to foster love for order and balance in society. Krause also displayed a traditional musical outlook when he characterized music as having an innate character, to which any text must accommodate itself. He observed that "Music arose out of a feeling of joy," that man uses music for pleasure and to lift his spirits, hence happiness and tranquility are the most natural subjects for music. The musical poet, Krause concluded, must work in alliance with this innate musical character.

Hiller and Ruetz, both university-educated and both musicians, rejected the full implications of the rationalistic limitations on musical content inherent in the neoclassic utterance theory by calling attention to the impossibility of giving names to music's special content and by asserting the mysterious means by which this content was communicated. Though they were, as we have seen, opponents in the debate over the applicability of Batteux's ideas to music, both echoed Augustine: Hiller spoke of music's "secret passageways" into the soul, and Ruetz of the "secret understanding" by which "harmonious souls" grasped the meaning of music's "peculiar expressions". (Ruetz actually called upon Augustine's authority by name.) Nicolai, the prominent *Aufklärer* who took it upon himself to defend instrumental music from its chief rationalistic enemy, felt certain that Gottsched would recognize that "music is indeed divine" if only he could see how Frederick the Great freed himself from the "cares of ruling" by means of the soothing and noble pleasure of playing his flute. For all these men traditional concepts formed a defense against the more radical rationalistic elements of neoclassic criticism. The need to defend music contributed to the perpetuation of some of these concepts.

When Junker, towards the end of his life, wrote the essay "Ueber den Werth der Tonkunst," he based his defense of music in part on an explicit reference to Luther's belief that music is valuable because it makes us happy. Similarly, Forkel's theory as to the proper affective sequences for sonata movements was based on the idea that music was supposed to arouse or maintain pleasant feelings or subdue unpleasant ones. He also wrote that music was beyond words the way faith was beyond reason, affirming the mystery and irrationality of music's content by suggesting an analogy with religious belief. Thus Forkel carried into the eighties two elements of traditional musical thought.

Despite the widespread use of many elements of the neoclassic aesthetic view, the covert persistence of traditional attitudes seems to have militated against any wholesale adoption on the part of German music critics of the narrow didacticism and antimusical bias frequently associated with neoclassic criticism. This persisting undercurrent eased the way for the Romantics' high opinion of music's spiritual significance, which was so in sympathy with pre-Enlightenment attitudes. There was, in addition, another native current, this one proceeding from the prominent philosopher Baumgarten, which was to play a major role in winning moral and aesthetic respectability for instrumental music. The dissemination of Baumgarten's "aesthetics" into the broader arena of German cultural life, at a time when neoclassic criticism was becoming quite influential, contributed to an evolutionary process profoundly affecting the aesthetic status of instrumental music: the neoclassic account of musical morality, which contained standards that instrumental music, by virtue of its specific nature, could not possibly meet, and according to which music per se was of little moral significance or human value, was gradually rejected in favor of theories of art, of morality, and of human perfection in which even music's specific abilities could play a useful and beneficial role. Such an evolutionary process, if not leading directly to Romantic views, certainly helped prepare the way for these views, just as did the persistence of traditional attitudes.

Coming to terms with the issue of instrumental music's spiritual and moral significance was essential if instrumental music was to rise above its position as the handmaid of poetry. For in the eyes of most eighteenth-century Enlightened critics, instrumental music's quesionable moral "use" was a major barrier to its being accorded a high aesthetic status. The neoclassic view, which we have seen exemplified most clearly in the views of Pluche and Gottsched, was that art's highest function was to instill moral wisdom and thus encourage moral action (for correct action was held to proceed from correct knowledge), and accordingly, that music's proper task was to render emphatic and appealing the words of the text, which themselves expressed moral precepts or in some way instilled moral wisdom. Music without words was seen as mere sensual diversion and as therefore morally impotent. This neoclassic view presented a formidable challenge to instrumental music: how indeed could such an unabashedly sensual and nonconceptual medium, whose meanings were indistinct at best, be of any redeeming human value?

Baumgarten's new philosophic discipline of "aesthetics" (its name derived from the Greek word meaning to percieve with the senses) provided a basis for the answer to this challenge. His ideas bore directly on the issues of the art's human and moral significance and on the proper standards for judging the arts. Though Baumgarten hardly spoke of music, his appreciation and definition of the arts in general was based on the very nonrational, even sensual, quality of art which neoclassic critics saw at the root of music's moral impotence. He defined artistic beauty as the "perfection of sensual cognition"; the arts, he explained, were addressed not to man's rational faculty, but to man's "lower cognitive powers," such as feeling, willing and desiring. Since then artworks engaged, stimulated, and nourished these lower powers of sensual cognition and fostered the activity of these "inner powers of soul," and since the activity of these inner powers constituted the ground of all moral action, the arts, even conceived as speaking a "sensual" language, were of inestimable human worth. For reason did not in fact govern all of men's actions, and the merely reasonable man had not achieved the perfection of his humanity. Not only is sensual cognition the basis of distinct cognition, Baumgarten asserted; aesthetic experience alone can lead to the harmonious functioning of all human powers—can "activate the whole man"—and only this inner activity can lead to the attainment of true human perfection. Thus, according to Baumgarten, the beneficial effects of the arts consisted in stimulating a process, rather than in instilling precepts. Since, too, the arts were addressed to man's sensual rather than rational faculties, they must have their own standards of excellence and intelligibility. One could not judge the content of a work of art by the same standards of clearness and distinctness by which one judged rational knowledge; for aesthetic cognition, by definition, is clear but not distinct. The implications of such a statement for instrumental music were not left to be drawn by chance.

Baumgarten's ideas made their impress for the most part through certain followers. In the case of music, Nicolai, Krause, and Sulzer put Baumgartnian notions to good use in the defense of music against the moralism of rationalistic aesthetics. Nicolai refused to apologize to Gottsched's party for music's inability to teach a moral lesson through the channels of the listener's rational faculties. Without mentioning Baumgarten by name, he grants, "to speak in philosophical language, that music causes not distinct, but rather only clear ideas, that it directly affects only the lower faculties and only indirectly the higher ones." He then proceeds to assert, still in a Baumgartnian vein, that emotions are the "very determinants of all human actions," and concludes that music does not require words or any "foreign" aid to function as a moral force. Krause also used the Baumgartnian principle that the arts evoke clear but not distinct ideas to justify the nonrational response to music typical of the "greatest connoisseurs" and to show the inappropriateness of the expectation that music should teach a moral lesson. Like Baumgarten, he held that sensual impressions were stronger than intellectual ones anyway and that reason does not in fact govern men's actions. Paraphrasing a traditional musical view, Krause asserted that virtue was "nothing other than a well-ordered and intelligently moderated disposition"; and since well-ordered music naturally contributed to this virtuous disposition and by its very nature strengthened those tendencies essential to virtue, music was itself a moral force. Krause concluded that since the beneficial sensual impressions of music were stronger than the rational impact of words, words must be made to accord with music rather than vice versa, as the neoclassic critics held. It is interesting that in both Nicolai's and Krause's thinking Baumgartnian principles and pre-Enlightenment musical attitudes work hand in hand to support the inherent worth of music.

Sulzer accepted Baumgarten's account of the arts as addressing and stimulating the lower faculties, and used this account to two very different ends. On the one hand Sulzer used Baumgartnian notions to construct a didactic account of art which was not dependent on the intellectual apprehension of moral precepts, but on a kind of conditioning of the lower faculties of desire and revulsion, accomplished by imbuing the truths of morality with "sensual power." More importantly, Sulzer used Baumgarten's idea that the arts' value derived from their stimulation and cultivation of man's active powers of soul to characterize and justify a second category of aesthetic endeavor which was just as valuable as the one which represented human passionate character and impressed moral truths. This second category was the sublime. Sublime artworks did not represent so much as they stimulated. Their immensity and incomprehensibility "shook the listener up," as Sulzer, and before him Hiller and Ramler, put it. The listener had to exert his inner powers of soul in order to comprehend them; and by virtue of this stimulation and "exercise" of these *Seelenkräfte*—which Sulzer called man's greatest treasure—the listener would be led to the very perfection of his humanity. Moreover, the inner activity so aroused was a precondition of all moral action. The chamber symphony, with its bewildering variety of content and its confusing, incoherent contrasts, was according to Sulzer's account such a sublime artwork. By implication, then, the symphony—that brilliant and confusing jumble of mere sounds—could contribute to man's spiritual perfection. In the eighteenth-century this was indeed an extreme claim even to imply. When the Romantic Wackenroder wrote that music "stimulates the very power of our being," he was not too far removed from Sulzer's second, "sublime," view of art.

However Sulzer was to be remembered for his moralism, as Baumgarten is known today for his rationalism. It remained for Kant and Schiller to dispel once and for all the notion that the content of artworks was the key to their definition and value, and to dissociate determinations of artistic value from determinations of their effect on moral action. Kant's emphasis on the form, rather than the content, of aesthetic representations—on "purposelessness without purpose"[1]—boded well for future appreciation and understanding of instrumental music; the same of course can be said for Sulzer's "sublime," with its focus on stimulating and activating, rather than informing and improving. Schiller's vision of the aesthetic experience (which was inspired by Kant's) as "the freedom of the spirit in the vivacious and purposeless play (*Spiel*) of its powers"[2] can be seen behind Tieck's vision of instrumental music as "independent and free" art—as art phantasizing "playfully and purposelessly."

But if we look back we can see already in Baumgarten's emphasis on the arts as "activating the whole man" an early stage of Schiller's theory that only through aesthetic experience do we bring our diverse powers into an inner harmony, hence only through beauty do we achieve the ideal of humanity.[3] This view of art's benefits to humanity, which focuses on process rather than precepts, was part of an evolution in critical thinking which actually can be traced back to the mid-century mark.

We have now completed our review of the critical developments that can be seen as leading up to the early Romantic aesthetic view of music. By focusing on the primary themes of content, intelligibility, vocality, contrast, counterpoint, and morality we have seen that certain constituents of the truly revolutionary view that instrumental music was the highest of the arts were already in the process of formation and preparation earlier in the eighteenth century. On the other hand, some elements constituted a more definite break with the past. The utter abandonment of the insistence on accurate representation in favor of conceiving music as a mysteriously evocative symbol, and the very intense relishing of music's obscure suggestiveness, stand out among the truly novel positions of the Romantics. The most notable evolutionary development leading to the Romantic view occurred with respect to the theme of contrast; all through the latter eighteenth century we can see that increasingly dynamic theories of the emotions were used to justify increasing levels of contrast in the instrumental idiom. The Romantic acceptance of sudden changes and struggling, contradictory elements both within music and within the psyche was only a final stage of a longer development, with which Enlightened critics had been much involved. Romantic ideas bearing on musical craft and on the spiritual significance of music were anticipated in another way. They were in part a return to the attitudes of pre-Enlightenment German musical culture; though here too we noted a preparation: beneath the mainstream of Enlightened music criticism in Germany we noted an undercurrent of persisting traditional attitudes towards music.

To conclude our summary I shall list, side by side, the "Enlightened" and "Romantic" positions on each of the issues which I isolated in the first chapter as relevant to the eighteenth-century critical debate over instrumental music. By reading over this concluding table one can readily see the critical distance that was traveled. Romantic attitudes, while bearing on the same issues as Enlightened attitudes, constitute a considerable transformation of opinion. Indeed it seems as though the Romantics took those aspects of instrumental music which previously had been grounds for complaints, or had been recognized as typical, but aesthetically unexplained, qualities, and made them essential parts of their new aesthetic vision of music as the highest of the arts. As I have tried to demonstrate in this summary, only a few elements of the Romantics' unprecedented appreciation of instrumental music were without preparation. The uniquely German critical synthesis that reached maturity in the ideas of the Romantics had been in the making over the course of the latter eighteenth century.

There are some themes or issues which were treated by one group and not by the other. For example, whereas earlier eighteenth-century writers complained continually about virtuosity, the Romantics rarely mention it explicitly. Nor do the Romantics refer frequently to *Verwunderung*, or wonderment, though they speak constantly of the "wonderful," and of the "wonder" of music. On the other hand, early eighteenth-century writers, in contrast to the Romantics, do not delve into the nature of the emotions; Cartesian models and notions drawn from the rhetorical tradition seem to have served them well enough. Sometimes it is difficult to ascertain whether the two groups are talking about the same thing or not, because terminology changed. When earlier writers talk of *Abwechselung* and later ones talked of *Mannigfaltigkeit*, are they referring to a comparable aspect of music? At other times the terms remain but one wonders whether the meaning persisted. Does the *Tändelei* that was so ridiculed by earlier eighteenth-century writers correspond to the same phenomenon that took on an almost profound significance for the Romantics? (For example, would they both have applied the term to the light-hearted and playful aspects of Haydn's symphonies?) It is difficult to answer such questions with certainty.

At times the transformation can be said to exist only by virtue of an implied divergence of opinion. For example, though contrast was recognized earlier in the century as a trait indigenous to Italian instrumental music, it had no recognized function within an aesthetic ideology that demanded the representation and arousal of the passions (indeed some called such contrasts "meaningless"). Thus, when the Romantics point enthusiastically to the role played by contrast and variety in a music which serves as a symbol of the multifarious reality of life, they have in fact brought about a certain reversal of opinion. In one case, contrast has no aesthetic function and in the other, it does.

Furthermore, as was the case at the end of the first chapter, the reference of many comments is unclear. Opinions are directed at times to instrumental music seen *a priori,* to music seen merely as an art in time using pitch, rhythm, etc., but lacking any innate power of reference to the real world. But at other times, as with the *manningfaltiger Strom,* it is the traits indigenous to a peculiar style of music which elicit opinions. The Romantics distinguished these two different points of reference even less clearly than earlier eighteenth-century writers. Thus, when mention is made of the "specific nature of music," we must be ready to interpret this term in either sense or as the blending of both senses.

Here, then, proceeding by theme, is the double listing. It makes clear the several fronts on which attitudes had to change in order to prepare the Romantic reevaluation of the significance of instrumental music. It also dramatizes the issues that had a bearing on eighteenth-century opinions of instrumental music. Since the earlier views, at least the complaints, can be seen as part of the larger cultural movement known as the Enlightenment, I shall label these earlier views with an E; Romantic views are then naturally designated with R. Implied views, conditions, or assumptions will be put into brackets.

1. Representation—Relation to real world—Significance
    E: Even instrumental music should represent, insofar as it can, aspects of the real world, especially the external signs of the passions. By such means does it acquire significance.
    R: It is a prostitution of the purity and "freedom" of instrumental music to demand that it represent a given reality outside of itself. Not only is it unable to do this by virtue of its very ambiguous and indefinite nature, but instrumental music does not even need to intend to represent in order to be significant. By its very nature, it can suggest, stimulate, embody, symbolize and celebrate the mysterious inner affective stream of man. [And in this stream dwells the truly real.]

2. Definitude—Verbalizability—Understandability
    E: Instrumental music's content is so dark and confused that words are necessary to overcome this defect and make its content clear and distinct. For its content must be intelligible; it must be determinate enough to be stated in words. However, instrumental music can express understandably the most obvious genres of feeling, such as happiness and sadness.
    R: This "defect" is fully justifiable. The content which music is supposed to express is not itself clear and distinct. The affective life cannot really

be analyzed into static, knowable emotional entities. Rather it is in a state of constant change which eludes all labels. Verbal labels do not convey the *way* it feels. No word—no clear and distinct concept—can penetrate the privacy of the emotional life or describe the realm of the infinite. Thus it is wholly appropriate that a wordless and ever-changing medium should suggest an ineffable, dynamic reality—that the sole subject of music should be the infinite.

3. Dramatic determinants—Specificity
    E: The passions represented or suggested by instrumental music are less potent than those of vocal music because instrumental music can provide no subject, object, or plot to make the passions seem real and moving. Since the listener cannot know who is suffering and why, he cannot feel sympathetic, he cannot enter into the emotion himself.
    R: The many affects suggested within a piece of instrumental music can act out a drama of their own without all these dramatic determinants. And the fact that subjects and objects of emotions are not specified enables the listener to imagine that the suggested affective flow is his own, and he can participate intensely in the music. Besides, one of the most profound and romantic of human emotions—infinite longing—itself possesses no object; instrumental music is therefore particularly suited to arousing or suggesting this emotion.

4. Coherence—Unity—Ordering—Contrast
    E: Affective contrasts and variety make no sense in instrumental music, because the reason for this variety, the motivation for this sequence of affects, cannot be explained. A piece that is first happy, than sad, is like a contradiction. Such instrumental music lacks *Charakter*.
    R: The affective life itself is full of change, both gradual and sudden; so too is life itself. Thus it is only natural that instrumental music should reflect this multifarious, at times even arbitrary, reality.

5. Relation to vocal music—Expressiveness
    E: Instrumental music should imitate vocal music. This is the only way to true beauty and expression. Expressiveness is a result of imitating the natural, understandable utterances of passion.
    R: Instrumental music speaks its own "pure" language. Emotions can be suggested, aroused, embodied, or symbolized independently of the models of vocal expression, that is by gestures and procedures natural to instrumental music. Besides, man's inner stream is often not even manifested in such external utterances.

6. Emotional effect—Moving the listener
    E: All music, including instrumental, should move the listener. But often, because the listener cannot discern the representation of any passion, instrumental music is only lifeless noise.
    R: Music possesses affective power—can evoke emotions and affect the course of the emotional stream—independently of any act of representation, or emotional communication from composer to listener. This effect is intuitive, immediate, even physical, and is not dependent on any cognitive act. The composer can "work upon the human soul" even though he does not intend to represent a passion or express his own real-life feelings.

7. Moral usefulness—Spiritual significance of the quality of life
    E: Instrumental music can neither teach a moral lesson nor confer any permanent uplift. Being purely sensuous, its effects are merely transitory.
    R: Instrumental music, by virtue of its innocence of reference to the real world, transports the listener to another world where he is liberated from all earthly concerns and struggles. Sometimes this liberation results in an ongoing serenity of soul where all antisocial traits dissolve, and a "universal acceptance" enters in. Instrumental music involves the soul with itself and nourishes the inner life. By bringing latent feelings to the fore it leads to a new awareness and understanding of oneself.

8. Relation to the other arts—Aesthetic status
    E: Instrumental music is the least among the arts; for its content, if indeed it has any, is obscure and indeterminate—it cannot be defined. Moreover, it does not move the passions and is of no redeeming moral value.
    R: Instrumental music is the highest of the arts, because it speaks the inarticulate mysterious language of the soul. By its very nature it has the closest affinity to the fluctuating ineffable quality of the inner affective life. Thus it is most able to suggest, embody, symbolize and stimulate this inner stream.

9. Attention-keeping
    E: Instrumental music is often just boring since it does not occupy the mind with any object, nor stir the passions. Or, if it succeeds in being entertaining, it must resort to procedures which are not sanctioned by the aesthetic of communicating the passions—such as surprise, novelty, variety, and meaningless contrasts.
    R: The Romantics seem to have had such a receptive "preparatory set" to

the new instrumental music, and to sheer tones, that music's power to hold the listener's attention was not an issue.

10. Sheer sensuality—Sensual pleasure—Sensual power of music
    E: The new instrumental music merely tickles the ears, and provides only sensual, transient pleasures. It fails to occupy the heart and the mind and it has no permanent effect. [Sensual pleasure must never be a law unto itself.]
    R: The very route of music into the soul is sensual. Music's powerful effects are achieved physically, through the sense organs. Music is so closely allied to the affective life because its impressions *feel* the way emotions feel. The very fleeting and variable nature of its sense impressions strikes a responsive chord in the ever-changing soul of the listener. Moreover, sheer sensual beauty—a beauty independent and free of reference to definite objects or concepts—can transport the listener into the realm of the infinite.

11. Compositional skill—Counterpoint—"System" of musical composition
    E: Counterpoint, or harmonic work, is in bad taste; its burdensome learnedness obscures the fundamental expression of a piece. It detracts from the beauty of a natural, flowing melody, and detracts from the intelligibility of music as the imitation of passionate utterance.
    R: The highly developed "science" of musical composition [including both counterpoint and thematic work] works mysteriously to reflect and affect the unity amid diversity of the complex, multifarious inner stream.

12. Virtuosity
    E: Music which serves merely to show off the skill of the performer is unworthy of the higher expressive goals of music. Virtuoso music is unvocal, unnatural, "fantastic," and inexpressive.
    R: [There is no deluge of complaints against virtuoso display in the Romantics' writings which we have surveyed. Of course, empty, wooden virtuosity is hardly in keeping with their aesthetic. However, virtuosity per se, insofar as it was unvocal, unnatural, fantastic, and nonrepresentative, was not inconsistent with their preferences—for they accepted the unnatural and the fantastic with relish.]

13. Contrast—Variety—Surprise—Expectation-Play—Abwechselung
    E: These are features indigenous to Italian instrumental music. They tickle the ears and insure the listener's attentiveness. They often cause the listener to be agreeably surprised and to feel astonishment (*Verwunder-*

ung). But they often make no sense and serve no purpose. [And what do they have to do with the representation and arousal of the passions?]

R: These elements are essential to a music which is to symbolize or reflect the ever-changing essence of the soul. For the affective life itself is characterized by such contrasts and changes, both gradual and abrupt. Fate itself is unpredictable.

14. *Verwunderung*

E: The arousal of *Verwunderung* by contrapuntal or virtuoso skill, by fantastic and unnatural instrumental gestures, or by sudden surprises is aesthetically undesirable. Rather, the passions should be moved.

R: [The Romantics do not speak much of *Verwunderung*, but of course they accepted most of the fantastic or ''unnatural'' things that caused it. Where eighteenth-century usage justifies the translation ''wonderment'' we can perhaps sense a certain acceptance of this emotion; for the Romantics loved anything which impressed upon them a sense of the mysterious, the unfathomable, the striking but unexplainable.]

15. Playfulness—Childishness

E: These qualities are not appropriate to art's highest manifestations; art must be serious and profound. Unfortunately, much of the new instrumental music is characterized by *Tändelei*.

R: The elements of the childlike and the playful transport us away from the purposeful concerns of the real world. The purposeless play of tones can be of profound significance. The nonreflective innocence of childhood brings us in closer touch with our primal, ineffable impulses.

16. Fire and Brilliance—Power and Grandeur

E: These are stimulating, enlivening, exhilarating qualities natural to instrumental music. [But again, what do they have to do with the communication of the passions?]

R: The ''grand'' symphonies with their manifold elements symbolize the luxuriant fullness and powerful currents of life. And the attentive soul rejoices in this full magnificence. Music celebrates the mystery of life.

Notes

Notes to Introduction

1. Leonard Meyer, *Emotion and Meaning in Music* (Chicago: University of Chicago Press, 1961), p. 73.

2. Ibid., p. 76.

3. We must not, of course, rule out the obvious possibility that critical ideas about music may have in some way affected the creative genius of a given composer in certain cases. But not only is this a more difficult assertion to defend in specific instances, and not only would it apply only to a small percentage of the music composed, it is not even necessary to assert this in order to hold that the ideas indeed had some relation to musical creation. There are other relations than causal ones; the whole question of priority, if indeed it is appropriate, should not be a focal or critical one.

4. Charles Rosen, *The Classical Style*, New York: W. W. Norton and Co., 1972. See, for example, pages 82–83. Rosen focuses particularly on the skill with which the classical composers—which he limits to Haydn, Mozart, and Beethoven—reconciled the opposing forces within their musical forms. "The simplest way to summarize classical form," Rosen writes, "is as the symmetrical resolution of opposing forces" (p. 83).

5. Alfred Einstein, *Mozart: His Character, His Work* (Arthur Mendel and Nathan Broder, trans., New York: Oxford University Press, 1945), p. 155.

6. See p. 10.

7. Roye Wates, "Karl Ludwig Junker (1748–1797): Sentimental Music Critic" (PhD. dissertation, Yale University, 1965), pp. 84 and 86–92.

8. Howard Serwer, "Friedrich Wilhelm Marpurg (1718–1795): Music Critic in a Galant Age" (PhD. dissertation, Yale University, 1969). For Serwer's adaptation of Abrams's "orientations," see Chapter VI: "Imitation, the Affections, and the Problem of Critical Orientation" (pp. 174–215).

9. See pp. 45 and 199.

10. See pp. 152–54 and 169.

11. See, for example, Joseph Martin Kraus, *Wahrheiten die Musik betreffend* (Frankfurt am Main, 1779), p. 96, where musical imitation is defined as the representation of inanimate nature and musical "expression" is defined as the "imitation of the tones uttered by men in various states of emotion, feeling, and passion."

12. See pp. 62–64 for Batteux's account of music as a natural language of the passions.

13. Schmid, *Bach und seine Kammermusik*, pp. 60 and 71.

14. See pp. 153–55 for Sulzer's use of the passionate utterance theory of musical expression.

15. See Chapter VI especially pp. 189–91.

16. See pp. 85–86.

17. The whole question of evolution vs. revolution is addressed in the Conclusion, Chapter VII.

Notes to Chapter 1

1. Problems with the rationalism-Romanticism and the imitation-expression frameworks are explored at length in the Introduction.

2. Georg Muffat, Preface to *Auserlesene mit Ernst und Lust gemengte Instrumentalmusik* [1701], in *Denkmäler der Tonkunst in Oesterreich*, vol. 23 (Vienna, 1895; reprint ed., Graz: Akademische Druck-u. Verlagsanstalt,1959), pp. 8–10. See below for Muffat's characterization of Corelli's style.

3. Wilhelm Friedrich Marpurg, *Der critische Musicus an der Spree* (Berlin, 1749–50; facsimile ed., Hildesheim: Georg Olms, 1970), Stück1 (March 4, 1749): 2–4.

4. Johann Joachim Quantz, *Versuch einer Anweisung die Flöte traversière zu spielen* [1st ed., Berlin, 1752], 3rd ed. (Berlin, 1789 facsimile ed. [ed. Hans-Peter Schmitz], Beverly Hills, Calif., 1953), Chap. 18, pars. 56–62. Vivaldi and Tartini are only mentioned by Quantz indirectly; his pointed remarks, however, clearly imply these two composers, as Edward R. Reilly has shown in his basic study, *Quantz and His Versuch* (American Musicological Society, Studies and Documents, no. 5, 1971).

5. Johann Adam Hiller, *Wöchentliche Nachrichten und Anmerkungen die Musik betreffend* (Leipzig, 1766–70; facsimile ed., Hildesheim: Georg Olms,1970) 3 (1768–69): 107–8.

6. Ferdinand Rochlitz, "Rhapsodische Gedanken über die zweckmässige Benutzunn der Materie der Musik," *Neue teutsche Merkur* 2 (October, 1798):169–70. All these views, only suggested here, will be discussed in the pages that follow.

7. I have found very useful the discussion of neoclassic criticism in the first volume of René Wellek's *History of Modern Criticism* (New Haven: Yale University Press, 1955). Cassirer's *Philosophy of the Enlightenment* is also quite helpful, especially on the relation of neoclassic criticism to later German aesthetics.

8. Pluche, *Le spectacle de la nature*, new ed., vol. 7: *Contenant ce qui regarde l'homme en société* (Paris, 1755), p. 111. Marpurg translated the sections on music in his *Historisch-Kritische Beyträge zur Aufnahme der Musik*, 5 vols (Berlin, 1754–78; facsimile ed., Hildesheim: Georg Olms, 1970), vol. 1 (1754–55), pp. 550–59 and vol. 2 (1756), pp. 145–80. Pluche is to be sure not a German writer, but as I mentioned in the preface, non-German writers whose ideas were taken up into the mainstream of German thought will at times be included; for they, too, affected aesthetic attitudes in Germany—sometimes very strongly.

9. Ibid., p. 111.

10. Gottsched, *Auszug aus des Herrn Batteux schönen Künsten aus dem einzigen Grundsatze der*

Nachahmung hergeleitet: zum Gebrauch seiner Vorlesungen mit verschiedenen Zusätzen und Anmerkungen erläutert (Leipzig, 1754), p. 201.

11. "Ein Körper ohne Geist," "ein todtes Ding," "deutlich erklären." Ibid., p. 202.

12. Johann Georg Sulzer, *Allgemeine Theorie der schönen Künste* [1st ed., Berlin, 1771–74], 2nd ed., 4 vols. (Leipzig, 1792; facsimile ed., Hildesheim; Georg Olms,1967), s.v. "Instrumentalmusik." It is known that J. A. P. Schulz and Johann Philipp Kirnberger helped Sulzer with the articles on music, especially their technical aspects. (Kirnberger worked with Sulzer on the articles up to *S*, with some help from Schulz; from *S* on, Schulz was alone responsible for drafting the music articles.) But since Sulzer was responsible for the music-aesthetic principles in these articles, and since the extent of Schulz's and Kirnberger's contributions has never been fully clarified, I shall not attempt to ascribe authorship of the articles to anyone other than Sulzer himself. (See *Die Musik in Geschichte und Gegenwart*, ed. Friedrich Blume [Kassel u. Basel: Bärenreiter Verlag,1949–68], s.v. "Sulzer, Johann Georg," by Peter Schnaus, vol. 12, cols. 1733–37.) Sulzer's encyclopedia will hereafter be cited as "Sulzer, ATdsK."

13. "Vermischte Gedanken," in Marpurg, *Beyträge* 5 (1760):19.

14. Although Sulzer's and Krause's complaints are very similar, I have put them into two separate classes. There is an important distinction: Sulzer, although admitting that the music makes a gentle or stormy impression, does not appear to hold that these pieces represent, in any way, gentleness or storminess. The pieces in question possess no content, because the composer did not consciously confer one. Krause's "kein *deutliches* Bild," however, allows for the possibility that the music he is discussing does in fact represent something, although in a confused way. But we are not dealing with careful, rigorous philosophical thinkers; their terminology and its implications do not necessarily benefit from vigorous analysis. They may, in fact, have held the same view; but the distinction between the two views they seem to hold is of the utmost importance.

15. Hiller, "Abhandlung von der Nachahmung der Natur in der Musik," in Marpurg, *Beyträge* 1 (1754–55): 528–29.

16. Junker, *Tonkunst* (Bern, 1777), pp. 97–98.

17. Herder, *Ob Malerei oder Tonkunst ein grösserer Wirkung gewähre [1781]*, in *Sämmtliche Werke*, ed. B. Suphan, 33 vols. (Berlin: Weidmann, 1877—99) vol. 15, p. 239.

18. "Obscure trifle." Marpurg, *Der critische Musicus*, p. 2.

19. Gotthold Ephraim Lessing, *Hamburgische Dramaturgie*, in *Gesammelte Werke*, ed. Wolfgang Stammler (Munich: Carl Hanser Verlag, 1959), vol. 2, Stück 27, p. 444.

20. Koch, *Musikalisches Lexikon* (Frankfurt am Main, 1802; facsimile ed., Hildesheim: Georg Olms, 1964), s.v. "Instrumentalmusik,"

21. Sulzer, ATdsK, s.v. "Instrmentalmusik."

22. Muffat, Preface to *Instrumentalmusik*, pp. 8–10.

23. Sulzer, ATdsK, s.v. "Sonate."

24. Mattheson, *Der Vollkommene Capellmeister* (Hamburg,1739; facsimile ed., Kassel: Bärenreiter, 1954), part 2, chap. 30 par.138. Subsequent citations will omit the designations for part, chapter, and paragraph; thus this reference would read merely "2. 30. 138."

25. Mattheson, "Musicalisches Ungeheuer." *Hamburgische Dramaturgie*, Stück 27, p. 445.

26. Reichardt, "Tausendfache Mannigfaltigkeit." *Schreiben über die berlinische Musik* (Hamburg, 1775), p. 14.

27. Quantz, *Versuch*, chap.10, par. 21. The frequent references to this work will also be shortened. The numbers refer to chapter and paragraph only, with an occasional third number in between indicating the part of the chapter. (I hope this will facilitate reference to other editions.)

28. Sulzer (ATdsK, s.v. "Vortrag") recommended that students practice these pieces so that they would learn how to express different *Charaktere*—one of the requirements of expressive performance. They were viewed as interpretative etudes, for each piece contained only one *Charakter* to express—each piece possessed affective unity.

29. Marpurg, *Der critische Musicus*, p. 37.

30. Mattheson, *Capellmeister*, 1. 10. 64.

31. Hiller, *Wöchentliche Nachrichten* 4 (1770):19.

32. Meyer (*Emotion and Meaning in Music*) has pointed out this very difficulty, which proved well-nigh insurmountable—for good reason, Meyer would say—to so many of the subjects of our study. ("The difficulty with an aesthetic of music based upon connotative and mood responses is not that the associations between music and referential experience are fortuitous or that there is no causal connection between music and feelings. . . . Though music can present the experiences themselves, if only metaphorically, it cannot stipulate the causal connection between them. There is no logical reason, either musical or extramusical, for any particular succession of connotations or moods" [pp. 271–72].)

33. *Christian Gottlob Neefens Lebenslauf von ihm selbst beschrieben*, ed. Walther Engelhardt (Cologne: Arno Volk, 1957), p. 23. He wrote, "Ich bin traurig und fröhlich. . . . Diese beiden Leidenschaften, Traurigkeit und Fröhlichkeit wechseln bei mir zu weilen sehr schnell ab" ("I am sad and happy. . . . Both these passions, sadness and happiness, sometimes alternate very quickly in me").

34. Pluche, *Spectacle*, pp. 115–16.

35. Junker, *Tonkunst*, p. 39.

36. Rochlitz, "Niedlich." "Rhapsodische Gedanken,"p. 170.

37. Quantz, *Versuch*, 18. 62. Quantz's entire discussion of the new Italian instrumental style is found in 18. 57–62.

38. Mattheson, *Capellmeister*, 1. 3. 89. Already in his *Neu-Eröffnete Orchestre* (Hamburg, 1713) Mattheson was emphasizing the difference between the "schöne singende Manier und geschwinde Brouillieren" (fast confusion): surprise and amazement are *not* the goals of music. Elsewhere he sums up the styles of the various countries thus: "Die Italiäner surprenniren; die Frantzösen wollen charmiren, die Teutschen studiren und die Engelländer recompensiren" (see pp. 83–84 and p. 220).

39. See Quantz, *Versuch*, 18. 78–86. Also, it should be noted that the statement most emphasized in Mattheson's mammoth work, *Der vollkommene Capellmeister*, is "Alles muss gehörig singen." He too would characterize the conflict of the present good musical taste and the past contrapuntally dominated style as one between the ear and the eye. C. P. E. Bach used the similar comparison "gearbeitet" versus "galant."

40. Marpurg, *Der critische Musicus*, p. 4.

41. *Carl Philip Emanuel Bach's Autobiography*, ed. William Newman [facsimile of the original edition of 1773, which was included in pp. 198–209 of the translation of Charles Burney's *The Present State of Music in Germany, the Netherlands, and the United Provinces*] (Hilversum: Frits A. M. Knuf, 1967), p. 209.

42. Mattheson, *Capellmeister*, 1. 10. 65. and 2. 12. 7; and Koch, *Lexikon*, s.v. "Instrumentalmusik."

43. Schubart, "Nachäffung des Menschengesprächs mit todten Instrumenten." *Ideen zu einer Aesthetik der Tonkunst* (Vienna, 1806; facsimile ed., Hildesheim: Georg Olms, 1969), pp. 335 and 360.

44. Koch, *Lexikon*, s.v. "Sinfonie."

45. It is important that we are aware that the emphasis many writers put on "moving" is due to their insistence that music have some moral affect. The tingling excitement of being put into an emotional state, just for its own sake, was not the outcome they envisioned for a moving music. Art was to improve morally and moving the passions was an essential means to this end.

46. See Sulzer, ATdsK, s.v. "Instrumentalmusik"; and Mattheson, *Capellmeister*, 1. 3. 89.

47. "Müssiges Zeitvertreib." According to Serauky (*Nachahmungs-aesthetik*, p. 96) this was the young *Aufklärer* Moses Mendelssohn's epithet for instrumental music. Sulzer uses a similar one: "blosses Zeitvertreib" is the label he applies again and again to music that does not express the passions in understandable language. As we recall, the "enlightened" rector Johann August Ernesti (J. S. Bach's superior at the Thomasschule in Leipzig) held a similar view of the uselessness of music. Many eighteenth-century defenses of music can probably be attributed to this new rationalistic disdain for music. Quantz in his *Versuch* (18.80) indirectly rebuts Ernesti's attitudes. And Junker, in his *Ueber den Werth der Tonkunst* (Bayreuth, 1786, pp. 82–83) answers similar charges of uselessness by none other than John Locke, who held that music is a waste of time and has no important role to play in education. For Junker music was one of the "noblest pastimes."

48. Krause, *Berlinische Musik*, p. 25. "Ihr seyd gebeten mit eurem Aberwitz/Und ohrenkitzelndem Klingklang zu gehn,/Ihr Possenreisser! . . . ihr Schander der edlen Harmonie!/Geht hin zum üppigen Hof, wo Albernheit,/Wo Gähnen, Ekel und Tandstoltz residirt;/Da könnt ihr Bravos die Menge, fürstlich Gold/Und fürstlich Lachen erbeuten, geht nur hin!"

49. Sulzer, ATdsK, s.v. "Musik," pp. 431–32.

50. "Ueber die aesthetische Erziehung des Menschen," 22nd Letter, in *Schillers Werke in fünf Bänden*, ed. Benno von Wiese (Cologne: Kiepenheuer & Witsch, n.d.), vol. 4, p. 547.

51. "Ueber das Pathetische," quoted in Rey Longyear, *Schiller and Music* (Chapel Hill: University of North Carolina Press, 1966), pp. 110–11. The entire passage, in Longyear's translation, is worth quoting, for it very graphically illustrates the "noble and manly" German disdain for merely sensually pleasing art: "The music of the moderns seems remarkably aimed only toward sensuality and thus flatters the dominating taste which wants only to be agreeably tickled, not affected, not powerfully stirred, nor exalted. All sweet melodiousness is therefore preferred, and if there is an even greater noise in the concert hall, suddenly everyone becomes all ears when a sentimental passage is played. An almost animal expression of sensuality then usually appears on all faces, the intoxicated eyes swim, the open mouth is lustful, a voluptuous trembling seizes the whole body, the breath is rapid and short; soon all the symptoms of intoxication appear as a clear indication that the senses are running riot but that the spirit or the principle of freedom has fallen

prey to the force of sensual impressions. All these feelings, I say, are excluded from art through a noble and manly taste because they please only the feelings, with which art has nothing to do.''(Sulzer, too, whose crude moralism was roundly rejected by Goethe's and Schiller's circle, associated the merely sensually pleasing with un-German effeminacy. [See Sulzer, ATdsK, s.v. ''Empfindung.''])

52. See Jean Jacques Rousseau, ''Lettre sur la musique francaise,'' in Oliver Strunk, *Source Readings in Music History* (New York: W. W. Norton & Co., 1950), pp. 642–48. Just as God-fearing Germans such as Mozart equated Voltaire's name with anti-Christ, to German defenders of *reine Satz* Rousseau's name came to symbolize anti-Harmony. (The eighteenth-century meaning of the word *Harmonie.* should be understood. In some contexts it can even be translated as counterpoint; in all cases it implies purity of voice leading; it would never mean something that could be reduced to symbols denoting merely vertical configurations. For example, if somebody's style were too *harmonisch*, then it was too contrapuntal, or had too much activity in the bass line or inner voices. It is in this light that the eighteenth century debate between melody and harmony must be understood—one had to be either on the side of Rousseau or Rameau, Melody or Harmony. Of course, Rousseau had nothing against harmony in our guitar stummer's sense of the word.)

53. *Dr. Browns Betrachtungen über die Poesie und Musik mit Anmerkungen und zween Anhängen begleitet,* trans. Johann J. Eschenburg (Leipzig, 1769), pp 316–17. My translation.

54. Quantz, *Versuch*, 18. 56–57.

55. Nichelmann, *Die Melodie nach ihrem Wesen sowohl, als nach ihren Eigenschaften* (Danzig, 1755), chap. 59.

56. Hiller, ''Nachahmung der Natur in der Musik,'' pp. 538–39. On page 539 Hiller speaks of musical bombast as excessive compositional art, which lacked taste and feeling. Later in the same essay, it should be noted, he goes on to admit as desirable a moderate admixture of the ''wonderful.''

57. Marpurg, *Der critische Musicus*, p. 2.

58. Quantz, *Versuch*,18. 65.

59. Krause, *Berlinische Musik*, p. 18.

60. See Sulzer, ATdsK, s.v. ''Vortrag''; and Bach, *Versuch über die wahre Art das Clavier zu spielen* [1st ed., Berlin, 1753, 1759]: *Kritisch revidierte Neudruck nach der unveränderten jedoch verbesserten zweiten Auflage das Originals, Berlin 1759 and 1762*, 5th ed., ed. Walter Neimann (Leipzig: C. F. Kahnt, 1925), Part I, Introduction, par. 4.

61. *Parallèle des Italiens et des Français* [1702], in Strunk, *Source Readings*, p. 474.

62. ''Aus der Mannigfaltigkeit in die Einförmigkeit.'' ''Herrn Johann Quantzens Lebenslauf, von ihm selbst entworfen,'' in Marpurg, *Beyträge* 1 (1754–55): 237.

63. ''Die Italiäner surprennieren; die Frantzosen wollen charmiren; die Teutschen studiren; und die Engelländer recompensiren.'' See Mattheson, *Das Neu-Eröffnete Orchestre*, p. 220.

64. Quantz, *Versuch*, Chapter 18, par. 67.

65. Junker, *Tonkunst*, p. 63.

66. Schubart, *Ideen zu einer Aesthetik der Tonkunst*, p. 179.

67. Quantz, *Versuch, 18. 59.*

68. Koch, *Journal der Tonkunst* (Erfurt and Braunschweig, 1795, pp. 92–93).

69. Ibid., p. 91.

70. Vol. 3 (1768–69): 107. Hiller opposes these qualities to the "wohl gearbeitete, prächtige, und affectvolle" ([contrapuntally] well worked out, splendid, and expressive).

71. Quoted in Ernst Fritz Schmit, *Carl Philipp Emanuel Bach und seine Kammermusik* (Kassel: Bärenreiter Verlag, 1939), p. 82.

72. See Sulzer's condemning use (in ATdsK) of "Tändelei" in the articles "Opera" and "Symphonie."

73. At times translations nearer the root meaning, for example, "alternation" or the awkward "alternatingness," are sufficiently accurate and clear. On the whole, however, the translation "contrast" best designates that stylistic procedure—namely, the use of thematic material of contrasting character—which eighteenth-century Germans usually designated with the word "Abwechselung"; for "contrast" is the word we in the twentieth century have come to use in discussing that very quality of latter eighteenth century music. Also, it should be remarked that Quantz and Junker use, respectively, the terms *Abwechselung* and *Kontrast* in part to refer to dynamic nuance, an interpretative procedure also known in the eighteenth century by the expression "light and shade." In addition, Junker, who was well-versed in English aesthetic writings, used the term *Kontrast* in a broader sense which corresponds with Quantz's broader usage of the word, as in the *Abwechselung* of the singing and the brilliant. See the examples on Quantz below, and the chapter on Junker for further discussion of what Burney called the "principle of contrast" in the "modern symphonic style" (*History* II, pp. 866 and 951).

74. "Charming alternation," "pleasant alternation," "delightful alternation." *Versuch einer gründlichen Violinschule* (Augsburg, 1756; facsimile ed., Vienna, 1922), pp. 33, 83, and 110.

75. Quantz, *Versuch, 18. 2.*

76. Ibid., 14. 18. Christian Gottfried Krause also pointed out at about the same time that without variety a composer could indeed write well worked-out and correct music; but if a composer wanted to be "pleasing" as well as "learned" he would have to use as many different ideas as were necessary to make the desired impression (*Von der musikalischen Poesie* [Berlin,1752], pp. 30–31).

77. Similarly, C. P. E. Bach, in warning the clavier player not to obscure the various characters of a piece with insensitive ornamentation, speaks of the *Vermischung* of the brilliant and the simple, the fiery and the faint, the sad and the happy *(Versuch, p. 94).*

78. Quantz, *Versuch, 18. 50.* "Solo" was another name used in the eighteenth-century for what we now call a "sonata."

79. "Betrachtungen über die Musik," in Hiller, *Wöchentliche Nachrichten* 1 (1766): 369–70. Hiller's translation is taken from Blainville's *L'esprit de l'art musical* (Geneva, 1754). Blainville's ideas clearly derive from those of Jean Baptiste Dubos, who will be discussed later. (The question of originality of thought is not relevant to our present survey; we are concerned rather with the currency of certain ideas.)

80. Raguenet, *Parallèle*, p. 479. Charles Rosen, in his book *The Classical Style* (New York: W. W. Norton & Co., 1972), places special emphasis on the "new coherence" Mozart and Haydn

achieved in spite of dramatic disruptions of texture. Part of the essence of Haydn's music—and hence part of the essence of the best of eighteenth-century instrumental music—was this very uniting of contrasting elements: "True civilized wit, the sudden fusion of heterogeneous ideas with an air paradoxically both ingenuous and amiably shrewd, characterizes everything that Haydn wrote after 1780" (pp. 154 and 159).

81. See Scheibe, *Der critische Musicus*, 2nd ed. (Leipzig, 1745), pp. 622—24; Mattheson, *Capell-meister*, 2. 4. 31; Mozart, *Versuch*, p. 200; Quantz, *Versuch*, 15. 5., 15. 11, and 15. 18; and Bach, *Versuch*, pp. 123 and 127. This represents of course only a small sampling.

82. Mattheson, *Capellmeister*, 2. 4. 31.

83. Bach, *Versuch*, chap. 41, pars. 8, 11, and 12.

84. Of course, it is the definition of emotion, or of the passions, which is the crucial question here. Leonard Meyer's book, *Emotion and Meaning in Music*, discusses at great length the relation of music to emotion and emotion to expectation. It is possible to see in remarks such as Blainville's (above, p. 19), C. P. E. Bach's (just cited), and Quantz's (above, pp. 18–19 and *Versuch*,15. 18, where he speaks of the moving quality of the unexpected) vaguely conceived adumbrations of Meyer's ideas.

85. Paris, July 3, 1778, to his father. In Mozart. *Briefe und Aufzeichnungen. Gesamtausgabe*, collected and annotated by Wilhelm A. Bauer and Otto Erich Deutsch, 4 vols. (Kassel: Bärenreiter Verlag, 1962–63), vol. 2, pp. 388–89. The English translation is Emily Anderson's, taken from her *Letters of Mozart and his Family*, 2nd ed. (New York: St. Martin's Press, 1966), vol. 2, p. 558.

86. Hiller, "Nachahmung der Natur in der Musik," pp. 537 and 542. Hiller used the words "Er-staunen" and "Bewunderung," not "Verwunderung," but judging from the context and from the historical account of the latter terms' usage in Grimms' dictionary (Jacob and Wilhelm Grimm, *Deutsches Wörterbuch*, 16 vols. [Leipzig, 1854–1954], s.v., "Bewunderung," and "Verwunderung," where the two terms are given as synonyms and very similar definitions are given—both could denote a feeling evoked by the novel, the unusual, and the unexpected), the difference in terminology does not always carry with it a conceptual difference. Moreover, I have not found in general in eighteenth-century musical writings distinct usage for each term.

87. Muffat, Preface to *Instrumentalmusik*, p. 9.

88. Quantz (see pp. 18–19) opposed the moving of an audience to the mere arousal of *Verwunderung*, as did Hiller in his essay "Abhandlung von der Nachahmung der Natur in der Musik" (p. 537). And Mattheson, in seeking to assign an affect to each genre of instrumental music, that is, to legitimize each genre by showing in what way it was moving, or what affect it aroused, took special pains to remind his disinclined readers that *Verwunderung*, the affect he assigned to the keyboard sonata, was indeed also an emotion: "Doch ist die Verwunderung über eine ungewöhn-liche Fertigkeit auch eine Art der Gemüths-Bewegung" *Capellmeister*, 2.13. 138). Obviously, many in his readership would not have granted that the arousal of *Verwunderung* could constitute the moving of the passions. *The* passions were those things which Mattheson characterized at the beginning of his book: love, sadness, joy, pride, patience, stubbornness, anger, jealousy, hope, dispair and such—which, by virtue of their objects (all passions were assumed to have objects), bore some relationship to the exterior world of moral integrity or moral turpitude. One could be possessed by love of honor, or of possessions, by anger at a tyrant, or anger at God, by hope of heavenly salvation, or by jealously of one's neighbor, and so on. *The* passions were thus spurs to either moral or immoral action; hence if music aroused one of them, music exerted moral influ-

ence on the listener. *Verwunderung* obviously did not have the same kind of effect on the social behavior of the person experiencing it.

Descartes lists "wonder" among the six primitive passions; but he also points out that it is the only passion of the six that does not have good or evil as its object, its object being only the knowledge of the thing we wonder at. Perhaps it was this amoral character which caused wonder to be rejected as a suitable response to an artwork. Wonder, according to Descartes, occurs "when the first encounter with some object surprises us, and we judge it to be new or very different from what we formerly knew, or from what we supposed that it ought to be." (See his *Passions of the Soul* [De passionibus animae, Amsterdam, 1649] in *The Philosophical Works of Descartes*, trans. E. S. Haldane and G. R. T. Ross [Cambridge: Cambridge Univeristy Press, 1911; reprint ed., New York: Dover Publications, 1955], vol. 1, p. 363.)

89. Burney, *History*, vol. 2, p. 981. We see how radical a shift of opinion took place here when we compare this unassuming observation of Burney's with the arch-neoclassic warning of Boileau, "License is a crime which is never permitted." (Quoted in Cassirer, *The Philosophy of the Enlightenment*, p. 281.)

90. Mattheson, *Capellmeister*, 2. 12. 26.

91. Ibid., 2. 12. 9.

92. Ibid., 1. 10. 64.

93. Hiller, *Wöchentliche Nachrichten* 4 (1770):18–19.

94. Burney, *History*, vol. 2, p. 981. The whole sentence reads: "The novelty and merit of Schobert's compositions seem to consist in the introduction of the symphonic, or modern overture style, upon the harpsichord, and by light and shade, alternate agitation and tranquility, imitating the effects of an orchestra." Elsewhere, (p. 945), in refuting Avison's opinion that the "torrent of modern symphonies" was causing the "corruption and decay of music," he claimed that the "variety, taste, spirit, and new effects produced by contrast and the use of *crescendo* and *diminuendo* had done more to advance the cause of instrumental music than all the "dull and servile imitations of Corelli, Geminiani, and Handel."

95. Junker, *Tonkunst*, p. 50.

96. Junker, *Betrachtungen*, pp. 82–85.

97. "Streams which embrace everything." See *Zwanzig Componisten: eine Skizze* (Bern, 1776), p. 42.

98. Scheibe's statement to this effect, although revealing, is rather modest; it refers only to instrumentation and appears as part of a long quotation from Scheibe which Lessing included in the 26th *Stück* of the *Hamburgische Dramaturgie* (p. 440). Quantz's is more embracing; he compares all chamber music, including vocal music, to church or theater music. Since chamber music has no plot, he writes, it requires more "Lebhaftigkeit und Freyheit der Gedanken" (liveliness and freedom of ideas); it could also be more carefully worked out and tolerate more "art"—we might say more contrapuntal artifice, or more compositional craft (*Versuch*, 18. 27).

99. See Mattheson, above n. 88 and more importantly his *Capellmeister*,1. 10. 106, where he says that the instrumental style of chamber music *requires* more diligence and elaboration, that is more contrapuntal interest and complexity, than other styles, even if the melody must suffer somewhat. Scheibe, although adamantly against a contrapuntally elaborate style in theatrical music, or anywhere when the words must be understood distinctly, nevertheless characterized concertos and trio sonatas as relying heavily on "Harmonic work" or "fugue-like work," for their interest

(*Critische Musicus*, pp. 635 and 676). (Sulzer's ideas on this topic follow immediately, and Quantz's are summarized in the preceding footnote.)

100. Sulzer, ATdsK, s.v. "Cammermusik."

101. Quantz, *Versuch*, 17. 32.

102. "Das Ueberraschende und Feurige." Ibid.

103. Quantz, *Versuch*, 14. 18 and 18. 33.

104. Mattheson, "Ermuntrenders." *Neu-Eröffnete Orchestre*, p. 226.

105. "Reissendes punctirtes Wesen." Mattheson, *Capellmeister*, 2.12.16

106. Ibid., 2. 12. 21.

107. "Untermischte Kantable." Quantz, *Versuch*, 16. 16.

108. Mattheson, *Capellmeister*, 2. 12. 35.

109. Ibid., 2. 12. 36.

110. Hiller, "Nachahmung der Natur in der Musik," pp. 536–40.

111. Ibid., p. 540.

112. Ibid., p. 542.

113. Sulzer, ATdsK, s.v. "Instrumentalmusik."

114. Gottsched, *Auszug aus Batteux*, p. 196.

115. For a representative assortment of such complaints see Malcolm Cole, "The Vogue of the Instrumental Rondo in the Late Eighteenth Century," *Journal of the American Musicological Society* 22 (1969): 425–55.

116. Junker, *Zwanzig Componisten*, pp. 31–36.

117. Bach, *Versuch*, chap. 3 par. 15. Bach based no aesthetic opinion on this recognition of a kind of expressiveness and effectiveness peculiar to an instrumental genre (the vocal form most like the fantasy is the accompanied recitative, he tells us): all his life he strove to make the clavier "sing." (See his *Autobiography*, p. 209.)

118. Ibid. Of course, the type of *Zwang* (compulsion) most eighteenth-century critics were worried about was contrapuntal, not metrical—for how could a composer move his audience when at the same time he was "working" to obey the laws of counterpoint?

119. Ibid., chap. 3 pars. 13 and 15; and chap. 41, pars. 8,11, and 12.

120. Mattheson, *Capellmeister*, 1. 10. 93.

121. It is important to keep in mind that neither sheer expression nor sheer arousal was considered sufficient. Both expression and arousal were widely held to entail a purposeful act of representation on the part of the composer. (Also complicating the situation is the fact that the word "expression," in eighteenth-century usage, usually did not mean self-expression of the artist's innermost feelings, in the nineteenth-century sense, but rather an act of considered representation or depiction.) In short, an act of *communication*, usually entailing a purposeful and understandable representation and then resulting in the arousal of the listener's feelings, was demanded.

122. "Mere clanging." (Gottsched). See p. 3.

123. "Nonsensical noise." See v.T., "Ueber die Tonkunst," *Allgemeine musikalische Zeitung* 1 (1798–99): 773.

124. "Uncertainty and confusion": (Lessing). See p. 5.

125. "Fantastische plötzliche Uebergänge" (Sulzer). See pp. 6–7.

126. "Incomprehensible mishmash" (Hiller); "formless clanging" (Mattheson). See pp. 25 and 7, respectively.

127. "Natural and lyrical" (Marpurg); "the wonderful in music" (Hiller). See pp. 10 and 13, respectively.

128. "Chatter which does not occupy the heart." See Sulzer, ATdsK, s.v. "Musik."

129. "Useless junk" (Mattheson). See p. 11.

130. "Marbled paper" (Pluche). See p. 8. Charles Batteux compared the absurdity of a music with no object of representation to the absurdity of what we would today call abstract art (see his *Beaux arts réduits à un même principe* [Paris, 1773; facsimile ed., Geneva: Slatkine Reprints,1969], p. 353).

131. "Empty sounds which put one to sleep." See Johann Nikolaus Forkel, *Musikalischer Almanach auf das Jahr 1784* (Leipzig, 1784), p. 28.

132. "Ear-tickling jinglejangle" (Reichardt). See p. 11.

133. See pp. 13 and 22–23.

134. "Nothing but acrobatics" (Hiller). See p 13.

135. "Oddity" (Junker). See p. 15.

136. For a discussion of *Verwunderung*, see pp. 9, 13, 15, 21–22, 25 and 26.

137. "Common frivolities" (Koch). See p. 16.

138. "Surprise and fire" (C. P. E. Bach). See p. 24.

Notes to Chapter 2

1. Ernest Eugene Helm, *Music at the Court of Frederick the Great* (Norman, Okla.: University of Oklahoma Press, 1960), pp. 73–74.

2. In all fairness to the English, it must be noted that the Germans made good use of English theories of the emotions in their labor of reconciliation. (See Chapter V, especially the sections on Junker and Forkel.)

3. Berlin, 1937. Most of the ideas she surveys come from either sermons or practical handbooks. Catholic as well as Protestant writers are surveyed, but with the latter predominating.

4. From the foreword to *Symphoniae jucundae* (Wittenburg, 1538), quoted in Karl Anton, *Luther und die Musik*, 3rd ed., (Zwickau, 1928), pp. 51–52.

5. "Sonderbare Kraft der Musik," "wunderbare Wirkungen der Musik." These terms recur fre-

quently throughout the literature Otto surveys. See especially pp. 75–130 for a survey of various views concerning the effects of music.

6.   These were of course some of the same stories of the "meravigliosi effetti" of music that had so tantalized musicians in sixteenth-century Italy. See D. P. Walker, *Der musikalische Humanismus im 16. und 17. Jahrhundert* (Kassel u. Basel, 1949).

7.   For example, in his *Lob und Preis der loblichen Kunst Musica* (Wittenburg, 1538):
      So Saul vom bösen geist geplagt/Nach Musiekunst als bald man fragt/Der David must zum König bald/Mit seiner harffen kunst gewalt/So offt des Davids harffen klang/So weich des bösen geistes zwang.

8.   See the discussion of Krause and Forkel in Chapters III and V.

9.   "So vertreibet sie [die Musik] den Teufel und machet die Leutet fröhlich."

10. Heinrich Albert, *Arien Etlicher theils Geistlicher theil Weltlicher Reijme . . . acht Teile* (1638ff). Verrede zum Vii. Theil, quoted in Otto, *Musikanschauung*, p. 66.

11. "Zur Ehre Gottes und zulässiger Ergötzung des Gemüts . . . zu Gottes Ehre und *Recreation* des Gemüths." From a rewording of Niedt's *Musikalische Handleitung* (1738) for the use of his students. Quoted in Albert Schweitzer, *J. S. Bach*, 6th ed. (Leipzig: Breitkopf und Härtel, 1928), p. 153.

12. Quoted in Anton, *Luther*, p. 47.

13. Augustine, *Confessiones*, 10. 34.

14. "Geheime Zugänge." *Abhandlung von der Nachahmung*, in Marpurg, *Beyträge 1*, (1754–55): 523.

15. "Unerklärliche Sympathie." See above, p. 49.

16. Mattheson, *Capellmeister*, I. 3. 49–52.

17. "Denn Gott ist ein Gott der Ordnung. Er wird seine Krafft in keine Unordnung, und verwirrtes Wesen mit einmengen." Andreas Werckmeister, *Cribrum musicum oder Musicalisches Sieb . . .* (Quedlinburg und Leipzig, 1700), p. 10, quoted in Otto, *Musikanschauung*, pp. 77–78.

18. Werckmeister, for example, demonstrated that God had used the proportions of the musical consonances in the creation of various biblical objects: "The proportions of the ark, with a length of 300 yards, a breadth of 50, and a height of 30, applied to the monochord, would yield a major chord." (Quoted in Jan Chiapusso, *Bach's World* [Bloomington: Indiana University Press, 1968], p. 136.)

19. Lorenz Mizler believed it should be possible "to calculate the effects of chords and melodies on the soul, and on the basis of these mathematical results establish aesthetic rules for composition (Ibid., p. 255); For Mattheson's account, see chapter 4.

20. Luther to Senfl (October 4, 1530). Quoted in Anton, *Luther*, p. 41. Luther placed music next to theology in the curriculum of the schools he instituted: "Ich gebe nach der Theologia der Musik den nähesten locum und höchste Ehre." Ibid., p. 49.

21. "Es sind auch ohne Zweifel viele Samenkörner köstlicher Tugenden in den Herzen, welche von der Musik ergriffen werden." Ibid., p. 41.

22. "Denn wer möchte, selbst in der Türkei den tadeln, der diese Kunst [Musik] liebt und den Künstler preist?" Ibid.

23. "Vorschmack himmlische Freude," "edle Gabe Gottes." See Otto, *Musikanschauung*, p. 35.

24. C. F. D. Schubart justified the popularity of comic opera in the eighteenth century by explaining that God gave music to man to make life less miserable (*Ideen zu einer Aesthetik der Tonkunst* [Vienna, 1806], p. 349.)

25. Anton, *Luther*, p. 48 (supposedly said in remarks praising several motets of Senfl). In 1717 Niedt described the sounds of music as "much more spiritual than material" ("vielmehr spirituel als materialisch"). Quoted from his *Heilung durch Musik* (Hamburg, 1717) in Otto, *Musikanschauung*, p. 83

26. Quoted in Anton, *Luther*, p. 52.

27. "Es ist ein feiner, frommer Mann gewesen; wenn er itziger Zeit lebte, so würde er's mit uns halten." Ibid., p. 46.

28. Quoted in Chiapusso, *Bach's World*, p. 137.

29. Johann Rist, *Sabbahtische Seelenlust...* (Luneburg, 1651), p. 31, quoted in Otto, *Musikanschauung*, pp. 48–49.

30. Ibid., p. 49

31. Scheibe, *Critischer Musicus*, p. [3].

32. Quoted in Serauky, *Nachahmungsaesthetik*, p. 96.

33. Maria Maniates, "'Sonate, que me veux-tu?': The Enigma of French Musical Aesthetics in the Eighteenth Century," *Current Musicology* 9 (1969), pp 117–40.

34. See Ernst Cassirer, *The Philosophy of the Enlightenment*, trans. Fritz C.A. Koelln and James P. Pettegrove (Princeton: Princeton University Press, 1951), pp. 278–331.

35. Useful discussions of neoclassic aesthetic views can be found in Cassirer, *Enlightenment*, Chap. VII, "Fundamental Problems of Aesthetics," pp. 275–360; and in René Wellek, *A History of Modern Criticism: 1750–1950*, Vol. 1: *The Later Eighteenth Century* (New Haven: Yale University Press, 1955), Chap. I, "Neoclassicism and the New Trends of the Time," pp. 12–30.

36. Maniates, "Enigma", p. 121.

37. For discussions of neoclassic views regarding music and opera see Cuthbert Girdlestone, *Jean-Philippe Rameau: His Life and Work* (London: Cassell & Co., 1957), Chap. 14, "Theories," pp. 513–46; and Rosalie Sadowsky, "Jean-Baptiste Abbe Dubos: The Influence of Cartesian and neo-Aristotelian Ideas on Music Theory and Practice," (Ph. D. dissertation, Yale University, 1959).

38. Jean-Baptiste Dubos, *Réflexions critiques sur la poésie et sur la peinture* (Paris, 1719), p. 441. Elsewhere Dubos paraphrases Longinus and writes that sounds in symphonies have only "half their being," and lead only "half of a life" ("Les symphonies . . . ne soient que de simples imitations d'un bruit inarticulé, et, s'il faut parler ainsi, des sons qui n'ont que la moitié de leur être, et une demi-vie," p. 431).

39. Dubos, *Réflexions critiques*, p. 441.

40. Ibid., pp. 429 and 438.

41. See Sadowsky, "Dubos," pp. 181–82.

42. See Claude Palisca, "Girolamo Mei, Mentor to the Florentine Camerata," *Musical Quarterly* 40 (1954): 1–20.

43. "Omnis motus animi suum quemdam a natura habet vultum, et sonum, et gestum," Cicero, *De oratore,* 3. Dubos's paraphrase runs, "Chaque sentiment a ses tons ses accens et ses soupirs propres" *Réflexions critiques,* p. 459.

44. Dubos, *Réflexions critiques,* p. 426. Dubos saw the "truth" of the recitative as residing in this imitation of passionate tones. But he also pointed out that "the same truth can be found in the harmony and in the rhythm of the whole composition" (La même verité peut se trouver dans l'harmonie et dans le rithme de toute la composition," p. 429).

45. "Tous ces sons . . . sont les signes des passions, institués par la nature dont ils ont reçu leur énergie; au lieu que les mots articulés ne sont que des signes arbitraires des passions." (Ibid., p. 426.)

46. *Le Neveu de Rameau,* ed. Herbert Dieckmann (Paris: Le Club du meilleur livre, 1957), p. 89.

47. Rousseau, *Dictionnaire,* s.v. "Harmonie."

48. Nöel Antoine Pluche characterized the objectionable new music of his day—"la musique barroque"—by saying that it offended the "bon esprits de l'ordre commun" by attempting to "mettre l'esprit en émotion sans qu'il sache pourquoi." (*Le Spectacle de la nature,* pp. 134–35.)

49. See the discussion of Batteux at the end of this chapter.

50. "[Les sons] commencent à nous ennuyer quand ils ne sont plus signes des rien" (*Spectacle,* p. 113). Pluche is a particularly relevant source of neoclassic opinion because Marpurg translated his remarks on music from the voluminous *Spectacle de la nature* in his *Historisch-Kritische Beyträge zur Aufnahme der Musik* 1 (1754–55): 550–59, and 2 (1756): 145–80.

51. "D'occuper l'esprit d'un objet, et d'aider le sentiment par la convenance toujours touchante du son avec la parole" (*Spectacle,* p. 133).

52. Ibid.

53. Ibid., p. 111.

54. *Traité de l'Harmonie réduite à ses principes naturels* (Paris, 1722), pp. 162–63. Quoted in Girdlestone, *Rameau,* p. 530.

55. "De la liberté de la Musique," in *Mélanges de littérature, d'Histoire, et de Philosophie,* nouvelle édition (Amsterdam, 1770), Vol. 4, pp. 455–57.

56. Ibid., p. 455.

57. *Oeuvres et correspondances inédites* (Paris, 1887), p. 155. Quoted in Girdlestone, *Rameau,* p. 529.

58. Pluche, *Spectacle,* pp. 115–116.

59. Ibid., p. 118.

60. Leipzig. Several editions followed.

61. Leonard Ashley Willoughby, *Classical Age of German Literature,* p. 19. His fall from this position was brought about by the Swiss partisans of the imagination and the "wonderful," Bodmer

and Breitinger, who both wrote treatises around 1740, and by the publication of the first three cantos of Klopstock's *Messias* ("the first practical justification of the Swiss theories") in 1748.

62. John George Robertson, *A History of German Literature*, 5th ed., ed. Edna Purdie (Edinburgh: William Blackwood and Sons, 1966), p. 214.

63. Gottsched, *Critischen Dichtkunst*, Vorrede to the 1730 edition, p. 125 of the third edition (1742), and p. 759 of the same, respectively. Unless otherwise noted, all subsequent references will be to the third edition of 1742.

64. Gottsched, *Critischen Dichtkunst*, p. 142.

65. Ibid., p. 144

66. In calling Bach's music "turgid and confused," Scheibe also said that the turgidity had rendered the music "artificial" rather than "natural," and that the "excess of art" obscured the natural beauty of Bach's pieces. (See Hans T. David and Arthur Mendel, eds., *The Bach Reader*, p. 238.)

67. Gottsched, *Critischen Dichtkunst,*, p. 150.

68. Ibid., p. 68. Note the paraphrase of Cicero.

69. Ibid., p. 69. (My italics.)

70. Ibid.

71. Ibid., p. 472.

72. Ibid., p. 466.

73. Ibid., p. 760.

74. Ibid., p. 757.

75. "Sammelplatz aller ersinnlichen Ergetzlichkeiten," "Zusammenfluss aller poetischen und musikalischen Schönheiten," "Meisterstück der menschlichen Erfindungskraft," "aus ihren Gründen hergeleitet." Ibid., p. 758.

76. Ibid., p. 759.

77. In 1754 Gottsched made explicit the negative implications of his view for the worth of instrumental music, which he characterized as "a dead thing, a body without a soul" ("ein todtes Ding, ein Körper ohne Geist"). See his *Auszug aus des Herrn Batteux . . . schönen Künsten* (Leipzig, 1754) and Chapter IV below.

78. First edition (Hamburg, 1738, 1740); second edition (Leipzig, 1745). All references are to the 1745 edition.

79. Scheibe, *Der critischer Musicus*, p. 375.

80. Ibid., p. 266.

81. *Musik in Geschichte und Gegenwart*, s.v. "Scheibe, Johann," by Paul Rubardt, vol. 11, cols. 1616–1617.

82. Scheibe, *Der critischer Musicus*, p. 266.

83. Ibid., p. 275.

84. Ibid., p. 274.

85. Ibid., p. 379.

86. "Es wird also zur Pracht, zur Lust und zum Lachen gebraucht"; "lebhaft und durchdringend." Ibid.

87. Ibid.

88. "Ein geschickter Componist kann in [die Synphonie wie sie anitzo beschaffen ist] alle Affecten, alle Leidenschaften . . . auf die deutlichste und angenehmste Art von der Welt ausdrücken." Ibid., p. 596.

89. Ibid., pp. 598–99.

90. Ibid., pp. 597–98.

91. In concluding his discussion of the theater symphony (ibid., p. 602) Scheibe does say that the symphony must be an imitation of nature; but the mimetic principle is used here only to oppose the constrained, the unnatural, the unpleasant, and the annoying. It seems that for Scheibe nature was at times merely the equivalent of pleasing melody.

92. Ibid., p. 598.

93. Ibid., p. 600.

94. Ibid., p. 622.

95. Ibid., p. 623.

96. Ibid., pp. 623–24.

97. "Sehr geschickte harmonische Arbeit," "ein blosses harmonisches Gewebe macht es nicht allein aus." Ibid., p. 633.

98. "Bey aller ihrer Kunst und mühsamen Arbeit." Ibid., p. 635.

99. "Beständiges Feuer," "natürliche Munterkeit," "edle Lebhaftigkeit." Ibid., pp. 667–71.

100. "Fugenmässige Ausarbeitung." Ibid., p. 676.

101. Ibid., p. 678.

102. Ibid., p. 677.

103. Paris. All references to Batteux's book will be to the Paris 1773 edition (facsimile ed., Geneva: Slatkine Reprints, 1969).

104. Manfred Schenker, *Charles Batteux und seine Nachahmungstheorie in Deutschland*, Untersuchungen zur neuern Sprach-und Literaturgeschichte, ed. Oskar F. Walzel, n.s., vol. 2 (Leipzig: H. Haessel Verlag, 1909), pp. [vii]-viii et passim.

105. Johann Adolph Schlegel, *Einschränkung der schönen Künste auf einen einzigen Grundsatz* (Leipzig, 1751); Philipp Ernst Bertram, *Die schönen Künste aus einem Grunde hergeleitet* (Gotha, 1751); Johann Christoph Gottsched, *Auszug aus des Herrn Batteux . . . schönen Künste* (Leipzig, 1754); Karl Wilhelm Ramler, *Einleitung in die schönen Wissenschaften* (Leipzig, 1756–58). The Schlegel and Ramler translations went through several editions; the fifth edition of Ramler's was published in Leipzig as late as 1802.

106. Arnold Schering, "Die Musikaesthetik der deutschen Aufklärung," *Zeitschrift der internationalen Musikgesellschaft* 8 (1907): 319. "Von Batteux an beherrscht französischer Geist die Musikaesthetik; die vorher bis zu einem gewissen Grade selbständige deutsche verliert ihre Selbständigkeit."

107. Batteux, *Beaux arts*, p. 8.

108. Ibid., p. 10.

109. Schenker, *Batteux*, pp. 27, 38, and 40.

110. Ibid., pp. 61–63.

111. "Tout sentiment, dit Ciceron, a un ton, un geste propre qui l'annonce." (This is Batteux's translation of Cicero's own words, quoted earlier in this chapter.) Batteux, *Beaux arts*, p. 357.

112. Dubos, *Réflexions critiques*, pp. 428–29.

113. "La plaint et la joie indépendamment des mots" (Batteux, *Beaux arts*, p. 336). See Dubos, *Réflexions critiques*, pp. 429–31.

114. Batteux, *Beaux arts*, p. 336–38.

115. Ibid., pp. 340–42: Batteux was adamant that the artist did not create objects, but only arranged, and made more agreeable and impressive the objects of nature: "L'Art ne crée les expressions, ni ne les détruit: il les regle seulement, les fortifie, les polit. Et de même qu'il ne peut sortir de la Nature pour créer les choses: il ne peut pas non plus en sortir pour les exprimer: c'est un principe." (Ibid., p. 351.)

116. "Toute musique doit avoir une signification, un sens." Ibid., pp. 336–42, and 350. Batteux was adamant that this meaning of music was not created but that it was found already existing in nature.

117. "Un sens net, sans obsurité, sans équivoque." Ibid., p. 353.

118. Ibid., p. 356.

119. Ibid., p. 353.

120. "Au moins, un commencement d'expression, comme une lettre, ou une syllable l'est dans la parole." Ibid., p. 355.

121. "La Musique me parle par des tons: ce langage m'est naturel: si je ne l'entends point, l'Art a corrompu la nature, plutôt que de la perfectionner." Ibid., pp. 351–52.

122. Ibid., p. 353.

123. "Les tons sont à demi formés dans les mots." Ibid., p. 345.

124. "Coherent discourse." Ibid., p. 357.

125. Ibid.

126. "Chaque ton, chaque modulation doit nous mener à un sentiment, ou nous le donner." Ibid., pp. 360–62.

127. Ibid., P. 364.

128. "Si le sentiment est rafiné, subtilisé, la musique ne le rend plus; ou ne le rendant qu'en partie, elle devient d'un sens obscur, équivoque." Ibid., p. 346.

129. "Pourquoi choisit-on certains objets, certaines passions, plutôt que d'autres? N'est-ce pas parce qu'elles sont plus aisées à exprimer, et que les spectateurs en saisissent avec plus de facilité l'expression?" Ibid., pp. 353–54.

130. Ibid., pp. 356–57.

131. See the discussion of Hiller and Ruetz below in Chap. IV.

132. Batteux, *Beaux arts*, p. 358

133. Schenker, *Batteux*, p. 11.

134. Batteux, *Beaux arts*, p. 343.

135. "Premier rang." Ibid., p. 356.

136. Ibid., p. 358.

Notes to Chapter 3

1. Hamburg, 1. 1. 6. References to Mattheson's *Capellmeister* indicate part, chapter, and para-graph. Unless otherwise noted all references in the part of the chapter devoted to Mattheson are to *Capellmeister*.

2. "Herzrührenden Gesang." 1. 3. 89.

3. *Die Musik in Geschichte und Gegenwart*, s.v. "Mattheson, Johann Georg," by Hans Turnow, vol. 8, cols. 1795-1815.

4. 1. 2. 15.

5. Beekman Cannon, *Johann Mattheson: Spectator in Music* (New Haven: Yale University Press, 1947), pp. 121-38 passim.

6. 1. 2. 22.

7. 1. 2. 24.

8. "Klingende Kräfte." 1. 3. 51.

9. "Der einige Sinn des Gehörs aber ist unsrer Seele und unsern Sitten bestimmet und vorbehal-ten." 1. 3. 26

10. "Naturlehre des Klanges." 1. 3. 1-89.

11. "Die Wirckungen der wol-angeordneten Klänge, welche dieselbe an den Gemüths-Bewegungen und Leidenschaften der Seele erwiesen." 1. 3. 49.

12. 1. 3. 49-54.

13. 1. 3. 89.

14. "Wol-eingerichtete und klüglich gemässigte Gemüthneigung." 1. 3. 52.

15. 1. 3. 53.

16. See his *Passions of the Soul*, pp. 358-427.

17. "Gleichförmige Verhältnisse der Klänge." 1. 3. 58.

18.   1. 3. 56.

19.   "Sinnlicher Begriff." 1. 3. 59.

20.   "Das sicherste und wesentlichste Handleitung zur Invention." 2. 4. 127.

21.   "Klang-rede" or "Ton-Sprache." 1. 10. 63.

22.   In the *Capellmeister* Mattheson never uses the word "imitation" to refer to musical depiction.

23.   2. 4. 66.

24.   "Eine solche Vergnügen des Gehörs, dadurch die Leidenschaften der Seele rege machen."

25.   "Redende Klänge." 2. 12. 36.

26.   1. 2. 37.

27.   2. 12. 38.

28.   1. 10. 1-108, 2. 13. 130-43, 2. 12. 1-47.

29.   "Alles spielen ist nur Nachahmung und Geleite des Singens." 1. 10. 65.

30.   1. 10. 63.

31.   2. 12. 38.

32.   "Unförmliches Geklängel." "Das wolgestalte und förmliche Wesen der Melodie bestehet."
      1. 10. 64.

33.   "Lebhafter Ausdruck der Gemüthsbewegungen." 1. 10. 72.

34.   "Als in einer Monarchie." 1. 10. 77.

35.   1. 10. 106.

36.   1. 10. 106.

37.   "Vieles Vergnügen." 1. 10. 105.

38.   2. 13. 1-143.

39.   "Mässige Lustigkeit," "jauchzende Freude." 2. 13. 81 and 87.

40.   2. 13. 130, 132, 134 and 136.

41.   2. 13. 137.

42.   "Flickwerck, auf lauter zusammengestoppelte Cläusulgen." 2. 13. 138.

43.   2. 13. 138.

44.   2. 13. 139.

45.   2. 13. 141.

46.   *Orchestre* p. 226.

47.   "Vom Unterschied zwischen Sing- und Spiel-Melodien." 2. 12. 1-47.

48.   2. 12. 2-3 and 47.

49.   2. 12. 4-6, 8-9, 11, 13-14, 16-17.

50.   2. 12. 7.

51.   2. 12. 4-9. "Man wird durch die grosse Freiheit bey Instrumenten zu lauter unförmliche Melodie gewohnet, und von der wahren Sing-Art so weit abgeräth."

52.   2. 12. 8.

53.   "Feuer und Freiheit." 2. 12. 12. "Absonderlich will der Violinen-Styl nicht viel schläfriges, es sey denn zur Abwechselung leiden, sondern fast immer eine gewisse lebhaffte Bewegung haben."

54.   2. 12. 13.

55.   "Reissendes punctirtes Wesen," "schön und munter," "geschärffte und spitzige Klang-Füsse." 2. 12. 20-21.

56.   2. 12. 26-27.

57.   2. 12. 30

58.   2. 12. 31.

59.   2. 12. 35.

60.   2. 12. 36.

61.   "Ohne Beilhülfe der Worte und Stimmen eben so viel zu sagen trachtet, als diese mit den Worten thun." 2. 12. 38.

62.   Frankfurt am Oder. Volume 2 was published in 1758. The basic outline of Baumgarten's theory can be found already in his *Meditationes philosophicae de nonnullis ad poema pertinentibus* (Halle, 1735).

63.   See the introduction to *Reflections on Poetry: Alexander Gottlieb Baumgarten's "Meditationes philosophicae de nonnullis ad poema pertinentibus,"* trans. and intro. Karl Aschenbrenner and William B. Holther (Berkeley: University of California Press, 1954), pp. [1]-32.

64.   See Cassirer, *Enlightenment*, "Taste and the Trend towards Subjectivism," pp. 297-312. Dubos and Bouhours are the principal figures discussed.

65.   "Eine seltne, eine abentheuerliche Erscheinung." "Von Baumgartens Denkart in seinen Schriften," Herder, *Sämmtliche Werke*, vol. 32, p. 184.

66.   Baumgartnians allowed that all or some arts imitated nature, but denied unequivocally that imitation was the fundamental principle of the arts.

67.   A version of Baumgarten's aesthetics, though not without lacunae, exists in German in the form of a student's lecture notes. This hand-written manuscript was published by Bernard Poppe as an appendix to his *Alexander Gottlieb Baumgarten: Seine Bedeutung und Stellung in der Leibnitz-Wolffischen Philosophie und seine Beziehungen zu Kant* (Leipzig: Robert Noske, 1907), pp. 65-258.

68.   3 vols. (Halle, 1748-50). For the purposes of this study, I shall, as have other students of eighteenth-century aesthetics, consider Meier's ideas to be those of Baumgarten.

69.   As Susanne Langer pointed out, "The belief that music is essentially a form of self-expression (or

we might add the imitation of a self-expression) meets with paradox in very short order. . . . For
. . . sheer *self—expression requires no artistic form."* See *Philosophy in a New Key,* p. 216. We
shall see that Sulzer actually recognized and dealt with this paradox.

70. I shall translate Baumgarten's "sinnliche" as "sensual," taken in its nonderogatory sense as
having merely to do with the senses. When other Germans use the word "sinnliche" in a derogatory way, I can then use the same English equivalent. In this way I preserve in English the hues of
meaning which the word "sinnlich" possessed in German: the word could be used merely to
oppose the intellectual, or to connote the sometimes suspect pleasures of the senses.

71. Meier, *Anfangsgründe,* vol. 1, pp. 5 and 9.

72. Throughout his work Meier refers to the nature of the senses and feelings to justify his rules. He
was quite aware of the basic role they played: "Ich habe die schöne Erkenntnis als einen hellen
und reinen Flus betrachtet, der eine eben so schöne Quelle haben muss. Bis zu dieser Quelle bin
ich hinaufgestiegen, und ich habe sie in dem Inbegriffe aller sinlichen Kräfte der Seele gefunden." (Ibid., vol. 3, p. 2.)

73. For the relation of Leibnitz's and Baumgarten's accounts of cognition see Cassirer, *Enlightenment,* pp. 342-44.

74. "Die strengen Wahrheit und Vernunft." Poppe, *Baumgarten,* p. 229.

75. Meier, *Anfangsgründe,* pp. 188, 190, and 204.

76. Poppe, *Baumgarten,* p. 66.

77. Ibid., p. 76. Meier writes that there is nothing more pitiful than a scholar who does not possess the
aesthetic spirit; and he goes so far as to assert that a woman is never safer than in the presence of
such a person. ("Man kann nicht genug sagen, wie elend ein Gelehrter ist, der kein schöner Geist
ist. Er ist ein blosses Gerippe ohne Fleisch. . . . Er hat in seinem Betragen so etwas starres,
rauhes, schulfuchsisches, ungeschliffenes, finsteres, dass er beydes unerträglich und lächerlich
ist. Alles an ihm schmeckt nach der Schule. . . . Ein Frauenzimmer ist, Vergleichungsweise zu
reden, nirgends sicherer für aller Gefahr, als wenn es mit einem Algebraisten und Metaphysicus
umgeht" [pp. 25 and 29].)

78. Ibid., p. 73.

79. Meier, *Anfansgründe,* vol. 1, p. 25.

80. Cassirer, *Enlightenment,* p. 352.

81. See Cassirer, *Enlightenment,* (pp. 27-36) for an extensive treatment of the significant differences
between Cartesian and Leibnitzian rationalism, which he sees as basic to an understanding of
Baumgarten's independent German aesthetic viewpoint.

82. Ibid., p. 29.

83. Quoted in Cassirer, *Enlightenment,* p. 29.

84. Ibid., p. 122.

85. Ibid., p. 127. The phrase "exaltation of being" is Leibnitz's own.

86. Meier, *Anfangsgründe,* vol. 1, p. 25.

87. J. A. Schlegel, who popularized and developed Baumgarten's concept of *das Sinnliche,* empha-

sized that neither the "precise and instructive" nor the "easy and flowing" was sufficient to make a moral effect on man but only *das Sinnliche*, which satisfied and brought into harmony both mind and heart. See Schenker, *Batteux und seine Nachahmungstheorie*, p. 102.

Schiller's theory of art as the mediator between reason and sense, between the formal and the sensual, is developed in his *Briefe über die Aesthetische Erziehung des Menschen* (1793-94). See Katharine Everett Gilbert and Helmut Kuhn, *A History of Aesthetics*, rev. ed. (Bloomington: Indiana University Press, 1954), pp. 363-69.

88. Cassirer sees Baumgarten's great contribution as the "humanization of sensuality" *(Enlightenment*, p. 354).

89. Gilbert and Kuhn, *History of Aesthetics*, p. 293.

90. Meier, *Anfangsgründe*, vol. 1, p. 49.

91. Gilbert and Kuhn, *History of Aesthetics*, p. 293.

92. Meier, *Anfangsgründe*, vol. 2, p. 79.

93. "Sensual life." Ibid., vol. 1, p. 422.

94. Ibid., p. 330.

95. Ibid., p. 215.

96. "Abwechselung is nötig, damit die Aufmerksamkeit erhalten werde." Poppe, *Baumgarten*, p. 242.

97. "Reichthum, Mannigfaltigkeit, und Abänderung." Meier, *Anfangsgründe*, vol. 3, pp. 275 and 288.

98. Ibid., vol. 3, pp. 268-332.

99. Ibid., vol. 3, p. 322.

100. Ibid., vol. 3, pp. 282-89.

101. Poppe, *Baumgarten*, p. 248.

102. "Die belustigende Abänderung." Meier, *Anfangsgründe*, vol. 3, p. 278.

103. Ibid., p. 321.

104. Ibid.

105. "Hauptsturm auf das Gemüth des Zuhörers." Ibid., p. 321.

106. Ibid., vol. 2, pp. 78-79.

107. Ibid., p. 79.

108. Ibid., vol. 1, pp. 263-64.

109. Ibid., vol. 3, p. 330.

110. Ibid., vol. 1, pp. 262-67.

111. "Anmuthige und abwechselnden Mannigfaltigkeit." Ibid., vol. 3, p. 297.

112. Ibid., vol. 1, p. 295.

113. Ibid., pp. 330-31.

114. "Inventer dans les Arts, n'est point donner lêtre à un objet, c'est le reconnoitre où il est, et comme il est"; "Man mus suchen ein Original zu werden, wenn man was neues denken wil." Batteux, *Beaux arts,* p. 32; Meier, *Anfangsgründe,* vol. 1, pp. 347-48.

115. Poppe, *Baumgarten,* pp. 252-53.

116. Meier, *Anfangsgründe,* vol. 1, p. 455.

117. Ibid., vol. 3 pp. 13-14.

118. Poppe, *Baumgarten,* p. 252.

119. "Das Unerwartete, das Wunderbare, und das auf eine angenehme Art überraschende." Meier, *Anfangsgründe,* vol. 2, p. 336.

120. Ibid., vol. 1, pp. 329 and 332.

121. Ibid., vol. 3, p. 298.

122. *Die Musik in Geschichte und Gegenwart,* s.v. "Krause, Christian Gottfried," by Hans Jancik, vol. 7, cols. 1717-21.

123. Berlin.

124. Krause, *Musikalischen Poesie,* p. 274. Unless otherwise noted, all page references in the remainder of this chapter are to this work.

125. "Die Musik ist zu einer eigenen Kunst geworden." P. 118.

126. Pp. 275-76.

127. P. 277.

128. Pp. 28-29.

129. "Skillful imitation of nature," "to paint the content," "nature beautifully presented," "instrumental painting of the affects."

130. "Bey allen schönen Wissenschaften kommt es auf die Nachahmung der Natur." P. 51.

131. P. 53.

132. "Nur in so weit musicalisch, als sie zur Erregung eines Affects oder eines besondern Wohlgefallens etwas beyträgen." P. 54.

133. Ibid.

134. Pp. 54 and 44.

135. "Vollkommene Uebereinstimmung," "genauesten Verhältnis," "Beschaffenheit unsers Geblütes und unserer Adern." Pp. 80-81.

136. "Die Musik brauchen wir zum Vergnügen"; "Durch Singen . . . sucht man sich die Zeit zu vertreiben, und das Gemüth zu erheitern, wenn man ganz allein ist"; "Wir singen und musiciren wenn Freude und Hofnung, Liebe, Traurigkeit, Schmerz und Verlangen sich unserer bemeistern. Wir thun es aber nicht, wenn Furcht, Verzweifelung, Kleinmuthigkeit, Zorn und Neid das Gemüth in Unruhe setzen." Pp. 98-99, 275, 69, and 93.

137. Pp. 93-94.

138. P. 368.

139. Pp. 26-27.

140. P. 59.

141. P. 290.

142. P. 198.

143. "Eine übermässige Liebe zur Ruhe." P. 92.

144. P. 94.

145. "Der Mensch kann seine Freude niemahls genug entdecken." P. 99.

146. P. 94.

147. P. 90.

148. "Die glückliche Nachahmung." P. 94.

149. P. 58. Elsewhere Krause wrote, in a similar vein, that all of the noblest virtures and inclinations were accompanied by the same emotions which were best expressed in music. ("Alle die edelsten Tugenden und Neigungen sind von den Affecten begleitet, die sich in ihr am besten ausdrücken lassen" [p. 89].)

150. P. 89.

151. Pp. 43-44.

152. Pp. 41-42.

153. P. 40.

154. Ibid.

155. "Vornehmste unter den Tugenden, natürlichen Neigungen und Leidenschaften." P. 89.

156. Pp. 277-78.

157. P. 278.

158. P. 290.

159. Pp. 289-90.

160. P. 32.

161. Pp. 29-30.

162. "Die Musici verbiethen auch in ihren Compositionsregeln solche Einförmigkeit." P. 30.

163. P. 30.

164. P. 31.

165. Pp. 30-31.

166. P. 316.

167.   P. 305.

168.   P. 314.

169.   "Um dadurch die immer während und *unausprechliche* Freude der himmlischen Einwohner auszudrücken." P. 309.

170.   Pp. 107-8.

171.   "Wunderbaren Wirckungen der alten Musik." P. 13.

172.   P. 41.

173.   "Durch die innerlichen Verhältnisse, so die Töne mit einander haben, und durch ihre äusserliche schöne Anordnung." Pp. 107-8.

174.   Pp. 369, 4l, and 102.

175.   "Unser Verstand will immer bey den Bewegungen der Seele mitarbeiten." P. 44.

176.   Pp. 44-45.

Notes to Chapter 4

1.   Gottsched, *Auszug aus des Herrn Batteux schönen Künsten aus dem einzigen Grundsatze der Nachahmung hergeleitet. Zum Gebrauch seiner Vorlesungen mit verschiedenen Zusätzen and Anmerkungen erläutert.* Leipzig, 1754.

2.   Ibid., p. 207.

3.   Ibid., p. 189.

4.   "Ein blosses Geklingel . . . das einem weder kalt noch warm machet." Ibid., pp. 201-202.

5.   Ibid., p. 200.

6.   Ibid., p. 201.

7.   Ibid., p. 200.

8.   Ibid., p. 199.

9.   Ibid., p. 202.

10.   "Ihr ausgeschütteter Sack voll Noten bedeuten sollte." Ibid., p. 201.

11.   Ibid., pp. 214-15.

12.   Ibid., p. 192.

13.   "Wunderlichen Vermischungen der Töne." Ibid., p. 207.

14.   Ibid., p. 205.

15.   Ibid., p. 208.

16.   Nicolai, *Musik in Geschichte und Gegenwart,* s.v., "Nicolai, Christoph Friedrich," by Günter Selk, vol. 9, cols. 1450-51.

17. Nicolai, *Briefe über den itzigen Zustand der schönen Wissenschaften in Deutschland*, (Berlin, 1755; reprint ed., Berlin: Gebrüder Paetel, 1894), p. 14. The second and third letters address Gottsched's translation and commentary on Batteux.

18. Ibid.

19. "Gar nichts ausdrükke, und unverständlich sei, . . . folglich auch zu allen Wirkungen, die man ihr sonst zuschreibet, ungeschikt sei." Ibid., p. 15.

20. Ibid., p. 23.

21. "Dass auch die Tonkunst göttlich sey!" Ibid., p. 24.

22. Ibid., p. 16.

23. Ibid., pp. 16-21.

24. "Die Vergnügen nur blos aus der Musik entspringet, und mit dem elenden Texte des Dichters gar nichts zu thun hat." Ibid., p. 19.

25. Ibid., p. 17.

26. Ibid., p. 20.

27. Ibid., p. 20.

28. Ibid., p. 21.

29. Ibid., pp. 21-22.

30. Ibid., p. 24.

31. "Harmonische Theil der Musik, und insbesondere die künstliche Verbindungen widrig scheinender Töne, die zu den Ausdrükken der meisten Leidenschaften nöthig sind." Ibid., pp. 24-25.

32. Ibid., p. 22. The following translation might be ventured: "Certainly fear itself trembles in his strings,/Grief, anxiety, and despair quarrel,/A languid tone follows, quivering slightly;/I feel, I feel, in breast and heart/Small uneasy unknown aches;/A noble sympathy surely moves me./At last I hear purity triumph,/Joy rushes through every stroke of the bow,/And every tone resounds with delight,/And every tone enraptures me./Intoxicated with pleasures/I hear how he strokes the high strings/In a carefree and gentle manner;/But then at the very time when he seems to subside/He brings delight with a quick ascent,/Until the tone dies away:/Then he rests in subtle indecisiveness,/He makes artfully deceptive movements,/Which he knows how to vary quickly and charmingly./Then he plays with much gentler strokes,/Tenderness and the purest love,/Fear draws out the slow sound;/The tones change, now they tremble,/Now they soar above the agile fingers,/Now he prolongs doubt:/In order to hear each tone I become,/Not soft and sentimental—but all ears./Who then is the magician?"

33. Ruetz, Vol. 1 (1754-55): 273-311.

34. Ibid., pp. 283-84.

35. Ibid., p. 292.

36. Ibid., pp. 306-7.

37. Ibid., p. 296.

38. "Junger Stutzer . . . verständliche Rede," "Vermögen der Seele das mit Empfinden und Begehren zu thun hat." Ibid., pp. 283-84 and 276.

39. Ibid., p. 296.

40. "Keine Sprache hinlänglich ist, allen besondern Empfindungen, die der Vorwurf der Musik seyn können, ihren eigenen Namen zu geben." Ibid., p. 276. See also pp. 292-93 and 296.

41. Ibid., pp. 301-302.

42. Ibid., p. 288.

43. Ibid., pp. 300-301.

44. Ibid., p. 305.

45. Ibid., p. 304.

46. Ibid., p. 305.

47. Ibid., p. 303.

48. Ibid., p. 309.

49. Ibid.

50. Ibid., p. 209.

51. Ibid., p. 277–78.

52. Hiller, *Historisch-Kritische Beyträge* 1(1754-55): 515-43. In all fairness to Hiller, it should be stated that in 1781 in the preface to his translation of Chabanon, *Ueber die Musik und deren Wirkung mit Anmerkungen* (Leipzig, 1781), he dismissed Batteux's theory of imitation and said that music was nature itself.

53. Koch, *Musikalisches Lexikon*, s.v. "Instrumentalmusik."

54. Hiller, "Abhandlung über die Nachahmung," pp. 515-518.

55. "Suche dich zu belustigen!"

56. Batteux, *Beaux arts*, p. 32.

57. "Ein Ton . . . ist das Gefühl selbst." Hiller, *Abhandlung über die Nachahmung*, pp. 520-21.

58. Ibid., p. 520.

59. Ibid., p. 521.

60. Ibid., p. 522.

61. Ibid., p. 523.

62. Ibid.

63. Ibid., p. 537.

64. "Lauter Blendwerk," "Unregelmässigkeit und Schwulst," "künstliches Unsinn," "unsinnige Meisterstücke," "ernsthaftscheinenden Kinderspielen," "unverständlichen Mischmasch." Ibid., pp. 537–40.

65. "Schwulst und Barbarey." Ibid., p. 538.

66. Ibid., p. 542.

67. "Die Bewunderung der Ohren und den Beyfall der Herzen zugleich." Ibid.

68. Ibid., pp. 540-42.

69. Ibid., pp. 541-42.

70. Ibid., pp. 542-43.

71. Ibid., pp. 528-29.

72. Ramler *Einleitung in die schönen Wissenschaften. Nach dem Französischen des Herrn Batteux, mit Zusätzen vermehret* (Leipzig, (156-58).

73. Marpurg, *Historisch-Kritische Beyträge* 5 (1760): 20-44.

74. "Wunderliche Einfälle, wo die Töne sich unter einander anstossen, ohne Absicht und ohne Bedeutung," "Künstlicher Abschilderung menschlicher Leidenschaften." Ibid., p. 27.

75. Ibid., pp. 27-28.

76. Ibid., p. 36.

77. Ibid.

78. Bremen, 1767-69; modern edition in *Gesammelte Werke,* ed. Wolfgang Stammler (Munich: Carl Hanser Verlag, 1959), vol 2. pp. 327-778. The review of Agricola's symphony occurs in the 26th and 27th *Stücke,* July 28 and 31, 1767), pp. 438-46.

79. Ibid., pp. 441-42.

80. Ibid., p. 440.

81. "Schranken der Musik," "unordentliche," "sich widersprechende." Ibid., pp. 443-44.

82. Ibid., p. 444.

83. Ibid.

84. Ibid.

85. Ibid., p. 445.

86. "Eitler Sandhaufen." Ibid., p. 445.

Notes to Chapter 5

1. Sulzer, "Nachahmung," vol. 3, p. 278.

2. "Würkliche, in ihnen vorhandene, nicht nachgeahmte Empfindungen ausgedrükt." Ibid.

3. 2 vols., Leipzig; also Leipzig, 1773–75 and 1777; 2nd ed., Leipzig, 1778, 1779; 2nd ed. enl., 4 vols., Leipzig, 1786–87, also 1792–99 [facsimile ed., Hildesheim: Georg Olms Verlag, 1967].

4. See *Musik in Geschichte und Gegenwart,* "Sulzer," by Peter Schnaus, vol. 12, cols. 1733–35.

5. Kirnberger worked with Sulzer on the articles up to *S*, with some help from Schulz; from *S* on,

Schulz was alone responsible for drafting the music articles. (Ibid., col. 1735.) I shall therefore for the purposes of this study treat all opinions as Sulzer's even though the possibility exists that the ideas expressed in some of the articles are more the property of his assistants than his own.

6. Sulzer, *Allgemeine Theorie der schönen Künste*, s.v. "Aesthetik," vol. 1, pp. 47–48, and s.v. "Künste," vol. 3, pp. 72–78 passim. All subsequent references to articles in Sulzer's encyclopedia will give only the name of the article and the page numbers. The volumes are divided as follows: Vol. 1, A–D, Vol. 2, E–J, Vol. 3, K–Q, Vol. 4, R–Z.

7. "Das Gute mitteilen," "wichtige Wahrheiten ausbreiten." Ibid., s.v. "Dichtkunst," p. 622.

8. "Kenner," Ibid., p. 11.

9. "Aus der Fülle lebhafter Empfindungen," "Schilderung der Sitten." Ibid., s.v. "Nachahmung," p. 488, and "Sitten," p. 414.

10. Ibid., "Erhaben," p. 108; "Erfindung," pp. 86–87; "Empfindung," p. 54; "Natur," p. 510; and "Feuer," p. 228.

11. Wellek, *History of Modern Criticism*, p. 21.

12. Sulzer, ATdsK, s.v. "Sitten," p. 414; and "Künste," p. 74.

13. Ibid., "Künste," p. 93

14. "Erkenntnis oder Aufklärung das höchste Gut ist." Ibid., "Werke des Geschmacks," p. 728.

15. Ibid., s.v. "Sitten," p. 414. The epic and drama are also called the highest forms of art in "Leidenschaften," p. 235, and elsewhere.

16. Ibid., "Charakter," p. 454.

17. Ibid., "Künste," p. 78.

18. Ibid., "Aesthetik," p. 48.

19. Ibid., "Sinnlich." p. 412.

20. Ibid., "Künste," pp. 74–76.

21. "Dass die durch getreue Schilderung leidenschaftlicher Scenen zu erlangende Kenntniss der Menschen eine höchst wichtige Sache sey, bedarf keines Beweises." Ibid., "Leidenschaften," p. 235.

22. Ibid., "Grösse," p. 447.

23. Ibid.

24. Ibid., "Empfindung," p. 55

25. "Abwechselung in den Vorstellungen und Empfindungen." Ibid., "Mannigfaltigkeit," p. 361.

26. Ibid.

27. Ibid., "Künste," p. 73. See also "Mannigfaltigkeit," p. 361.

28. Ibid., "Weichlich, schwach, und unmännlich." "Mannigfaltigkeit," p. 361.

29. Ibid., "Grösse," p. 447.

30. Ibid., "Grösse," p. 436.

31. Ibid., "Bewunderung," p. 397.

32. Ibid., "Erhaben," p. 97.

33. "Wo man den Seelenkräften einen grossen Reiz zur Würksamkeit geben, oder sie mit Gewalt Zurükhalten will." Ibid., "Erhaben," p. 98.

34. Ibid., "Grösse,"p. 440 and "Erhaben," p. 98.

35. "Blosses Spiel der Leidenschaften," "lachende und tänzende Bilder," "vorübergehendes Kützel." Ibid., "Künste," p. 75 et passim.

36. Ibid., "Leidenschaften," p. 224.

37. Ibid., "Empfindung," p. 59.

38. Ibid., "Leidenschaften," p. 225.

39. Ibid., "Instrumentalmusik," pp. 677–78.

40. Ibid., "Ausdruck in der Musik," p. 271.

41. Ibid.

42. M. H. Abrams, in his *Mirror and the Lamp: Romantic Theory and the Critical Tradition* (New York: Oxford University Press, 1953, pp. 88–90) attributes to Sulzer an important role in the supplantation of old theories of imitation with new theories of emotional outpouring, citing in particular Sulzer's statements to the effect that art is not an imitation but a spontaneous outpouring, and that the artist forgets the outer world when creating. However correct Abrams may be in his assessment of Sulzer's anti-imitation stance, Sulzer clearly paid more than token allegiance to Abrams's "pragmatic" theory of art, where the artist is primarily concerned with his effect on his audience, especially his moral effect. Witness Sulzer's description of poetry, where imitation is indeed not the described act, but where also the artist's self-expression and his moving of his audience is seen chiefly as contributing to the social good:

"Der Ursprung der Dichtkunst ist unmittelbar in der Natur des Menschen zu suchen. Jedes Volk . . . hat seine Dichter gehabt, die keinen andern Beruf, keine andre Veranlassungen gehabt, was sie stärker, als andre gedacht und empfunden, unter sinnlichen Bildern und in harmonischen Reden ihnen vorzustellen, als die Begierde, die jede edle Seele fühlt, andern das Gute, davon sie durchdrungen ist, mitzutheilen. Ohne Zweifel sind die ersten Dichter jeder Nation Menschen von grössern Genie und wärmern Empfindungen, als andre, gewesen; Menschen, die in ihrem Verstand Wahrheiten und in ihrem Herzen Empfindungen entdeket, deren Wichtigkeit sie lebhaft gefühlt, und aus Liebe fur ihre Mitbürger auszubreiten gesucht haben." (ATdsK, "Dichtkunst," p. 622)

(The origin of poetry stems directly from the nature of man. . . . Every nation has had its poets, who had no other calling than to represent what they thought and felt more intensely than others with sensual images and harmonious speech, no other motivation than the desire which every noble soul feels, to impart the good, with which they are permeated. Without a doubt the first poets of every nation were men of great genius and warmer feelings than others; men who discovered truths in their minds and feelings in their hearts, the importance of which they keenly sensed, and who then sought to spread them abroad out of love for their fellow citizens.)

The theme of art's social and moral value runs throughout Sulzer's work. And it would be a mistake to see in his views an anticipation of the Romantic vision of art as unencumbered self-expression.

43. Sulzer, ATdsK, "Melodie," p. 37.

44. Ibid., "Ausdruck in Musik," p. 272.

45. "Die Menschen nur in diesem Gesichtspunkt sehen." Ibid.

46. Ibid.

47. Ibid., "Gesang," p. 369.

48. Ibid., "Musik," p. 422. "Die Natur hat eine ganz unmittelbare Verbindung zwischen dem Gehör und dem Herzen gestiftet; jede Leidenschaft kündiget sich durch eigene Töne an, und eben diese Töne erweken in dem Herzen dessen, der sie vernimmt, die leidenschaftliche Empfindung, aus welcher sie entstanden sind."

49. Ibid., "Instrumentalmusik," p. 677.

50. Ibid., "Gesang," p. 369.

51. Ibid.

52. "Eine Empfindung so bestimmt und richtig ausdrüken, dass der Zuhörer ganz genau den Gemüthzustand der singenden Person daraus erkennt." Ibid., "Hauptsatz," p. 488.

53. Ibid.

54. Ibid.

55. Ibid., "Musik," p. 423.

56. Ibid., "Hauptsatz," p. 488. Other sources of musical unity isolated by Sulzer include tonality, meter, and correct harmony (see "Musik," pp. 423 and 238, and "Einförmigkeit," p. 21). The variety of the newer galant style, with which Sulzer was quite taken, he describes as deriving largely from rhythmic variety ("Musik," p. 438).

57. Ibid.

58. Ibid., "Mannigfaltigkeit," p. 362.

59. Ibid., "Ausdruck in der Musik." p. 273.

60. Ibid., "Ausdruck in der Musik," p. 273, "Singen," p. 377, "Bewegung," p. 386.

61. Ibid., "Vortrag," p. 710.

62. "Gewissen Empfindungen und Leidenschaften in denen sich das Gemüth gleichsam immer nur um einen Punkt herum bewegt." Ibid., "Ausdruck in der Musik," p. 274.

63. Ibid.

64. "Durch alle Entwickelungen des Affects." Ibid., "Einförmigkeit," p. 22.

65. Ibid., "Leidenschaften," p. 231.

66. "Romantische" "Spiel der Empfindungen," "die wahre Entwicklung und die mannichfaltigen Wendungen, die jeder Leidenschaft eigen sind." Ibid., "Leidenschaften," pp. 235–36.

67. Ibid., "Melodie," p. 378.

68. Ibid., "Ausdruck in der Musik," p. 272.

69. Ibid., "Instrumentalmusik," p. 677.

70. Ibid., "Singen," p. 375.

71. Ibid., "Instrumentalmusik," p. 677. See also "Singen," p. 375.

72. Ibid., "Singen," p. 375.

73. Ibid., "Leidenschaften," pp. 230–31.

74. "Künstliches Geräusch." Ibid., p. 231. See also "Musik," p. 431.

75. Ibid., "Instrumentalmusik," p. 677.

76. Ibid., "Vornehmsten Werke," p. 678.

77. "Festgesetzten Charakter," "keinen bestimmten Endzweck." Ibid.

78. "Ein wolklingendes Geräusch, das stürmend oder sanft in das Gehör fällt." Ibid.

79. "Pathetische, feurige, oder sanfte, zärtliche Stellen." Ibid.

80. Ibid., "Instrumentalmusik," p. 678.

81. "Nichtsbedeutende Folge vön Tönen," "gleichgültige, blos das Ohr ergötzende Variationen," "Gesang selbst in eine Instrumentalstimme verwandelt." Ibid., "Singen," p. 377.

82. Ibid., "Sonate," p. 425.

83. "Blos wohlklingend lärmen," "ohne Kraft und Ausdrück." Ibid., "Symphonie," pp. 479–80.

84. "Nichts, als eine Uebung für Setzer und Spieler, und eine ganz unbestimmte, weiter auf nichts abzielende Ergötzung des Ohres," "keinen bestimmten Charakter; denn niemand kann sagen, was er vorstellen soll." Ibid., "Concert," p. 573.

85. Ibid., "Musik," pp. 431–32.

86. Ibid., p. 432.

87. "Freaks," Ibid., "Vortrag," p. 711, and "Erfindung," p. 90.

88. "Nehmen in ihrem Vortrag einen unmännlichen, tändelnden und manierlichen Schwung." Ibid.

89. Ibid., "Vortrag," p. 711.

90. "Dem feurigsten Strom," "welches sehr überraschend ist, und wodurch hernach die Folge sich wieder lebhafter ausnimmt." Ibid., "Ouvertüre." p. 644.

91. "Unerwartete Fortschreitungen, fremde und schwere Passagen, übernaturliche hohe Töne, Sprünge, Läufer, Doppeltriller und der gleichen Schwierigkeiten." Ibid., "Solo," p. 423.

92. Mattheson held a similar position, as we saw in Chapter 3.

93. Ibid., "Sonate," pp. 424–25.

94. Ibid., p. 425.

95. Ibid., "Symphonie," pp. 478–79.

96. Ibid., p. 479.

97. Ibid., "Mannigfalhgkeit," p. 361.

98. "Wiedersprechend erscheinendes." Ibid., "Bewunderung," p. 397.

99. Ibid., "Feuer," p. 288.

100. See *Die Musik in Geschichte und Gegenwart*, s.v. "Junker, Karl Ludwig," by Ulrich Siegele, vol. 7, cols. 387–89.

101. Junker, *Tonkunst* (Bern, 1777); *Betrachtungen über Mahlerey, Ton-und Bildhauerkunst* (Basel, 1778).

102. This is the characterization of Roye E. Wates in her study, *Karl Ludwig Junker (1748–1797): Sentimental Music Critic* (Ph.D. dissertation, Yale University, 1965).

103. *Musik in Geschichte und Gegenwart*, "Junker," col. 389.

104. "Erwekkung des leidenschaftlichen Mitfühlens." *Betrachtungen*, p. 73.

105. Junker, *Tonkunst*, p. 97.

106. "Richtige Ausdrück der Empfindungen," "Studium des leidenschaftliehen Ton." Ibid., pp. 26–27.

107. Junker, *Tonkunst*, pp. 27–32.

108. Junker, *Betrachtungen*, p. 63.

109. Junker, *Zwanzig Componisten: Eine Skizze* (Bern, 1776), p. 17.

110. "In immer gleichen Gang, ohne Kontrast." Junker, *Tonkunst*, p. 53.

111. "Sinnlich fassbar." Junker, *Tonkunst*, Vorbereitung.

112. Ibid., p. 1. Webb had written, "Pleasure is not, as some have imagined, the result of any fixed or permanent condition of the nerves or spirits, but springs from a succession of impressions, and is greatly augmented by sudden or gradual transitions from one kind of strain of vibrations to another" (*Observations on the Correspondence between Poetry and Music* [London, 1769], p. 47).

113. Junker, *Tonkunst*, p. 2.

114. Junker, *Betrachtungen*, pp. 27–28.

115. Junker, *Tonkunst*, p. 5.

116. "Die Tonkunst ist fortschreitende Kunst." Junker, *Ueber den Werth der Tonkunst* (Bayreuth, 1786), p. 17, and *Betrachtungen*, p. 19.

117. Junker, *Werth der Tonkunst*, p. 15, and *Betrachtungen*, p. 93.

118. Ibid., p. 88.

119. "Die fortschreiten sinnliche Vorstellung des Fühlens durch Töne." Junker, *Betrachtungen*, p. 63.

120. Junker, *Tonkunst*, pp. 54–72 passim.

121. Junker, *Werth der Tonkunst*, pp. 12–13.

122. Junker, *Betrachtungen*, p. 74.

123. Junker, *Tonkunst*, pp. 67–69.

124. Junker, *Betrachtungen*, p. 79.

125. Junker, *Tonkunst*, p. 60.

126. "Abwechselnde,—unangenehme—ihre Wendung schnell verwechselnde Leidenschaften." Ibid.

127. "Mannigfaltige, und zweideutige Wendung der Leidenschaften." Ibid., p. 61.

128. Junker, *Betrachtungen*, p. 90.

129. "Zwischen dem Mechanischen der Tonkunst, und dem Mechanismus beyder Leidenschaften, als Geschlechter, ist Analogon." Ibid., p. 65.

130. Junker, *Tonkunst*, pp. 12–13.

131. Ibid., p. 13.

132. Ibid., p. 17.

133. Junker, *Betrachtungen*, p. 64.

134. "Bestimmung." Junker, *Tonkunst*, p. 75.

135. Ibid., pp. 97–98.

136. "Unbestimmte, unerklärliche Leidenschaft," "bestimmte Bedeutung." Ibid., pp. 38–39.

137. Junker, *Betrachtungen*, p. 66.

138. Ibid., p. 67.

139. "Begreiflich," "fasslich." Ibid. and Junker, *Tonkunst*, p. 101.

140. Junker, *Tonkunst*, pp. 100–101.

141. Ibid., p. 50.

142. Junker, *Betrachtungen*, pp. 84–85. Junker previously characterized "Handlung" as proceeding from the development of a single theme.

143. Junker, *Zwanzig Componisten*, p. 100.

144. *Die Musik in Geschichte und Gegenwart*, s.v. "Forkel, Johann Nikolaus," by Franz Peters-Marquardt, cols. 514–20. This acticle states that Forkel was in no way in sympathy with the Romantic movement (Wackenroder was at Göttingen at the same time as Forkel). But we shall see in Forkel some adumbrations of Romantic notions of the musical embodiment of dynamic emotional patterns. Indeed Junker by comparison seems a conservative.

145. Forkel, "Schilderung und Mittheilung jeder Art von Empfindung." *Allgemeine Geschichte der Music*, 2 vols. (Leipzig, 1788, 1801), vol. 1, p. 20.

146. Forkel, *Musikalischer Almanach für Deutschland auf das Jahr 1784* (Leipzig, 1784), p. 26.

147. Ibid., p. 35.

148. "Mit allen ihren Beziehungen und Modificationen," "Schilderung einer Empfindung mit allen ihren unendlichen Modificationen." Forkel, *Geschichte*, pp. 20 and 37.

149. "Aesthetische Anordnung," "mannigfaltig Modificationen." Forkel, *Ueber die Theorie der Musik* (Göttingen, 1777). p. 26.

150. Henry Home (Lord Kames), *Elements of Criticism*, 3 vols. (London, 1753), vol. 2, p. 163.

151. David Hume, *A Treatise of Human Understanding* [1739] (Oxford: Clarendon Press, 1896), p. 283.

152. Forkel, *Geschichte*, p. 8.

153. Hume, *Treatise*, p. 283.

154. Forkel, *Almanach*, pp. 31–32.

155. "Zusammenhang der Empfindungen unter einander." Forkel *Geschichte*, p. 8.

156. "Einzelne von allen übrigen abgesonderte Leidenschaft." Forkel, *Musikalisch-Kritische Bibliothek*, vol. 2, pp. 132–135.

157. Ibid., pp. 65–67.

158. "Feinen Verhältnisse und Uebereinstimmungen dunkler Gefühle." Ibid., vol. 3, p. 349.

159. "Inner geistigen Bilde," "geheimsten Winkel unsers Wesens." Forkel, *Almanach*, p. 24.

160. Ibid.

161. Forkel, *Theorie der Musik*, pp. 31–35 passim; and *Musikalisch-Kritische Bibliothek*, vol. 3, pp. 349–50

162. "Geübtesten Gefühle," "inneres Gepräge." Forkel, *Theorie der Musik*, pp. 23, 28, and 31.

163. Forkel, *Geschichte*, p. 22.

164. "Sprache für die Empfindungen," "einzig und allein auf die Art und Weise, sie sich Empfindungen . . . auseinander entwickeln." Forkel, *Geschichte*, p. 50.

165. "Unwillens," "betrachtend Ueberlegung," "melancholische Beruhigung." Forkel, *Almanach*, pp. 34–36.

166. Review of Bach's fourth collection "Für Kenner und Liebhaber," in C. F. Cramer, *Magazin der Musik* 1 (1783): 1238–55.

167. Forkel, *Geschichte*, pp. 2–20 passim. Forkel most likely got from Herder the notions that language and music were born together and that there were no distinct faculties. It is not clear why Forkel insisted on the analogy with linguistic development. Most probably he hoped to fortify his belief that music was as highly developed and hence as meaningful as verbal language.

168. "Eine allgemeine Sprache der Empfindungen . . . deren Umfang eben so gross ist und seyn kann, als der Umfang einer ausgebildeten Ideen-Sprache," Ibid., p. 19.

169. "Für sich selbst bestehende und ganz aus eigenen Kräften würkende Kunst." Ibid., p. 12.

170. Ibid., p. 49.

171. "Unendliche mannigfaltige Modificationen der Empfindung." Ibid., pp. 13–16.

172. "Means of determination." Ibid., pp. 13–14.

173. "Die künstliche Art der Vereinigung mehrerer Melodien." Ibid., p. 14.

174. Ibid., pp. 16–18.

175. Ibid., p. 47.

176. "Leeres Spielwerk," Ibid., p. 15.

177. Ibid., pp. 47–48.

178. Ibid., p. 55.

179. "Je heftiger aber die Empfindung ist, deren Lauf schleunig unterbrochen werden soll, desto fremder und entfernter muss auch die Cadenz seyn, in welche die gewöhnliche verändert wird." Ibid., p. 57.

180. "Wodurch einzelne Theile eines Satzes bald verändert bald unverändert, bald vergrössert bald verkleinert, bald aus dem Anfange und der Mitte, bald aber auch aus dem Ende desselben wiederholt werden, so wie man ungefähr glaubt dass Empfindungen auf verschiedene Weise sich verändern und wiederkehren." Ibid., p. 58.

181. "Ein lebhaftes nicht unangenehmes Geräusch, oder ein artiges und unterhaltendes, aber das Herz nicht beschäftigendes Geschwätz." "Zur genauere Bestimmung einiger musikalischen Begriffe: Ein Einladungsschrift" [Göttingen, 1780], in C. F. Cramer, *Magazin der Musik* 1 (1783): 1068–69.

182. "Innern Kreis der Kunst," "feinsten und bedeutungsvollesten Idealen."

Notes to Chapter 6

1. E. T. A. Hoffmann, *Sämtliche Werke,* ed. Carl Georg von Maassen, vol. 1: *Fantasiestücke in Callots Manier* (Munich: Georg Müller, 1912), p. 55.

2. Ludwig Tieck, "Symphonieen," in "Die Beyträge Ludwigs Tiecks zu den Herzensergiessungen eines Kunstliebenden Klosterbruders und zu den Phantasien uber die Kunst," in Wilhelm Heinrich Wackenroder, *Werke und Briefe,* ed. Friedrich von der Leyen, 2 vols. (Jena: Eugen Diedrichs, 1910), vol. 1, pp. 304-5.

3. Ibid., p. 306

4. Ibid., p. 303.

5. The qualification "definite" is important. The Romantics seem to have been consciously defending music against the pervasive demand that it represent "definite" feelings, as the opening quotation of this chapter indicates. It is important to understand, however, that they did not deny any relationship between music and emotional, or "inner," life. This relationship is explored below.

6. Hoffmann, *Fantasiestücke,* p. 55. The English translation is from Strunk, *Source Readings,* pp. 775-76.

7. "Das eigenthümliche innere Wesen der Tonkunst und die Seelenlehre der heutigen Instrumentalmusik," in Wackenroder, *Werke und Briefe,* vol. 1, pp. 188 and 194.

8. The Romantics were not the first to rebel against the "truth"-conferring arrogance of the word (although they may well have been the first to apply this rejection of the word to a novel and positive appraisal of instrumental music). Goethe and Schiller both saw that the word often conferred misunderstanding rather than true insight. Schiller's epigram, "Sprache," uses two puns

to point up the incommensurability of verbal language and the soul's life: "Warum kann der lebendige Geist dem Geist nicht erscheinen?/*Spricht* die Seele, so spricht, ach! schon die *Seele* nicht mehr." ("Why can the living spirit not appear to the mind?/If the soul *speaks,* then alas, it is no longer the *soul* itself who speaks.") And Goethe's Faust, when rebelling against the idea of using the name "God," said, "Gefühl ist alles/Name ist Schall und Rauch." ("Feeling is every-thing/Name [is only] sound and smoke.")

9.   "Herzensergiessungen," in Wackenroder, *Werke und Briefe,* vol. 1, p. 133.

10.   "Dieser grosse ungeheure Wunsch hebt unsern Geist empor." Johann Paul Friedrich Richter [Jean Paul], *Hesperus,* 2nd ed., vol. 2 (Berlin, 1798), p. 133.

11.   August Wilhelm Schlegel, *Vorlesungen über schöne Litteratur und Kunst* (Heilbronn, 1884), pp. 256-57.

12.   Wackenroder, "Eigenthümliche innere Wesen der Tonkunst," p. 193.

13.   Berglinger, "Herzensergiessungen," p. 132.

14.   Tieck, *Beiträge,* pp. 302-3.

15.   Tieck, "Meerstrudel." Ibid., pp. 293-94.

16.   Wackenroder, "Die Wunder der Tonkunst," in *Werke und Briefe,* vol. 1, p. 164.

17.   Schlegel, *Vorlesungen,* p. 249. Similarly, Luther esteemed singing because "Es hat nichts zu tun mit der Welt."

18.   Wackenroder, "Die Wunder der Tonkunst," p. 168.

19.   Tieck, *Beiträge,* pp. 292-93.

20.   For Junker's views, see above, p. 26.

21.   "Fragment aus einem Briefe Joseph Berglingers," in Wackenroder, *Werke und Briefe,* vol. 1, pp. 178-79.

22.   Hoffmann, "Beethovens Instrumental-Musik," from *Kreisleriana,* in his *Sämtliche Werke,* vol. 1, pp. 62-63.

23.   In the eighteenth century it was a much repeated remark that every emotion or passion had a particular tone by which it was expressed. The source was the classical orator, Cicero: "Omnis motus animi suum quemdam a natura habet vultum at sonum et gestum" (Every motion of the soul has from nature a certain countenance, sound, and gesture). For an excellent treatment of the pervasiveness in the seventeenth and eighteenth centuries of this doctrine of emotional "expres-sion" based on clearly distinguishable external manifestations (itself a heritage of classical ora-torical pedagogy), see Brewster Rogerson's "The Art of Painting the Passions," in *Journal of the History of Ideas,* 14 (1953): 68-94.

24.   It was not widely discussed whether these utterances to be imitated were nonverbal ones such as "Ouch!" "Whee!" or "Ooooooo—" or verbal ones. Some writers speak of inarticulate pas-sionate utterances such as the "cry of pain," but others seem to be speaking of the manner in which a verbal utterance was declaimed—hence the reference to declamation in the first quota-tion in this chapter. As that quotation illustrates, imitation of "definite" feelings was associated with the imitation of certain patterns of declamation.

25.   "Schilderung leidenschaftlicher Aeusserungen." Sulzer, ATdsK, s.v. "Leidenschaften."

26. Junker, *Betrachtungen,* pp. 71-72.

27. See above, the annotation on p. 193.

28. "Weltmenschen." "Er hasste und floh während seiner Empfindungen alle Aufmerksamkeit auf fremde Aufmerksamkeit." *Hesperus,* vol. 2, p. 129.

29. Perhaps two of the most difficult Romantic concepts for us to understand today are those of "the infinite," and of "infinite longing." both of which played such an important role in the definitive opinions of A. W. Schlegel and E. T. A. Hoffmann. I would like merely to offer a few observations and suggestions as to their meaning. The Romantic talk of "transport" must of course be understood metaphorically; it is, in other words, important to recognize that the concept of the infinite does not have to be taken in any spatial sense. "Infinite" means without limits, boundaries, definitions, or delimitations. It conveys the notion of incomprehensibility, as when we speak of "God, in His infinite wisdom . . . ." Thus an "infinite" longing could arise out of a recognition that the felt qualities of what could be intensely experienced could never be known in any verifiable sense, because these felt qualities themselves are undefined—they are private, they have no intersubjective verifiability. Or it could arise out of the recognition of the incommensurability of feeling and knowing, of what could be felt and what could be known, of what could be envisioned and of what, in this finite world, could be attained—hence the incommensurability of fantasy and reality. As A. W. Schlegel suggested, this feeling of infinite longing stems from "a sense of gap between actual and ideal, hence an unsatisfied longing." (See Monroe Beardsley, *Aesthetics from Classical Greece to the Present* [New York: T. Macmillan Co., 1966], p. 245.)

    Another useful angle is to give the concept a sort of existentialist interpretation: the longing is a kind of objectless emotion, a lack of satiety, a desire for which one knows neither the cause nor the cure, hence a longing which cannot be satisfied, a longing that is an endlessly recurring aspect of experience, and the object of which is itself unknowable, undefined—or "infinite." Jean Paul characterizes it so:

    > "In man there is a great desire, never fulfilled; it has no name, it seeks no object, it is nothing that you call it nor any joy; but it returns, when on a summer's night you look toward the north or toward the distant mountains, . . . or when you are very happy. This great monstrous desire exalts our spirit, but with sorrows: Alas, prostrate here below, we are hurled into the air like epileptics. But this desire, to which nothing can give a name, our songs and harmonies name it to the human spirit—the longing spirit then weeps the more vehemently and can control itself no longer and calls amid the music in sobbing rapture: Truly, all that you name, I lack.
    >
    > "The enigmatic mortal likewise has a nameless, monstrous fear that has no object, that is awakened when one hears ghostly apparitions." *(Hesperus,* vol. 2, p. 133. The translation is from Strunk, *Source Readings,* p. 767.)

    Infinite longing, or longing for the infinite, is thus a desire for something undefined, hence unattainable. But the elemental forces of life propel us onward, in intense involvement, and the awareness of these forces exalts us. And we celebrate in music this feeling and this process. That is, at any rate, one construction that could be offered.

30. The concept of "the wonderful" is, again, difficult for us today, especially inasmuch as the word has degenerated into merely a term of approbation. I have already pointed to its usage in the eighteenth century as the opposite of verisimilitudinous. And I would like here to emphasize the potency this word possessed for a generation which could still recall vividly the indoctrination that art imitated nature and possessed verisimilitude, that nothing was beautiful but the true, and so on. The wonderful on the other hand included the world of fastasy, of the marvellous, the

incomprehensible and the awesome—a world which for the Romantics was full of aesthetic riches and excitement. Allegiance to the wonderful implied the rejection of the principle of understandable real-worldly representation. Gottsched chastised instrumental music for being "wunderlich" rather than "verständlich." And *Verwunderung* or wonderment was the little respected emotional reaction to the nonrepresentative aspects of instrumental music as described by Hiller. Thus the title of Wackenroder's essay, "Die Wunder der Tonkunst," itself implies a new attitude—a new allegiance to this art which from the beginning was marked out as unsuited to the display of verisimilitude. The title is a testimonial to a new aesthetic ideology which valued the fantastic, the marvelous, the distant, the dark, the incomprehensible, and the "wonderful," and to the importance of music's role in this new aesthetic.

31.   *Vorlesungen,* p. 115. It should be observed that Schlegel viewed the emotional life as not only less compartmentalized and less static than was previously held, but as more inclusive. Whatever reality was inadequately referred to by the verbal labels for *the* emotions or *the* passions, this reality did not comprise the whole of the sensitive life. More than *"the* passions" were involved. Thus, this phrase, "the whole quality of our existence," can be seen to have opened the door to the aesthetic validation of such things as less intense and obtrusive and more gentle and subtle shadings of feeling, to childlike pleasure taken in the dance or in beautiful sounds, to that ostracized emotion *Verwunderung,* and even to what might be called "specifically musical" emotions—for the Romantics recognized the existence of affective responses to music which were not like any affect experienced in "real life." Jean Paul's Victor, for example, spoke of the "artificial suffering" aroused by music, which nevertheless could ennoble the listener just as could real suffering. (See *Hesperus,* vol. 3, p. 98.) And Wackenroder believed that even the dry scholarly system of composition could be used to bring forth "ganz wunderbar neue Wendungen und Verwandlungen der Empfindungen" (completely new and wonderful turns and transformations of feelings). (See "Eigenthümliche innere Wesen der Tonkunst," p. 189.) And thus music which did not represent or even move "the passions" could nevertheless be viewed as affectively significant—both in the sense of symbolizing some aspect of the inner life and in the sense of affecting this life. Most importantly, perhaps, "infinite longing" was not counted among "the passions," either.

32.   *Allgemeine Musikalische Zeitung,* 1 (1798-99): 433-35.

33.   Ibid., p. 437.

34.   Herder, too, pointed to the expressive potentialities in the transitoriness of music's tones and effects: "In coming and going, in beginning and ceasing, lies the conquering power of tone and feeling" ("Im Kommen und Fliehen, im Werden und Gewesenseyn liegt die Siegskraft des Tons und der Empfindung"). The waxing and waning, the dynamism of his own spirit and emotions obeyed the same inexplicable laws as the changing, transitory patterns of music. Sulzer and Kant, on the other hand, held, as did many Enlightened thinkers, the transitoriness of music's effects to be a defect. But for Herder, in 1800, this transitoriness enabled tones to be extremely affecting, to instill, as he said, that feeling of "endless longing." (See Herder's *Kalligone,* in *Sämmtliche Werke,* vol. 22, p. 187.)

35.   L. A. Willoughby, *The Classical Age of German Literature: 1748-1805* (London: Oxford University Press, 1926), p. 69.

36.   "Gesang der Geistern über den Wassern." Similarly, when Goethe's Faust asked the Earth Spirit where he was to be found, the spirit answered, "In the flood of life, in the storm of deeds/I wax and wane/Weave hither and yon/Birth and death,/An eternal sea/A life of change!" (In Lebensfluthen im Thatensturm/Wall ich auf und ab/Webe hin und her/Geburt und Grab, Ein ewiges Meer/Ein wechselnd Leben!) See *Urfaust* [c. 1770-75], lines 149-54.

37. Wackenroder, "Eigenthümliche innere Wesen der Tonkunst," pp. 188-89.

38. In the same essay from which the above quotation is taken Wackenroder does indeed speak in terms of emotional entities, such as love, hate and fear; but of course the entities he describes are very changeable and variegated essences. The Romantics were not completely averse to using the vehicle of common language—only they were painfully aware of its limitations.

39. Ibid., p. 190.

40. "Infinite longing" is a difficult enough concept to tackle without attempting to explain how it might be represented, evoked, or embodied by music. However, it is difficult to resist the suggestion that the "longing" part of the formula is not somehow related to the element of expectation-arousal and attention-keeping, as well as the more open-ended and extended forms which are found in so much of the music the Romantics savored. (The namelessness, objectlessness, and indeterminateness of music's effects [or affects] might well enough correspond to the "infinite" part of the formula; but surely the "longing" aspect was also sensed in some way as proceeding from the music itself.)

41. "Die eigenthümliche innere Wesen der Tonkunst und die Seelenlehre der heutigen Instrumental-musik."

42. See p. 203.

43. I wish to make clear my usage of the term *Affektenlehre* here. Although Mattheson himself used the term in the literal, and narrower, sense to refer to a doctrine of the affects (as is found in a doctrine such as Descartes's *Passions of the Soul*), music historians have made it into a composite including not only a doctrine of the emotions as static, separable entities, but also a detailed theory as to what specific musical elements (rhythm, intervals, figures, etc.) should be used in the representation of these various emotions, and, as well, the belief in the aesthetic propriety of representing only one affect (emotion, passion) in any one piece of music—thus resulting in a highly unified style of music. I use the term here not in Mattheson's sense (which would have been a better usage to have adopted) but in the complex sense which embraces a whole theory of what music expresses and how.

44. This view seems very close to Suzanne Langer's: that music reflects the "morphology of feelings." But it must be remembered that the outcome of the listening experience, on Langer's account, was not an emotive one, but a "wealth of wordless *knowledge*—[my italics] of emotional and organic experience, of vital impulse, balance, conflict, the *ways* of living and dying and feeling." (See Chap. 7, "On Significance in Music", of her *Philosophy in a New Key,* 3rd ed. [Cambridge: Harvard University Press, 1957], pp. 238, 244, et passim.) Nevertheless the parallels between Langer's and the Romantics' ideas are sometimes quite striking.

45. Wackenroder, "Innere Wesen der Tonkunst," p. 189.

46. Ibid.

47. Hoffmann, "Beethovens Instrumental-Musik," pp. 62-63. See also the final quotation of this chapter.

48. Wackenroder, "Innere Wesen der Tonkunst," p. 185.

49. Ibid., pp. 183-84.

50. Ibid., p. 192.

51. v. T., "Ueber die Tonkunst, "*Allgemeine musikalische Zeitung* 1 (1798-99): 772-73.

52. Herder, *Kalligone*, p. 182.

53. See following quotation.

54. Wackenroder, "Innere Wesen der Tonkunst," p. 183.

55. Hoffmann, "Beethovens Instrumental-Musik," pp. 62-63. (The work under discussion is Op. 70, No. 1.) The translation is from Strunk, *Source Readings*, p. 39.

56. Wackenroder, "Innere Wesen der Tonkunst," p. 183.

57. That these specifically musical instincts of the composer had in their origins a close, mysterious (or unconscious) relation to the composer's own affective patterns and experience, no Romantic would have denied. But I wish to make it clear that in no way did the Romantics surveyed in this chapter—those who saw in instrumental music an art of profound significance—treat music as the vehicle for the composer's expression of his own personal, real-life emotions.

Notes to Chapter 7

1. See Monroe C. Beardsley, *Aesthetics from Classical Greece to the Present* (New York: Macmillan Co., 1966), pp. 214–17 and 224–25, for a treatment of his concept of "purposelessness without purpose" and a discussion of the relation of his aesthetics to morality. Kant's definitive work in the field of aesthetics was his *Kritik der Urteilskraft*, first published in 1790.

2. See Beardsley's *Aesthetics*, p. 229. Kant had already laid the groundwork for Schiller when he wrote that the experience of formal purposiveness evokes the "free harmonious play" of the imagination and the understanding (Beardsley, *Aesthetics*, p. 216).

3. Schiller's unprecedented claims for the human benefits of art were put forth in his *Briefe über die ästhetische Erziehung des Menschen* (1793–95); his arguments are succinctly summarized in Beardsley's history (pp. 225–230).

Bibliography

I. Primary Sources

D'Alembert, Jean le Rond. "De la liberté de la musique." In *Mélanges de littérature, d'histoire, et de philosophie*. Nouvelle édition. Amsterdam, 1770. Vol. 4, pp. 383–462.

Augustine, Saint. *Confessions*.

Bach, Carl Philip Emanuel. *Carl Philip Emanuel Bach's Autobiography*. Facsimile of original edition of 1773. Edited by William S. Newman. Hilversum: Frits A. M. Knuf, 1967.

_____. *Versuch über die wahre Art das Clavier zu spielen* [1st edition, Berlin, 1753, 1759]: *Kritisch revidierter Neudruck nach der unveränderten jedoch verbesserten zweiten Auflage des Originals. Berlin 1759 und 1762*. 5th ed. Edited by Walter Niemann. Leipzig: C. F. Kahnt, 1925.

Batteux, Charles. *Les beaux arts réduits à un même principe* [Paris, 1746]. Paris, 1773; facsimile ed., Geneva: Slatkine Reprints, 1969.

Baumgarten, Alexander Gottlieb. *Aesthetica*. 2 vols. Frankfurt am Oder, 1750, 1758.

_____. *Reflections on Poetry [Meditationes philosophicae de nonnullis ad poema pertinentibus*, Halle, 1735]. Translated, with the original Latin text, and introduction and notes by K. Aschenbrenner and W. B. Holther. Berkeley: University of California Press, 1954.

Brown, John. *Dr. Brown-s Betrachtungen über die Poesie und Musik mit Ammerkungen und zween Anhängen begleitet*. Translated by Johann J. Eschenburg. Leipzig, 1769.

Burney, Charles. *A General History of Music* [London, 1776–1789]. London: G. T. Foulis and Co., 1935; reprint ed., New York: Dover Publications, 1957.

Cramer, Carl Friedrich, ed. *Magazin der Musik*. 2 vols. Hamburg, 1783–1786; reprint ed., Hildesheim: Georg Olms Verlag, 1971.

Descartes, René. *The Passions of the Soul [De passionibus animae*, Amsterdan, 1649]. In *The Philosophical Works of Descartes*. Translated by E. S. Haldane and G. R. T. Ross. Cambridge: Cambridge University Press, 1911; reprint ed., New York: Dover Publications, 1955. Vol. 1, pp. [330]–427.

Diderot, Denis. *Le neveu de Rameau*. Edited by Herbert Dieckmann. Paris: Le Club du meilleur livre, 1957.

Dubos, Jean Baptiste. *Réflexions critiques sur la poesie et sur la peinture*. Paris, 1719.

Forkel, Johann Nikolaus. *Allgemeine Geschichte der Musik*. 2 vols. Leipzig, 1788, 1801.

_____. *Musikalischer Almanach für Deutschland auf das Jahr 1784*. Leipzig, 1784.

_____. *Musikalisch-Kritische Bibliothek*. Gotha, 1778–1779.

_____. *Ueber die Theorie der Musik insofern sie Liebhabern und Kennern notwendig und nützlich ist*. Göttingen, 1777.

_____. "Zur genauere Bestimmung einiger musikalischen Begriffe: Ein Einladungsschrift" [Göttingen, 1780]. In C. F. Cramer, *Magazin der Musik* I (1783): 1039–1072.

Gottsched, Johann Christoph. *Auszug aus des Herrn Batteux Schönen Künsten aus dem einzigen*

Grundsatze der Nachahmung hergeleitet. Zum Gebrauch seiner Vorlesungen mit verschiedenen Zusätzen und Anmerkungen erläutert. Leipzig, 1754.

————. *Versuch einer critischen Dichtkunst.* 3rd ed. Leipzig, 1742.

Herder, Johann Gottfried von. *Sämtliche Werke.* Edited by B. Suphan. Berlin: Weidmann, 1877–1899.

Hiller, Johann Adam. *Ueber die Musik und deren Wirkung mit Anmerkungen.* Leipzig, 1781.

————. "Abhandlung von der Nachahmung der Natur in der Musik." In F. W. Marpurg, ed., *Historisch-Kritische Beyträge* 1 (1754–1755): 515–543.

————. *Wöchentliche Nachrichten und Anmerkungen die Musik betreffend.* Leipzig, 1766–1770; facsimile ed., Hildesheim: Georg Olms Verlag, 1970.

Hoffmann, Ernst Theodor Amadeus. *Sämtliche Werke.* Edited by Carl Georg von Maassen. Munich: Georg Müller, 1912.

Home, Henry (Lord Kames). *Elements of Criticism.* 3 vols. London, 1753; facsimile ed., New York: Johnson Reprint Co., 1967.

Hume, David. A Treatise of Human Nature [1739]. Oxford: Clarendon Press, 1896.

Junker, Karl Ludwig. *Betrachtungen über Mahlerey, Ton-, und Bildhauerkunst.* Basel, 1778.

————. *Musikalischer Almanach auf das Jahr 1782.* Alethinople, 1782.

————. *Tonkunst.* Bern, 1777.

————. *Ueber den Werth der Tonkunst.* Bayreuth, 1786.

————. *Zwanzig Componisten: Eine Skizze.* Bern, 1776.

Koch, Heinrich Christoph. *Musikalisches Lexikon.* 2 vols. Frankfurt am Main, 1802; facsimile ed., Hildesheim: Georg Olms Verlag, 1964.

Kraus, Joseph Martin. *Wahrheiten die Musik betreffend.* 2 vols. Frankfurt am Main, 1777–1779.

Krause, Christian Gottfried. *Von der musikalischen Poesie.* Berlin, 1752.

Lessing, Gotthold Ephraim. *Gesammelte Werke.* 2 vols. Edited by Wolfgang Stammler. Munich: Carl Hanser Verlag, 1959.

Luther, Martin. *Lob und Preis der löblichen Kunst Musica.* Wittemburg, 1538.

Marpurg, Wilhelm Friedrich, ed. *Der critische Musicus an der Spree.* Berlin, 1749–1750; facsimile ed., Hildesheim: Georg Olms Verlag, 1970.

————. *Historisch-Kritische Beyträge zur Aufnahme der Musik.* 5 vols. Berlin, 1754–1762, 1778; facsimile ed., Hildesheim: Georg Olms Verlag, 1970.

Mattheson, Johann. *Das Neu–Eröffnete Orchestre.* Hamburg, 1713.

————. *Der vollkommene Capellmeister.* Hamburg, 1739; facsimile ed., Kassel: Bärenreiter, 1954. Internationale Gesellschaft für Musikwissenschaft. Documenta musicologica. 1. Reihe: Druckschriften-Facsimiles, 5.

Meier, Georg Friedrich. *Anfangsgründe aller schönen Wissenschaften.* 3 vols. Halle, 1748–1750.

Mozart, Leopold. *Versuch einer gründlichen Violinschule.* Augsburg, 1756; facsimile ed., Vienna, 1922.

Mozart, Wolfgang Amadeus. *Briefe und Aufzeichnungen. Gesamtausgabe.* 4 vols. Collected and annotated by Wilhelm A. Bauer and Otto Erich Deutsch. Kassel: Bärenreiter Verlag, 1962–1963.

Muffat, Georg. *Auserlesene mit Ernst und Lust gemengte Instrumentalmusik* [1701]. *Denkmäler der Tonkunst in Oesterreich,* vol. 23. Vienna, 1895; reprint ed., Graz: Akademische Druck-u. Verlagsanstalt, 1959.

Neefe, Christian Gottlob. *Christian Gottlob Neefens Lebenslauf von ihm selbst beschrieben.* Edited by Walther Engelhardt. Cologne: Arno Volk, 1957.

Nichelmann, Christoph. *Die Melodie nach ihrem Wesen sowohl, als nach ihren Eigenschaften.* Danzig, 1755.

Nicolai, Christoph Friedrich. *Briefe über den itzigen Zustand der schönen Wissenschaften in Deutschland.* Berlin, 1755; reprinted., Berlin: Gebrüder Paetel, 1894.

Pluche, Noël Antoine. *Le spectacle de la nature. Nouvelle édition.* Vol. 7: *Contenant ce que regarde l'homme en societé.* Paris, 1755.

Quantz, Johann Joachim. *Versuch einer Anweisung die Flöte traversière zu spielen* [1st ed., 1752]. 3rd ed. Berlin, 1789; facsimile ed., ed., Hans-Peter Schmitz, Berverly Hills, Calif., 1953.

Raguenet, François. *Paiallèle des Italiens et des François* [1702]. Translated in *Source Readings in Music History*, edited by Oliver Strunk, pp. 473–488. New York: W. W. Norton and Co., 1950.

Rameau, Jean-Philippe. *Traité de l'Harmonie*. Paris: Ballard, 1722; facsimile ed., New York: Broude Brothers, 1965.

Ramler, Carl Wilhelm. "Auszug aus der Einleitung in die schönen Wissenschaften, nach dem Französischen des Herrn Batteux mit Zusätzen vermehret." In F. W. Marpurg, ed., *Historisch-Kritische Beyträge* 5 (1760): 29–44.

Reichardt, Johann Friedrich. *Schreiben über die berlinische Musik*. Hamburg, 1775.

Richter, Johann Paul Friedrich [Jean Paul]. *Hesperus*. 2nd ed. Berlin, 1798.

Rochlitz, Ferdinand. "Rhapsodische Gedanken über die zweckmassige Benutzung der Materie der Musik." *Neue teutsche Merkur* 2 (Oct. 1798); 153–71.

———. "Vorschläge zu Betrachtungen über die neuste Geschichte der Musik." *Allgemeine musikalische Zeitung* 1 (1798–1799): 625–29.

Rousseau, Jean Jacques. *Dictionnaire de Musique*. Paris, 1768.

Ruetz, Caspar. "Sendschreiben eines Freundes an den andern über einige Ausdrücke des Herrn Batteux von der Musik." In F. W. Marpurg, ed., *Historisch-Kritische Beyträge* 1 (1754–1755): 273–311.

Scheibe, Johann Adolph. *Der critische Musicus* [1st ed., Hamburg, 1738, 1740]. 2nd ed. Leipzig, 1745.

Schlegel, August Wilhelm. *Vorlesungen über schöne Litteratur und Kunst. Erster Teil (1801–1802): Die Kunstlehre*. Deutsche Litteraturdenkmäle des 18. und 19. Jahrhunderts, vol. 17. New ed. Heilbronn: Gebrüder Henninger, 1884.

Schubart, Christian Friedrich Daniel. *Ideen zu einer Aesthetik der Tonkunst*. Vienna, 1806; facsimile ed., Hildesheim: Georg Olms Verlag, 1969.

Sulzer, Johann Georg. *Allgemeine Theorie der schönen Künste* [1st ed., Berlin, 1771–1774]. 2nd ed., enl. Leipzig, 1792; facsimile ed., Hildesheim: Georg Olms Verlag, 1967.

v. T. "Ueber die Tonkunst." *Allgemeine Musikalische Zeitung* 1 (1798–1799): 721–727, 737–743, 753–760, and 769–777.

Tieck, Ludwig. "Die Beiträge Ludwig Tiecks zu den Herzensergiessungen eines kunstliebenden Klosterbruders und zu den Phantasien über die Kunst." In Wilhelm Heinrich Wackenroder, *Werke und Briefe*, vol. 1, pp. 195–310. Edited by Friedrich von der Leyen. Jena: Eugen Diederichs, 1910.

Wackenroder, Wilhelm Heinrich. *Werke und Briefe*. 2 vols. Edited by Friedrich von der Leyen. Jena: Eugen Diederichs, 1910.

Webb, Daniel. *Observations on the Correspondence between Poetry and Music*. London, 1769.

II. Secondary Sources

Abrams, Meyer Howard. *The Mirror and the Lamp: Romantic Theory and the Critical Tradition*. New York: Oxford Univesity Press, 1953.

Anton, Karl. *Luther und die Musik*. 3rd ed. enl. Zwickau, 1928.

Beardsley, Monroe C. *Aesthetics from Classical Greece to the Present*. New York: Macmillan Co., 1966.

Becker, Heinz. "Krause, Christian Gottfried." *Musik in Geschichte und Gegenwart*, vol. 7, cols. 1718–1721.

Bukhofzer, Manfred. *Music in the Baroque Era*. New York: W. W. Norton & Co., 1947.

Cannon, Beekman. *Johann Mattheson: Spectator in Music*. New Haven: Yale University Press, 1947.

Cassirer, Ernst. *The Philosophy of the Enlightenment*. Translated by Fritz C. A. Koelln and James P. Pettegrove. Princeton: Princeton University Press, 1951.

Chiapusso, Jan. *Bach's World*. Bloomington: Indiana University Press, 1968.

Cole, Malcolm. "The Vogue of the Instrumental Rondo in the Late Eighteenth Century." *Journal of the American Musicological Society* 22 (1969): 424–455.

Dadelsen, Georg von. "Kirnberger, Johann Philipp." *Musik in Geschichte und Gegenwart*, vol. 7, cols. 950–956.

David, Hans T., and Mendel, Arthur, eds. *The Bach Reader*. Rev. ed. New York: W. W. Norton and Co., 1966.

Gatz, Felix Maria, ed. *Musik-aesthetik in ihren Hauptrichtungen: Ein Quellenbuch der deutschen Musikaesthetik von Kant und der Frühromantik bis zur Gegenwart*. Stuttgart: F. Enke, 1929.

Geck, Martin. "Ruetz, Caspar." *Musik in Geschichte und Gegenwart*, vol. 11, cols. 1072–1074.

Gilbert, Katharine E. and Kuhn, Helmut. *A History of Esthetics*. 2nd ed., rev. and enl. Bloomington: Indiana University Press, 1954.

Girdlestone, Cuthbert. *Jean-Philippe Rameau: His Life and Work*. London: Cassell and Co., 1957.

Goldschmidt, Hugo. *Geschichte der Musikaesthetik im achtzehnten Jahrhundert*. Zürich: Rascher, 1915; reprint ed., Hildesheim: Georg Olms Verlag, 1968.

Gottwaldt, Heinz. "Schulz, Johann Abraham Peter." *Musik in Geschichte und Gegenwart*, vol. 12, cols. 245–253.

Grimm, Jacob and Wilhelm. *Deutsches Wörterbuch*. 16 vols. Leipzig, 1854–1954.

Helm, Ernest Eugene. *Music at the Court of Frederick the Great*. Norman, Oklahoma: University of Oklahoma Press, 1960.

Langer, Susanne K. *Philosophy in a New Key*. 3rd ed. Cambridge, Mass.: Harvard University Press, 1957.

Longyear, Rey. *Schiller and Music*. Chapel Hill: University of North Carolina Press, 1966.

Maniates, Maria. "'Sonate, que me veux-tu?': The Enigma of French Musical Aesthetics in the Eighteenth Century." *Current Musicology* 9 (1969): 117–40.

Meyer, Leonard B. *Emotion and Meaning in Music*. Chicago: University of Chicago Press, 1956.

Die Musik in Geschichte und Gegenwart. Edited by Friedrich Blume. 15 vols. Kassel: Bärenreiter Verlag, 1949–1968.

Otto, Imgard. *Deutsche Musikanschauung im siebzehnten Jahrhundert*. Berlin, 1937.

Palisca, Claude. "Girolama Mei, Mentor to the Florentine Camerata." *Musical Quarterly* 40 (1954): 1–20.

Poppe, Bernhard. *A. G. Baumgarten, seine Bedeutung und Stellung in der Leibniz-Wolffschen Philosophie und seine Beziehungen zu Kant. Nebst Veröffentlichung einer unbekannten Handschrift der "Aesthetica."* Berne-Leipzig, 1907.

Reilly, Edward R. *Quantz and His Versuch*. American Musicological Society, Studies and Documents, no. 5, 1971.

Robertson, John George. *A History of German Literature*. 5th ed. Edited by Edna Purdie. Edinburgh: William Blackwood and Sons, 1966.

Rogerson, Brewster. "The Art of Painting the Passions." *Journal of the History of Ideas* 14 (1953): 68–94.

Rosen, Charles. *The Classical Style*. New York: W. W. Norton and Co., 1972.

Rubardt, Paul. "Scheibe, Johann." *Musik in Geschichte und Gegenwart*, vol. 11, cols. 1616–1617.

Sadowsky, Rosalie. "Jean-Baptiste Abbé Dubos. The Influence of Cartesian and neo-Aristotelian Ideas on Music Theory and Practice." Ph. D. dissertation, Yale University, 1959.

Schäfke, Rudolf. *Geschichte der Musikaesthetik im Umrissen* [Berlin, 1934]. 2nd ed. Tutzing: Hans Schneider, 1964.

Schenker, Manfred. *Charles Batteux und seine Nachahmungstheorie in Deutschland*. Untersuchungen zur neuern Sprach-und Literaturgeschichte. Edited by Oskar F. Walzel. Neue folge, 2. Heft. Leipzig: H. Haessel, 1909.

Schering, Arnold. "Die Musikaesthetik der deutschen Aufklärung." *Zeitschrift der Internationalen Musikgesellschaft* 8 (1907): 263–271, 316–322.

Schmid, Ernst Fritz. *Carl Philipp Emanuel Bach und seine Kammermusik*. Kassel: Bärenreiter Verlag, 1939.

Schnaus, Peter. "Sulzer, Johann Georg." *Musik in Geschichte und Gegenwart*, vol. 12, cols. 1733–1735.

Schweitzer, Albert. *J. S. Bach*. 6th ed. Leipzig: Breitkopf und Härtel, 1928.

Selk, Günter. "Nicolai, Christoph Friedrich." *Musik in Geschichte und Gegenwart*, vol. 9, cols. 1450–1451.

Serauky, Walter. *Die musikalische Nachahmungaesthetik im Zeitraum von 1700 bis 1850*. Münster, 1929.

Serwer, Howard J. "Friedrich Wilhelm Marpurg (1718–1795): Music Critic in a Galant Age." Ph. D. dissertation, Yale University, 1969.

Siegele, Ulrich. "Junker, Carl Ludwig." *Musik in Geschichte und Gegenwart*, vol. 7, cols. 387–389.

Strunk, Oliver, ed. *Source Readings in Music History*. New York: W. W. Norton and Co., 1950.

Turnow, Hans. "Mattheson, Johann." *Musik in GELE, Ulrich. "Junker, Carl Ludwig." Musik in Geschichte und Gegenwart*, vol. 7, cols. 387–389.

Strunk, Oliver, ed. *Source Readings in Music History*. New York: W. W. Norton and): Sentimental Music Critic." Ph. D. Dissertation, Yale University, 1965.

Wellek, René. *A History of Modern Criticism: 1750–1950*. Vol. 1: *The Later Eighteenth Century*. New Haven: Yale University Press, 1955.

Willoughby, Leonard Ashley. *The Classical Age of German Literature*, 1748–1850. London: Oxford University Press, 1926.

Index